Making Minds Less Well Educated Than Our Own

Making Minds Less Well Educated Than Our Own

Roger C. Schank

 LAWRENCE ERLBAUM ASSOCIATES, PUBLISHERS

2004   Mahwah, New Jersey   London

Lawrence Erlbaum Associates, Inc., Publishers
10 Industrial Avenue
Mahwah, New Jersey 07430

Cover design by Kathryn Houghtaling Lacey

CIP data can be obtained from the Library of Congress.

    p.   cm.
Includes bibliographical references.
ISBN 0-8058-4877-0 (cloth : alk. paper)

Books published by Lawrence Erlbaum Associates are printed on acid-
free paper, and their bindings are chosen for strength and durability.

Printed in the United States of America
10 9 8 7 6 5 4 3 2 1

Contents

Preface

What Is an Educated Mind?

For a few years in the early 1990s, I was on the Board of Editors of the Encyclopedia Britannica. Most everyone else on the board were octogenarians—the foremost of these, since he seemed to have everyone's great respect, was Clifton Fadiman, a literary icon of the 1940s. When I tried to explain to this board the technological changes that were about to come that would threaten the very existence of the Encyclopedia, there was general disbelief. There would always be a need for a great encyclopedia and the job of the board, as they perceived it, was to determine what knowledge was the most important to have in the book. Only Clifton Fadiman seemed to realize that my predictions about the internet might have some effect on the institution they guarded. He concluded sadly, saying "I guess we will just have to accept the fact that minds less well educated than our own will soon be in charge."

He didn't say "differently educated," but "less well educated." For some years the literati have held sway over the commonly accepted definition of education. No matter how important science and technology seem to industry or government, or indeed to the daily life of the people, as a society we believe that those educated in literature and history and other humanities are in some way better informed, more knowledgeable, and somehow more worthy of the descriptor "well educated."

Now if this were an issue confined to those who run the elite universities and prep schools or those whose bible is the New York Review of Books, this really wouldn't matter all that much to anybody. But this out of date conception of the educated mind weighs heavily on modern notions of how we educate our young. We are not educating our young to work or to live in the nineteenth century, or at least we ought not be doing so. Yet, when universities graduate thousands of English and history majors it can only be because we imagine that such fields form the basis of the educated mind. When we choose to teach our high schoolers trigonometry instead of, for example, basic medicine or business skills, it can only be because we think that trigonometry is somehow more important to an educated mind or that education is really not about preparation for the real world.

When we focus on intellectual and scholarly issues in high school as opposed to more human issues like communications, or basic psychology, or child raising, we are continuing to rely upon out dated notions of the educated mind that come from elitist notions of who is to be educated. In that ubiquitous view, education for the masses is the same as education for the intellectual elite and education for the intellectual elite is anything but practical. So while the goal seems to be to educate everyone equally, the reality is that those who survive the current system are educated in a particular way that is less and less relevant to operating in today's world.

While we argue that an educated mind can reason, curiously there are no courses in our schools that teach reasoning. When we say that an educated mind can see more than one side of an argument we go against the school system which holds that there are right answers to be learned and that tests can reveal who knows them and who doesn't.

Now obviously, telecommunications is more important than basic chemistry and HTML is more significant than Latin in today's world. These are choices that have to be made, but they never will be made until our fundamental conception of erudition changes or until we realize that the schools of today must try to educate the students who actually attend them as opposed to the students who attended them in 1892.

The 21st-century conception of an educated mind is based on old notions of erudition and scholarship not germane to this century. The curriculum of the school system bears no relation to the finished products we seek. We need to rethink what it means to be educated and begin to focus on a new conception of the very idea of education.

To do this, we start by looking at the very people whose work was so admired by Clifton Fadiman and the other editors of the Encyclopedia Britannica (EB). Mortimer Adler, who was the Chairman of the Board of EB was greatly involved in something called the Great Books Program. In fact, EB published a series of volumes called the Great Books which included the works of all the people deemed to have been the greatest writers of the last three millennia. Those volumes were edited by Clifton Fadiman. I asked Mortimer Adler how it was that such a small amount of 20th-century writing was included in the Great Books series and he told me that most of it wasn't all that new and wasn't all that interesting. That remark alone would tell you a great deal about the mind-set of those who created the series with respect to education. The "great ideas are forever" they would say. They may well be right about that, but perhaps this is not such an important issue for students as it is for scholars.

In the spirit in which I started this enterprise, that is, an honest attempt to understand what it means to be educated in today's world, I perused the works of the writers of the Great Books to see what they had to say about education. I did not do this because I thought that these thinkers were likely to teach me or the reader about education. Rather, I did it because I wondered whether the collective conception of education in those books was at odds with Clifton Fadiman's notion of what it means to be educated. And, of course, Fadiman is not the real issue. Fadiman's view is pretty mainstream, and that is the issue because his thoughts drive our education system.

So my question is: Is our system of education broken because no one has understood education until now, or is it broken because the world has changed so much that we need new and more up-to-date ideas? Would reading what the writers of the Great Books have to say about education change what we do in education? If these writers disagreed with what we do in schools today should we pay them heed or should we just insist that students read them? Why do we pay homage to great minds when we fail to grasp their message? Does being educated necessarily entail having read a lot or is there another, larger issue behind the notion of education in its deepest sense?

Acknowledgments

Sometime in the late 1920s, Columbia University was the home to three people whose lives and attitudes had a great deal to do with the creation of this book. Mortimer Adler studied there at that time and also taught there. Clifton Fadiman was a student at Columbia at that time. And my father, Maxwell Schank, was in law school. Adler taught in the law school (I don't know why) but he didn't remember my father, nor did my father remember him. These men have all passed on so it is too late to ask about possible interactions. But they have interacted in the creation of this book. Adler inspired me to think about the Great Books, and over many a great meal, we talked about education. Fadiman and I interacted only briefly, but it was his remark that set me on the course for writing this book. My father had an important role too, beyond the obvious. He talked with me night after night when I was in high school about what had happened to him in college. He complained bitterly about taking irrelevant courses and listening to endless lectures the sole purpose of which, in his view, was to see if you could tell the professor on an exam what he had just told you in the lecture. He promised me that college would be different for me as surely things would have improved 35 years later. This book is in part due to each of these men, who once upon a time, I like to think, sat down for a good talk in the Columbia cafeteria in 1928 but they just didn't remember it.

Most of this book is the result of many years of thinking and talking about education, and I could not possibly list all the people and experiences that have influenced my thinking on these issues. My thinking has been influenced by many people over the years. In college, my thinking was provoked a great deal by Allan Newell and Herb Simon, neither of whom I actually met in college although we too were all in the same place. We did become friends over the years and they continued to influence my thinking about learning and the proper way to approach Artificial Intelligence and Cognitive Science problems. In graduate school, Eugene Pendergraft and Jacob Mey taught me a great deal and allowed me the opportunity to try out new ideas. At Stanford, I gained perspective from Ken Colby and also from Jerry Feldman. At Yale, I had many conversations over the years about all kinds of issues with Bob Abelson and Alan Perlis (who, truth be told, was an influence much earlier than that—from the time I was 16 to be exact). And there is always Marvin Minsky, who many people assume to have been my thesis advisor. I never attended MIT, but Marvin has played that role well in my life nevertheless.

But all that is just preparation. I was, after all, during those years not really working on education. I was simply being educated or working as a professor in computer science. When I moved to Northwestern (in 1989) I began to work on education seriously. There I began to create a team to work on these issues. Key members of that team then and now were Chris Riesbeck (who has been working with me for so long it is hard to remember when he wasn't); Alex Kass, who has been invaluable for quite some time; Ray Bareiss, a more recent addition to the team (only ten years or so); Kemi Jona, Greg Saunders, and Steve Feist. Recent PhDs who are now key team members include Tammy Berman and Adam Neaman.

Educational innovation isn't an easy road. You need a lot of help to make change. David Cohen, the Provost of Northwestern while we were all there, was my champion. None of what followed in later years would have happened without him. He helped us survive at Northwestern, and later, to start to work with Columbia when he moved there. It was during the course of that work we began to develop the ideas for Web mentoring that are an important aspect of the work described here. Chris Riesbeck was simultaneously trying his apprenticeship ideas at Northwestern and these became part of what we did at Columbia, and formed the backbone of what we accomplished at CMU West. John Smith, the head of training at Andersen Consulting (now Accenture) was vital to our success. Without Andersen's sponsorship, none of our ideas about how learning can be facilitated by computers could ever have seen the light of day. Both men took risks for me and for what we were trying to do that were critical to the ventures described here.

I went to Carnegie Mellon because of Raj Reddy, who shares my vision about education. None of what happened at CMU West would have happened without his endless support. CMU West is his baby and he has reason to be proud. He has tried valiantly to simply make new things happen at a university, which I can tell you, is no easy task.

I was able to start the Grandview experiment because Jeffrey Epstein, my friend and neighbor, gave me the money to pay my team to do the work. The

Grandview experiment didn't work out as well as the CMU experiment. It did as far as the kids were concerned of course, but kids don't get a vote in school. Nevertheless, the people who took the risk to give it a try have my gratitude, specifically Tom Janton, the technology consultant who I met on a plane one day; Gene and Carolyn Ehlers, who founded the school; and Jackie Westerfield, the headmaster who tried valiantly to hold off the hordes of parents who were insisting on making sure nothing changed at all.

The team that built the story centered curricula at CMU and at Grandview, besides those mentioned previously, included Allan Collins, Diana Joseph, Suzanne Furlong, George Ganat, Jennifer Wright, Samina Sami, Jennifer Gorman, and Nathan Benjamin. The Grandview teachers who worked hard to make the curriculum work in their respective grades were Jonathan Berman, Betsy Mayell, Michelle Henne, Rob Rosenholtz, and Judy Kern.

We sought help from John Bransford's team at Vanderbilt and he sent us Kadira Beylene and Jill Ashworth, who contributed mightily to our Fifth grade offerings. My good friend Elliot Soloway from Michigan sent us Steven Best to help us use his curriculum in the Fifth grade. Renelle Rae from the EPA helped us plan the EPA portion of the Twelfth grade curriculum. Dan Shannon at the University of Chicago agreed to work with us to build new curricula, and he convinced Judith Stein from the University of Chicago to help us plan the Twelfth grade writing curriculum. Shyamala Reddy, my student at CMU West, also helped with that curriculum.

Making these curricula work requires experts who care about them working. At CMU West, Lynn Carter worked very hard to learn how to teach in a new way and has become our leading evangelist for this new kind of teaching. Mike Shamos made sure e-Business curriculum was a success. Lisa Jacinto has been critical to the success of CMU West in general.

Tammy Berman, Cristen Torrey, Kemi Jona, and Franci McFarland all helped with the write ups of the later chapters of this book that deal with the specifics of how the new curricula fared.

Finally, I would like to thank my wife Annie, who knows how to let me alone when I am working and knows how to play when I am not.

November, 2003
Palm Beach, Florida

Prologue

1892

About 1993, I was invited to give a keynote lecture at a conference on intelligence held at Darwin College in Cambridge, England. Many American professors feel, although they are not likely to openly admit it, intimidated by Oxford and Cambridge. The Oxbridge professors are not only quite aggressive in their attacks when you say something they don't like, but they are quite erudite as well, and are likely to cite some ancient scholar you were supposed to have read but didn't in their rebuttals, leaving you in the intellectual dust as it were. Some ten years earlier in a similar circumstance at Cambridge, exactly that had happened to me as I made reference to presuppositions and how they affected our understanding of intention by referring to our expectations of the Dutch military as being unlikely to engage in outright aggression. I was quickly informed that as an ignorant American I had obviously not known that the Dutch had burned the British fleet in the Thames in 16 something or other. Of course, the fact that this point had nothing to do with what I was saying didn't make it any less irritating.

So, this time I decided to come forearmed. I decided that it would be a nice touch if I read Darwin before coming to his namesake college. I was talking about intelligence and was concerned with some issues around consciousness, and I figured that Darwin might have had something to say about animal intelligence that might be relevant to my talk and make me look a little better in the eyes of the intellectually aggressive British faculty types.

I was armed with the Great Books and with the Syntopicon which made sifting through them that much easier. So, I read Darwin. And, I found Darwin to be very interesting. He had a great many good examples of animal intelligence that related to the things I was going to talk about. I thoroughly enjoyed the experience. And, it seemed the audience thoroughly enjoyed my lecture; I was hardly attacked at all.

Why am I telling you this?

Because I was more than 40 when I read Darwin. Had I read him even 10 years earlier or, heaven forbid, when I was in high school or college, I would have certainly not appreciated his ideas. To appreciate Darwin I had to have thought about intelligence on my own first. In fact, reading Tacitus in my freshman year in college so turned me off to history, a subject I now love to read, that I never read another history book for 10 years. Reading Dickens in junior high school kept me from reading Dickens for 20 years. It turns out, I really like Dickens. In fact, I dedicated one of my recent books to him.

And, why am I telling you this?

Here is the point. I am about to embark on a curious enterprise. In the first part of this book I am going to attack our common conceptions of education by seeming to accept the most basic tenet of those conceptions. Here is my attack: There are only two things wrong with modern education: what we teach and how we teach.

I discuss both in this book. To address the *what to teach* issue, I look at what is typically taught in schools and then propose some alternative conceptions of what school should be about. Of particular concern to me is what we might call the *academic approach* to education. To explain what I mean by this, let me tell you another story.

In the 1970s and 1980s I was a professor at Yale University. During much of that time, the President of Yale was Bart Giamatti. He was a Renaissance scholar and I was a professor (and chairman) of computer science. As both of us were combative types, we used to get into vociferous arguments about a range of subjects. Once I asked him to approve a master's degree program in computer science and he responded by saying: "That sounds like training, Roger. We don't do training at Yale."

I was taken aback by this remark. Most masters degree programs are training, although they are not specifically acknowledged as being training. Of course, masters degree programs aren't actually training in the English department I suppose, since they don't necessarily lead to a job.

But I was taken aback by this remark for another reason entirely. Yale, and institutions like Yale, are most certainly training institutions. What are they training students for? Originally, they were training students for the ministry. Now, although this isn't an idea that is openly acknowledged (most faculty members, when pressed, will admit that it is true, however)—they are training professors. Professors at Yale like nothing better than to spot the student who is the best in the class and to nurture him on to a top graduate school, or better yet, to encourage him to be his very own PhD student. The idea that Yale is inherently about training for an academic life can be seen by looking at any department's requirements. In computer science, the bulk of the required courses are theoretical in nature, basically math courses, that are of no use to a programmer, what most computer science undergrads want to be. But, they are part of the education of a professor of computer science. Similarly, in psychology, despite the fact that most students take psychology courses to learn about themselves and their psychological problems, most courses are about experimental psychology. The faculty is preparing students to conduct experiments despite the fact that basically, only professors conduct experiments. Those who work in the practical aspects of psychology, where the jobs are, never run an experiment. The courses of study at major universities are designed by academics for future academics. You bet Yale is a training institution, it just isn't very loud about it. All those investment bankers and lawyers that it graduates are seen as failures of the system to encourage bright young people into academia, although this isn't a sentiment that you will hear voiced out loud very often.

And, why does this matter to us?

When we think about fixing what ails education, specifically the *what to teach* part, we need to understand why we teach what we teach now. Curiously it was all decided in 1892, a fact I alluded to earlier, by a meeting of academics.

In the summer of 1892 in Saratoga Springs, New York, the National Council on Education held a meeting. (The group that met was referred to as the Committee of Ten.) The chairman of the group was Charles Eliot, President of Harvard. Charles Eliot is well known today as a champion of education. He is known as the man who made Harvard into the place it is today, with a varied curriculum and an emphasis on science as well as the liberal arts.

Also present were President Angell of Michigan, President Taylor of Vassar, and President Jesse of Missouri, three headmasters of various preparatory schools, the U.S. Commissioner of Education, President King of Oberlin, President Baker of Colorado, and the only "high school man," Principal Robinson of Albany, the sole representative of the public secondary schools.

They were there to discuss the possibility of creating uniform high school programs and establishing admissions requirements for universities. The issue was uniformity. Each was a specialist in a different subject, Latin, Greek, English, modern languages, mathematics, physics, astronomy, chemistry, biology, history, civil government, and geography.

The question before them was whether "any given subject should be treated differently for pupils who are going to college, for those who are going to a scientific school, and for those who, presumably, are going to neither."

They decided "that every subject which is taught at all in the secondary school should be taught in the same way and to the same extent to every pupil as long as he pursues it, no matter what the probable destination of the pupil may be, or at what point his education is to cease."

"There shall be nine core subjects and that each high school shall arrange these subjects to reflect equal seriousness, dignity, and efficacy. Every high school would offer the recommended subjects."

Of course this was pure elitism. It was obvious that most high school students would drop out of school with such a boring and irrelevant curriculum at hand. They noted that

> only an insignificant percentage of the graduates of the secondary schools go to colleges or scientific schools. A secondary school programme intended for national use must therefore be made for those children whose education is not to be pursued beyond the secondary school. The preparation of a few pupils for college or scientific school should in the ordinary secondary school be the incidental, not the principal object.

But alas, this never happened, or at least alternative secondary schools never became important. Today, nearly all high school students follow the program decided on in 1892 by the Committee of Ten. And, of course, more than half of all high school students do go on to college. The problem, not anticipated by the Committee of Ten, was that college became ordinary, not the refuge of "an insignificant percentage." And, because of that, the elitist, impractical, high school curriculum, intended to serve only the few, began to serve the many. This is where our current problems in school began. We teach the average child what the children of the elite (in 1892), who never intended to be anything but scholars (real world training if needed involved going into the family business typically), were supposed to learn. The high school curriculum took this notion of scholarship for the elite and made it into a virtue for the masses. Why not give everybody a taste of what they were missing while at the same time preparing the elite for college? One good reason not to do this is that scholarly pursuits are probably not what the average person needs. The committee didn't bother to concern itself with issues of learning how to deal with the world students would enter after graduation. For the elite this didn't matter. Their world took care of that education. For the rest, they continue to suffer because of the lack of regard for their welfare by the Committee of Ten.

Although this was surely not their intention, this committee had established the national curriculum for the next 100 years. When we wonder why students study algebra or Latin or physics in high school, it is simply because that is what the president of Harvard and his cohorts thought would make a good program for preparing one for entry into their institutions in 1892. Never mind that it is no longer 1892. It is also no longer the case that only the elite go on to college. Thus, a training ground for future academics has become the training ground for everyone in the country. An insignificant percentage of them are going to become academics. Still, there remains the notion that even a little exposure to academic subjects is somehow good for those who do not intend to pursue academics as a career. One wonders why they thought this, or if in fact they really did think it. In any case, it seems a wrong headed notion to teach trigonometry instead of basic medicine, ancient history instead of basic business skills, or English literature instead of simple human skills such as parenting or marriage. Academic notions dominate high school today at a time when they are less relevant to the majority of the student body than ever. Why then, can't we change the curriculum so that it is not about academics and the preparation for academic careers? This seems to me to be a reasonable question.

I am going to propose something in this book that, at first glance, looks very radical. The idea is that being well educated does not necessarily entail being able to cite the Great Books. To put this another way, education does not mean or ought not to mean preparation to be an academic, and therefore, does not require studying the various academic disciplines in the traditional way. While this may seem to be a wild and radical notion, it is my contention that this is actually a very old notion indeed and I am by no means the first one to put it forward. To make my case, I am going to do exactly what I say one does not have to do: I cite the many brilliant people who wrote the works that comprise the Great Books. I do this not to show my erudition, indeed I have simply used the Syntopicon to find what I need, but precisely to show that so many of the folks who are seen as the intellectual heroes of the ages have put forth very similar ideas.

It may well be ironic that I am citing the Great Books in order to destroy them. But of course I have no intention of destroying them. I believe there is great wisdom in them. I also believe that when one is over age 40 (or when one knows what one is interested in intellectually) one can begin to appreciate the ideas contained in them. But to require knowledge of them for children, or what is worse, to define the very definition of education in terms of knowledge of them, entails creating exactly the education system we have created and it isn't working. New (or old) ideas are needed. We cannot continue to be dictated to by Charles Eliot or by Mortimer Adler, or by Clifton Fadiman.

Of course, neither Charles Eliot and his colleagues nor the EB Board, were operating in a vacuum. They were part of a tradition of education in this country, a tradition that deserves a look. To start, let's go back to the 1600s in New England:

Here is a lesson from the New England Primer:

I will fear God, and honour the King.
I will honour my father and mother
I will obey my superiors.
I will submit to my elders.

This was typically followed by a catechism to be memorized:

Q: What rule hath God given to direct us how we may glorify and enjoy him?

A: The Word of God which is contained in the Scriptures of the Old and New Testament, is the only Rule to direct us how we may glorify and enjoy him.

We have, in the 20th century, adopted the notion as a society that schools are for learning. But, our notions of schooling have consisted of successive adaptations of what has passed for learning since schools were started in this country. The unfortunate truth is that schools were certainly not about learning in the 17th century. That was simply not their purpose.

School was primarily intended to each submission to authority. The children learned to read and write so as to better understand and submit to the laws of religion and government.

While today we imagine that memorization is not a really effective learning methodology, this method still has its proponents and has not been entirely abandoned. Certainly it was still a major method of instruction in the beginning of the 20th century. No one was trying to teach thinking. While today we talk about thinking skills we still use conceptions of teaching that come from an era when the teachers felt that they already knew what to think and their job was to transmit this to children. Of course the real question is: Has anything really changed?

John Dewey reflected on this issue when he noted that:

While we may lead a horse to water we cannot make him drink; . . . while we shut up a man in a penitentiary we cannot make him penitent. . . . We need to distinguish between physical results and moral results. A person may be in such a condition that forcible feeding or enforced confinement is necessary for his own good. . . . But no improvement of disposition, no educative effect, need follow. . . . When we confuse a physical and an educative result, we always lose the chance of enlisting the person's own participating disposition in getting the result desired and thereby of developing within him an intrinsic and persisting direction in the right way.

Of course, Dewey was talking about learning, but schools have always been about preparation. The phrase Grammar School actually refers to an idea that has typically been forgotten in the 21st century. The children who attended schools like Hopkins Grammar School in New Haven in the 17th, 18th, and 19th centuries were preparing for Yale, by learning the grammar rules of Latin and Greek, "reciting them, parsing and construing, translating from Latin to English and back again, 'making Latin,' translating Greek, and puzzling over its rules—this was the course the scholar followed until his master declared him ready for college." They were learning these languages so they could recite Justin, Virgil, Horace, Juvenal, and Persius, and then turn a Psalm into Latin Verse. They were learning the wisdom of the Greeks and Romans as preparation for civic and religious responsibilities and leadership. The idea was simple enough. Great leaders had already thought all that was needed to be thought about leadership, so the way to make great leaders was to have them memorize the words of those who had gone before. This was the reason why Latin and Greek were so important. While Hopkins still requires Latin of its students even to this day, the reasons have been lost. Hopkins is not about learning grammar anymore, but, and this is the important point, it is still about getting its students prepared for Yale.

Again, Dewey's remarks are relevant:

> Not until he knew what it was about and performed the act for the sake of its meaning could he be said to be "brought up" or educated to act in a certain way. To have an idea of a thing is not just to get certain sensations from it. It is to be able to respond to the thing in view of its place in an inclusive scheme of action.

The idea behind reading works in Latin was that one learned to govern or lead by reading about what others have done in that area. That idea while abhorrent to some, is still the basis of today's educational system. While it might seem more reasonable to have students learn to govern or lead by having them try to govern or lead, schools have not attempted to provide such opportunities within the curriculum. Typically those things are left for very unstructured, and often untutored, extracurricular activities that students may choose to partake in. Thus, they are required to read about government but are not required to participate in government.

These notions made sense to schools in the 17th century because they indeed had no other choice. There weren't that many teachers available and there were very few books. A teacher's job could easily be construed as helping students read the books that were available because there really was no alternative. But, this assumes that the goal of the school was to produce educated minds, according to the definition of them at the time. That definition revolved around Latin and Greek (and being able to cite author's who had written the great works of that era). In other words, the conception of what constituted an educated mind dominated (not surprisingly) what constituted an education. Not much has changed in our education system and even in our conception of what it means to be educated. But the world has changed considerably.

In the 18th century, Benjamin Franklin led the drive for a "common school movement" (as opposed to Latin schools). Common school academies were formed that relied on Franklin's idea:

We strive to teach "every Thing that is useful, and every Thing that is ornamental: But Art is long, and their Time is short. It is therefore proposed that
they learn those things that are likely to be most useful and most ornamental.
Regard being had for the several Professions for which they are intended."

Franklin's intention was to create schools that would prepare students to
be useful citizens of the new republic. He wanted people to be trained in the
practicalities of life. Franklin's conception of the educated mind was probably predicated on his own experience of self-educating about the things that
were of interest to him or he thought might be useful. Franklin learned
through the apprenticeship method and it is that method that tells the tale.
You can't apprentice unless you are apprenticing to do something. Learning
by listening is, by its nature, passive and not related to the active doing of
anything at all. Of course this was a kind of class struggle. Franklin was interested in teaching all the people.

Although Franklin preached practical education, the entrance requirements for Harvard were as follows:

When any Schollar is able to read Tully or such like classicall Latine Authour
ex temporare, and make and speake true Latin verse and prose *Suo (ut aiunt)
Marte*, and decline perfectly the paradigms of Nounes and verbes ine the
Greeke tongue, then may hee bee admitted into the Colledge, nor shall any
claim admission before such qualification.

The question, of course, was whether high school was for preparing students for college or preparing people for life. Throughout the 19th and much
of the 20th century there were high schools of both sorts. Because the Latin
school movement insisted that Latin was the cornerstone of the educated
mind, those students who attended Franklin's academies were considered by
them to be uneducated. Harvard did then, and does now, hold sway on what
an educated mind should know.

Of course the battle was not solely about Latin. Each and every aspect of
the Latin school movement was challenged by the Academies. Horace
Greeley wrote:

We can shed no tears for algebra. We can be thankful that algebra had not yet
been thrust into our rural common schools, to know the brains and squander
the time of those who should be learning something of positive and practical
utility.

Today algebra holds a prominence in our schools that would have sick-
ened the proponents of the common school movement. Each president of
the United States worries aloud about the nation's mathematics competence
despite the fact that the presidents themselves are unlikely to recall any of

what they learned from their high school math classes and certainly would have used none of it in their professional lives. Is this reverence for mathematics also attributable to Harvard?

Of course it is. Mathematics was the core of the curriculum established in 1892 by the Committee of Ten. While it is clear why academics like mathematics, its relevance for population at large remains in doubt. Here is one of the most famous mathematicians of the 20th century on this subject:

> The fact is that there are few more "popular" subjects than mathematics. Most people have some appreciation of mathematics, just as most people can enjoy a pleasant tune; and there are probably more people really interested in mathematics than in music. Appearances may suggest the contrary, but there are easy explanations. Music can be used to stimulate mass emotion, while mathematics cannot; and musical incapacity is recognized (no doubt rightly) as mildly discreditable, whereas most people are so frightened of the name of mathematics that they are ready, quite unaffectedly, to exaggerate their own mathematical stupidity.
>
> (G. H. Hardy, A *Mathematician's Apology*, 1940)

Hardy noticed that while mathematics was generally approved of as an important subject, in fact most people had no real ability or interest in it. Despite studying it in every grade in school, they rarely can do more than basic arithmetic. It is really hard to understand the generally held belief that forcing students to study mathematics for 12 years is all that important. One possible explanation was offered by another famous mathematician:

> Mathematics knows no races or geographic boundaries; for mathematics, the cultural world is one country.
>
> David Hilbert (1862–1943)

There is no ideology in mathematics. It is pure and unadulterated by politics. Perhaps that is why politicians love it so. Here is Hardy on why he loves mathematics:

> The mathematician's patterns, like the painter's or the poet's must be beautiful; the ideas, like the colors or the words must fit together in a harmonious way. Beauty is the first test: there is no permanent place in this world for ugly mathematics.
>
> (G. H. Hardy, A *Mathematician's Apology*, 1940)

Indeed, there is much to love about mathematics. But this is a subject for intellectuals not for the general school population. Students don't see the beauty of mathematics or understand what Hardy could possibly have meant by ugly mathematics. They understand that they have a math test in the morning and someone is making them memorize a lot of formulas and that they will never use them in their lives. That is not the kind of mathematics that Hardy was talking about. The kind of mathematics mathematicians talk about was best summed up in a toast given by a 19th-century mathematician:

> Pure mathematics, may it never be of any use to anyone.
> Henry John Stephen Smith (1826–1883)

This book treads on some sacred cows. It is important to take a look at why we teach what we teach and how we should teach what we decide it is important to teach. While it is all well and good to have read what great thinkers have thought, it is not necessarily right to see an educated mind as being one which has read these works. Academics cite great thinkers when they want to prove a point. Of course, these citations prove nothing except perhaps the erudition of the citer, but then that is usually their intent. Indeed, I do exactly that in this book. But being able to cite great thinkers is not the same as being able to think for oneself. A good education system produces minds capable of independent thought. While it may seem heretical to suggest this, that may not have been the goal of the Committee of Ten or their predecessors. In fact, independent creative thought seems like a more modern idea. But the very thinkers whose work is most cited by scholars were not trying to produce minds who simply repeated what they were told, as I show in this book. They didn't necessarily believe that the hallmark of an educated mind was the ability to cite what had been previously said. I discuss what they did believe and make a case for what an educated mind in the 21st century ought to look like.

REFERENCE NOTES

The description of the 1892 meeting was taken from Angus and Mirel, *The Failed Promise of the American High School*, Teachers College Press, New York, 1999. The details of what was said and done at that meeting are available at:

http://www.blancmange.net/tmh/books/commoften/mainrpt.html

I used Rippa, 1997, Education in a Free Society, Longman for some of the background on requirements on early American schools. The New England Primer was the most popular text from primary instruction in the 1600s in the new colonies. Instruction meant memorization of the text in most cases. Taken from Paul Leicester Ford, Ed. *The New England Primer* (New York: Teachers College Press, 1962); discussed in Spring (1997), McGraw Hill.

Dewey's comments are taken from John Dewey, Democracy and Education, Free Press, 1966.

Benjamin Franklin's remarks come from *Benjamin Franklin, Proposals* relating to the education of youth in Pennsylvania, in *The Age of the Academies*, Ed. Theodore Sizer, New York, 1964, cited in Reese, William, *The Origins of The American High School*, Yale University Press, New Haven, 1995.

Greeley's remarks made in 1869 (Reese, *The Origins of the American High School*, Yale University Press).

Hardy's statement come from a little book that is very much worth reading called *A Mathematicians Apology*, by G.H. Hardy, Cambridge University Press (originally 1940).

The other mathematician's quotes I got from the Web. A particularly good source is found at:

http://math.furman.edu/~mwoodard/ascquoth.html

1

The Great Minds on Education: Plato Meets Grandview Prep

Nothing in education is so astonishing as the amount of ignorance it accumulates in the form of facts.

Henry Adams

It is possible to store the mind with a million facts and still be entirely uneducated.

Alec Bourne

Factual knowledge is at the center of modern-day education. In fact, in an increasingly test-oriented school system, it is not only the center of the day, it is the basis on which everything else rests. One need not venture very far into the school system to see why this is so. It takes a little work, however, to see why this is a problem. It seems, at first glance, that an educated person is someone who has a great deal of information at his fingertips and that a large part of the role of a teacher would be to impart that information to the student. One problem with this idea was stated by Plato (*The Republic*, Book X):

And whenever anyone informs us that he has found a man knows all the arts, and all things else that anybody knows, and every single thing with a higher degree of accuracy than any other man—whoever tells us this, I think that we can only imagine to be a simple creature who is likely to have been deceived by some wizard or actor whom he met, and whom he thought all-knowing, because he himself was unable to analyze the nature of knowledge and ignorance and imitation.

1

Knowing only creates more understanding of what one doesn't know, after all. It is odd that an educational system that depends so much on understanding the works of the great thinkers of history managed to miss this idea.
Plato seems somewhat skeptical of the idea that there is some finite amount
of knowledge. If that were the case there might be some possibility of knowing everything. But knowledge doesn't work like that. Of course, there is
value in knowing a great many things. However, consider the following from
the Phaedrus Dialogue, also written by Plato:

> SOCRATES: But he who thinks that in the written word there is necessarily
> much which is not serious, and that neither poetry nor prose, spoken or writ-
> ten, is of any great value, if, like the compositions of the rhapsodies, they are
> only recited in order to be believed, and not with any view to criticism or in-
> struction; and who thinks that even the best of writings are but a reminiscence
> of what we know, and that only in principles of justice and goodness and nobil-
> ity taught and communicated orally for the sake of instruction and graven in
> the soul, which is the true way of writing, is there clearness and perfection and
> seriousness, and that such principles are a man's own and his legitimate off-
> spring;—being, in the first place, the word which he finds in his own bosom;
> secondly, the brethren and descendants and relations of his idea which have
> been duly implanted by him in the souls of others;—and who cares for them
> and no others—this is the right sort of man; and you and I, Phaedrus, would
> pray that we may become like him.

Socrates doesn't seem to be that big a fan of explicit knowledge either. It
isn't knowledge that is basis of the educated mind, but the ability to deal
with ideas based on knowledge. Socrates is making a key point about education, namely that simply knowing something isn't of much value. You have
to make it your own and that doesn't happen simply by being able to reiterate what a teacher has told you. But surely that isn't what modern education
is about. Surely, we do let students come to grasp ideas and make them their
own. Don't we?

To answer this question more clearly I present next the 2nd-grade social
studies curriculum from a school I have been working with in Florida. Following is the curriculum that I found there when they asked for my help:

Department of History
Second Grade Social Studies Curriculum

TIME REQUIREMENTS: 43 minutes

TEXT: *Living in Communities*: Silver, Burdett and Ginn (with corresponding
workbook). (Note: Texts listed in section III are supplemental and can be
used at the teacher's discretion)

OTHER MATERIALS: Maps, globe, audio-visual materials, multi-media sources

COURSE EMPHASIS: The purpose of a second grade social studies curriculum is to reinforce the study of family, to study about neighborhoods and communities and the country as a whole, to learn about living in groups and working in communities. The students will also learn about communities from the past and communities around the world. The students will also reinforce their understanding of our country today and to reinforce the study of our country's holidays. The Internet will be used extensively as a resource for students to enhance their studies.

I. OBJECTIVES

    A. Social Studies Skills

        1. Nature and Character of the Community

           a. how the individual plays a role in the family unit—*reinforce*

           b. how the student's family compares with that of different cultures—*new*

        2. Nature and Process of Change

           a. how the study of early man helps to develop a sense of time

           b. how early man's life compares with our own lives today

        3. Nature and Character of Peoples, Civilizations, and Cultures

           a. how to compare different cultures and identify different reasons for similarities—*reinforce, develop*

           b. how to contrast different cultures and identify reasons for differences—*reinforce, develop*

        4. Nature and Character of Heritage

           a. how famous individuals have a significant impact on a country's heritage—*reinforce, develop*

           b. how individual ethnic groups have a significant impact on a country's heritage—*reinforce, develop*

        5. Content and Methods of Various Social Studies Disciplines—Geography

           a. how natural features that appear on the surface of the earth can be represented on maps using lines, shapes, colors, simple drawings, and symbols—*reinforce, develop*

           b. how man-made features that appear on the surface of the earth can be represented on maps using lines, shapes, colors, simple drawings, and symbols—*reinforce, develop*

B. Learning, Studying, and Growing skills
  1. Map Study skills
     a. How to interpret different kinds of maps—*reinforce, develop, prepare.*
     b. How to identify and use map symbols—*reinforce, develop, prepare.*
     c. How to distinguish a map from a picture—*reinforce, develop, prepare.*
     d. How to use a map legend (key)—*reinforce, develop, prepare.*
     e. How to use cardinal and ordinal directions on a map and globe—*new, prepare.*
     f. How to use map coordinates—*new, prepare.*
     g. How to use map colored pencils and crayons to color maps—*reinforce, develop, prepare.*
     h. Identify major cities, rivers, lakes, and boundaries in Florida—*new, prepare.*
  2. Examination Skills
     a. How to review class information as a review for a test—*new, prepare.*
     b. How to read over all questions while taking a test—*new, prepare.*
  3. Classroom Study Skills
     a. How to listen, follow instructions, etc.—*reinforce, develop, prepare.*
     b. How to participate in discussion—*reinforce, develop, prepare.*
  4. Information Gathering, Recording, Organizing, and Communication Skills
     a. How to gather materials—*reinforce, develop, prepare.*
     b. How to organize materials—*reinforce, develop, prepare.*
  5. General Maturity Skills
     a. How to assume responsibilities—*reinforce, develop, prepare.*
     b. How to cooperate with others in group activities—*new.*
  6. How Geographic Setting and Important Historical Events Influence the Daily Life and the Current Situation of a single State—*reinforce, develop.*

II. IMPLEMENTATION
  A. Design and Sequence
    1. Community

   a. Own Family
   b. Style of Families—Cultures
  2. Change
   a. Early Man
   b. Men of the Middle Ages
   c. Modern Man
  3. People, Civilizations, and Cultures
   a. American Indians
   b. Indians native to Florida
  4. Heritage
   a. Famous Americans
   b. Famous Floridians
   c. Famous Natives

 B. Methods
  1. Community
   a. Own Family
    (1) Interaction with Family Members
    (2) Location of families on maps—city, state, world
   b. Style of Families—Cultures
    (1) Selected Literature
    (2) Discussions
    (3) Locations of Cultures
  2. Change
   a. Early Man
    (1) Selected Literature
    (2) Discussion
    (3) Timeline
    (4) Booklet
   b. Medieval Man
    (1) Selected Literature
    (2) Discussion
    (3) Timeline
    (4) Booklet
   c. Modern Man
    (1) Selected Literature
    (2) Discussion
    (3) Timeline

        (4) Booklet
    3. People, Civilizations, and Culture
        a. American Indians
            (1) Discussions
            (2) Migration from Asia Map and Worksheet
            (3) Major groups of Indians—migration and settlement patterns
            (4) Charts and maps
        b. Five major groups—Eastern Woodland, Southeast, Plains, Desert, and Western Coast
            (1) Selected Literature
            (2) Charts
            (3) Maps
            (4) Pictures
        c. Indian Sign Language
            (1) Charts
            (2) Alphabets
            (3) World Lists
            (4) Original Stories
        d. Word Searches and Crossword Puzzles
        e. Homes of Various Tribes
        f. Clothes of Various Tribes
        g. Clothes of Various Tribes
        h. Indian Crafts in Art

    C. Heritage
        1. Famous Americans
            a. Christopher Columbus
                (1) Selected Books
                (2) Worksheets
                (3) Illustrations
                (4) Film
            b. Pilgrims
                (1) Selected Books
                (2) Worksheets
                (3) Illustration
            c. Daniel Boone
                (1) Selected Books

    (2) Worksheets

    (3) Illustration

   d. George Washington, Abraham Lincoln, and Benjamin Franklin

    (1) Selected Books

    (2) Reports

    (3) Worksheets

    (4) Illustrations

    (5) Word Searches and Crossword Puzzles

 2. Florida

   a. Major Units

    (1) Florida as an Indian Land

    (2) Florida Under Spain

    (3) Florida as a State

    (4) Florida Sites and Symbols

   b. Activities

    (1) Vocabulary

    (2) Lifestyle—charts and illustrations

    (3) Worksheets

    (4) Time Line

    (5) Discussion of Major Events

 3. Geography

   a. Land Areas

   b. Indian Adaptation

   c. Exploration

   d. Agriculture

   e. Resources

 4. People—Discussed with Florida Vocabulary

   a. Ponce de Leon

   b. Vasco da Gama

   c. Black Caesar

   d. Thomas Edison

   e. Other noted Floridians

 5. Field Trips

   a. Graves Archaeological Museum

   b. Miami Museum of Science

   c. Fort Lauderdale IMAX

      6. Florida Play
      7. Florida Wildflower Study
      8. Florida Map Test
      9. Florida Test
    10. Boca Raton
        a. Boca Facts
        b. Use of Local Phone Directory
        c. Interviews
        d. Charts
        e. Graphs
        f. Grids
        g. Maps
        h. Word Searches and Crossword Puzzles
        i. Illustrations
        j. Field Trips
           (1) Industrial
           (2) Downtown

  D. Social Studies Disciplines—Geography
      1. Map Skills Unit
        a. Map Show the Earth Kit
        b. Success with Maps Workbooks
        c. Multi-Media Sources
        d. Worksheets
        e. Original Maps

III. TEXTS AND MATERIALS

  A. Texts
      1. Down Bright Roads—Economy
      2. Tales to Enjoy—Economy
      3. Lincoln and Washington—Highlights

  B. Additional Books
      1. *Early Man* by F. Clark Howell
      2. *The How and Why Book of Primitive Man* by Donald Barr
      3. *People of the Ice Age* by Goode
      4. *The Story of Christopher Columbus* by Ann McGovern
      5. *A Man Named Columbus* by Gertrude Norman

6. *Columbus* by Ingri and Edgar Parin
7. *Daniel Boone* by Katherine E. Wilke
8. *George Washington* by Stewart Graff
9. *Abraham Lincoln* by Ann Colve
10. *The Pilgrims' Party* by Sadybeth Lowitz
11. *The American History Scene*—Creative Teaching Press
12. All Junior Biographies
13. *World of the American Indian*—National Geographic
14. *The Rain Dance People* by Richard Erdoes
15. *Indian Crafts and Lore* by W. Ben Hunt
16. *Highlights Book About the American Indian*
17. *The Coloring Book of the American Indians* by Cathy Bodmer
18. *American Indian* by Bruce Grant
19. *Indians* by Edwin Tunis
20. *The American Indian* by Sydney Fletcher
21. *Western Indians* by Ralph Andrews
22. *Indians of the Plains* by Eugene Rachles
23. *America and Its Indians* by Jerome Leavitt
24. *Indian Music Makers* by Robert Hofsinde
25. *The Cherokee* by Sonia Bleeker
26. *Indian Festivals* by Paul Showers
27. *Kachina Dolls* by Julie Staheli
28. *Indian Myths* by Berstein and Kabrin
29. *Facts About Our Fifty States* by Sue Brandt

C. Labs
   1. Maps Show the Earth
   2. Map Skills for Beginners

D. Multi-Media

E. Maps
   1. Nystrom Readiness U.S. and World Map
   2. American Geographics Map of Florida

F. Globes

G. Second Grade Curriculum Binder

H. Teacher made Materials

IV. EVALUATION

    A. Observation to Determine:
        1. Degree of Interest and Enthusiasm
        2. Skill Application
        3. Readiness for Third Grade Work

    B. Groups Discussions

    C. Student Response to Informal Questions

    D. Performance on Stanford Achievement Tests

    E. Class Participation

There is no reason to believe that the curriculum I have detailed here is much different from any other being used in the US today. So, the question is: What would Socrates have to say about such a curriculum? Seven-year-old children may well be able to understand that there was a person named Vasco da Gama and that he had something to do with the establishment of the current state of Florida. This student may be able to understand that there are people called Indians and that they told stories to each other. They may be able to learn about Daniel Boone and George Washington. But to what end? What are they learning? How long will these facts stay with them? What will have been the value of learning such facts in their future lives? Most adults live full lives without ever having heard of Vasco da Gama.

    Actually there are a few things of value in the curriculum just detailed—use of the local phone directory for one—the ability to read a map for another. But, clearly, this curriculum is about indoctrination, not education. There is some fun stuff, Indian rain dances for example, which might be at least enjoyable to learn. But simply telling a seven-year-old about Abraham Lincoln or the Pilgrims or "Indian adaptation" is simply making sure that students know whatever the official story is this year about the conquest of America. It is, in fact, the exact opposite of what Socrates was talking about. He was suggesting that the real issue was getting students to be able to understand principles by having used the principles in some way that made them real to the student and allowed them to see many sides of an issue. Do you think that students in second grade are arguing about whether Abraham Lincoln was right in pursuing the Civil War or whether Columbus was a just man or when it is okay for one nation to conquer another? I doubt it. It seems rather obvious that they are only learning the names and then being tested on them.

Let's again consider what Plato had to say (this time from the Sophist dialogue):

Str.   When a person supposes that he knows, and does not know, this appears to be the great source of all the errors of the intellect.

Theaet.   True.

Str.   And this, if I am not mistaken, is the kind of ignorance which specially earns the title of stupidity.

Theaet.   True.

Str.   What name, then, shall be given to the sort of instruction which gets rid of this?

Theaet.   The instruction which you mean, Stranger, is, I should imagine, not the teaching of handicraft arts, but what, thanks to us, has been termed education in this part the world.

Str.   Yes, Theaetetus, and by nearly all Hellenes. But we have still to consider whether education admits of any further division.

Theaet.   We have.

Str.   I think that there is a point at which such a division is possible.

Theaet.   Where?

Str.   Of education, one method appears to be rougher, and another smoother.

Theaet.   How are we to distinguish the two?

Str.   There is the time-honoured mode which our fathers commonly practiced towards their sons, and which is still adopted by many-either of roughly reproving their errors, or of gently advising them; which varieties may be correctly included under the general term of admonition.

Str.   For all these reasons, Theaetetus, we must admit that refutation is the greatest and chiefest of purifications, and he who has not been refuted, though he be the Great King himself, is in an awful state of impurity; he is uninstructed and deformed in those things in which he who would be truly blessed ought to be fairest and purest.

Theaet.   Very true.

Is refutation is the greatest method of teaching? Socrates thought so. It is also clear that Grandview Prep (and most other schools) do not believe this at all. Where is the refutation to be had in the second grade? Do second graders argue both sides of important questions? More importantly, how would we teach them to do that? If the time honored method of teaching by fathers to their sons is by showing them where they are wrong, where in the second grade does anyone get a chance to be wrong? What could they be wrong about? They could only not have the right answer to a factual question and that is not the same thing at all. Argument matters in training the mind to think but argument can only happen when there are issues that have (at least) two sides and it is politically acceptable to be on one of those sides. What do you think happens when a second grader in this school suggests that perhaps Columbus was a murderer and no hero at all? Nothing happens of course, because the event never takes place.

Of course, one cannot argue if one has had no experience. Argument comes from experiential knowledge that contradicts assertions of another. Before we teach second graders to refute a premise therefore, they must have some familiarity with the premise, not because they were told about it, but because they experienced it in some way.

So, when Grandview teaches about Lincoln, the question is: what experiences have they had that would make such knowledge both relevant and refutable? If there are no such experiences in their repertoire they will understand nothing about Lincoln and the facts they gather will be retained, if they are retained at all, as inert knowledge to be retrieved for quizzes but of no other use.

Machiavelli, in his advice to princes, also gives advice to schools about teaching history:

> But to exercise the intellect the prince should read histories, and study there the actions of illustrious men, to see how they have borne themselves in war, to examine the causes of their victories and defeat, so as to avoid the latter and imitate the former; and above all do as an illustrious man did, who took as an exemplar one who had been praised and famous before him, and whose achievements and deeds he always kept in his mind, as it is said Alexander the Great imitated Achilles, Caesar Alexander, Scipio Cyrus.

Will our second graders be imitating Vasco da Gama? Will they in any way be able to understand Vasco da Gama? A second grader can only comprehend aspects of the world to which he can relate. Further, there is some issue as to the veracity of what our second graders are reading. This is what Montaigne had to say about the writing of history:

> The only good histories are those that have been written by the very men who were in command of the affairs, or were participants in the conduct of them, or who at least had the fortune to conduct others of the same sort. . . . What can you expect of a doctor discussing war or a schoolboy discussing the intention of princes?

We might ask about the texts the children are reading. Who wrote them? With what purpose were they written? Are they accurate accounts of events or stories written for children that have no more value than do fairy tales?

Minds less well educated than those of the EB board members are produced by just such a system. When students read about events that they cannot possibly comprehend in any real way, because they have no basis in any experience they could possibly have had, they may as well not bother. To make matters worse, they are reading simplified stories about complex events that quite often didn't actually take place just the way the author of these texts describes. And then, in a test-oriented society, they are being made to say what facts they have just read. The successful student is the one who has memorized what he was told, not the one who has analyzed what he has been told. Plato would have been appalled.

> The classics, and their position of prerogative in the scheme of education to which the higher seminaries of learning cling with such a fond predilection, serve to shape the intellectual attitude and lower the economic efficiency of the new learned generation. They do this not only by holding up an archaic ideal of manhood, but also by the discrimination which they inculcate with respect to the reputable and the disreputable in knowledge.
>
> *Veblen*

Veblen saw the teaching of classic texts as a way of keeping people down. He saw the classic idea of the educated mind as being little more than a way of giving certain ideas prominence and keeping everyone unproductive. In fact, graduating with a degree in classics or literature is not a ticket to economic status. It is odd that these things are so highly valued at great universities when society does not value them much at all.

Gibbon commented on the effect of such teaching on the Greeks who lived after the classic Greek period:

> In our modern education, the painful though necessary attainment of two languages which are no longer living may consume the time and damp the ardour of the youthful student. . . . But the Greeks of Constantinople . . . acquired the free use of their ancient language . . . and a familiar knowledge of the sublime masters who had pleased or instructed the first of nations. But these advantages only tend to aggravate the reproach and shame of a degenerate people. They held in their lifeless hands the riches of their fathers, without inheriting the spirit of which had created and improved their sacred patrimony: they read, they praised, they complied, but their languid souls seemed alike incapable of thought and action. In the revolution of ten centuries not a single discovery was made to exalt the dignity or promote the happiness of mankind.

Reading the Great Books it seems, even in the original Greek, did not in-spire a millennium's worth of Greeks to do much. They were quite well edu-cated in Clifton Fadiman's sense, but as Gibbon pointed out, they didn't do anything of importance. History teaches us to do, or not to do, or it ought to. Doing should be informed by history, but history without the anticipation of doing is a lifeless affair. We can tell all we want about da Gama to second graders, but what will they do with that information? Of course, the problem is not only that second graders cannot possibly have use for what they are be-ing taught. There is also a bigger problem. Typically, what they are being taught is simply wrong. To really deal with history is a complex undertaking, well beyond the abilities, interests, or experience of any second grader.

Plutarch, the great biographer wrote a preface to his biography of Alexan-der that helps delineate the real issue in history education:

> It being my purpose to write the lives of Alexander the king, and of Caesar, by whom Pompey was destroyed, the multitude of their great actions affords so large a field that I were to blame if I should not by way of apology forewarn my reader that I have chosen rather to epitomize the most celebrated parts of their story, than to insist at large on every particular circumstance of it. It must be borne in mind that my design is not to write histories, but lives. And the most glorious exploits do not always furnish us with the clearest discoveries of virtue or vice in men; sometimes a matter of less moment, an expression or a jest, informs us better of their characters and inclinations, than the most famous sieges, the greatest armaments, or the bloodiest battles whatsoever. Therefore as portrait-painters are more exact in the lines and features of the face, in which the character is seen, than in the other parts of the body, so I must be allowed to give my more particular attention to the marks and indications of the souls of men, and while I endeavour by these to portray their lives, may be free to leave more weighty matters and great battles to be treated of by others.

Even a great biographer admits that he writes only part of the story. So, before we expect any child to learn history, we need to ask who is writing what they read. Some parts of the story they read have been left out. Which parts? Are these the parts that are likely to be controversial in some way? To put this another way, are these the parts that are likely to be the very reason why anyone would learn anything at all, namely to discuss it, to see many sides of an issue, to form a judgment about the issues complexity and to make one's conclusions one's own?

History, a subject that surely Clifton Fadiman believed comprised an es-sential part of the make up of an educated mind, is not such a simple affair. When we say that we want our children to learn history we need to under-stand what we are letting them in for. We cannot be satisfied with simple as-sertions about knowing the father of our country or understanding the plight of the Indians. They can never really know who the father of our country is since the idea is complicated. Simple answers to simple questions are not what Fadiman or anyone who has thought about education had in mind.

To teach history one needs to relate what one is teaching to a situation that is on the minds or can be made to be on the minds of students. Decision making is well informed by precedent. Instead of making children into trivial historians we need to cause children to make decisions and make those decisions using historical precedent. While this is not a simple undertaking it is also not impossible. It requires considering history less as a subject and more as data. In other words, the subject is planning, achieving goals and such, not history. Unless we are trying to train scholars, and no one is suggesting doing that in the second grade, we must think about what we should be trying to do. Teaching reasoning, and taking the idea of critical thinking seriously, one sees that history ought not be a subject at all, no matter what the Committee of Ten dictated. History should be learned, but only in a way that facilitates complex thought.

Now let's take a look at the science curriculum for fourth grade in this school:

Fourth Grade General Science Curriculum

COURSE TITLE: General Science

TIME REQUIREMENTS: 43 Minutes every other day

TEXT: *Science Anytime Series*: Harcourt-Brace

OTHER MATERIALS: Various hand on materials, notebooks, and computer access

COURSE EMPHASIS: The goals of this course are to foster in children curiosity and delight about the wonders of science. Emphasis is placed on strengthening student's investigative skills while developing knowledge of Science vocabulary, facts and theories. Experimentation and hands on- applications are employed to allow flexible, independent science experiences. Students also pursue mature citizenship through value judgements and peer relationship activities. Students use the Internet throughout the course to enhance their knowledge of their scientific studies.

I. OBJECTIVES

    A. Identify parts of the respiratory system, know functions, learn health care and study certain diseases of the lungs.

    B. Know the four basic food groups, concept of proper nourishment, personal eating habits, deficiency effect and awareness of labeling and advertising practices

C. Student's will learn the process of digestion, names and functions of the system parts. Digestive track ailments, health care system and the purpose of enzymes and hormones in regard to the digestive process.

D. Students will understand how and why vertebrates and classified—common characteristics, adaptations, reproduction and methods for identifying unfamiliar animals

E. Students will recognize parts of the reproductive system, sperm and ovum development, growth of a baby, correct terminology, events and puberty, simple genetic principles, and endocrine system relationship

F. Students will identify parts and functions of their circulatory system, blood passage components blood, advances in the treatments of heart disease, and health care

G. Students will learn sources of energy, vocabulary of basic ecology, types of pollution, and animal and plant interaction with the environment

H. Students will major bones and muscles, their functions, and malformations

I. Students will recognize parts of the brain and nervous system, along with the causes and treatments of certain diseases and health care of the system

J. Students will reference objects, basic directions, relative motion, and be able to interpret all in set circumstances

K. Students will use the specific method and recognize and define the science process skills

II. IMPLEMENTATION

A. Life Sciences

1. Through worksheets, teacher demonstration and discussion, and the Internet, students will study animal classification and adaptations, their environment and habits, and animals and reproduction

2. Students will research an animal and develop a computer project for the animal

3. Students again by using various forms of study, will learn more about the human body, including the body systems, nutrition, human reproduction and sexuality, and staying fit.

    4. Students will also study plant life by examining the ways people use plants, and the need for conservation, and plants and their photosynthesis.

    5. Students will complete a gardening project during this period of study.

B. Earth Sciences

    1. By using numerous forms of study and experimentation, students will learn about weather erosion, the protection and conversation of natural resources, and what is inside the earth.

    2. Students will study the movements of the ocean water, tidal pools and ocean resources, and the causes of the ocean pollution

    3. Students will visit and observe an ocean environment

    4. Students will create a model ocean environment

C. Physical Sciences

    1. Students will various types of energy sources, e.g. heat, light sound, electricity

    2. Students will study communications technologies, especially the increasing use of the internet for scientific research

    3. Students will experiment with elementary chemistry

    4. Students will also experiment with various sources of matter

    5. Students will also be asked to demonstrate one energy type in a project

D. Future Sciences

    1. Students will spend much time using the Internet as a scientific tool.

    2. Students will work extensively with the microscope and understand its many purposes

    3. Students may do research in the library and/or the Internet to learn about famous inventors and scientists.

    4. Students my have inventions convention, at which they would present an original invention

III. MATERIALS

The curriculum will be supplemented using aims, prisms, and gems activities. Also, students will obviously be provided with necessary scientific, tools to perform laboratory experiments.

IV. EVALUATION

Students will be assessed by their class participation, their lab experiences and performance tasks. Quizzes, tests and various projects. Tests will be given after each unit taught.

Students will go to the ocean and do some gardening. In fact, this is not so bad. At least they are doing something. Is it science? Maybe it is in a funny sort of way. Gardening is undoubtedly much more the actual doing of science than "experimenting with elementary chemistry," which probably means watching the teacher do one of those so-called science experiments. The problem of course is what the students will actually be doing is taking tests on naming the organs of the body and various types of energy sources. Yet again, there is nothing wrong with knowing that sort of stuff. But where does it lead? Does it teach science? What follows is what Alfred North Whitehead had to say about teaching science:

> My own criticism of our traditional educational methods is that they are far too much occupied with intellectual analysis, and with the acquirement of formularized information. What I mean is, that we neglect to strengthen habits of concrete appreciation of the individual facts in their full interplay of emergency values, and that we merely emphasize abstract formulations which ignore this aspect of the interplay of diverse values.

Science is about reasoning within a scientific environment. It is not the facts that matter but their interplay. Here again, it is the issue of argumentation and refutation that matters. Following is Descartes on the same subject:

> SCIENCE in its entirety is true and evident cognition. He is no more learned who has doubts on many matters than the man who has never thought of them; may be appears to be less learned if he has formed wrong opinions on any particulars. Hence it were better not to study at all than to occupy one's self with objects of such difficulty, that, owing to our inability to regard the doubtful as certain; for in those matters any hope of augmenting our knowledge is exceeded by the risk of diminishing it. Thus in accordance with the above maxim we reject all such merely probable knowledge and make it a rule to trust only what is completely known and incapable of being doubted. No doubt men . . . have believed that it was unbecoming for a man of education to confess ignorance on any point.
>
> But if we adhere closely to this rule we shall find left but few objects of legitimate study. For there is scarce any question occurring in the sciences about which talented men have not disagreed. But whenever two men come to opposite decisions about the same matter one of them at least must certainly be in the wrong, and apparently there is not even one of them who knows; for if the reasoning of the second was sound and clear he would be able so to lay it before the other as finally to succeed in convincing his understanding also.

Descartes noted that science really isn't all that full of incontrovertible facts. Here again we see that our problem is that we conceive of school as the vehicle for the transmission of truth. The problem is that truth is not so easy to determine in science. In fact, it is the determination of truth that is what makes science interesting to scientists. It is not the facts but getting at the facts that makes science fun. While school wants to teach things that are true in science this may be not exactly the real issue. It is a situation not so different from history after all. What will the children do with the facts they learn? Can't we find some situations in which scientific knowledge would be of benefit to something the children were trying to accomplish? Then they might want to know the facts of the matter, and might possibly, if they were really interested in science, attempt to determine how to determine the truth of these facts for themselves.

Of course, the recent emphasis on testing in the name of educational reform in the US has made this situation worse instead of better. You can't test what isn't true so the schools teach true things. What could be wrong with teaching the truth? Descartes points out that not all that much actually is true in the end. It is his appreciation of nontruth that needs to be taught. Descartes and Plato agree. Unfortunately, the governors of most of the states in the US wouldn't know about that. They haven't read much Plato. The solution is not to have them remedy their educations by reading Plato of course, but to have employed in their own education the principles espoused by Plato.

Aristotle (in Nicomachean Ethics) wondered about science in a way that makes clear what scientific study is for:

> Every science is thought to be capable of being taught, and its object of being learned. And all teaching starts from what is already known . . . for it proceeds sometimes through induction and sometimes by syllogism. Now induction is the starting-point which knowledge even of the universal presupposes, while syllogism proceeds from universals. There are therefore starting-points from which syllogism proceeds, which are not reached by syllogism; it is therefore by induction that they are acquired. Scientific knowledge is, then, a state of capacity to demonstrate . . . for it is when a man believes in a certain way and the starting-points are known to him that he has scientific knowledge. Let this, then, be taken as our account of scientific knowledge.

Aristotle was saying that having scientific knowledge meant being able to reason about things in a logical manner. It is the data that matters in science, from which one can draw conclusions. It is really not the conclusions themselves that matter. In fact, Aristotle points out that if only the conclusions are known, this is not very important. And, what do we teach in school? The conclusions of course.

What then does it mean to know history and science? The educated mind certainly would know both of these subjects. Or would it? This is actually the wrong question. In discussions of education we seem to always be asking what we want children to know. This is really such a bad question that even playwrights remark upon it.

Here is what Shakespeare had to say (from *The Taming of the Shrew*, act 1 scene 1):

Tranio

Mi perdonato, gentle master mine,
I am in all affected as yourself;
Glad that you thus continue your resolve
To suck the sweets of sweet philosophy.
Only, good master, while we do admire
This virtue and this moral discipline,
Let's be no stoics nor no stocks, I pray;
Or so devote to Aristotle's cheques
As Ovid be an outcast quite abjured:
Balk logic with acquaintance that you have
And practise rhetoric in your common talk;
Music and poesy use to quicken you;
The mathematics and the metaphysics,
Fall to them as you find your stomach serves you;
No profit grows where is no pleasure ta'en:
In brief, sir, study what you most affect.

Study what you most affect. This is advice from the 16th century. Or to put this another way, nothing much has changed. Then, as now, students studied subjects that were assumed to be good for them and were most likely not really much absorbed by what they studied. Tranio's advice is advice to be listened to today. What should we teach? Why, what would most affect the students of course. Motivation is a key issue in education.

What do students care about? What are they thinking about? Aren't they worrying about issues in their own lives? To get them to expand their horizons don't we have to start with what they have already experienced and build on that? How can we motivate interest out of the realm of experience? These must be the guiding questions of the curriculum designer. They should have been the issue for the Committee of Ten, but, alas, they were not.

To enable students to study what they most affect we must allow them to be who they are. What does this mean in practice? It certainly means allowing students to be individuals. They are not all equally interested in, nor moved by, the same phenomena. John Dewey, writing in the early 20th century agreed with Shakespeare:

It is no reflection upon the nutritive quality of beefsteak that is not fed to infants. It is not an invidious reflection upon trigonometry that we do not teach it in the first or fifth grade of school. It is not the subject per se that is educative or that is conducive to growth. There is no subject that is in and of itself, or without regard to the stage of growth attained by the learner, such that inherent educational value can be attributed to it Failure to take into account adaptation to the needs and capacities of individuals was the source of the idea that certain subjects and certain methods are intrinsically cultural or intrinsically good for mental discipline. There is no such thing as educational value in the abstract. The notion that some subjects and methods and that acquaintance with certain facts and truths possess educational value in and of themselves is the reason why traditional education reduced the material of education so largely to a diet of predigested materials.

We simply cannot go on assuming that we are certain what students should know and therefore must teach it to them. We need to pay attention to what students can do with any knowledge we choose to teach. Temporary memorization of knowledge that never comes up later in life is really not a reasonable goal for students or for schools.

We must attempt to understand what students will be able to do with what they learn. Here again is Dewey:

> Almost everyone has had occasion to look back upon his school days and wonder what has become of the knowledge he was supposed to have amassed during his years of schooling. . . . Indeed, he is lucky who does not find that in order to make progress, he does not have to unlearn much of what he learned in school.

Dewey was frustrated throughout his life that he could not create schools that would change this state of affairs. Can we succeed where Dewey could not? It has always been possible to change one school for a short period of time. Dewey was able to do that as well. But his changes couldn't create systemic changes. We need a plan that not only produces one good school, but thousands of good schools. Fortunately, the world is quite different than it was 100 years ago. New technologies can play a crucial role this time. To take advantage of these new technologies, we must stop asking what knowledge to transmit and begin to talk about doing. We must ask, in a new way, what it means to be educated.

Next is Dewey's characterization of what it meant to be educated in the early 20th century:

> It was enough to regulate the quantity and difficulty of the material provided, in a scheme of quantitative grading, from month to month and from year to year. Otherwise a pupil was expected to take it in the doses that were pre-

scribed from without. If the pupil left it instead of taking it, if he engaged in physical truancy, or in the mental truancy of mind-wandering and finally built up an emotional revulsion against the subject, he was held to be at fault. No question was raised as to whether the trouble might not lie in the subject-matter or in the way in which it was offered. The principle of interaction makes it clear that failure of adaptation of material to needs and capacities of individuals may cause an experience to be non-educative quite as much as failure of an individual to adapt himself to the material.

Nothing much has changed in the last 100 years. We still fail to consider what it is the child wants to learn. We still have lists of facts we think children should know independent of their use for that material in their future lives. We still believe that information can be simply told to children and that they will retain it, no matter how much our own experience in school fails to confirm this.

School ought not be about factual knowledge. That simply shouldn't matter. Facts aren't so clear cut any way and it is hard to remember them unless you can make regular use of them. Education ought to be about preparation for real life. The intellectual issue in real life is reasoning, not recitation. We need to avoid telling students how things are and instead help them discover things for themselves. The job of a school and a teacher is to serve as the catalyst for that discovery.

Men are born ignorant, not stupid; they are made stupid by education.

Bertrand Russell

REFERENCE NOTES

The short quotes I found on the Web. There are many sources. A good one is:

http://www.etni.org/il/quotes/education.htm

The long quotes from Plato, Aristotle, Descartes, Shakespeare, Veblen, and others are from the Great Books series edited by Clifton Fadiman and published by The Encyclopedia Britannica. There are 60 volumes in the series containing many but not all the works of many great thinkers. Plato gets two volumes and I believe that every work of his that is known is in there.

The Grandview Preparatory School has its curriculum on file for use by its teachers. It is not published. I believe they got the curriculum they use from an independent school in Texas whose headmaster they hired.

The Dewey quoted in this chapter is from the Great Books series but only a very small amount of Dewey is represented in that series. Mortimer Adler studied under Dewey at Columbia and there was no love lost between the two men (personal communication—from Adler, not Dewey.)

2

Thinking and Experience
in School

THE ROLE OF EXPERIENCE

The best way to come to truth being to examine things as really they are, and not to conclude they are, as we fancy of ourselves, or have been taught by others to imagine.

John Locke, An Essay Concerning Human Understanding

True information is mainly derived from experience; and if the Americans had not been gradually accustomed to govern themselves, their book-learning would not help them much at the present day.

Tocqueville

For centuries, it has been understood by the great scholars that experience and knowledge are intricately woven together.

That all our knowledge begins with experience there can be no doubt. . . . no knowledge of ours is antecedent to experience, but begins with it.

Immanuel Kant, The Critique of Pure Reason

But if knowledge begins with experience, one is prone to wonder why the teaching of knowledge doesn't typically begin with experience. To see what I mean here we can consider teaching any subject not typically taught in school. Let's imagine we want to teach someone to play baseball. How might we begin? We might take them to a baseball game before we start, perhaps as a way of motivating them and perhaps as a way of letting them see what it is they will be expected to do. But, it won't be too long into the start of the course of instruction, that they attempt to hit the ball, or catch the ball, or throw the ball. It is virtually inconceivable that the teaching of baseball would proceed in any other way. Would we make them first be baseball students and have them pass an exam on the physics of the curve ball before we let them play?

The same would be true of learning to cook, learning to do carpentry, photography, or nearly any other subject one might voluntarily choose to learn. Except somehow in school, where the choices are not voluntary, all bets are off. Suddenly, since a student cannot vote with his feet, those in charge subject students to endless theory and allow very little in the way of practice. Experience does not get to be the teacher in school. Part of the problem is that we have decided what subjects must be taught independent of what a student might eventually do with the knowledge taught in those subjects. We have decided that history and science need to be taught, without asking why a student will ever need the information or theory provided. We never allow the possibility of practice to arise in the first place.

Of course, the truth is we don't usually decide to teach someone to play baseball or any of the other subjects listed above. We usually wait to be approached by the prospective student in some way. They want to play baseball, and they ask for help. Students don't usually want to learn history or science in the same way. So, four questions are obvious. Why don't they want to? How can we make them want to? Should we make them want to? And, how do we go about teaching these subjects once we have established that the students do indeed want to learn them?

> According to my view, any one who would be good at anything must practise that thing from his youth upwards, both in sport and earnest, in its several branches: for example, he who is to be a good builder, should play at building children's houses; he who is to be a good husbandman, at tilling the ground; and those who have the care of their education should provide them when young with mimic tools. They should learn beforehand the knowledge which they will afterwards require for their art. For example, the future carpenter should learn to measure or apply the line in play; and the future warrior should learn riding, or some other exercise, for amusement, and the teacher should endeavour to direct the children's inclinations and pleasures, by the help of amusements, to their final aim in life.
>
> *Plato*

We can admit the possibility that we don't know how to make science, for example, a doing-based subject, but certainly Plato understood the issue well enough. So, perhaps the school system just forgot. True education, according to Plato (and according to nearly anyone else who has thought about education seriously), is about practice. You can't learn anything without constant practice. You can teach a child to hit a baseball for example, but it will take years of practice before he is any good at it.

How do we get the child to be interested in what we want to teach him? Plato again provided some insight into this:

> The most important part of education is right training in the nursery. The soul of the child in his play should be guided to the love of that sort of excellence in which when he grows up to manhood he will have to be perfected.

The real issue for education is figuring out how to make a child love something and then begin to make them practice it. We can see how this works in the modern day with respect to music lessons. You can force a child to practice the piano after having spent a great deal of money on piano lessons. But, unless a child has a natural love of and curiosity about music, it is unlikely you will meet with much success. A child who grows up in a house of musicians is far more likely to develop such an interest than one who grows up in a house where music is never played.

But what about mathematics? Can we simply wait for a child to love it or must we force it down their throat because hardly anyone ever loves mathematics? It is clear what the school system's answer to this is. It is much less clear how this force feeding of mathematics does much good.

The same applies to history and science. What would make a child love history or science? Let's go back to the curriculum of Grandview Prep:

B. Learning, Studying, and Growing skills
  1. Map Study skills
     a. How to interpret different kinds of maps—*reinforce, develop, prepare.*
     b. How to identify and use map symbols—*reinforce, develop, prepare.*
     c. How to distinguish a map from a picture—*reinforce, develop, prepare.*
     d. How to use a map legend (key)—*reinforce, develop, prepare.*
     e. How to use cardinal and ordinal directions on a map and globe—*new, prepare.*
     f. How to use map coordinates—*new, prepare.*
     g. How to use map colored pencils and crayons to color maps—*reinforce, develop, prepare.*
     h. Identify major cities, rivers, lakes, and boundaries in Florida—*new, prepare.*

Of all the material that was listed in the history second grade curriculum, the only thing that seems to be obviously about interests a student might have is map reading. Why? Because one can imagine that possibility that a child might need to acquire that skill. On a road trip with their parents they might be interested in the map. Alternatively, the school could devise an activity that was fun in which could only succeed by knowing how to read a map. Is map reading important? Perhaps. That is not the question. The point is that it is something a second grader could get excited about, practice, and maintain as a life long skill.

As an alternative let's consider Medieval Man (another of the units in the curriculum.) At first glance this seems hopeless. How can a second grader relate to the life of medieval man? Why should he have to? What relevance will it have in his life? What could he practice going forward based on what he learned by finding out about medieval man? And more importantly, why is this in the curriculum in the first place?

But of course, one can make such a subject of interest to a child. One can easily imagine a child in England or France becoming curious about castles that he sees when he is driven around his country. Curiosity is a good starting place for instruction. Second graders are just at the age where they find castles to be cool. They could be charged with trying to build a castle. They would certainly learn a great deal from the experience, but here again we need to ask whether they would retain that knowledge since castle building isn't a subject that will come up all that much in their future lives. The conundrum is always the same: Simply because we know it and want to tell it, and even because a child enjoys it, does that mean that a child needs to hear it or will retain what he does hear?

I can recall a visit to Brazil a few years ago. I was taken to what was supposed to be the best school in Sao Paolo. In a first grade class I watched as the students discussed Greek theater. They had built dioramas of a typical theater and were discussing the plays.

How relevant is this to the life of these children? Even if this were great fun (it didn't look like it), the children would soon forget the experience because it really isn't germane to the lives they are living or will live. The curriculum made no sense.

Of course, this is not a new problem:

> I'm sure the reason such young nitwits are produced in our schools is because they have no contact with anything of any use in everyday life.
> *Petronius (d. circa 66 CE) The Satyricon*

Imagine that. Two thousand years later, and still no one has figured this out.

A curriculum should focus on problems that may come up again and again in a child's life. Does history actually come up? It can. I just used history to make a point for example. History informs decision making. But a child would have to be making decisions to make use of it then, wouldn't he?

Suppose that instead of teaching history per se, we taught decision making. Or suppose we taught how to listen in order to determine the veracity of what you hear. These are not academic subjects of course. But shouldn't they be?

For example, there have been many movies made about various historical events. Some of these movies can be understood by second graders. But are these movies right? Do they accurately depict events as they happened? How would the child know the truth? These are, in fact, questions that matter very much in the future life of a child—not whether the particulars of some history are true, but how to determine truth. In real life truth is not so easily determined:

I never give them hell. I just tell the truth and they think it's hell.

Harry Truman

Men stumble over the truth from time to time, but most pick themselves up and hurry off as if nothing happened.

Winston Churchill

So, reversing things for a moment, instead of teaching about medieval man, how about getting kids interested in any subject, historical or otherwise, that would call on their ability to determine truth, either by experimentation, or by reading, or by argument? Surely this ability matters more than the facts being studied. And curiously, this is what it means to love history. Historians don't love the facts, they love uncovering the facts, disputing the facts, reinterpreting the facts. Instead we teach children the least interesting aspect of history and claim that they need to know it. No one needs to know who Daniel Boone was. We can all live fine lives without this information. But can we live well if we don't understand how to verify whether something we hear about has actually taken place?

The real issue is that we cannot artificially impose knowledge on children nor tell them what they need to know. In a sense, they need to tell us what they need to know. Every parent understands this when they answer their children's questions and do things that their children demand to do. Why should school be different? The parent can take the child to the zoo because they hope they will like it, but the second visit must be demanded by the child. So it should be in school. Schools don't behave this way, at least in part because there are many different children each with different interests. But there are other less benign reasons as well. While it may not be possible to build individuated curricula (it is not impossible, just costly), it is certainly possible to take advantage of what can be taught in relation to the needs children already have. Let's hear from John Dewey:

Try the experiment of communicating, with fullness and accuracy, some experience to another, especially if it be somewhat complicated, and you will find your own attitude toward your experience changing; otherwise you resort to expletives and ejaculations. The experience has to be formulated in order to be communicated. To formulate requires getting outside of it, seeing it as another would see it, considering what points of contact it has with the life of another so that it may be got into such form that he can appreciate its meaning. . . . It may fairly be said, therefore, that any social arrangement that remains vitally social, or vitally shared, is educative to those who participate in it. Only when it becomes cast in a mold and runs in a routine way does it lose its educative power.

In final account, then, not only does social life demand teaching and learning for its own permanence, but the very process of living together educates. It enlarges and enlightens experience; it stimulates and enriches imagination; it creates responsibility for accuracy and vividness of statement and thought.

Dewey was suggesting that simply having experiences, communicating them, sharing ideas, functioning as a group, perhaps those are the issues that demand treatment in the schools. One wonders why they never were the main issues in school. They certainly are some of the main issues in life. But because school has been intellectualized, because it is about scholarship, despite the fact that few students actually go on to become scholars, we persist in teaching subjects that have no value.

Chief among these is, of course, higher mathematics. Mathematics has reached the pinnacle of success as an academic discipline in this country despite the fact that it is of so little use in real life. Here is what Descartes had to say about it:

Among the branches of philosophy, I had, at an earlier period, given some attention to logic, and among those of the mathematics to geometrical analysis and algebra—three arts or sciences which ought, as I conceived, to contribute something to my design. But, on examination, I found that, as for logic, its syllogisms and the majority of its other precepts are of avail—rather in the communication of what we already know, or even as the art of Lully, in speaking without judgment of things of which we are ignorant, than in the investigation of the unknown; and although this science contains indeed a number of correct and very excellent precepts, there are, nevertheless, so many others, and these either injurious or superfluous, mingled with the former, that it is almost quite as difficult to effect a severance of the true from the false as it is to extract a Diana or a Minerva from a rough block of marble.

So, Descartes had little use for logic. But what about algebra?

Then as to the analysis of the ancients and the algebra of the moderns, besides that they embrace only matters highly abstract, and, to appearance, of no use, the former is so exclusively restricted to the consideration of figures, that it can exercise the understanding only on condition of greatly fatiguing the imagination; and, in the latter, there is so complete a subjection to certain rules and formulas, that there results an art full of confusion and obscurity calculated to embarrass, instead of a science fitted to cultivate the mind. By these considerations I was induced to seek some other method which would comprise the advantages of the three and be exempt from their defects.

Descartes (on Method) Part II

Descartes was of course, among other things, a famous mathematician. If algebra seemed useless to him, for whom is it useful? The answer, of course, as we saw in the Prologue, is that it isn't meant to be useful. Nevertheless we teach it and test it and teach it and test it.

Mathematics is not within the realm of the normal experience of even the most educated adult. I am quite sure that Clifton Fadiman would have had trouble with the math portion of the SATs. It is imperative that we make school relate to the experiences we anticipate that children will actually have as they mature into adults. School is about preparation for experience, the enhancement of experience, the simulation of experience, and the comprehension of experience, or it should be.

If school is not about experience, then the consequences can be awful. Dewey again:

Indeed, he is lucky who does not find that in order to make progress, he does not have to unlearn much of what he learned in school. These questions cannot be disposed of by saying that the subjects were not actually learned, for they were learned at least sufficiently to enable a pupil to pass examinations in them. One trouble is that the subject-matter in question was learned in isolation; it was put, as it were, in a water-tight compartment. When the question is asked, then, what has become of it, where has it gone to, the right answer is that it is still there in the special compartment in which it was originally stowed away. If exactly the same conditions recurred as those under which it was acquired, it would also recur and be available. But it was segregated when it was acquired and hence is so disconnected from the rest of experience that it is not available under the actual conditions of life.

THE ROLE OF ORIGINAL THOUGHT

Of course, there are some experiences that would never happen if it weren't for someone thinking they need to cajole someone into having them. It is really a question of what form the cajoling might take and what experiences are deemed worthy of the effort. Convincing a child to go to the zoo the first time may take a little effort, but curiously convincing him to learn to drive a car does not. As long as the child has already experienced something, their interest is aroused and they can be cajoled into trying some of it. Here is Montaigne on the normal methodology for this:

> 'Tis the custom of pedagogues to be eternally thundering in their pupil's ears, as they were pouring into a funnel, while the business of the pupil is only to repeat what the others have said: now I would have a tutor to correct this error, and, that at the very first, he should, according to the capacity he has to deal with, put it to the test, permitting his pupil himself to taste things, and of himself to discern and choose them, sometimes opening the way to him, and sometimes leaving him to open it for himself; that is, I would not have him alone to invent and speak, but that he should also hear his pupil speak in turn.

Montaigne was talking about 16th-century France, but nothing ever really changes in education. How can we fix this? Unfortunately, the reason that school changes so slowly is that governments see no need for the change:

> No one will doubt that the legislator should direct his attention above all to the education of youth; for the neglect of education does harm to the constitution. The citizen should be molded to suit the form of government under which he lives. For each government has a peculiar character which originally formed and which continues to preserve it. The character of democracy creates democracy, and the character of oligarchy creates oligarchy; and always the better the character, the better the government.
>
> *John Stuart Mill*

Mill was talking about 19th-century England, but the lessons are the same. Government cares about making the citizens do their job as citizens. Even so, we might want students to experience government in some way. The problem is that the scholars want students to be scholars and the government wants them to be citizens. What is left out of this confrontation is the real experiences outside of these two realms. Mill had something to say about that as well:

> No one's idea of excellence in conduct is that people should do absolutely nothing but copy one another. No one would assert that people ought not to put into their mode of life, and into the conduct of their concerns, any impress whatever of their own judgment, or of their own individual character. On the other hand, it would be absurd to pretend that people ought to live as if nothing whatever had been known in the world before they came into it; as if experience had as yet done nothing towards showing that one mode of existence, or of conduct, is preferable to another. Nobody denies that people should be so taught and trained in youth, as to know and benefit by the ascertained results of human experience. But it is the privilege and proper condition of a human

being, arrived at the maturity of his faculties, to use and interpret experience in his own way.

John Stuart Mill
On Liberty Chapter III on Individuality, as One of the Elements of Wellbeing

Here then is the problem. We want students to have their own experiences and learn from them. Yet so many adults have had important experiences and we want students to learn from those experiences before having their own. We want individuality, but we have large classrooms and that makes that difficult. We want to tell students about our collective experiences, but students don't pay attention unless you test them so we have to test them to see if they were listening. We want originality, but we don't. This is the issue.

Here again is Mill:

The human faculties of perception, judgment, discriminative feeling, mental activity, and even moral preference, are exercised only in making a choice. He who does anything because it is the custom, makes no choice. He gains no practice either in discerning or in desiring what is best. The mental and moral, like the muscular powers, are improved only by being used. The faculties are called into no exercise by doing a thing merely because others do it, no more than by believing a thing only because others believe it. If the grounds of an opinion are not conclusive to the person's own reason, his reason cannot be strengthened, but is likely to be weakened by his adopting it.

Even Mill, who wants people to learn from others and thinks governments need to be teaching students to be good citizens, realized that it is the individuality of the educational experience that makes it valuable. He doesn't want people to simply adopt the viewpoints of others. He wants originality in thinking:

He who lets the world . . . choose his plan of life for him, has no need of any other faculty than the ape-like one of imitation. He who chooses his plan for himself, employs all his faculties. He must use observation to see, reasoning and judgment to foresee, activity to gather materials for decision, discrimination to decide, and when he has decided, firmness and self-control to hold to his deliberate decision.

There we have it. This is all there is to know about education. Fadiman probably read this essay of Mill's since he edited the book, but one wonders if he understood it. This is what education must be about: enabling children to create their own life plans. This would include, at some point, one's own educational plan one would hope. This point must be much earlier than college, perhaps as early as the third grade. Why? Because after you are used to letting others define for you what will constitute your own education, it is hard to become your own educational master once again.

Mill realized that this was an issue for society as a whole. In a government that is repressive, education cannot allow individuals to flourish. But, in the United States where individuals have a great deal of freedom, is this really an issue? Why isn't there freedom in school too?

> Whoever thinks that individuality of desires and impulses should not be encouraged to unfold itself, must maintain that society has no need of strong natures—is not the better for containing many persons who have much character—and that a high general average of energy is not desirable.
>
> In some early states of society, these forces might be, and were, too much ahead of the power which society then possessed of disciplining and controlling them. There has been a time when the element of spontaneity and individuality was in excess, and the social principle had a hard struggle with it. The difficulty then was, to induce men of strong bodies or minds to pay obedience to any rules which required them to control their impulses. . . . But society has now fairly got the better of individuality; and the danger which threatens human nature is not the excess, but the deficiency, of personal impulses and preferences.

Here again, I need to point out that Mill was writing about 19th-century England. He worries about inducing individuality. In our schools, ruled as they are by standardized tests, there is no individuality at all. The real reason for encouraging individual thought was stated by Alfred North Whitehead in the early 20th century:

> The rate of progress is such that an individual human being, of ordinary length of life, will be called upon to face novel situations which find no parallel in his past. The fixed person for the fixed duties, who in older societies was such a godsend, in the future will be a public danger. In the second place, the modern professionalism in knowledge works in the opposite direction so far as the intellectual sphere is concerned.

Whitehead believed that those who could not think on their own would be a public danger! He thought society was changing too fast and that education had to be about how to handle novel situations. I wonder what he would think now.

Let's hear from Plato (Phaedrus dialogue):

> SOCRATES: But he who thinks that in the written word there is necessarily much which is not serious, and that neither poetry nor prose, spoken or written, is of any great value, if, like the compositions of the rhapsodies, they are only recited in order to be believed, and not with any view to criticism or in-

struction; . . . this is the right sort of man; and you and I, Phaedrus, would pray that we may become like him.

It is not the things that are taught that matter but our understanding and criticism of the idea presented to us. It is original thought that is worthy of emulation. So said Socrates. We would have better schools if anyone had listened.

The Role of Curiosity

One cannot be original in thought if there is nothing to be original about. It makes sense to present situations, problems, issues, and various conundra to children in the attempt to awaken their ability to think. But, we also must put them in situations about which they become curious:

> The whole art of teaching is only the art of awakening the natural curiosity of young minds for the purpose of satisfying it afterwards.
>
> *Anatole France*

This relates strongly to the idea of experience. We must allow students to have experiences so that they can become curious about them. This is an idea to which many people pay lip service. The key word is "exposure." Children are constantly being exposed to mathematics or physics or literature, just in case they might like it. The entire country is exposed to physics in case they might like it. I can only speculate on what percentage of our children become physicists but I know that nearly all of those who go to college are exposed to it. Curiously none of them are exposed to medicine or law and great many more of them go on to work in these fields.

The idea of exposure is fine, but the reality is that we teach what was dictated in 1892 and that is that. (We could teach physics to teach scientific reasoning, but what we actually do is have students memorize formulas for tests.) To change this we must understand 1892 as an essentially random event, and ignore everything done at that meeting. Then we need to ask ourselves, what kinds of experiences would be useful for children to have and see if we can begin to provide them in school. One part of the answer to this question of what to provide to children in the way of experience is that we need to think about experiences that will make them curious.

> My own criticism of our traditional educational methods is that they are far too much occupied with intellectual analysis, and with the acquirement of formularized information. What I mean is, that we neglect to strengthen habits of concrete appreciation of the individual facts in their full interplay of emergency values, and that we merely emphasize abstract formulations which ignore this aspect of the interplay of diverse values.
>
> *Whitehead (Science and the modern world)*

Whitehead was concerned here with the idea that professional education makes everyone a specialist. This is not a problem in our current schools of course. His main point was as follows:

> Wisdom is the fruit of a balanced development. It is this balanced growth of individuality which it should be the aim of education to secure. The most useful discoveries for the immediate future would concern the furtherance of this aim without detriment to the necessary intellectual professionalism.

The relevance of his concerns are these: We cannot expect to create a balanced development if we compartmentalize knowledge in the way that we do. Students study history and later science and later math. They go from period to period and subject to subject. They do none of this because they have expressed an interest or shown curiosity about a subject. If they do express curiosity, they cannot delve into that interest because the curriculum has a pace of its own and the student must move with it. The student becomes a kind of professional student, good at being a student.

The balance to his development is determined by the school and the state which has demanded to which tests the school must adhere. Thus, every student is narrow in exactly the way that Whitehead was worried about. Being broad in thoughts and wise in ideas depends on being able to think about complex issues at one's own pace according to one's own interests. This cannot happen in our current schools without extraordinary measures being put into place. Students are compartmentalized in the same way that the subjects they study are departmentalized. They are narrow in multiple subjects.

People who propose curricula of necessity make divisions that can be studied. But the subjects are not always English, history, mathematics, and science. Here are Plato's proposed divisions (from The Republic):

> At any rate, we are satisfied, as before, to have four divisions; two for intellect and two for opinion, and to call the first division science, the second understanding, the third belief, and the fourth perception of shadows, opinion being concerned with becoming, and intellect with being.

But alas, Charles Eliot, noted scholar and, one would assume, a man who could read Plato in the original Greek, failed to take seriously what he had read.

Learning to Think for Oneself

Of course, it is learning to think on one's own that is the real purpose of education, or at least it should be. Here again, this is hardly a new idea. Let's listen again to Plato:

Until the person is able to abstract and define rationally the idea of good, and unless he can run the gauntlet of all objections, and is ready to disprove them, not by appeals to opinion, but to absolute truth, never faltering at any step of the argument—unless he can do all this, you would say that he knows neither the idea of good nor any other good; he apprehends only a shadow, if anything at all, which is given by opinion, and not by science; dreaming and slumbering in this life, before he is well awake here, he arrives at the world below, and has his final quietus.

Plato; Republic, book 7

The issue is simple enough and Plato understood it well. One cannot train leaders by telling them what to think.

And surely you would not have the children of your ideal State, the future rulers, to be like posts, having no reason in them, and yet to be set in authority over the highest matters?
Certainly not.
Then you will make a law that they shall have such an education as will enable them to attain the greatest skill in asking and answering questions?

It is easy to find scholars who agree with Plato on this. The reason is obvious. People who think about thinking conclude that thinking is the most important thing there is to teach. Unfortunately, "teaching people to think" is what teachers often claim they are doing. Consider the following:

A great truth is a truth whose opposite is also a great truth.
Mann, Thomas (1875–1955) Essay on Freud. 1937.

College teaches people to think. We hear this all the time. Let me make a simple statement. If the course a student is taking has a multiple choice test at the end, it is not teaching the student to think. If there is argumentation, if it is possible to hold opposite points of view from the teacher and still be right, indeed if it is possible to hold opposite points of view from your own and still be right, then perhaps one is learning to think. But, if there are right answers that the teacher knows and your job is to reiterate them, no thinking is taking place.

Be not astonished at new ideas; for it is well known to you that a thing does not therefore cease to be true because it is not accepted by many.
Spinoza

Spinoza was talking hear about the same issue. The value of a seminar in school is not to learn the material but to deal with new ideas. New ideas are the currency of thinking. Can a second grader deal with new ideas? Of course they can. This might be the best time for them to do so. How to deal with issues in their own lives would have to be the subject matter however, otherwise the new ideas will be just so much air.

> Creativity is a central source of meaning in our lives . . . most of the things that
> are interesting, important, and *human* are the results of creativity . . . [and]
> when we are involved in it, we feel that we are living more fully than during
> the rest of life.
>
> Mihaly Csikszentmihalyi, *Creativity: Flow and the Psychology*
> *of Discovery and Invention*

Csikszentmihalyi is not dead, so maybe he doesn't qualify as a great author to
be quoted. Certainly Clifton Fadiman is unlikely to have met him, although
they were both in Chicago. He studies how people feel about themselves and
how they think and has observed how students feel in school. He notes that
students feel good in school when they are being creative, that this is what
makes people feel alive. It is important to remember this when we think
about school.

Let's again hear from Plato (the Phaedrus dialogue):

> SOCRATES: Until a man knows the truth of the several particulars of which
> he is writing or speaking, and is able to define them as they are, and having de-
> fined them again to divide them until they can be no longer divided, . . . and
> discover the different modes of discourse which are adapted to different na-
> tures, until he has accomplished all this, he will be unable to handle arguments
> according to rules of art, . . . either for the purpose of teaching or persuading.

It is strange to realize that Plato (or Socrates) knew so well that true
learning depends on the ability to persuade, analyze, examine truth, and
teach, yet these things are so completely absent from our schools even today.

Because we have relied on Plato heavily in this chapter, I let him have the
final word:

> Ath. Then let us not leave the meaning of education ambiguous or ill-defined.
> At present, . . . we call one man educated and another uneducated, although
> the uneducated man may be sometimes very well educated for the calling of a
> retail trader, or of a captain of a ship, and the like. For we are not speaking of
> education in this narrower sense, but of that other education in virtue from
> youth upwards, which makes a man eagerly pursue the ideal perfection of citi-
> zenship, and teaches him how rightly to rule and how to obey. . . . Those who
> are rightly educated generally become good men.

REFERENCE NOTES

The sources are the Great Books series for the extended quotes and the Web for the
short pithy ones.

3

What Uneducated Minds Need

It is time to rethink our basic tenets of education. We need to see education not as a process for the transmission of knowledge to children, but as a process of the opening of children's minds to the world around them. Because typically government and religion have been in charge of education, the former was always the model. Governments want citizens who follow the rules of society. Religions want students to take in and believe the basic tenets of the faith. In the modern era these can no longer be the hopes of our education system. What we need to do is enable children to think for themselves. In an ever changing and complex world, the winners will be those who can do more than recite what they were taught.

> Genius, in truth, means little more than the faculty of perceiving in an unhabitual way.
>
> *William James*

Do we want to create geniuses? Well, of course we do, but there is a more important lesson in James' words. The question raised by James is: How do we teach children to perceive in an unhabitual way? To put this differently, it is obvious that we cannot teach children to perceive unhabitually. What we can do is teach them to perceive habitually. We can teach them about what they see and about what they hear and we can supply beliefs that will allow them to interpret complexity. In other words, we can supply simple answers to complex questions. This is, in fact, what the school system does on a regular basis. In fact, this is pretty much the intent of the school system. This is why there are tests—to see if the student has learned the answers. It is the very concept that the answers are there to be learned that is the heart of the problem. In a school where there are right answers, there is the intention to make students learn those answers, or in James' terms, to cause students to perceive in a habitual way. Knowing the answers is in many ways less valuable than people suppose. Certainly generations of students have memorized answers only to forget them after the exam. There can be little value in this exercise. But more importantly, reverence for the answers can tend to obscure the questions. Pascal, the most famous mathematician of the 17th century had this to say:

> If it is a question of knowing who was the first king of France, where the geographers put the first meridian, what words are used in a dead language and everything of this sort, how could we find it out except from books? And who can add anything new to what they tell us about it, since we desire to know only what they contain? Authority alone can give us light on such matters.
>
> It is quite otherwise with subjects accessible to sense or reasoning; here authority is useless, only reason can know them.
>
> Thus it is that geometry, arithmetic, music, physics, medicine, architecture and all the sciences subject to experiment and reason must be added to if they are to become perfect. The ancients found them merely sketched by their predecessors, and we shall leave them to our successors in a more perfected state that received them.
>
> Blaise Pascal, Scientific Treatises, Preface to the Treatise on the Vacuum

Pascal was worrying about advancing science rather than teaching students, but in many ways these are the same issue. Original thought does not come from first learning all the answers. A mind cluttered with the right way to see things cannot necessarily be original about things. A certain amount of naiveté is valuable for creativity. To make students curious one must allow for them to delve into unanswered questions, to see the mysteries that make up the whole world rather than the facts that make up a small subset of the world that is well understood.

Descartes addressed the question of the value of knowing a set of facts:

> If, after we have recognized intuitively a number of simple truths, we wish to draw any inference from them, it is useful to run over them in a continuous and uninterrupted act of thought, to reflect upon their relations to one another, and to grasp together distinctly a number of these propositions so far as is possible at the same time. For this is a way of making our knowledge much more certain, and of greatly increasing the power of the mind.
>
> Descartes (Rule XI)

To put this more simply, Descartes was suggesting that it's not the truths that are of value, but the inferences that can be drawn from them. Or in other words, it is thinking about what you know that is of value, not the knowledge. In a school system concerned with tests and grades, the facts, not the inferences have value. Inferences can be wrong. Or they can be very insightful, leading to new, more significant truths. But how often are the tests about the inferences? In a world where there are only correct answers you can't test possible conclusions. In a world dominated by multiple choice tests, your new insight is not likely to be one of the choices. The currency of a good education cannot be facts, it must be insights.

With this is mind, let's go back to the curriculum of the school in Florida. This time let's look at the sixth grade World Cultures curriculum (I have highlighted the parts that are germane to our subsequent analysis):

TIME REQUIREMENTS: 74 minutes every other day

TEXT: *Global Insights* (with corresponding workbook); Glencoe, McGraw-Hill

OTHER MATERIALS: Globe, maps, notebooks, laptop computers, worksheets

COURSE EMPHASIS: This course will emphasize the new global issues that students will face in the 21st century. Students will develop an understanding and appreciation of diverse cultural backgrounds, the reason being that we now all share our Global Home. **Students will investigate some of the political, economic cultural and social institutions of different global regions.** Students will study struggles of independence, economic reality and what denotes peace from a regional, non-Western perspective. The major areas studied include Africa, China, Middle East, Australia, New Zealand, and the World today, and if time permits, students will briefly Japan, Latin America, and India. Current events will be a unifying thread throughout this course. The students to learn more about the cultures they are studying will use the Internet extensively.

I. OBJECTIVES

    A. History/Social Studies Skills

        1. Integration

           a. Using special days, integrate all academic activity into one coherent unit

           b. Discover the interconnections between different phases and periods and periods of cultural history

        2. Methods and Concepts of Various Social Studies Disciplines

           a. Utilize the knowledge and skills from various social studies disciplines to trace the process of change

      b. Use a wide variety of materials as sources to exemplify the process of change

      c. Utilize geography to see how physical location affects the history of an area

   3. Nature and Process of Change

      a. Practice comparing and contrasting two separate cultures

      b. Determine the process and patters of change, during declines, the rise of new structures, and radical changes in a culture

   4. Nature and Character of Peoples, Civilizations, and Cultures

      a. To characterize a civilization and its culture

      b. To characterize a particular civilization and its culture

      c. To characterize a particular civilization and its culture during various stages.

B. Learning, Study, and Growth Skills

   1. Classroom study skills: listening, note taking discussion, following instructions, etc.

      a. Gather the main ideas, tracing change in patterns during the lectures and student presentations—*new*.

      b. Note taking practice for speed using abbreviations and arrows to relate—*new*.

   2. Homework Study Skills

      a. Practice outlining a chapter

      b. Take note cards on chapter.

   3. Examination preparations and note taking skills

      a. Review class notes effectively—outlining and highlighting during review—tracing change over several days' records—*new*

      b. To organize test answers, tracing cause and effect (re-reading answers with the goal to make sure the teacher will not have to write "why").

   4. Reading Skills

      a. Reading for main ideas—*reinforce*

   5. Writing Skills

      a. Writing in clear and complete sentences—*reinforce*

      b. Writing short reports with high clarity—*reinforce*

   6. Map Study Skills

      a. Read maps to grasp physical features

7. Information Gathering, Recording, Organizing, communication Skills

   a. To gather materials and present small groups project several times a year using technology.

8. Research Paper Skills

   a. To use paper skills from 5th grade—reinforce

   b. To use parenthetical notation

9. General Maturity skills

   a. Examine other cultures and peoples objectivity.

   b. To listen to other opinions objectively.

   c. To break down ethnocentrisms.

II. IMPLEMENTATION

A. Design, Sequence, and Method

   1. Design—the course examines a variety of cultures at different stages and usually during periods of rapid and significant change. A quick static view of a society is taken followed by a study of that society undergoing change.

   2. Sequence

      a. Africa

         1) Adapting to the Environment

         2) African Heritage

         3) Nigeria

         4) South Africa

         5) Kenya

         6) The Arts in Daily Life

         7) Challenges to Development

      b. China

         1) The Land Under Heaven

         2) The mandate of Heaven

         3) The Few and the Many

         4) The Chinese Heritage

         5) The Chinese Revolution

         6) China after Mao

         7) Daily Life in Modern China

      c. Japan

         1) The Great Island Country

    2) Traditional Japan
    3) Modern Japan
    4) Religion and the Arts
    5) Japanese Society
    6) Work and Leisure

d. India
    1) Land and Water
    2) The Indian People
    3) Religions of India
    4) An Old and New Land
    5) Developing India
    6) The Arts

e. Latin America
    1) Vast and Varied Environment
    2) The Human Diversity
    3) The Social Fabric
    4) Prayer and Politics
    5) Change Takes Many Forms
    6) Dictatorships and Democracies

f. Middle East
    1) Environment and People
    2) A Mosaic of Peoples
    3) The Way of Life
    4) Religion and State
    5) The Great Bitterness
    6) The Middle East Theory

g. Commonwealth of Independent States
    1) Giant Among the Gigantic
    2) The Russian Past
    3) The Soviet Era
    4) A New Revolution
    5) The European Republics
    6) Republics of the Caucasus
    7) Central Asian Republics

h. Europe
    1) Varied Lands and Peoples
    2) Roots of European Civilization

> 3) **Conflict and Change**
>
> 4) **The New Europe**
>
> 5) **A Sense of Themselves**
>
> 6) **Arts and Thought**

3. **Methods**

   a. **Lectures**

      1) To connect phases and trace changes as well as to provide background material.

   b. Slides/art to exemplify the thought of a period and a culture-visually

   c. Class Discussion

      1) Reinforce ideas

   d. Computer Software programs

   e. Small group reports where small groups investigate particular areas in more detail

      1) This method helps communication and research skills using reference works, ideas, etc., while teaching the important lesson of good teamwork.

   f. Integrated Units where several disciplines come together and produce a unified whole.

III. EVALUATION

A. **Full period tests**

B. **Quizzes**

C. **Evaluation of Class Discussions**

D. **Computer Assessment Tools**

E. **Cumulative Examinations at the Conclusion of both Semesters**

IV. TEXTS AND MATERIALS

A. *Global Insights*—Glencoe

B. *Teacher's Resource Binder*—Glencoe

C. *Review Book*—Glencoe

D. *Transparency Package*—Glencoe

E. *Testmakers*—Glencoe

When I first saw this curriculum I almost fell over. In 74 minutes, every other day, mostly by listening to lectures, 11-year-old children will know about Africa, China, Europe, India, Japan, Russia, and the Middle East!

I travel a great deal. When my children were young they would travel with me. My daughter spent a week in England with me when she was 8 and a week in Italy, Belgium, and France, when she was 10. When she was 13, we lived in Paris for a year. On those trips she visited many castles (which she really liked) and archeological sites (especially Pompeii, which she loved) and met, played with, and had dinner with many local children and adults. I would say that, on the whole as a result of these visits, she knew more about Europe than most American children and considerably more than one could ever know spending 74 minutes every other day for one school year listening to lectures and reading other material.

Why am I telling you this? Because she knew next to nothing about Europe prior to moving to Paris. After living in Paris she knew a great deal about kids from other parts of the world (she was in a multicultural class) and something about France, but not much. Who are we kidding here? What students learn from such a curriculum is a bunch of facts that they can use for passing tests and promptly forget. What else could they learn from such a whirlwind, and most likely boring, tour of the world? One can't help but wonder what the designers of this curriculum thought they were accomplishing. How can we fix this?

To fix it, we need to ask what the point was in teaching this stuff in the first place. One obvious answer is that it is not unreasonable that 11-year-olds should be exposed to the world around them, a world that is larger than the town they live in or the country they were born in. This is the reason I took my children on trips with me. I figured maybe they would learn more about themselves by seeing others who were different from them.

First let's consider what are the stated goals of this curriculum:

Students will investigate some of the political, economic cultural and social institutions of different global reasons.

2c. Utilize geography to see how physical location affects the history of an area

3b. Determine the process and patters of change, during declines, the rise of new structures, and radical changes in a culture

4c. To characterize a particular civilization and its culture during various stages.

Are they serious? How many adults can do this? Why would children care about this? In fact, these two questions must dominate any thinking we are to do about curriculum reform. All too often curricula are written as if children were to be made into scholars, debating complex issues about which they have no conceivable concern. While, at the same time, there are interesting issues that children are quite willing to concern themselves with. We are interested in turning children into adults who can make sensible decisions about the world in which they live, not into scholars. Do you know how to characterize a particular civilization and its stages? Why would you want to know how to do that? One can only assume that there is some sort of answer in the textbook that children will learn in order to make such characterizations, a methodology they will use for the sixth grade and never again think about in their lives. They will pass tests but they will learn nothing. That said, and realizing that we do not want to make them into scholars but into functioning adults, what can we teach them that will interest them? (If it doesn't interest them they will forget it.)

> Ideas in the mind quickly fade, and often vanish quite out of the understanding, leaving no more footsteps or remaining characters of themselves than shadows do flying over fields of corn, and the mind is as void of them as if they had never been there.
>   There seems to be a constant decay of all our ideas, even of those which are struck deepest, and in minds the most retentive; so that if they be not sometimes renewed, by repeated exercise of the senses, or reflection on those kinds of objects which at first occasioned them, the print wears out, and at last there remains nothing to be seen.
>
>   John Locke (Concerning Human Understanding)

The awful truth is that it is very hard to remember anything one has learned unless that learning is repeated over and over again. Or, if that learning had a great emotional impact, it would be remembered. So, what shall we teach? It seems obvious, since people forget what they learn, that the substance of what we teach isn't the point. Unless we are teaching a skill that can be practiced, the only other point to teaching is to open worlds that a student, knowing of their existence, can willingly enter later on his own.

Following is what Montaigne had to say about his own memory:

> It has befallen me more than once to forget the watchword I had three hours before given or received, and to forget where I had hidden my purse. . . . Memory is the receptacle and case of science: and therefore mine being so treacherous, if I know little, I cannot much complain. I know, in general, the names of the arts, and of what they treat, but nothing more. I turn over books; I do not study them. What I retain I no longer recognize as another's; 'tis only what my judgment has made its advantage of, the discourses and imaginations in which it has been instructed: the author, place, words, and other circumstances, I immediately forget; I am so excellent at forgetting, that I no less forget my own writings and compositions than the rest.
>
>   Montaigne (Of Presumption)

It really comes down to skills that can be practiced again and again and opening the eyes of students to the world around them. What skills might matter here? Following are the skills to be learned that were listed previously in this curriculum:

B. Learning, Study, and Growth Skills

1. Classroom study skills: listening, note taking discussion, following instructions, etc.

    a. Gather the main ideas, tracing change in patterns during the lectures and student presentations—*new*.

    b. Note taking practice for speed using abbreviations and arrows to relate—*new*.

2. Homework Study Skills

    a. Practice outlining a chapter

    b. Take note cards on chapter.

3. Examination preparations and note taking skills

    a. Review class notes effectively—outlining and highlighting during review—tracing change over several days' records—*new*

    b. To organize test answers, tracing cause and effect (re-reading answers with the goal to make sure the teacher will not have to write "why").

4. Reading Skills

    a. Reading for main ideas—*reinforce*

5. Writing Skills

    a. Writing in clear and complete sentences—*reinforce*

    b. Writing short reports with high clarity—*reinforce*

6. Map Study Skills

    a. Read maps to grasp physical features

7. Information Gathering, Recording, Organizing, communication Skills

    a. To gather materials and present small groups project several times a year using technology.

8. Research Paper Skills

    a. To use paper skills from 5th grade—*reinforce*

    b. To use parenthetical notation

9. General Maturity skills

    a. Examine other cultures and peoples objectivity.

    b. To listen to other opinions objectively.

    c. To break down ethnocentrisms.

Are these skills reasonable? Simply put—no. The first three are school skills. I don't consider doing homework or taking tests a skill. I realize that I am out of touch on this since every student in the United States practices this skill daily, but as no adult does, I believe this is a phenomenal waste of time. School ought not be concerned primarily with preparing people for school.

No one can object to teaching reading or writing. But one can object to having students read things in which they have no interest or writing papers that they are doing simply because it has been assigned to them. Such readings and writings fade from the mind the moment they are finished.

Perhaps our task was anticipated by David Hume (writing in the 18th century):

> Should a traveler, returning from a far country, bring us an account of men, wholly different from any with whom we were ever acquainted; men, who were entirely divested of avarice, ambition, or revenge; who knew no pleasure but friendship, generosity, and public spirit; we should immediately, from these circumstances, detect the falsehood, and prove him a liar, with the same certainty as if he had stuffed his narration with stories of centaurs and dragons, miracles and prodigies.
>
> We must not, however, expect that this uniformity of human actions should be carried to such a length as that all men, in the same circumstances, will always act precisely in the same manner, without making any allowance for the diversity of characters, prejudices, and opinions. Such a uniformity in every particular, is found in no part of nature. On the contrary, from observing the variety of conduct in different men, we are enabled to form a greater variety of maxims, which still suppose a degree of uniformity and regularity.
>
> Are the manners of men different in different ages and countries? We learn thence the great force of custom and education, which mould the human mind from its infancy and form it into a fixed and established character. . . . Even the characters, which are peculiar to each individual, have a uniformity in their influence; otherwise our acquaintance with the persons and our observation of their conduct could never teach us their dispositions, or serve to direct our behaviour with regard to them.
>
> *David Hume (Concerning Human Understanding)*

The issue, of course, is that children should learn, as well as they can, what David Hume knew: that we are basically all the same. With that understanding, it possible to appreciate difference, but you can only do that by really experiencing the people of a place, not by reading about it. In today's world we have a variety of ways of experiencing a place without actually going there: movies and television, music, and conversing by Internet to name a few. In Florida, all types of people could actually come to the school. There are people from every country who are retired nearby with little to do who would be glad to visit. Wouldn't the real issue be to get children to experience another world as well as they can, rather than have them pretend to analyze the cultural influences of the Russian Revolution?

Let them write about what they've experienced. Let them debate about issues that they discover are current in the lives of the people they find out about. Let them talk to real people and become impassioned by some aspect of another world and learn more about it and express what they have learned. But, above all, let them choose where they want to go and what they want to do when they get there. If they care about what they experience they will remember it. Otherwise, like Montaigne, they will struggling to remember what happened three hours earlier.

> In all pedagogy the great thing is to strike the iron while hot, and to seize the wave of the pupil's interest in each successive subject before its ebb has come, so that knowledge may be got and a habit of skill acquired—a headway of interest, in short, secured, on which afterward the individual may float.
> William James (Principles of Psychology)

The issue is interests. The job of the educator is to understand what student might be interested in and lead him there.

> To detect the moment of the instinctive readiness for the subject is, then the first duty of every educator.
> William James (Principles of Psychology)

With these thoughts in mind, let's take a look at the seventh grade English curriculum in our Florida school (key points are highlighted):

Department of English/Language Arts
Seventh Grade Curriculum

TIME REQUIREMENTS: 74 minutes every other day

TEXT: *Introduction to Literature*, Glencoe, *The Writer's Choice 7*, Glencoe, *Worldly Wise Book 4*, Educator's Publishing Service, *Grammar Practice Book 7*, Glencoe, *Ridgewood Analogies (3)*, EPS, supplementary novels chosen by the instructor.

OTHER MATERIALS: Library books, laptop computers (provided by the school), spiral notebooks, Internet access.

COURSE EMPHASIS: Goals for reading in the seventh grade extend far beyond merely improving the physical process if reading. Literature is more closely analyzed for plot, character setting, conflict and theme. Point of view is also carefully examined. Works now are studied by genres. Students learn to recognize and use their own writing the concepts of irony, poetic justice, foreshadowing, metaphor and simile, Writing assignments are base don the reading, form their text and their supplemental reading. The focus is on expository writing beginning with an extensive unit on the paragraph and its development of a thesis and long papers. Subject matter for these papers rangers form topics taken form the literature under study. Opinions, on current events, to the results of interviews with other people. The Holocaust is introduced at this level, and a number of the supplemental books deal with the subject, Guest speakers also introduce this event on a personal level. Library time is scheduled, and students are again responsible for choosing books for both oral and written book projects. Other special skills covered in this course include such things as outline, note taking, using the dictionary and thesaurus, and using the correct manuscript form. (MLA guidelines are followed for research). Students also study roots, prefixes and suffixes at this level. Grammar and vocabulary continues to be stressed. Research skills are reinforced. Students use the computer and the Internet extensively, both to improve written work and to improve their research skills.

READING

I. OBJECTIVES

    A. To reinforce the concepts of plot, characterization, setting, conflict and theme

    B. To introduce the concept of point of view, and how point of view affects how a story is viewed by the reader

    C. To introduce the concept of genre

    D. To introduce the concepts of irony, poetic justice, foreshadowing, metaphor and simile

    E. To examine how historical events (e.g. the Holocaust) are the basis for both fiction and nonfiction

II. IMPLEMENTATION

The teacher will assign reading from the text as well as from the supplemental reading. Students will be encouraged to take chapter summaries at home to use for a closer examination of what they are reading. Daily discussions of the reading will focus on the above goals. The discussion will not merely focus on the literal meaning of the text, but will also examine the various layers of what is being read. Students will be encouraged to constantly dig deeper into what is being read, by learning to ask *why* questions. For example, the motives of a character can be examined more closely, as can the relationship between characters. The teacher will give a historical account of the Holocaust when this reading unit is studied, so students have a background of this historical event. Students will also be asked to do research on the Holocaust, using the library and the Internet for research purposes. Students will also choose books from the library on their own for outside reading, and will present at least one oral report during the year, as well as reading projects based on their choices.

III. MATERIALS AND TEXTS

    A. *Introducing Literature*: Glencoe

    B. Supplemental texts chosen by the teacher

    C. Library books chosen by the student

IV. EVALUATION

    A. Quizzes and texts based on the class assigned reading

    B. Writing assignments based on the literature

    C. Oral presentations by individual students

    D. Student participation in class discussions of the literature read

SPELLING

OBJECTIVES

    A. To individualize the spelling instruction

    B. To encourage the application of good spelling in all subject areas

    C. To review the basic spelling rules and generalizations

    D. To learn the content area words currently used in each subject area

    E. To encourage students to enter the yearly spelling competition

    F. To learn and practice methods for learning to spell a word

IMPLEMENTATION

The spelling area of grade 7 English is a continuation of the same guidelines as grade 6. Lists of words are taken from their text, as well as words generated by the teacher, for students to study. Students may be pre-tested on these words, and then are asked to practice learning how to spell each word. Since students learn differently, no one method is pushed as the "best" way to learn to spell a work. At times, different students may have different spelling words, based on their level of achievement. Students are given spelling quizzes when appropriate.

MATERIALS

    A. Teacher generated lists

    B. Lists of words from supplementary reading

C. *Worldly Wise*: Educator's Publishing Service

EVALUATION

Quizzes and texts based on the class assigned reading

Writing assignments based on the literature

Oral presentations by individual students

Student participation in class discussions of the literature read

VOCABULARY

I. OBJECTIVES

To increase the number of words students know.

To improve student's skills in getting a word's meaning from context.

To encourage students to consult a dictionary to choose the appropriate definition.

To encourage the proper use of words through knowledge of parts of speech

IMPLEMENTATION

One lesson from *Worldly Wise* is covered each week. The teacher introduces each lesson and discusses the words. He/she also draws attention to the additional information within the lesson, which includes such things as word roots, or the story behind the words. Class time is given for the students to work the exercises, which are checked orally. Quizzes are given after each lesson, with a major vocabulary test after several lessons.

Vocabulary is also taught through the literature studied at this level. Students should keep a 3×5 file card for each word covered. On the front of the card are the word and its part of speech. On the back of the card is the definition of the word as it is used in the story, and an original sentence using the word correctly.

MATERIALS

Wordly Wise

Teacher generated vocabulary lists

Teacher vocabulary lists from supplemental reading

EVALUATION

Quizzes and texts based on the class assigned reading

Writing assignments based on the literature

Oral presentations by individual students

Student participation in class discussions of the literature read

GRAMMAR

I. OBJECTIVES

   A. To increase the student's knowledge of the basics of grammar.

   B. To encourage students to write in complete sentences and to give the practice in writing both simple and complex sentences.

   C. To increase the student's ability to identify adverb and adjective phrases.

   D. To improve punctuation by concentrating on the guidelines concerning capitals, commas, apostrophes, and quotation marks.

II. IMPLEMENTATION

   A. Determine the student's ability to identify parts of speech

   B. Exercises are assigned from text

   C. Discussions involving other resources and computer sources

III. MATERIALS

   A. *Writer's Choice*

   B. Teacher generated worksheets

IV. EVALUATION

   A. Quizzes and texts based on the class assigned reading

   B. Writing assignments based on the literature

   C. Oral presentations by individual students

   D. Student participation in class discussions of the literature read

LITERATURE

I. OBJECTIVES

   A. To provide enjoyment to literature.

   B. To expose the students to a variety of quality authors.

   C. To improve skills of reading for fact and detail.

    D. To introduce basic terminology of literary analysis.

    E. To teach students to identify literary terms and devices.

    F. To emphasize the short story's narrative form and potential for interpretation (distinguishing between abstract and concrete subjects).

    G. To help students appreciate the craftsmanship that makes literature a work of art.

II. IMPLEMENTATION

The short story is the core of the seventh grade reading program. It is a good introduction to literature because its brevity allows the student to experience a wide range of authors, styles, and themes throughout the early part of the year without extended concentration required for a novel. The type of story read in the seventh grade introduces students to a greater degree of complexity than they might have encountered in the past, and the stories are of recognized literary merit. Thus begins the process of helping students develop a taste for good literature.

    The short stories are usually given an overnight reading assignments, with discussions the following day. Reading check quizzes are given to encourage students to keep up with assignments. Class discussions aim first for a factual understanding of the plot. The following elements of the short story are also covered:

    A. Characterization

    B. Conflict
        1. Man vs. Man
        2. Man vs. Nature
        3. Man vs. Himself

    C. Setting

    D. Mood

    E. Plot
        1. Rising action
        2. Climax
        3. Falling action, resolution, denouement

    F. Point of View
        1. First person
        2. Third person

    G. Flashback

   H. Foreshadowing

   I.   Protagonist/antagonist

   J.   Symbolism

   K. Theme

   L. Style

A great deal of time is spent giving the students practice in analyzing the stories for the elements listed previously. Literary devices are also identified and discussed and include (although they are not limited to):

   A. Irony

   B. Poetic Justice

   C. Simile

   D. Metaphor

   E. Realism

   F. Stereotype

   G. Allusion

III. MATERIALS AND TEXT

   A. *Introducing Literature*

   B. Short Stories Read by the Teacher

   C. Short Stories Chosen by the Teacher

IV. EVALUATION

   A. Quizzes and texts based on the class assigned reading.

   B. Oral presentations by individual students.

   C. Student participation in class discussions of the literature read.

THE PARAGRAPH

I.   OBJECTIVES

   A. To identify topics sentences.

   B. To write topic sentences.

   C. To develop topic sentences through details, incident, or example.

   D. To write a coherent paragraph through the use of chronological order, spatial order, and the order of importance.

II. IMPLEMENTATION

Primarily, this unit is completed in class, although some exercises can be assigned as homework. Extensive oral drill is given on topic sentences, on listing details, and on developing a topic sentence through incident or examples. A homework assignment is given in which students find a factual newspaper or magazine article and identify topic sentences. We also do an in-class exercise on topic sentences in which each student writes a topic sentence, then exchanges papers and adds to the body of other students' paragraphs until it is finished. We then read aloud and evaluate for unity. Students are required to put at least one paragraph on the counter and use editing program before submitting a final copy.

III. MATERIALS AND TEXT

A. *Writer's Choice*

B. PowerPoint

C. Teacher generated worksheets

IV. EVALUATION

A. Quizzes and texts based on the class assigned reading

B. Writing assignments based on the literature

C. Oral presentations by individual students

D. Student participation in class discussions of the literature read

LETTER WRITING

I. OBJECTIVES

A. To teach students the parts of a letter

B. To introduce the different types of letters and emphasize the social guidelines concerning the occasions when each type of letter is appropriate.

C. To provide practice in using each type of letter.

D. To emphasize the psychology of writing requests and complaints.

II. IMPLEMENTATION

Practical situations, such as thank you notes for Bar Mitzvahs are emphasized. To integrate with the history curriculum, students are asked to assume the character of a famous person in Florida or American History and turn in a portfolio of his or her letters. For example, the student may be Davy

Crockett describing life in the Alamo to a friend, or Betsy Ross writing her mother about her problems sewing a flag. They also design and issue humorous invitations, such as an invitation to come for dinner from a cannibal society, etc. The unit can also tie in with current events by requiring the students to write a letter to the editor on some current topic of interest. In-class practice in complaining, whether by letter, over the Internet, by telephone, or in-person, is given through role-playing, simulated situations, and writing letters to manufacturers, either real or imaginary.

III. MATERIALS AND TEXTS

   A. *Writer's Choice*

   B. Different Letter Formats

   C. Newspaper Letters to the Editor

   D. The Internet

IV. EVALUATION

A file of letters evaluates the unit. Several situations are described; students choose one of these and follow directions, writing four different types of letters based on the chosen situation.

THE HOLOCAUST

I. OBJECTIVES

   A. To understand the historical importance of the Holocaust.

   B. To sensitize students as to the nature and characteristics of prejudice, hatred and man's inhumanity to man.

   C. To explore the themes associated with the historical occurrence of the Holocaust.

   D. To discover representative samplings of Holocaust literature.

   E. To model journal writing after Anne Frank's diary.

   F. To write an extensive essay, which blends student research into the Holocaust with the literary testimonials, provided by the literature under study.

II. IMPLEMENTATION

The students are assigned readings and view several short films that will provide them with an overview of this period of world history, and we will invite a Holocaust survivor into the classroom to discuss his/her personal reflections. Throughout the study of the Holocaust, students will keep a journal in which they reflect on their own feelings about what they are learning. They will also keep a designated notebook that will be kept and graded at the conclusion of the unit.

III. MATERIALS AND TEXTS

    A. *Number the Stars*

    B. *Night*

    C. *Anne Frank: Diary of a Young Girl*

    D. Magazines

    E. Internet

    F. Library Research

IV. EVALUATION

An essay will be written on the text on their choice from the three in-class readings and students will be required to work in groups to develop a multimedia presentation on some specified area of our study of the Holocaust. All students will also write a letter of thank-you to our guest speaker.

SUMMER READING

I.   OBJECTIVES

    A. To encourage summer growth through continued reading

    B. To expose students to books they might enjoy and / or should experience

    C. To begin the year with meaningful discussions of summer reading experiences the students had in common

    D. To enable early detection of the strengths and weaknesses of individual students and the class as a whole.

II. IMPLEMENTATION

Summer reading lists are distributed in the spring. Each student is required to read three books form the summer reading list. the list is comprised of books selected for their grade and age level appropriateness, of theme, and subject matter which have a high degree of readability. Books range from popular fiction and nonfiction to the 'classics'. Consideration should be given to choosing some books that integrate with other disciplined and cultures

III. MATERIALS

    A. The summer reading list

B. A notebook to record the students summaries

IV. EVALUATION

   A. Grading the summaries the students are required to write of each book

   B. A test on the required summer reading book.

This is pretty standard stuff. We all studied literature and grammar and leaned about poetry and simile and irony and plot, didn't we? Who can fault this school for this curriculum? Well, Descartes for one does:

> I esteemed eloquence highly, and was in raptures with poesy; but I thought that both were gifts of nature rather than fruits of study. Those in whom the faculty of reason is predominant, and who most skillfully dispose their thoughts with a view to render them clear and intelligible, are always the best able to persuade others of the truth of what they lay down, though they should speak only in the language of Lower Brittany, and be wholly ignorant of the rules of rhetoric; and those whose minds are stored with the most agreeable fancies, and who can give expression to them with the greatest embellishment and harmony, are still the best poets, though unacquainted with the art of poetry.
>
> *Descartes (On method)*

We cannot simply assume, because it has always been so as far as we can recall, that learning about grammar rules or the structure of literature is a valuable enterprise. If one thinks it is of value then one needs to ask what purpose it serves. Does knowing the structure of literature make one a better writer? Perhaps it does, but you can be pretty sure that many great writers had no formal training in writing whatsoever. More importantly, does this curriculum have the intent of training professional writers? I think not. What then might its intent be?

One would hope that its intent would be as Montaigne would have it:

> Let him make him examine and thoroughly sift everything he reads, and lodge nothing in his fancy upon simple authority and upon trust. Aristotle's principles will then be no more principles to him, than those of Epicurus and the Stoics: let this diversity of opinions be propounded to, and laid before him; he will himself choose, if he be able; if not, he will remain in doubt.
>
> *Montaigne (On Education)*

According to Montaigne, one should read not for the appreciation of literature but for the possibility of learning to understand diverse points of view and come to one's own views.

From my childhood, I have been familiar with letters; and as I was given to believe that by their help a clear and certain knowledge of all that is useful in life
might be acquired, I was ardently desirous of instruction. But as soon as I had
finished the entire course of study, at the close of which it is customary to be
admitted into the order of the learned, I completely changed my opinion. For I
found myself involved in so many doubts and errors, that I was convinced I
had advanced no farther in all my attempts at learning, than the discovery at
every turn of my own ignorance. And yet I was studying in one of the most cel-
ebrated schools in Europe, in which I thought there must be learned men, if
such were anywhere to be found.

Descartes (On Method)

Descartes saw the world this way as well as have many others. Taking into
account what William James said earlier, together with what we know of
children at this age, wouldn't it be a better idea to find out where their interests lie and encourage them to read diverse writings about those interests?
How do we determine that they should study the Holocaust, for example?
For those who feel compelled to say something politically correct here, let me
say that I lost quite a few relatives in the Holocaust and it is an issue of great
seriousness to me. Nevertheless, that does not make it a literary theme to be
force-fed to every seventh grader.

Picture the poor seventh grader in this curriculum, being regularly tested
on grammatical rules and plot structure, reading what has been assigned to
him whether he cares for it or not and being told to write about what he has
read. Unless his interests miraculously match up with the selections made for
him to read, he is more likely to be turned off to reading than to be turned
on. And isn't that the real intent here? Don't we simply want children to
learn to enjoy reading? Here again is Montaigne:

As for Cicero, the works of his that can best serve my purpose are those that
treat of philosophy, especially moral. But to confess the truth boldly . . . his
way of writing and every similar way, seems to me boring.

Montaigne (On Books)

Children typically are not allowed to find something boring. My daughter
told her teacher in her final essay in a high school course on Faulkner that
she found Faulkner boring. She got an F for the paper. Now, my daughter
wrote extremely well and made fine arguments, so it wasn't her writing or
her thinking that was being judged. It was her opinion. Perhaps Montaigne
failed his Cicero paper. All I can tell you is that every time a child has to
read *The Red Badge of Courage* or *The Rime of the Ancient Mariner* at this age
it is a sad thing indeed.

Students learn to enjoy reading if we suggest readings that relate to what
they care about. They will learn to enjoy thinking about issues if we suggest

literature concerning those issues that presents opposing points of view.
They will learn to enjoy writing if they can write about things about which
they are passionate. They will never learn to enjoy gerunds and there is no
reason whatever to talk about them. If you never use what you have learned
you cannot possibly have any reason to learn it. Learning grammatical rules
does not make one better at reading, writing, or speaking. Reading, writing,
speaking, and being corrected and helped through the process by a teacher
makes one better at those things. One doesn't have to know the rules of
grammar, one needs to know how to employ them, which is a different thing
entirely.

> It is little short of a miracle that modern methods of instruction have not al-
> ready completely strangled the holy curiosity of inquiry. . . . I believe that one
> could even deprive a healthy beast of prey of its voraciousness if one could
> force it with a whip to eat continuously whether it were hungry or not.
>
> *Albert Einstein*

The issue is "the classics." I began this book with the issue of their value.
Obviously there is much wisdom in them. The question is whether there is
importance in making children who are not ready to understand them, read
them.

> The classics have scarcely lost in absolute value as a voucher of scholastic re-
> spectability, since for this purpose it is only necessary that the scholar should
> be able to put in evidence some learning which is conventionally recognized as
> evidence of wasted time; and the classics lend themselves with great facility to
> this use. Indeed, there can be little doubt that it is their utility as evidence of
> wasted time and effort, and hence of the pecuniary strength necessary in order
> to afford this waste, that has secured to the classics their position of preroga-
> tive in the scheme of higher learning, and has led to their being esteemed the
> most honorific of all learning. They serve the decorative ends of leisure-class
> learning better than any other body of knowledge, and hence they are an effec-
> tive means of reputability.
>
> *Veblen*

Veblen was trying to understand the make up of the leisure class. It is interesting that he considered the classics to be wasted time. In Veblen's day
the entire school population was not being subjected to them as they are today.

> In this respect the classics have until lately had scarcely a rival. They still have
> no dangerous rival on the continent of Europe, but lately, since college athlet-
> ics have won their way into a recognized standing as an accredited field of
> scholarly accomplishment, this latter branch of learning—if athletics may be
> freely classed as learning—has become a rival of the classics for the primacy in

leisure-class education in American and English schools.

Veblen

Veblen wrote about football before it was the behemoth on college campus that it is today. In fact, football may have taken the place of the classics in the spending of leisure time, and perhaps some school time as well. But still the idea persists that there is a body of literature that everyone must read or forever remain ignorant.

We have carried our respect for antiquity so far today, in matters in which it should have less influence, that we treat all its ideas as revelations and even its obscurities as mysteries; we can no longer advance new opinions without danger, and an author's text is enough to destroy the strongest arguments.

Blaise Pascal, Scientific Treatises

Pascal put it very well. School is about the respect for antiquity. We convey to students that everything that is of interest has already been thought of by minds more educated than our own. No wonder that Mencken concluded:

School days, I believe, are the unhappiest in the whole span of human existence. They are full of dull, unintelligible tasks, new and unpleasant ordinances, brutal violations of common sense and common decency.

H. L. Mencken

REFERENCE NOTES

The sources are the Great Books series for the extended quotes and the Web for the shorter ones.

4

The Formally Educated Mind

DEFINING A REAL EDUCATION

There is little doubt that when we refer to an educated person, or an educated mind, we are talking about something rather specific. For example, we would expect an educated person to know something about Chaucer, to have read Plato, to understand the implications of the industrial revolution, to be able to relate the foreign policy of the United States to that of the Romans, to know about the origins of the Cold War and the demise of the Soviet empire. In any case, Clifton Fadiman knew about all these things and this is what he would have meant by an educated mind. Fadiman knew nothing about artificial intelligence, cognitive science, or e-learning. This I know from personal experience with the man.

Fadiman was not alone. His is the majority opinion in the world about the educated mind. For most people education is the same as erudition. Someone who is well read, and this most certainly would include having read most of the Great Books, is considered educated. The problem with this definition is that no one actually agrees with it. Yes, many people spout it, but if you are an officer in a corporation and you need to hire someone, do you care if that person is well read? If you are hiring a professor in a university, it is nice to find out that they are well read, but you much more concerned with the quality of their research. In other words, skill at what one is supposed to do is paramount in earning our respect. Most of the time one acquires these skills through education, but apparently that type of educational experience is just the sort of experience for which Fadiman had a certain disdain.

In fact, disdain for school is everywhere, although there isn't a general consensus on where exactly that disdain is most warranted:

> We are shut up in schools and college recitation rooms for ten or fifteen years, and come out at last with a bellyfull of words and do not know a thing. The things taught in schools and colleges are not an education, but the means of education.
>
> *Ralph Waldo Emerson*

For Emerson, the disdain is about facts. They are most certainly the currency of education—indeed Fadiman not only knew a great many facts, he was quite famous for running a quiz show in the 1940s that has various folks showing off their factual knowledge. Such shows exist today in other forms of course, and we are impressed when someone knows what is the largest body of water in the Northern Hemisphere.

I am not sure I agree with Emerson though. Are these facts really the means of an education? Or was he just being kind?

> The end of study should be to direct the mind towards the enunciation of sound and correct judgements on all matters that come before it.
>
> *Descartes: Rule 1*

For Descartes, it is clear, this disdain is focused on those who cannot make use of what they have learned to help them make judgments. But we need to realize when people talk about judgments they mean for unanticipated events. In other words, the question is: What can we teach somebody that will help them decide about things that we have not taught them about at all?

Montaigne also has a certain disdain for education of the traditional sort:

> For a boy of quality then, who pretends to letters not upon the account of profit, nor so much for outward ornament, as for his own proper and peculiar use, and to furnish and enrich himself within, having rather a desire to come out an accomplished cavalier than a mere scholar or learned man; for such a one, I say, I would, also, have his friends solicitous to find him out a tutor, who has rather a well-made than a well-filled head; seeking, indeed, both the one and the other, but rather of the two to prefer manners and judgment to mere learning, and that this man should exercise his charge after a new method.
>
> *Montaigne, On the education of children*

Montaigne's disdain is clear enough. He is worried that a student might want to become a man of letters to make money on it, or to make himself look good. Indeed I am not so concerned about the former, Montaigne was writing about the 16th century after all, as the latter. Much of this kind of learning, that which makes one a "man of letters" is ornamental. The problem is that those who subsidize this kind of education, typically parents although sometimes for inexplicable reasons it is the government, may very well not understand that that is what they are doing. Where they are attempting to provide value to the future of the child, they are providing mere ornamentation without realizing they are doing so.

Shakespeare was disdainful of education in another way. Next are excerpts from *Loves Labours Lost*:

Biron

I can but say their protestation over;
So much, dear liege, I have already sworn,
That is, to live and study here three years.
But there are other strict observances;
As, not to see a woman in that term,
Which I hope well is not enrolled there;
And one day in a week to touch no food
And but one meal on every day beside,
The which I hope is not enrolled there;
And then, to sleep but three hours in the night,
And not be seen to wink of all the day—
When I was wont to think no harm all night
And make a dark night too of half the day—
Which I hope well is not enrolled there:
O, these are barren tasks, too hard to keep,
Not to see ladies, study, fast, not sleep!

Ferdinand

Your oath is pass'd to pass away from these.

Biron

Let me say no, my liege, an if you please:
I only swore to study with your grace
And stay here in your court for three years' space.

Longaville

You swore to that, Biron, and to the rest.

Biron

By yea and nay, sir, then I swore in jest.
What is the end of study? let me know.

Ferdinand

Why, that to know, which else we should not know.

Biron

Things hid and barr'd, you mean, from common sense?

Ferdinand

Ay, that is study's godlike recompense.

Biron

Come on, then; I will swear to study so,
To know the thing I am forbid to know:
As thus,—to study where I well may dine,
When I to feast expressly am forbid;
Or study where to meet some mistress fine,
When mistresses from common sense are hid;
Or, having sworn too hard a keeping oath,
Study to break it and not break my troth.
If study's gain be thus and this be so,
Study knows that which yet it doth not know:
Swear me to this, and I will ne'er say no.

Ferdinand

These be the stops that hinder study quite
And train our intellects to vain delight.

I realize that the section above is a little long, so for those of you that have skimmed it (you wouldn't be the first to have skimmed a Great Book) let me summarize. Basically, Shakespeare noted that you have to give up a lot to learn things that may not be of very much value in the long run. Biron, the student, wonders how abstaining from the real world will teach him more about the real world. He has to give up doing what he likes doing to learn how to do it better. He wonders why; I wonder about that as well.

The classics ... serve to shape the intellectual attitude and lower the economic efficiency of the new learned generation. They do this not only by holding up an archaic ideal of manhood, but also by the discrimination which they inculcate with respect to the reputable and the disreputable in knowledge. This result is accomplished in two ways: (1) by inspiring an habitual aversion to what is merely useful, as contrasted with what is merely honorific in learning ... and (2) by consuming the learner's time and effort in acquiring knowledge which is of no use, except in so far as this learning has by convention become incorporated into the sum of learning required of the scholar, and has thereby affected the terminology and diction employed in the useful branches of knowledge.

Veblen, The Higher Learning as an Expression of the Pecuniary Culture

Veblen's disdain is economic. He wonders if inculcating a disdain for useful knowledge and raising up to a idealized level the kind of education Fadiman had in mind, was really all that useful for society as a whole. Now note that Veblen was writing a century ago, but nothing much has changed. In fact, he was a professor at Stanford—and you can be sure Stanford hasn't changed.

In fact very little has changed. I was astonished to discover, when my daughter attended a private high school in New Haven, that she was required to take Latin. What could possibly be the reason for this? Ask and you will find many who will say things like Latin is the basis of all languages (certainly untrue) or Latin helps you understand English (studying English would work as well) or other justifications for what is in fact an idea that is simply old (and meant to have people read Latin texts) and hasn't gotten fixed. I once got into a public argument with the poet laureate of Brazil on the value of Latin. He exclaimed: "I feel sorry for those who haven't studied Latin, those who don't know Latin can't think." I responded that I felt sorry for the Chinese in that case.

Here again is Veblen:

A knowledge of the ancient languages, for instance, would have no practical bearing for any scientist or any scholar not engaged on work primarily of a linguistic character. ... The fact that classical learning acts to derange the learner's workmanlike attitudes should fall lightly upon the apprehension of those who hold workmanship of small account in comparison with the cultivation of decorous ideals.

The ability to use and to understand certain of the dead languages of southern Europe is not only gratifying to the person who finds occasion to parade his accomplishments in this respect, but the evidence of such knowledge serves at the same time to recommend any savant to his audience, both lay and learned. It is currently expected that a certain number of years shall have been spent in acquiring this substantially useless information, and its absence creates a presumption of hasty and precarious learning, as well as of a vulgar practicality that is equally obnoxious to the conventional standards of sound scholarship and intellectual force.

Veblen, The Higher Learning as an Expression of the Pecuniary Culture

Veblen was a kind of a jokester in his way. He is saying that, in his day, everyone learned Latin because not knowing Latin made them seem rather practical and of course, uneducated. It kind of makes you wonder whether

Fadiman knew Latin. And you know the answer was that he just had to have known it.

WHY SCHOOL MATTERS

The standard definition of the educated mind then, is one that is thoroughly familiar with great works of literature and other old stuff. Here is something I found on the Stanford web site about Clifton Fadiman:

> Anxious to avoid the problems encountered by his parents, who spoke English imperfectly, Fadiman consciously set out to master the language. This commitment led to his "interest in the whole Western cultural tradition," he told CCT in a Fall 1982 interview. He traced his lifelong involvement with books to age 4, when he read his first one; by 10, he was reading Homer, Sophocles, Dante, and Milton. "By the end of high school I was not of course an educated man," Fadiman said, "but I knew how to try to become one."

Of course, it is really not my concern to further understand the make up of Clifton Fadiman. Fadiman was a voice of a generation and that generation holds sway over our schools today despite the fact that most of them are no longer with us. I enjoyed the above quote because it made me realize (no surprise really) that this remark he made in my presence was probably an overriding concern for him all his life. He strove to be an educated man. I was clearly striving to be nothing of the sort. It as clash of cultures (although we are both from Brooklyn, so maybe it was more a clash of generations).

The question really is not about Fadiman, but it is instructive to note that while I was searching the web for tidbits about Fadiman, I found an item that said he had read more than 25,000 books in his life. I guess he was sort of the Wilt Chamberlain of literature. And like Wilt, one can't help but wonder at the truth of it. He did live well into his nineties, but that would be more than one book a day. Not so hard to believe except that, to write this book I have been living with the Great Books, which Fadiman edited of course, and I can tell you that reading Plato in a day would take some doing. Maybe he just skimmed Kant. Bacon is tough going, let me tell you.

> Reading, after a certain age, diverts the mind too much from its creative pursuits. Any man who read too much and uses his own brain too little falls into lazy habits of thinking.
>
> *Albert Einstein*

All of this is beside the point. If Fadiman wanted to define himself by how much he had read that was his business. Unless of course, that is how we define the educated mind. In that case we have a problem.

But, of course, we do have a problem. The people in control of education do not find this absurd. They find it laudable. Veblen, Montaigne, and Descartes may not have found it laudable, but they are not running our schools.

> Let us reform our schools, and we shall find little need of reform in our prisons.
>
> *John Ruskin*

This matters for the reason Ruskin says it matters, which is not unrelated to Veblen's point. We cannot have a reasonable society without reasonable schools. And the reason for this was well stated by Spinoza:

> As we know not anything among individual things which is more excellent than a man led by reason, no man can better display the power of his skill and disposition, than in so training men, that they come at last to live under the dominion of their own reason.
>
> *Baruch Spinoza*

Ah, but that is not what is done in school. Next is a curious thing I found in the curriculum of Grandview Prep:

Social Science Department
Middle/Upper School Curriculum: Grade 6–12

LIFE SKILLS

TIME REQUIREMENTS: 45 minutes every day

TEXT: NONE

COURSE EMPHASIS: Life skills are an elective course that focuses on developing skills that prepare students for the future. The goal of this course is to help students become more confident about themselves and the world around them.

I. OBJECTIVES

    A. Student will be able to identify effective communication skills

    B. Student will be able to demonstrate healthy coping skills

    C. Student will be able to identify constructive elements in a relationship and destructive elements in a relationship.

II. IMPLEMENTATION

    A. Lecture

    B. Classroom projects and assignments (i.e. worksheets)

III. MATERIALS

    A. The health teachers Book of lists—Patricia Rozzo—Toner, M.d.

    B. Videos

    C. Worksheets

IV. EVALUATION

    A. Quizzes

    B. Classroom participation

    C. Homework, assignments

Life skills are an elective course! Really? Why wouldn't life skills be the centerpiece of education? Why is the only stuff worth knowing in school always extracurricular?

> There are two types of education . . . One should teach us how to make a living, And the other how to live.
>
> *John Adams*

It is comforting to note that not all American Presidents were out of it when it came to making a judgment about education. However, Adams seems to have had no effect since our schools fail to do what Adams suggested.

But the real problem is not that. The real problem lies in the objectives:

    A. Student will be able to identify effective communication skills.

    B. Student will be able to demonstrate healthy coping skills.

    C. Student will be able to identify constructive elements in a relationship and destructive elements in a relationship.

First, I should point out that learning objectives are one of the main evils in the school system.

Learning objectives seem like a good idea for the basis of curriculum design. Every curriculum designer makes use of them. "At the end of the course the student will know X." Sounds good.

The problem of course is that when you decide that any student who takes a given course should come out knowing X it is very tempting to test to see if they do in fact know it. To make sure they know it, a teacher tells it to them a lot, makes them read about it, gives them short quizzes about it, and finally examines them to see if in fact they know X.

In the confusion about learning objectives, which tend to be stated rather factually (the student should know X), there is always the underlying hope that the student might come away from the experience being able to do something he couldn't do before. No one is really interested in having students spouting X. But having that as ones explicit objective tends to make that the goal that is uppermost in everyone's mind.

What did the writers of the previous objectives mean when they said:

A. Student will be able to identify effective communication skills.

You know and I know that they meant there would be a test. But what would they test be about? Well, it would pretty well have to be about the list of effective communication skills that were given to the student. So, you see the problem here. It isn't that there will be a test to see if the student knows X. It is that the curriculum now has to have in it some explicit statement of X that may not be so important to learn. Do we in fact learn to communicate by being able to say a set of rules about effective communication? I don't think so. I doubt that teachers that have to teach this think so either. Communication involves actually communicating, not saying stuff about communicating.

Now examine the third learning objective:

C. Student will be able to identify constructive elements in a relationship and destructive elements in a relationship.

Are we trying to make these students into clinical psychologists or are we trying to help them get along with each other? It is that word "identify" again. What we want is for them to be able to be constructive in a relationship. It is easy to say words about being helpful to someone else. Being helpful is harder. Learning objectives tend to trivialize complex issues by making them into sound bites that can be told and then tested to see if a student were listening.

One can see why learning objectives play the role that they do. Since we can't state what we want students to be able to do in any easy way, we can simply state what we want them to know, hoping that knowing substitutes for doing in learning. The bad news is that it does not. Furthermore, students know this. The passive "tell them and test them" approach to education is deadly dull and students don't like it. They want to learn to do something.

How then, can we teach people to communicate or relate to each other? Obviously we must put them in situations that cause them to have to communicate and relate. These situations should implicitly entail the learning objectives so it is unnecessary to tell students what we might want them to know. Rather, students should naturally pick up what we want them to know (being mentored when they err in some way) while being involved in doing something that is of interest to them. Or to put it another way, we need to transform learning objectives into performance goals.

Schools are often paralyzed by an inability to do the kind of teaching they should do. Nowhere is this more obvious than in education about real life issues. A good example of this, perhaps the most extreme example, is sex education. Somehow we would like schools to teach sex without having students engage in any. That is a conundrum, but one I only use to make a point; no one is going to suggest that students should start having sex in class and be helped by the teacher to understand what they were doing and how it all worked. But it is important to realize that no one is going to suggest that for sociological reasons, not for pedagogical ones. This would certainly be the best way to teach this topic. Unfortunately, our society often has prohibitions against students actually performing material that would be best learned through performance.

Here is the important point. No such prohibitions exist for many other subjects that we treat exactly as if there were such a prohibition. Learning to think is a performance act. All of the above items could be transformed into performance goals instead of learning objectives, and none of them are socially taboo.

Despite the well intentioned motives of people who list learning objectives, there is no set of such objectives that cannot be perverted into a vapid educational experience that meets the letter of those objectives. The spirit of these objectives can only be met if learning objectives are eliminated from curricula and replaced by performance objectives.

> Education is an admirable thing, but it is well to remember from time to time that nothing that is worth knowing can be taught.
>
> *Oscar Wilde*

Next are the learning objectives that were listed in the twelfth grade Comparative Mythology curriculum that Grandview. It is a long list, feel free to skim:

Objectives

The Creation Myths

Students will be able to describe the myth of creation, the story of how the cosmos began and developed.

Students will understand that the creation story is metaphor of birth.

Students will analyze the mythic motif of the hero's birth.

Students will understand the creation myth, then, establishes our reason for being the source of significance.

The Afterlife Myths

Students will be able to understand that belief in some sort of afterlife is ubiquitous.

a. Students will be able to identify the religious cultures that stress the struggle between good and evil in this.

b. Students will be able to understand that in the more mystical religions that stress the illusory nature of life. The afterlife may be distinctly a nonphysical realm.

c. Students will be able to understand that all afterlife myths, and even the lack of such myths, reflect cultural perceptions of the world.

d. Students will be able to understand that in myth, afterlife is an almost inevitable result.

Myths of gods

1. Students will be able to chronicle the pantheons, the officially recognized gods of a culture.

   a. Students will be able to contrast the Egyptian Pantheon that speaks directly to the culture's obsession with death and resurrection, with the Hebrew development of a single Patriarchal God concerned with the actions of 'chosen people'

   b. Students will be able to identify the Gods of Heliopolis, Athens and Rome.

   c. Students will be able to describe the God as archetype, in the global intellectual, political, economic, social and cultural developments.

   d. Students will be able to recognize in any god or goodness or pantheon both the mask, or metaphor that is worshipped by the culture that created it and the spiritual or psychological source of that mask.

   e. Students will be able to recognize the Supreme Being who emerges from many world myths about the chief god is one who embodies the prevalent patriarchal arrangement of society.

   f. Students will be able to understand the concept of the Supreme Being that has developed in patriarchal society.

Goddesses

1. Students will be able to understand that many of the stories in this unit have religious significance, and many will be read in the light of the archetypal global categories.

    a. Students will be able to compare the archetypal gods who help human-
       kind.
    b. Students will be able to identify these stories, as all of them part of the
       general vocabulary of the cultures from which they come.
    c. Students will be able to recognize revenge in global mythology.
    d. Students will be able to recognize in myth, the archetypal 'femme fatale'
    e. Students will be able to recognize the myth of patriarchal perversion as
       a story that reflected the meaning of Pandora's name.

The Hero Myths

1. Students will be able to understand that mythology comes alive most
   clearly in the stories of heroes, and that the hero is our persona, our representative in the world dream.
   a. Students will be able to understand the process by which the hero
      leaves the ordinary world of waking consciousness to enter the dark
      world of the supernatural, and how he overcomes.
   b. Students will be able to understand the myth of Dionysus, Orpheus,
      Isis, and Jesus contains examples of journeys of quest into the world
      mysteries.
   c. Students will be able to understand that the myth that emerges from
      the many cultural versions of the hero must be seen as a universal met-
      aphor for the human search for self-knowledge.
   d. Students will be able to recognize that the monomyth contains as
      many elements by comparing mythical heroes form all over the world.

Stories of Places and Objects

1. Students will be able to recognize the significance of places throughout
   the world, and how they relate to the significance of myths themselves.
   a. Students will be able to understand that in the world of myth, objects
      and places are endowed with properties of the sacred, the 'other'.
   b. Students will be able to understand the process of 'opening' as a com-
      mon concern of the religious person and the creative artist.
   c. Students will be able to understand that the sacred mountain in global
      mythology is the moon veneries of Mother earth the cosmic center on
      which the temple or city is placed.
   d. Students will be able to understand that the city is humanity's stand
      against chaos.
   e. Students will be able to understand that Jerusalem is the city of the be-
      loved God, and how it sacred to Christians and Muslims as well as to
      Jews.

Maybe it's just me, but I find this list frightening.

Students will be able to understand the myth of Dionysus, Orpheus, Isis, and Jesus contains examples of journeys of quest into the world mysteries.

Students will be able to chronicle the pantheons, the officially recognized gods of a culture.

Students will be able to understand that belief in some sort of afterlife is ubiquitous.

Students will in fact be able to understand that they will have to say stuff like this to pass the test. What does it mean to know what students will understand before they understand it? Does this mean that there is no possibility of understanding anything else?

The problem with sort of thing is that it is basically a backward approach to education. To see how this works, following is something that I found on the Web site of the National Science Foundation:

Science and Technology: Public Attitudes and Public Understanding

- Most Americans do not know a lot about S&T. In 2001, only about 50 percent of NSF survey respondents knew that the earliest humans did not live at the same time as dinosaurs, that it takes Earth one year to go around the Sun, that electrons are smaller than atoms, and that antibiotics do not kill viruses.
- A majority of Americans (about 70 percent) lack a clear understanding of the scientific process. Although more than 50 percent of NSF survey respondents in 2001 had some understanding of probability, and more than 40 percent were familiar with how an experiment is conducted, only one-third could adequately explain what it means to study something scientifically.

Most readers find this sort of information upsetting. Americans know very little about science. So, we decide to fix this state of affairs. How do we fix it? By making a list of learning objectives and drilling the answers into student's heads and then getting higher test scores on the questions for which we have prepared them, then patting ourselves on the back. What is the point of this exercise? Does it really matter when Americans think dinosaurs lived or what they think about the size of electrons? People don't know this stuff not because they weren't taught it, but because they were taught it in a foolish, irrelevant way. People don't forget information that they use regularly or information that has made some impact on them.

It may very well matter that people understand that antibiotics don't kill viruses. But telling them that won't make them know it. Having them work in a biology lab might help them know it, or putting them through some complex simulation that uses these ideas might help.

In the end education is an issue of breadth versus depth. There is so much we want people to know that we are forced to hurry up and tell it them real fast. We can, of course, adopt an alternative strategy and have them know much less but live with what we are trying to impart in away that makes them recall the experience. In that case, one would impart the scientific process by having students live in that process for a while, not learn the facts about the process so that they can pass a test.

My favorite part of the NSF Web site is the following:

- Belief in pseudoscience, including astrology, extrasensory perception (ESP), and alien abductions, is relatively widespread and growing. For example, in response to the 2001 NSF survey, a sizable minority (41 percent) of the public said that astrology was at least somewhat scientific, and a solid majority (60 percent) agreed with the statement "some people possess psychic powers or ESP." Gallup polls show substantial gains in almost every category of pseudoscience during the past decade. Such beliefs may sometimes be fueled by the media's miscommunication of science and the scientific process.
- Alternative medicine, defined here as any treatment that has not been proven effective using scientific methods, has been gaining in popularity. One study documented a 50 percent increase in expenditures for alternative therapies and a 25 percent increase in the use of alternative therapies between 1990 and 1997. Also, more than two thirds of those responding to the NSF survey said that magnetic therapy was at least somewhat scientific, although no scientific evidence exists to support claims about its effectiveness in treating pain or any other ailment.

National Science Foundation, Division of Science Resources Statistics

There is a reason for people to be educated. If they are not they adopt all kinds of beliefs not grounded in reality. Should we try to dispel those beliefs? Sure, but only if we do it in a fashion that is more than simply saying it. We need to spend a lot of time on it. This is what learning objectives looks like when students really spend a lot of time on something. Next is a list of the eleventh grade mathematics objectives in our Florida school:

Department of Mathematics
Integrated Math

TIME REQUIREMENTS: 74 MINUTES

TEXT: Algebra and Trigonometry: Prentice-Hall (with corresponding workbook.)

OTHER REQUIREMENTS: Pencils, graphing, calculators, notebooks, use of the computer with corresponding software (provided by school)

COURSE EMPHASIS: Integrated math is a one-year course for students who have completed Algebra 2, but are not ready to take college Algebra. The purpose of this course is to complete a mastery of basic algebraic concepts and manipulations by stressing why and how mathematics. Topics include: equations and inequalities, word problems and factoring, fractions, graphs, complex numbers, systems of equations, conic sections, exponents and logarithms, trigonometric functions and right angle trigonometry.

I. OBJECTIVES

The students will be able to:

Identify the properties for the addition and multiplication of real numbers

Give examples of the field properties and identify fields

Manipulate and evaluate polynomials

Solve equations in one variable and classify these equations as consistent, inconsistent, or conditional and applications of the above

Work with integral exponents

Solve and graph inequalities

Solve compound inequalities

Solve equations and inequalities involving absolute value, including some involving more than one absolute value term

Handle special products by inspection, including the cubing of a binomial

Factor polynomials using common monomial factors, grouping and special factoring terms

Using polynomial division to factor a polynomial when one-first-degree factor is determined by inspection

Solve problems involving variation

Identify the domain and draw the graph of a relation

Find the values of a function and draw its graph

Distinguish between a function and a relation

Find the slope of a line given a pair of points on that line

Find the zeros of a function and graph it

Put equations into y ñ form, find the slope and the intercepts, and graph the equations

Use the two points and slope—intercept forms of an equation or a line

Determine if two line are parallel, perpendicular, or coinciding

Find equations of lines given sufficient information about them

Find the solution set of pair of linear equations in two variables

Determine if a system of linear equations is inconsistent, dependent and independent and consistent, and graph the system

Find the solutions set of a system of three equations in three variables

Use equations and systems of linear equations in two and three variables to solve word problems

Graph the solution set of a linear inequality and a system of linear in two variables

Graph parabolas and determine the vertices and the axes of symmetry, discovering the role of a, h, and k in the determining the shape and the position of the parabolas

Use factoring to find the solution of a quadratic equations

Solve quadratic equations by using the quadratic formula

Solve word problems involving quadratic equations

Use algebraic methods to solve quadratic inequalities

Give a graphical solution of quadratic inequalities

Solve systems of quadratic/quadratic and quadratic and quadratic/linear inequalities

Determine the nature of the roots of a quadratic equation by using its discriminant

Use the number 'I' to simplify square roots of negative numbers

Solve the quadratic equation involving imaginary roots using the discriminant and the quadratic formula

Add, subtract, multiply and divide complex numbers

Identify roots of real numbers

Simplify radical expressions, paying attention to necessary restrictions

Extend the meaning of exponents to include rational numbers

Manipulate expressions containing radicals

Factor expression containing radical

Solve radical equations

Determine the degree of a polynomial

Add, subtract, and multiply polynomials

Divide a polynomial by one that is of lower or equal degree

Write rational expressions in simplest form

Multiply and divide rational expressions

Add and subtract rational expressions

Solve rational expressions

Use synthetic division to factor a polynomial

Find the distance between any two points and the mid point of a line segment joining them

Learn the relationship between the focus, directrix, vertex, and axis of symmetry of a parabola and the equation of a parabola

Learn the relationship between the center and radius of a circle and the equation of the circle

Graph polynomials

Graph rational equations

Extend the meaning of exponents to include irrational numbers

Define and graph exponential functions

Define an inverse relation and find the inverse of a function

Define logarithmic functions and lean how they are related to exponential functions

Learn the basic properties of logarithms

Evaluate common logarithms and antilogarithms

Use interpolation to find logs and antilogs

Use logarithms in simple computations to illustrate how these computations were done before the introduction of calculators

Solve the exponential and logarithmic equations

Solve problems involving exponential growth and decay

Graph the trigonometry functions sine, cosine, tangent

Solve problems involving right angle trigonometry

Identify amplitude, and vertical shit, in working with graphs of sine and cosine

Learn some basic identities and use them to prove other identities, including
double and half angle formulas

Work with the addition properties of sine and cosine

Solve triangles using the laws of sine and cosine

Work with reference angles

Notice how long this list is. Notice how it is a list of things students will be
able to do. It is pretty real. There is a lot of depth here. There is only one
problem. No student who finishes this course is likely to ever use any of these
abilities at any point during the rest of their life. We teach math in depth but
we ignore subjects that actually come up later in life. Nothing new in the following, of course:

> Whence it comes to pass, that for not having chosen the right course, we often
> take very great pains, and consume a good part of our time in training up chil-
> dren to things, for which, by their natural constitution, they are totally unfit.
> *Montaigne (On Education)*

THE ROLE OF GOVERNMENT

In the end, it is those who mandate learning objectives that are the culprits
in the educational travesty that we have in this country. Who mandates
them? Education schools teach curriculum designers how to write them, so
at first glance it may seem that it is the curriculum publishers who are at the
root of it, but really it is the government that starts the process.

> If the government would make up its mind to require for every child a good
> education, it might save itself the trouble of providing one. It might leave to
> parents to obtain the education where and how they pleased, and content it-
> self with helping to pay the school fees of the poorer classes of children, and
> defraying the entire school expenses of those who have no one else to pay for
> them.
> *JS Mill*

Interpreted in a modern context, this looks like a plea for school vouchers but I take it a different way. I take it as a plea for the government to get the heck out of the education business. Any school reformer can tell you that between politicians, parents, and faculty members it is hard to change anything at all. Add in economic interests like those of book publishers and the testing industry and you can't change a thing. The fact that someone thinks that issues in education should be determined democratically, by politicians, astonishes me. It also seems to have astonished Mark Twain.

> First, God created idiots. That was just for practice. Then He created school boards.
>
> *Mark Twain*

John Dewey was more serious about education than was Mark Twain, but their opinions aren't that different.

> The realization of the new education destined to produce a new society was, after all, dependent upon the activities of existing states. The movement for the democratic idea inevitably became a movement for publicly conducted and administered schools.
>
> *John Dewey*

And therein lies a story. Why should democracy be the problem? Before there were democracies no one much thought about having governments be in charge of education. In that case, rich people could do what they wanted and if what they wanted was to outfit their sons with the ornaments of education, with the pretense of letters rather than with an education useful for living, that was their choice. When the government got in on the act and institutionalized this nonsense is when the problem began.

> Under the influence of German thought in particular, education became a civic function and the civic function was identified with the realization of the ideal of the national state. . . . To form the citizen, not the "man," became the aim of education. . . . The German states felt . . . that systematic attention to education was the best means of recovering and maintaining their political integrity and power. Externally they were weak and divided. Under the leadership of Prussian statesmen they made this condition a stimulus to the development of an extensive and thoroughly grounded system of public education.
>
> *John Dewey*

Dewey is writing here in the early 1900s. The full effect of what the Germans tried to do was unknown to him, but the idea hasn't escaped the attention of governments since that time. Governments can help make citizens behave in ways they want them to behave. It may not seem obvious but this is one of the real goals of any government, to create a set of citizens who believe in the status quo.

> This change in practice necessarily brought about a change in theory. The individualistic theory receded into the background. The state furnished not only the instrumentalities of public education but also its goal. When the actual practice was such that the school system, from the elementary grades through the university faculties, supplied the patriotic citizen and soldier and the future state official and administrator and furnished the means for military, industrial, and political defense and expansion, it was impossible for theory not to emphasize the aim of social efficiency. . . . The educational process was taken to be one of disciplinary training rather than of personal development.
>
> *John Dewey*

So, why don't we teach life skills? Because personal development is not what the government concerns itself with.

> One of the fundamental problems of education in and for a democratic society is set by the conflict of a nationalistic and a wider social aim.
>
> *John Dewey*

To fix education we either have to get government out of the picture or get a more enlightened government. We may well indeed have a more enlightened government, at least more enlightened than any we have ever had before. They may simply do not know what they are doing. When the President insists that everyone know the Pythagorean Theorem, I for one am willing to believe that he is not doing this so as to make more docile citizens who follow arbitrary rules. I believe he is doing it because he is clueless about education.

> No one will doubt that the legislator should direct his attention above all to the education of youth; for the neglect of education does harm to the constitution The citizen should be molded to suit the form of government under which he lives. For each government has a peculiar character which originally formed and which continues to preserve it. The character of democracy creates democracy, and the character of oligarchy creates oligarchy; and always the better the character, the better the government.
>
> *Aristotle, Politics*

This is, of course, the prevailing view. It has been around a long time as you can see. Here is Mill on the same subject:

The objections which are urged with reason against State education, do not apply to the enforcement of education by the State, but to the State's taking upon itself to direct that education: which is a totally different thing. That the whole or any large part of the education of the people should be in State hands, I go as far as any one in deprecating. All that has been said of the importance of individuality of character, and diversity in opinions and modes of conduct, involves, as of the same unspeakable importance, diversity of education. A general State education is a mere contrivance for moulding people to be exactly like one another: and as the mould in which it casts them is that which pleases the predominant power in the government.

J. S. Mill, On Liberty

And that is the issue. Are we molding students to be exactly like one another? No American would admit to this, but what else are we to make of a curriculum so rigid that every student takes all the subjects set out for him by the Committee of Ten in 1892. No one intentionally planned that high schools would be solely focused on college admittance, thus allowing colleges to dictate what one needs to do to prepare for college. But, the government has mandated Harvard's 1982 requirements as law. They may not have intended to do so, but it is what they have done.

That education should be regulated by law and should be an affair of state is not to be denied, but what should be the character of this public education, and how young persons should be educated, are questions which remain to be considered. As things are, there is disagreement about the subjects. For mankind are by no means agreed about the things to be taught, whether we look to virtue or the best life. Neither is it clear whether education is more concerned with intellectual or with moral virtue.

Aristotle, Politics

Aristotle thought about the problem as well. The problem isn't that the government is involved, it is at what level they are involved. How does the government decide what to teach?

The existing practice is perplexing; no one knows on what principle we should proceed- should the useful in life, or should virtue, or should the higher knowledge, be the aim of our training; all three opinions have been entertained.

Aristotle, Politics

Here is that same issue again. What is education for? Is it for life skills, job skills, or scholarly skills? Aristotle wondered about this, but in our day this is not a question. Life skills are an elective and job skills aren't taught in our Florida school. Lots of mathematics, science that doesn't last in one's mind, random facts about history and literature. It is not a great story.

Education would be much more effective if its purpose was to ensure that by the time they leave school every boy and girl should know how much they do not know, and be imbued with a lifelong desire to know it.

Sir William Haley

Yes, it would be, but sadly that doesn't happen too often, does it?

REFERENCE NOTES

The sources are the Great Books series for the extended quotes and the Web for the shorter ones. The NSF site was the source for the NSF information. Harvard provides an extensive Web site which includes its internal publications from 1892 on curriculum, faculty, and so on.

5

What Is Required
for a Good Education?

Every society believes in educating its children, that much is clear. What is less clear is why a society wants to educate its children. One would think that the subject matter that is taught would inform us about the presumed purpose of education, so let's look at what is taught and see if we can figure out why it is taught. But while doing this, we need to realize that Plato was in a quandary about this as well:

> There yet remains one difficulty which has been raised by you about the sons of good men. What is the reason why good men teach their sons the knowledge which is gained from teachers, and make them wise in that, but do nothing towards improving them in the virtues which distinguish themselves?
>
> *Plato (Protagorus)*

What subjects should be taught? Plato continued:

> Good men . . . think virtue capable of being taught and cultivated both in private and public; and, notwithstanding, they have their sons taught lesser matters, ignorance of which does not involve the punishment of death: but greater things, of which the ignorance may cause death and exile to those who have no training or knowledge of them—aye, and confiscation as well as death, and, in a word, may be the ruin of families—those things, I say, they are supposed not to teach them—not to take the utmost care that they should learn. How improbable is this, Socrates!

Plato had a great deal to say about virtue and thought it important to teach. In modern times, the equivalent might the attempt to teach children to get along with each other, to work in groups, to volunteer their help to people in need, to debate ethical issues. And indeed we may do this sort of thing in school or in religious settings, but we decidedly do not treat these subjects as subjects of study. We ask how a student is doing in school and we mean how he is doing in math or English, not in life skills. This mystified Plato and it ought to mystify us as well. Plato noted how children are raised and then contrasts it with how they are educated:

> Education and admonition commence in the first years of childhood, and last to the very end of life. Mother and nurse and father and tutor are vying with one another about the improvement of the child as soon as ever he is able to understand what is being said to him: he cannot say or do anything without their setting forth to him that this is just and that is unjust; this is honourable, that is dishonourable; this is holy, that is unholy; do this and abstain from that. And if he obeys, well and good; if not, he is straightened by threats and blows, like a piece of bent or warped wood.

Plato then noted how this differed from the schooling of the time:

> At a later stage they send him to teachers . . . And when the boy has learned his letters . . . they put into his hands the works of great poets, which he reads sitting on a bench at school; in these are contained many admonitions, and many tales, and praises, and encomia of ancient famous men, which he is required to learn by heart, in order that he may imitate or emulate them and desire to become like them. Then, again, the teachers of the lyre . . . introduce him to the poems of other excellent poets, who are the lyric poets; and these they set to music, and make their harmonies ana rhythms quite familiar to the children's souls, . . . Then they send them to the master of gymnastic, in order that their bodies may better minister to the virtuous mind, . . . The state again compels them to learn the laws.

Plato is amazed that all this is deemed to be more important than the teaching of virtue:

> But why then do the sons of good fathers often turn out ill?

Why indeed? Perhaps because school is about whatever has been deemed to comprise the educated mind of the era in which one lives. For the Ancient Greeks, history, poetry, and the lyre, and certainly gymnastics, were critical for education. Plato didn't quite get how that was the most important stuff. In our day, poetry is out, and gym is much less important, but little else has changed.

No, now that I think about it, maybe gym is still real important. At least it was in my day. It was June 6, 1966, graduation day at Carnegie Tech. My parents were there. My friend Ralph's parents were there. And my friend Arthur's parents were there too. As we marched down the aisle in the hot sun wearing dark robes, I waved to my parents and saw the frantic look on Arthur's parents faces. Where was Arthur? Nowhere to be found. It was a very sad day for them. The party at their house was canceled. There was nothing to celebrate.

This is not a story about insanity or violence—except in a metaphorical sense. Arthur is alive and well today—doing fine in most any of life's measures. What happened that day? Arthur was told that he would not graduate. He had been admitted to the MBA program at Columbia. He had a respectable B average in college. So, what had happened? Arthur had failed gym.

While his parents were hopelessly trying to find his face in the crowd, Arthur was trying to negotiate with the powers that be at Carnegie Tech. He was trying to convince them that he should graduate, that his life would be ruined, that this gym requirement was silly, that he was a superb athlete—but none of this worked. What had happened? Arthur had simply blown off gym. He didn't show up. He found the jumping jacks boring and the attitudes of the gym teachers tyrannical. Too bad then—no diploma.

Arthur did eventually graduate—it took two more years. He managed to get the officials at Carnegie Tech to accept some statement or other from the 92nd Street Y in New York. He does not get invited to class reunions however, since he is officially a member of the class of '68.

Do schools know what they are doing when they set requirements? Do they think about what subjects are really important for students to know, or is something else going on?

The story of modern American is intimately bound up with the history of Harvard University. Harvard (and Yale) were established as Divinity Schools. This made sense for a society whose first son inherited the family business and whose second son became a minister. Ministers were classically educated. What this meant in practice was that in addition to teaching subjects directly related to training for the ministry, it made sense to teach students what the educated people of the time knew. It is by no means my intent here to get into the history of education in any detail. The issue is why education exists in the first place.

In a New England dominated by religion and concerned with creating a new country, it is clear that the answer to that question was, from the very beginning, in America:

Answer #1

To make sure that people fit into the society in which they live.

This is clear from looking at The New England Primer as we saw in the Prologue. It was also clear to outside observers of the American scene:

> But it is by the mandates relating to public education that the original character of American civilization is at once placed in the clearest light. "Whereas," says the law, "Satan, the enemy of mankind, finds his strongest weapons in the ignorance of men, and whereas it is important that the wisdom of our fathers shall not remain buried in their tombs, and whereas the education of children is one of the prime concerns of the state, with the aid of the Lord . . ."
>
> Here follow clauses establishing schools in every township and obliging the inhabitants, under pain of heavy fines, to support them. Schools of a superior kind were founded in the same manner in the more populous districts. The municipal authorities were bound to enforce the sending of children to school by their parents; they were empowered to inflict fines upon all who refused compliance; and in cases of continued resistance, society assumed the place of the parent, took possession of the child, and deprived the father of those natural rights which he used to so bad a purpose.
>
> The reader will undoubtedly have remarked the preamble of these enactments: in America religion is the road to knowledge, and the observance of the divine laws leads man to civil freedom.
>
> Tocqueville (Democracy in America)

Put another way, learning meant learning what religion expected of you, and no one was able to escape its rules. School was about learning the truth, and religious truth at that.

Now, in a society that was religiously based, in which it was thought that the real issues were making children into good citizens of a new country this made a great deal of sense at the time. The issue for us is how relevant this point of view is today.

The answer, it should be obvious, is that the state is always interested in inculcating its citizens with its core tenets. It is also true that the more totalitarian the society, the more germane it is. Certainly children in each and every country learn the history of their country in a way that is biased toward its current rulers and against its current enemies. Certainly the U.S. history that American students learn is biased in this way as well, but that is not my concern here.

The issue is: Do we, as a society, believe that the purpose of education is to teach our society's official view of the world so students will function well in that society? Be aware that this is a trick question. While it is easy to suggest that school should not be a place of indoctrination anymore, it is foolhardy to believe that any government will eschew that opportunity, nor is it reasonable to believe that its citizens really want it to. We are all appalled when we hear that students don't know who George Washington is. To explain why this is an issue I take as an example something from American history that is less of basic belief. (I assume most every American citizen believes that children should know who George Washington was.)

I am a baseball fan. I root for the New York Mets. Some years back the Mets got a veteran left fielder from the St. Louis Cardinals who was an excellent base stealer. He is also Black. He was interviewed extensively on his arrival in New York, and was asked about his feelings about playing where Jackie Robinson had played. He replied that he "ain't heard of no Jackie Robinson, man." (For my non-American readers, Jackie Robinson was the first Black man to play major league baseball, which had been barred to Black men from its inception. He was a superstar and important national figure. He suffered quite a bit of abuse in his early years as he "broke the color line.") Baseball fans everywhere were horrified that Vince Coleman could know so little of what a man had gone through, in some sense for him, some 40 years earlier.

So, the question I ask is should Vince Coleman have known who Jackie Robinson was? And if your answer is "yes," who should have taught it to him? This is not a simple issue.

Either we adopt the stance that education entails a certain amount of indoctrination or we don't. If we believe, as the cultural literacy advocates would have it, that education is about learning the basic tenets of one's culture, then we have the issue of who gets to define what tenets must be learned and just how much of that sort of things should make up the totality of the educational experience.

The alternative is to say that education simply ought not be about indoctrination of any sort. This latter view would cause us to have to rethink a great deal of what goes on in today's schools.

Answer #2

To prepare people for more education.

Another possible answer to what education is for can be understood by looking closely at what is actually done in school. A great deal of school is about preparation for more school. Harvard required Latin and Greek of all its students in the 18th century as we saw. But what was the underlying intent? Why were these the requirements of Harvard? It was believed at that time that an educated man was one who could read all the works of the important thinkers of mankind (all of whom happened to have been Romans or Greeks). I can't help but wonder here whether Fadiman read Greek. Somehow I doubt it. I guess minds better educated than his were around in the 18th century.

Admission to Harvard mattered then and it matters now, not just for those people who actually want to go to Harvard. The idea that an educated person is one who knows what Pliny the Elder said has been perhaps replaced with knowing what Descartes said, but anyone who has not read at least some Aristotle is seen in educated circles as being not very educated. (A student who actually had the temerity to say that he "ain't heard of no Euripedes, man" would be snickered at, but the snickerers might well have never read, or seen, anything by Euripedes either.)

The impact of Harvard's requirements in 1745 mattered a great deal in shaping today's schools, but they were nowhere near the significance of what the meeting to the Committee of Ten in 1892.

The requirements set down in 1892 were meant to make life easy for professors at universities. No longer would students show up knowing different stuff. Now professors could presume some basic knowledge for entering students and could begin their courses at a more advanced level. What was good for faculty was bad for students, however. This standardization took away any flexibility high schools might have in providing an interesting intellectual experience for students.

This problem persists today. One cannot innovate in the schools because Harvard doesn't allow it. When we suggest that algebra might not be a very important subject to learn or that a student who does not care for taking economics might just as well skip it, a chorus will be heard from parents quoting Harvard's entrance requirements. No longer do they require Latin, but they certainly require algebra and economics. Proceed without these subjects at your own peril. So in effect, Harvard controls the high schools and what they teach. Harvard does not do this because it cares about high school education. It cares about making life easier for its faculty, then as now.

Answer #3

To prepare students for the world of work.

I put this here in homage to Ben Franklin but we all know perfectly well that schools do nothing of the kind. One cannot help but wonder how this happened.

Most students imagine that a university education will prepare them for life and for work. They expect to get a job after graduation because they believe they will have learned certain skills in school that will make them valuable to corporations. Nothing could be further from the truth.

Students do indeed get jobs on graduating from college. Then, most corporations put new graduates through a job training program that makes them potentially useful employees. Corporate universities are springing up all over the country in an effort to remedy the failures of the university system.

Why is it that universities have been incapable or simply uninterested in meeting the needs of their customers? Universities are run by professors. Professors have a pecking order that makes clear that the most highly valued skill is research. At top universities professors who are great researchers have very little in the way of teaching duties. Universities "punish" bad researchers by making them teach more. Teaching is not valued at top universities. Furthermore, the preferred subject matter of the professors is their own research. They don't teach real world job skills because, for the most part, they know nothing about them. Professors don't really live in the real world.

This is the situation at the top research universities. Students at these universities don't complain all that much about this state of affairs because they are valued simply for having graduated from elite institutions. Corporate America pays the price for this when it has to retrain the graduates.

At the second tier universities, the situation is not much different. The faculty aspires to be like their colleagues at the better schools and thus they still have a research orientation. This means that even the subject matter of these schools is dictated by the elites. So, the liberal arts are emphasized and practical skills are looked down on. When practical skills are taught, typically at the third tier schools, the education is devalued, because it is not intellectual and the graduate is seen as someone who really couldn't go to a "good school."

Our best and brightest are being trained to be academics and the least successful students are being taught to be low level practitioners. Who teaches the leaders of tomorrow who are not intending to be professors but are nevertheless very bright? Top universities do not expend much effort on very bright students who do not want to be academics.

No existing university could possibly invent a really new curriculum. Faculty control is too strong and the vested interests would prevent any meaningful change. Faculty do not want to teach what their students want to learn and no one can make them. It is really not solely an issue of preparation for work. It is also an issue or preparation for life. Why don't schools teach life skills?

Some subjects that are typically not covered in college that belong to this set are: childrearing, basic medicine, basic law, dealing with government, the basics of business, interaction with other people, and various skills that are part of everyday life in the modern world.

Mental skills include reasoning, argumentation, research, experimentation, invention, exploring new uses for technology, and mental exercise in general. These courses should be taught backwards from the way modern universities teach. Universities present complex new problems to seniors or graduate students after years of basic subjects have been taken. Students are forced to take general survey courses as introductions and may never get to the hard problems in a field, the ones that are unsolved. Instead students are given the facts that are well known to learn. The hard problems of a field should be presented first. Students should be encouraged to learn the basics of a field on their own after they have determined their need for them. Instead of learning calculus as some kind of rite of passage prior to learning economics, for example, students would learn calculus at their moment of need, after they have decided that it will help in pursuit of a goal in economics.

Answer #4

To certify, assess, and differentiate between people.

This may seem like a facetious answer but it's not. I cannot tell you how much the issue of assessment seems to drive education. And it has always been like this.

> One had to stuff all that jumble into oneself for the exams, whether one liked it or not. This compulsion had such a deterrent effect that, having passed the final exam, I lost all taste for any reflection on scientific problems for a whole year.
>
> *Albert Einstein*

When I was just starting out as an Assistant Professor at Stanford, I had a radical idea. I never believed that grades were worthwhile. I had always done badly in school unless I was super excited by something. Grades, it seemed to me, were keeping the education system down, rewarding those who studied hard and did what they were told, but keeping students focused on pleasing the teacher rather than focused on learning. So, in the first course taught at Stanford I announced that everyone would get an A. My intention was to focus the course on ideas rather than on requirements laid down by me. I wanted people to think about things, argue, propose their own ideas. This was my deal. What I got was quite different. I got a bunch of students who realized that they had one less course to worry about and thus they paid more attention to their other courses and little or none to mine.

Grades, clearly, were the motivating factor for Stanford students. What could I have been thinking? How could one become a Stanford student without being motivated by grades? I was naive in the extreme. School, for nearly all students is about grades, not about learning.

In many ways it is obvious that if there is one belief that students, teachers, parents, and colleges agree on it is that grades are important. Grades have become the raison d'etre of school. Whenever I propose any other idea people ask me: "but how will we know how they are doing?" Indeed.

Do we ask this question about life? We make subjective evaluations about how our friends and family are doing, but there is no number associated with each person's life. We simply muddle on not knowing for sure. "But how will the colleges know who to take?"

How did this become a high school's problem? Why should all of education in the U.S. be subverted so Harvard can have a more efficient admission process? Why is it the high school's job to tell employers who to hire? Why isn't it the high school's job to educate?

Answer #5

To ensure that students proceed through a set of requirements that satisfy the people who set up the requirements.

Who sets these requirements? How is it determined which courses are required? As I began to think about these things I asked my graduate students and associates what they recalled about the requirements at their colleges. Here are some responses:

At MIT there is a swimming requirement. You can't get your degree unless you either pass the swimming test (4 laps, any stroke) or take a swimming class. Apparently this requirement is quite serious, because as seniors we were sent a memo reminding us to get the requirement taken care of. With the memo came a story about a young man who didn't pass the swimming test and didn't take the class. The University refused to give him his degree even though he had met all the academic requirements. He had already found a job and didn't think having the actual degree mattered . . . till he was looking into a promotion at his company. Turned out he had to have the degree before promotion, so we went back, took the swimming class, got his degree, and everyone was happy.

I'm not absolutely sure about the history behind the requirement, but I think it had something to do with a student drowning in the Charles River and MIT's attempt to prevent that from happening in the future.

Sam Kwon

MIT is not alone in this nonsense:

All students at Columbia College must pass a swimming test, or submit a waiver from the University Health Service. This is from Columbia's Web site: http://www.columbia.edu/cu/college/bulletin9798/index.html.

All students are required to pass a swimming test or submit a waiver from the University Health Service. The swimming tests are administered the first day of classes and those who do not pass are encouraged to take a beginner swimming course at the first opportunity. The test consists of swimming three laps of the pool (75 yards) without resting, using any stroke or combination of strokes. If a student takes beginner swimming for one term and is still not able to pass the swimming test, the requirement is waived.

This is, of course, a really good exemplar of the mentality in a non-learn by doing institution. Here we have something that one can demonstrate having learned. The very essence of learning by doing is inherent in a subject such as swimming and Columbia has nevertheless decided to settle for the old model of education. *As long as you take the course it makes no difference if you can swim.* Who thinks this stuff up? Either swimming is a requirement or it isn't. Of course I vote against. The Columbia position on this only makes it clear how odd a requirement this is.

One of the main reasons that colleges set up requirements has to do with breadth. The idea is that the college doesn't want you only know one subject very well. They have decided, and nearly every university agrees on this, that a student should know a little bit about a lot of different things. Of course, there have been periods in various colleges' histories where these requirements reduced to taking one from column A and one from column B, but more typically these days, specific courses or specific areas of study are fixed by the college. The rationale behind this is, as we have noted, is not always what is going on. Quite often it is university politics that is the real issue. In any case, let's see what some other of my students had to say:

As a part of the General Education requirement, Cal State Chico (and, I believe, the entire Cal State system) required that students be exposed to other cultures and their ways of thinking, or something like that. The official standardized way of doing this was to require that every student take one class which had been officially designated "Non-Western," and one class which had been officially designated "Ethnic."

Part one of the silliness is that the distinctions weren't always clear or consistent. For example, I satisfied my Ethnic requirement by taking a religious studies class in Judaism. However, the analogous religious studies class in Buddhism was designated as Non-Western, not Ethnic, and the analogous class in Christianity was neither. Of course, there were also classes which satisfied both requirements.

Part two of the silliness is the somewhat politically correct, liberal guilt mentality behind the whole thing; I'm not sure that anyone's consciousness was actually raised by any of these classes, and that seems to be (at least implicitly, if not explicitly) the whole point.

Brendon Towle

At Washington University in St. Louis, I graduated without taking a single course in history, poly sci, psych, literature, etc. How? All I did was take a few AP and Achievement Tests in high school to nail down English and Spanish, and then I took piano lessons for credit the rest of the time. If I recall correctly, I was required to take 6 classes outside of the engineering school, 3 of them in the same discipline, and one of those three at or above the 300 level. My English counted for 1, Spanish for another 2 (maybe even 3), and piano lessons took care of the rest. In fact, I *started* piano at the 300 level, so I didn't even need to get any better to meet the requirements.

But during my time as an undergrad, they fixed this "problem." They divided the arts courses into two categories: performance and non-performance. Piano lessons, language discussion groups, etc were considered performance. For each performance course you wanted to use to fill requirements, you needed to take one non-performance course in the same discipline to match, like music theory, or Spanish literature, or whatever. By those rules (which I didn't have to follow), I never would have graduated, because none of my piano lessons would have counted.

Michael Wolfe

Bowdoin had a requirement that all students had to take two semesters of "Non-Eurocentric Study." The rationale was to broaden the experience of all the students beyond the standard Western cultural tradition. It also increased enrollment in those departments enough to allow Bowdoin to continue to offer a broader slate of courses in that area than most other schools that size. I fulfilled the requirement with two semesters on the history of India, which were fascinating, and were courses I would never have taken without the requirement.

Any class covering the history, religion, art or politics of India, sub-Sarahan Africa or the Far East qualified. Stuff that *didn't* fill the requirement included studies on the Middle East, and East Asian language courses. That always seemed a bit bizarre to me—how to speak the language seems like one of the most useful things you can learn about a culture. I can't remember if Latin American studies counted or not. I think not, since most of the modern culture is derived from the Spanish, and I don't think there were any courses on the indigenous cultures.

Brian Davies

All MIT undergraduates, even liberal arters or philosophers, are required to take a science curriculum.

All students must take:

Two courses of Physics—Basic Laws of Kinetics and Electromagnetism
Two courses of Calculus—Basic and Advanced
One course of Inorganic or Material Chemistry

At the time no Biology course was required, according to some Biology was not viewed a necessary science to know. However since my departure in 93, MIT has reevaluated their stance and have mandated a Biology class.

These requirements may have been on par for students in the Engineering or Basic Science departments but students in Philosophy and Linguistics, Architecture, Urban Planning, Political Science, Brain and Cognitive Science, Humanities, and Management, these reqs are just plain stupid and a waste of time.

Adebisi Lipede

At Caltech (over 40 years ago), biology majors, but not some other majors, had to take introductory German to graduate. I entered CIT with a solid high school and other background in German. So, as a sophomore, I registered for an advanced course, Scientific German. The only requirement in that course was to translate a book capably. I selected a German genetics textbook. Because there were no real pressures, I would work on my other courses instead of my translating. I forget how many times I registered for Scientific German and then dropped it. But eventually I turned in a solid job. Cool. I got an A. Shortly before graduation, the registrar told me I wouldn't be graduating. What?! I had never taken introductory German. But, said I, I have here in my records an A in an advanced course. Too bad, or words to that effect, was the answer. Eventually, I had to go to the German professor and get him to devise a special test on "introductory German" that I could take. Fortunately, I passed it.

Bill Purves

Of course, not only universities make requirements, each individual department makes them as well:

Students in every department of Texas' college of Natural Sciences, except CS, were required to take a foreign language to graduate. Some clever person in CS had succeeded in convincing the administration that learning programming languages should count.

Ray Bareiss

When I was an undergrad at Harvard, I double majored in Art History and Studio Art. The studio arts program required me to take some unbelievably stupid art theory class taught by a complete idiot, Prof. Dilnot, who could never in a million years have held a position in Harvard's art history program. No matter how much pleading I did, pointing out all of the hardcore methodology classes I was taking in the art history department, studio arts would not exempt me.

Dilnot taught two art theory classes. I took the "advanced" one. It was a class which focused on "the difference between the real and the real." Yes, that is a direct quote. "This sneaker is not the same as this picture of a sneaker," was another notable quote. Inexplicably, we spent a lot of the class looking at slides he had made from pornographic magazines. I decided to write my midterm on "A formalist analysis of Ms. January." My final "research" paper was 20 pages long. I wrote it as fast as I could type it. I got an A (no doubt for my hard work).

Adam Neaman

At Yale, the CS department had a requirement that all majors take at least one math course numbered above 220 (I could be wrong about the number, but the concept is right). My senior year, I was called into Alan Perlis' office because my highest math course was Math 230, which was not considered by the CS department to be a math course numbered over 220.

As I remember it, the issue was that Math 230 was a sort of extended version of a lower numbered course, so the CS department didn't think it counted. I eventually convinced him to make an exception.

Steven Feist

Are there a set of courses that every student should take? Is there stuff everyone should know? Does breadth matter? To answer this question I am tempted to tell one more story. It really has nothing to do with what I am about to discuss, except that it exemplifies so well, how I feel about requirements. The story is from my time in high school.

I attended Stuyvesant High School in New York City, a school that emphasized science and required a test for admission. It was a very competitive place. But this story is about gym not science. Stuyvesant had a gym requirement, as do most high schools. We can wonder why there should be such a requirement, although no one would doubt the idea that being physically fit is a good thing. The issue is why such requirements are mixed up with ideas about educational achievement. In any case, I digress.

Stuyvesant was located in an old school building and it simply wasn't built to accommodate the number of students that it had. As a result it was impossible for each student to shower after gym class. In any case, there were 45-minute periods and the showers that did exist were very far from the lockers, so for everyone to shower after the class, the class would have had to have been absurdly short. The powers that be worried about this, and so for reasons I will never quite understand, they decided that every student would shower once a week. This shower was to be taken for one period of the five allotted in the week to gym. Or, to put this another way, showers lasted 45 minutes, and occurred say, every Friday.

As you might expect, students found this idea absurd, so they often skipped the shower period. Schools find such behavior intolerable of course so they set up the idea that one had to "make up" any showers that were missed. What this meant, in actuality was that some students were actually forced to shower for entire days and sometimes an entire week at the end of the year to graduate.

In retelling this story, I found it to be so absurd that I have at times thought my memory was failing. And then, in an unlikely place, I found a cohort of mine from those days and he confirmed my story to my astonished companions.

One of my students heard me tell this story and responded with one of her own:

In order to graduate high school, I had to pass "drown proofing." In other words we had to prove that we could float. Why? So we could survive in the ocean long enough for rescue crews to save us. I kid you not. I'm assuming the people who wrote this up were emotionally-scarred survivors of the Titanic.

They put great big rubber bands around our legs so we couldn't really kick, told us that we couldn't use our arms and hands to aid us, made us jump into a 12 ft deep diving pool, and "float" for 10 minutes—allowing us to lift our heads every so often to breath (well, they weren't barbarians).

Back then, I had little body fat, so I didn't float. I was an "A" student . . . with very little body fat . . . who was already accepted into Stanford, Harvard, Yale, Princeton, etc. . . . and I wasn't going to be able to graduate because I couldn't float. I finally got the head P.E. person to agree to let me use my toes to propel my body to the water's surface when I sank to the bottom of the pool (which happens 10 seconds after jumping in). He said that he would "unofficially" allow it. So that's what I did for 10 minutes. Sink for 10 seconds, do a big toe push, will myself to the water's surface, gasp, sink to the bottom (repeat for 10 minutes).

So, I guess this was ok because I learned that when I do get stranded in the middle of the ocean, all I have to do is sink for several hundred feet and do a big toe push to the water's surface. . . .

Kim McPherson

What is one to make of all this? The first thing to see is that whatever requirements get set down, with some rationale one would assume behind them, they eventually get perverted in some way by circumstance. Because requirements get screwed up in this way, should we just forget the whole idea, or is there some right way to do this?

These various swimming requirements are actually quite interesting. Schools, from my point of view, consistently err on the side of teaching subjects that have no real relevance to the future lives of students. Every high school requires geometry and algebra, yet it hard to discern a reason why these subjects are likely to ever matter in the life of your average adult. Yet, school seems most absurd when we look at things like swimming requirements. My student (referred to previously) couldn't graduate because she couldn't float? You have to be kidding. On the other hand, swimming might actually matter to an adult. Moreover, it is precisely the kind of "doing requirement" that makes sense. Students can actually learn to do it, will know when they have done it, and can continue to practice and therefore be able to do it all the rest of their lives. Swimming is indeed worth learning. The real question is what schools should be teaching? If we all agree on swimming, shouldn't we also require that all students learn to drive? This doesn't seem unreasonable after all. What about maintaining an effective relationship with another person? This is very important in adult life. Why don't we teach that?

The issue is really about two things. First, we have the question of what constitutes an academic subject. School is about academics and we have the sense that math is an academic subject and swimming isn't. That's why students remark on the absurdity of this requirement. Second, we have the idea of a requirement. We have the idea that schools should require things that are essential. The question is: Do they know what's essential? Also, we can ask: If they did know what was essential, would that mean that those things should be required? We will take these two questions (academics and requirements) in turn.

Answer #6

To ensure that every student has a well rounded educational experience covering the major areas of intellectual study.

What constitutes an academic subject? That is, what is the intellectual turf that a good education must cover? We have evolved a set of answers to this question that, as a culture, we all subscribe to. We believe that education is about science, humanities, and the arts. Inside universities we find Colleges of Arts and Sciences. These are usually the cornerstone of the university and typically predate the founding of other schools within the university. Many universities have Engineering Schools or Drama Schools or Music Schools or Journalism Schools. These are roughly grouped as "professional schools" and are looked down on by those in the College of Arts and Sciences. Business Schools, Medical Schools, and Law Schools, are part of a modern university but are so looked down on by the other schools that they typically do not teach undergraduates and their faculty are often made to feel that they are not really part of the university at all. (This doesn't mean that the university itself isn't proud of these schools. After all, if a university has a great medical school it will ballyhoo it when it can.) At Northwestern, the Medical and Law Schools are located 10 miles away from the main campus. This is not at all unusual. The other universities where I worked (Stanford and Yale) had similarly quite separate medical schools. Some state university systems put these schools in entirely different cities from the main campus.

There is a general ethos in any university that says that members of the professional schools are really not like the rest of the faculty since they are not really academics. They do stuff in the real world, they often get paid a great deal more money, they quite often don't have tenure, and are not really engaged in "pure" research.

The idea of pure research dominates the modern university. Those who engage in it are members of the elite ruling class. Those who do no research, either because their research careers are over or because their fields are not research oriented (true of most of the professional schools), have little or no clout when it come to things like setting requirements. This is why you will never see a required course at any university for undergraduates in law, medicine, journalism, music, business, or art. Those who set the requirements for what constitutes a liberal academic curriculum—those who say what should go on in a college—are simply not from those fields so they never get to vote for their own subjects.

Now, if one thinks about this for a moment, one can see that this state of affairs is basically absurd. Many colleges require a mathematics course in order to graduate but none require a course in medicine or law. Most adults need to know something about basic medicine or law at many times in their lives while they somehow can muddle through without ever solving a quadratic equation. Clearly, the requirements are not about practical issues in daily life. They are about power.

They are also about structures that are immune to change. Let's for a moment consider the idea that any good university should require its students to take a year-long course in basic medicine that would supply them with knowledge that would be quite valuable in their future lives. Many universities have some very impressive faculty members who could teach such a course. But, there are a few problems. First, where are these people located? At the University of Texas, the main campus is in Austin but the Medical School is in Dallas. It is actually not surprising that the medical schools of these universities are far away from the undergraduates. Medical schools are meant to be learn by doing institutions. This means they need hospitals, research labs, and other things that require enormous campuses of their own. The kind of teaching is different, the lives of the faculty are different (since they are usually practicing physicians), and the connection between the medical school and the rest of the university is quite tenuous. So, how would such a course get taught? Even if you could get the right people to the right city, it would be difficult to provide the incentives for such teaching since the faculty of the medical school are busy enough as is. The fact is that it would be darn near impossible to require such a course for every undergraduate, so no one in their right mind would suggest such a thing. It hardly matters if it would be a good thing or not.

So, when we assume that an education is about academic subjects we must recognize that we believe this to be so because it has always been so and because the infrastructure we have created tends to preserve the status quo. There are alternative colleges, ones which emphasize much more practical curricula. The problem is that these schools are perceived as being second rate and they often are second rate. The best minds in the country do not teach at them and the best students in the country do not attend them. This does not mean, however, that the curriculum in the schools that the best and the brightest do teach at and attend is in any sense right or reasonable.

Practical education is seen as vocational in nature and the vocational schools have always been for the least talented students. The best students go to more academically oriented schools but the problem is that the curriculum of these schools is determined by academics. Academics may not be the best people to determine what a college student should learn since they have a vested interest in preserving the status quo. I end with a remark by a retired colleague of mine:

> We academics and ex-academics know that the final, key ingredient in tightly-defined curricula (especially the "breadth" requirements) is the matter of politics, full-time-faculty-equivalents, and so forth. The college I retired from has an extremely tightly defined core curriculum, required of all students. Ask anyone the reason: BREADTH, the need to be prepared to select a major after three semesters without being "behind," and various platitudes. Of course the final, determining element is "If we don't include physical chemistry the world will end, and besides, there are already five required semesters of math and OUR department will have only TWO required semesters."

REFERENCE NOTES

The sources are the Great Books series for the extended quotes and the Web for the shorter ones. The New England Primer material was taken from Ford, 1962 as mentioned earlier. The quotes from graduate students at Northwestern were collected by me in the mid-1990s. The Columbia requirements were taken from their Web site. The retired colleague I quote chose to remain nameless but I can give a hint: He is a biologist living in California.

6

How High School Got That Way (the Search for the Smoking Gun)

Since there is no single set of abilities running throughout human nature, there is no single curriculum which all should undergo. Rather, the schools should teach everything that anyone is interested in learning.

John Dewey

My son Joshua was cramming for his final exams in his senior year in high school. Joshua was taking History. He was studying material that would help him answer questions like the following:

1. The Wilmot Proviso was aimed at:
2. Who objected to the "Ostend Manifesto?"

He was taking Calculus. He was trying to answer questions like the following:

3. The average value of $\sqrt{x}$ over the interval $\leq x \leq 2$ is:
   a. $1/3 \sqrt{2}$ b. $1/2 \sqrt{2}$ c. $2/3 \sqrt{2}$ d. 1 e. $4/3 \sqrt{2}$
4. if $f(x) = \ln(\ln x)$ then $f'(x) =$
   a. $1/x$ b. $1/\ln x$ c. $\ln x /x$ d. x e. $1/x \ln x$

He was studying Chemistry. Here are two of the questions he had to answer:

5. What is the mass of 0.34 mole of CH_3COOH in grams?
6. Draw electron dot diagrams for the elements Sr, Sn, Sb.

What is going on here? This is high school? Why?

Can your average high school graduate answer of these questions? Can your average college graduate answer any of these questions? Why is this what a high school student should know? Who determined this? What were they thinking?

> What we want is to see the child in pursuit of knowledge, and not knowledge in pursuit of the child.
>
> *George Bernard Shaw*

Joshua was having trouble with his Calculus homework. He called the teacher at nine o'clock at night, one of the privileges of going to an elite private school. However, his teacher refused to provide him with the information that he needed. She said it would be unfair to the other kids in the class. I was dumbfounded when he told me this. Aren't teachers supposed to await with great anticipation the day that a student actually wants to know more stuff? Isn't that the thrill of teaching? What a shame that grades impede learning in this way. Well, Joshua replied, if there were no grades, he wouldn't have wanted to know the answer to the question he asked his teacher in the first place.

Joshua didn't want to know Calculus. His school wanted him to know Calculus. Why? It is tempting to say that they wanted this because they knew it would be of importance to him in some way. A committee sat down and decided what an educated mind should know. We would like to believe this. But here is the problem. Who should ask this question? If you let universities ask it, it is good to remember that universities are already divided into departments, and departments tend to be self perpetuating. No department would ever decide that what they teach isn't critical to knowledge and to the make up of the educated mind.

An English Department assumes that an educated mind should know literature and that an educated mind should know how to write. An English Department already knows, because their faculty must teach something to someone or else they would lose their jobs, that it is important for all students to take (one, two, or many) English courses, the amount determined in direct proportion to the power of that department's faculty relative to other departments within the university. No one asks if an educated mind should know literature. There is no possibility to ask it anew since a negative answer would threaten the livelihood of a great many professors.

So, we assume that an educated mind should know literature because universities have always had English Departments whose specialty is literature.

Let us not be confused. We are not making it up when we are asked what an educated mind must know. We are not left fumbling for ideas on the subject. We have been spoon fed an answer to this all our lives. An educated mind should know something about every subject offered at Harvard in 1892.

What? That is a crazy answer, you say? Why Harvard you ask? And why every subject offered at Harvard, isn't that a bit much? And why 1892? If you have to model this on Harvard, why not Harvard 2002?

No, this a completely crazy answer. That's what you think, I say. Read on. Here is the smoking gun in the story of education (don't skim this one):

The secondary schools of the United States, taken as a whole, do not exist for the purpose of preparing boys and girls for colleges. Only an insignificant percentage of the graduates of these schools go to colleges or scientific schools. Their main function is to prepare for the duties of life that small proportion of all the children in the country—a proportion small in number, but very important to the welfare of the nation—who show themselves able to profit by an education prolonged to the eighteenth year, and whose parents are able to support them while they remain so long at school. There are, to be sure, a few private or endowed secondary schools in the country, which make it their principal object to prepare students for the colleges and universities; but the number of these schools is relatively small. A secondary school programme intended for national use must therefore be made for those children whose education is not to be pursued beyond the secondary school.

The Committee of Ten, 1892

How was it determined that Joshua needed to know Calculus and obscure facts about history and chemistry in high school? First, it was assumed that a high school student would not be going to college so he'd better get his college in high school. Then college professors were asked how to teach college in high school.

The Committee of Ten decided in that summer of 1892, to hold conferences on each subject to determine the answer to the following questions:

1. In the school course of study extending approximately from the age of six years to eighteen years—a course including the periods of both elementary and secondary instruction—at what age should the study which is the subject of the Conference be first introduced?
2. After it is introduced, how many hours a week for how many years should be devoted to it?
3. How many hours a week for how many years should be devoted to it during the last four years of the complete course; that is, during the ordinary high school period?
4. What topics, or parts, of the subject may reasonably be covered during the whole course?

5. What topics, or parts, of the subject may best be reserved for the last four years?

6. In what form and to what extent should the subject enter into college requirements for admission? Such questions as the sufficiency of translation at sight as a test of knowledge of a language, or the superiority of a laboratory examination in a scientific subject to a written examination on a textbook, are intended to be suggested under this head by the phrase "in what form."

7. Should the subject be treated differently for pupils who are going to college, for those who are going to a scientific school, and for those who, presumably, are going to neither?

8. At what stage should this differentiation begin, if any be recommended?

9. Can any description be given of the best method of teaching this subject throughout the school course?

10. Can any description be given of the best mode of testing attainments in this subject at college admission examinations?

Notice the question that was not asked. Left out from this list because its answer was already known was the only question that mattered: Should this subject be studied in high school (or elementary school)? Nine conferences were set up, each devoted to a particular discipline. These conferences met in December, 1892.

The places of meeting were as follows:

for the Latin and Greek Conferences, the University of Michigan, Ann Arbor, Mich.;

for the English Conference, Vassar College, Poughkeepsie, N.Y.;

for the Conference on Other Modern Languages, the Bureau of Education, Washington, D.C.;

for the Conference on Mathematics, Harvard University, Cambridge, Mass.;

for the Conferences on Physics, Astronomy, and Chemistry, and on Natural History, the University of Chicago, Chicago, Ill.;

for the Conference on History, Civil Government, and Political Economy, the University of Wisconsin, Madison, Wis.,

for the Conference on Geography, the Cook County Normal School, Englewood, Ill.

And what were the results of these conferences? I have an amazing surprise for you. In each conference, a group of professors of the discipline being discussed by that conference decided that their subject was critical for study in high school. In most cases they decided that their subject was critical in elementary school as well. What a shock! Job security for them and their colleagues for the rest of their lives (and for many more generations to boot). Here in brief are the results of the conferences:

1. Latin

An important recommendation of the Latin Conference is the recommendation that the study of Latin be introduced into American schools earlier than it now is. They recommend that translation at sight form a constant and increasing part of the examinations for admission to college and of the work of preparation.

The committee on Latin decided that Latin should be taught in elementary school too. And they made clear that the end goal of Latin study was to pass entrance examinations for college. Clearly, for this group at least, college entrance was the driving force behind their high school curriculum, which was curious for a time in which very few people went to college.

2. Greek

The Conference on Greek agree with the Conference on Latin in recommending the cultivation of reading at sight in schools, and in recommending that practice in translation into the foreign language should be continued throughout the school course. They urge that three years be the minimum time for the study of Greek in schools; provided that Latin be studied four years.

The Greek scholars knew their place. Only three years of Greek if there are four years of Latin. Sounds like a good old political compromise to me. The Greek faculty probably knew their day was over and were holding on to what they could get.

3. English

The Conference on English found it necessary to deal with the study of English in schools below the high school grade as well as in the high school. Their opening recommendations deal with the very first years of school, and one of the most interesting and admirable parts of their report relates to English in the primary and the grammar schools.

The Conference are of the opinion that English should be pursued in the high school during the entire course of four years;

I love the wording here. "The Conference on English found it necessary to deal with the study of English below the high school grade." Oh the pain of it all. They had to deal with other grades because people might need to learn how to read before high school. But, they could at least be sure there would be plenty of work for English teachers by making sure that English was required all four years of high school.

So there it is, the first part of the smoking gun. Why do we study English for four years in high school? Because that is what this report says. Now, I know that there are those for whom it is so ingrained in them that what they did was the right thing because they did it, that this doesn't sound funny at all. "English? Well sure we take English every year." Of course you should read literature all through school. I just have one simple question: Why?

No answer is given in the report. The clear answer is what I have said, because it was English professors writing their report and it was very self-serving. The "why" question deserves an answer.

4. Other Modern Languages

The most novel and striking recommendation made by the Conference on Modern Languages is that an elective course in German or French be provided in the grammar school, the instruction to be open to children at about ten years of age.

Remember these are their words, not mine. "The most novel and striking recommendation is that an elective course in German and French be provided in grammar school." Funny that the only really right-headed recommendation made by this committee was more or less ignored. Some schools offer foreign language instruction in early grades, but most do not. Are foreign languages worth studying? Sure. The best way to learn them: immersion as early as possible.

5. Mathematics

The Conference on Mathematics maps out a course in arithmetic which, in their judgment, should begin about the age of six years, and be completed at about the thirteenth year of age. The Conference next recommend that a course of instruction in concrete geometry with numerous exercises be introduced into the grammar schools; and that this instruction should, during the earlier years, be given in connection with drawing. They recommend that the study of systematic algebra should be begun at the age of fourteen; but that, in connection with the study of arithmetic, the pupils should earlier be made familiar with algebraic expressions and symbols, including the method of solving simple equations. The Conference believe that the study of demonstrative geometry should begin at the end of the first year's study of algebra, and be carried on by the side of algebra for the next two years, occupying about two hours and a half a week.

And there you have it. Why do we teach ninth graders algebra, followed by geometry, followed by more algebra? Because that was what this group decided in 1892. Who were these people? I think you should know since they made 100 years of high school students miserable:

Professor WILLIAM E. BYERLY, Harvard University, Cambridge, Mass.

Professor FLORIAN CAJORI, Colorado College, Colorado Springs, Colo.

ARTHUR H. CUTLER, Principal of a Private School for Boys, New York City.

Professor HENRY B. FINE, College of New Jersey, Princeton, N.J.

VV. A. GREESON, Principal of the High School, Grand Rapids, Mich.

ANDREW INGRAHAM, Swain Free School, New Bedford, Mass.

Professor SIMON NEWCOMB, Johns Hopkins University, and Washington, D.C.

Who were these people? William Byerly got the first PhD in mathematics ever awarded at Harvard. A chair in mathematics is named after him at Harvard. Henry Fine was a professor and chairman of mathematics at Princeton. His main accomplishments in life were the writing of a variety of mathematics textbooks. His *College Algebra* was not found easy by beginning students who, when first confronted with it according to a Princetonian of that era, "decided that no one could understand it but Professor Fine and God." This is the man who decided high school students should study algebra.

It is of course no surprise that such men would want everyone to study their subject. It is certainly no surprise that a man who wrote textbooks would want people to have to buy them.

6. Physics, Chemistry, and Astronomy

The Conference on this subject were urgent that the study of simple natural phenomena be introduced into elementary schools; and it was the sense of the Conference that at least one period a day from the first year of the primary school should be given to such study. As regards the means of testing the progress of the pupils in physics and chemistry, the Conference were unanimously of opinion that a laboratory examination should always be combined with an oral or written examination, neither test taken singly being sufficient. There was a difference of opinion in the Conference on the question whether physics should precede chemistry, or chemistry physics. The logical order would place physics first; but all the members of the Conference but one advised that chemistry be put first for practical reasons which are stated in the majority report.

And so, everyone takes chemistry first. Not that big a deal. It is the fact that they take chemistry at all that I find troublesome. Actually a conversation that I got into recently will make clear my concern. I was talking to a man who is high up in the administration at an Ivy League University about my ideas in education. I should mention that I like and respect this man. He is one the best people I have ever known in a University administration. I suggested eliminating chemistry. He was upset.

"How will the students be ready for college chemistry then?" he asked.

"Very few high school graduates take college chemistry," I replied.

"Besides that, as you well know, the introductory courses start at the beginning because faculty never assume that anyone learned anything in high school."

"Yes," he replied, "but if you eliminate chemistry from high school how will those people who become chemists ever know about chemistry?"

"Why is it the job of the high schools to make every single student take chemistry just in case someone wants to be a chemist?" I asked.

"How many people become chemists after all? Far more become lawyers and no one suggests that they take pre-law in high school." I answered.

Why is that? Why chemistry and physics instead of law, psychology, computer science, business, or medicine? No law (medicine, psychology, business, computer science) faculty were given a conference to run by the Committee of Ten, that's why.

Why not? Read on.

7. Natural History

The Conference on Natural History unanimously agreed that the study of botany and zoology ought to be introduced into the primary schools at the very beginning of the school course, and be pursued steadily, with not less than two periods a week, throughout the whole course below the high school. The report on Natural History emphasizes the absolute necessity of laboratory work by the pupils on plants and animals; The Conference give their reasons for recommending the postponement to the latest possible time of the study of physiology and hygiene.

Did you ever wonder why hygiene is only presented as you get older? Now you know why. And why were we cutting up frogs? Because it was an "absolute necessity." And, thus, tenth grade biology was born.

8. History

The Conference on History, Civil Government, and Political Economy had a task different in some respects from those of other Conferences. It is now-a-days admitted that language, natural science, and mathematics should each make a substantial part of education; but the function of history in education is still very imperfectly apprehended. Accordingly, the eighth Conference were at pains to declare their conception of the object of studying history and civil government in schools, and their belief in the efficiency of these studies in training the judgment, and in preparing children for intellectual enjoyments in after years, and for the exercise at maturity of a salutary influence upon national affairs. They believed that the time devoted in schools to history and the allied subjects should be materially increased; and they have therefore presented arguments in favor of that increase.

So, the history faculty wasn't perceived in 1892 as being as good as everybody else apparently. They had to explain why people needed to study history. So, they said it was for training one's judgment. Funny how that turned into memorizing the dates and places of famous battles.

9. Geography

Considering that geography has been a subject of recognized value in elementary schools for many generations, and that a considerable portion of the whole school time of children has long been devoted to a study called by this name, it is somewhat startling to find that the report of the Conference on Geography deals with more novelties than any other report; exhibits more dissatisfaction with prevailing methods; and makes, on the whole, the most revolutionary suggestions. Their definition of the word makes it embrace not only a description of the surface of the earth, but also the elements of botany, zoology, astronomy, and meteorology, as well as many considerations pertaining to commerce, government, and ethnology. No one can read the reports without perceiving that the advanced instruction in geography which the Conference conceive to be desirable and feasible in high schools cannot be given until the pupils have mastered many of the elementary facts of botany, zoology, geometry, and physics. It is noteworthy also that this ninth Conference, like the seventh, dealt avowedly and unreservedly with the whole range of instruction in primary and secondary schools. They did not pretend to treat chiefly instruction in secondary schools, and incidentally instruction in the lower schools; but, on the contrary, grasped at once the whole problem, and described the topics, methods, and apparatus appropriate to the entire course of twelve years.

I have included as much of this report as I have because I found it fascinating. The geography faculty seems to have actually understood something about education. They didn't think geography was something that needed four years of study in its own right. They thought geography was everywhere. Those who were to implement their ideas immediately decided that every other subject was therefore, prerequisite to geography, so geography came last and suddenly, amazingly, disappeared entirely from the high school curriculum. You can't help but wonder who these men were, these geography

committee members who were so ineffective and yet were right headed. Next
I show who they are:

Professor THOMAS C. CHAMBERLIN, University of Chicago, Chicago, Ill.

Professor GEORGE L. COLLIE, Beloit College, Beloit, Wis.

Professor W. M. DAVIS, Harvard University, Cambridge, Mass.

DELWIN A. HAMLIN, Master of the Rice Training School, Boston, Mass.

Professor EDWIN J. HOUSTON, Central High School, Philadelphia, Pa.

Professor MARK W. HARRINGTON, The Weather Bureau, Washington,
D.C.

CHARLES F. KING, Dearborn School, Boston, Mass.

FRANCIS W. PARKER, Principal of the Cook County Normal School,
Englewood, Ill.

G. M. PHILIPS, Principal of the State Normal School, West Chester, Pa.

Professor ISRAEL C. RUSSELL, University of Michigan, Ann Arbor, Mich.

Collie was the President of Beloit, but he was an anthropologist so he had
no ax to grind about geography. I can't find out about the other professors. I
do note that four of the conference members were from high schools and one
of them, Francis Parker, was famous for advocating active learning rather
than traditional classes and lectures. There are schools that follow in his ideology even today. So, we can guess that this was a weird conference. It was-
n't trying to put forth some professor's agenda. It was trying to do the right
thing. No wonder it wasn't listened to.

At the end of this report a curious thing is found. Remember the questions each conference had to address? Here is a part of their answer:

7. Should the subject be treated differently for pupils who are going to college,
for those who are going to a scientific school, and for those who, presumably,
are going to neither?

8. At what stage should this differentiation begin, if any be recommended?

The 7th question is answered unanimously in the negative by the Conferences,
and the 8th therefore needs no answer.

Or to put this another way, let's treat every student as if he were going to
college. This answer had profound implications for anybody who went to
school after 1892 until the present day. To see why let's take a look at Harvard in 1892.

All students at Harvard were required to take what they called *elementary
studies* and then they could select from what they called *advanced studies*.
Here are the elementary studies offered at Harvard in 1892:

Harvard 1892
elementary studies
English
Greek
Latin
German
French
Ancient History
Modern History
Algebra
Plane Geometry
Physical Science (descriptive)
Physical Science (experimental)
Advanced studies

Here were the advanced studies at Harvard in 1892:

Greek
Latin
Greek Composition
Latin Composition
German
French
Logarithms and Trigonometry
Solid Geometry
Analytic Geometry
Mechanics or Advanced Algebra
Physics
Chemistry

This would mean that each member of the faculty at Harvard fit into one of the departments that taught something on the list, there being no possibility in those days that there was a faculty member who taught something not on the list. So, let's see if we have this right. There were nine conferences:

Latin
Greek
English

Modern Languages
Mathematics
Physics, Chemistry, and Astronomy
History
Natural History
Geography

There were the following faculties at Harvard in 1892:

Greek
Latin
English
German, French
Mathematics
Physical Science, Chemistry
Ancient History, Modern History

I am shocked—shocked that geography didn't make it onto the list of what is required for high school students, since it wasn't required at Harvard either.

No, I'm just kidding here. I am not shocked. Let's say this was all perfectly reasonable. Let's assume for a moment that the high school curriculum should be exactly equal to the requirements at Harvard, enabling students to prepare properly for Harvard by taking each and every subject offered at Harvard so they will be ready.

Here are the subjects offered at Harvard in 2002:

2002–2003 FAS Courses of Instruction
    African Studies
    Afro-American Studies
    Anthropology
    Applied Mathematics
    Applied Physics
    Archaeology
    Architecture, Landscape Architecture, and Urban Planning
    Asian Studies Programs
    Astronomy
    Biological Sciences
    Biological Sciences in Dental Medicine

Biological Sciences in Public Health
Biophysics
Business Studies
Celtic Languages and Literatures
Chemical Physics
Chemistry and Chemical Biology
The Classics
Comparative Literature
Computer Science
Dramatic Arts
Earth and Planetary Sciences
East Asian Languages and Civilizations
Economics
Engineering Sciences
English and American Literature and Language
Environmental Science & Public Policy
European Studies
Expository Writing
Ethnic Studies
Folklore & Mythology
Germanic Languages and Literatures
Government
Health Policy
History & Literature
History of American Civilization
History of Art and Architecture
History of Science
Inner Asian & Altaic Studies
Latin American and Iberian Studies
Linguistics
Literature
Mathematics
Medical Sciences
Medieval Studies
Middle East Program
Mind, Brain and Behavior
Music

Near Eastern Languages and Civilizations
Oceanography
Philosophy
Physics
Political Economy and Government
Psychology
Public Policy
The Study of Religion
Russia, Eastern Europe & Central Asia
Romance Languages and Literatures
Sanskrit and Indian Studies
Slavic Languages and Literatures
Social Policy
Social Studies
Sociology
South Asian Studies
Special Concentrations
Statistics
Ukrainian Studies
Visual and Environmental Studies
Women's Studies

Why isn't Ukrainian Studies as important as Physics in high school?
While this may seem like a silly question, I can assure you that the members
of the Psychology, Computer Science, Linguistics, Anthropology, Philosophy,
and Sociology departments think their subject is just as important as Physics.

But really, who cares what Harvard is teaching its undergraduates? Should
that really be the basis of high school and elementary school, namely, preparation for Harvard? Oh, you think it should be? Then fine, let's have them
prepare for Harvard in 2003, not 1892.

Is there something sacrosanct about what subjects happened to be at
Harvard in 1892? Are they somehow more important than other subjects
because they were there first? You can't claim that that is the case lest I
show you Harvard's faculty in 1750 and you realize that Harvard taught
what it happened to have people available to teach. Departments in universities are, as I said, self perpetuating. Faculties survive at all costs. So of
course the ones from 1892 are still around, but that doesn't make them
more important than the newer ones. In fact, the newer ones might just be
more relevant today.

But after all, this is not what I am suggesting. The educated mind is not created by study of all the subjects that happened to be at Harvard at 1892, nor is it likely that it would be created by studying those of 2003. Preparation for college ought not be the hallmark of K through 12 education. This made little enough sense when it was unlikely that your average high school student was going to college. It makes less sense when your realize that colleges could easily teach college subjects and high schools could attend to their own business, whatever that might be determined to be.

The colleges ought not be in a position to determine what a K–12 education ought to look like. We need to define what it means for a high school graduate to be educated by something other than the standards of Harvard in any century.

We need to create a high school experience that is not meant to prepare people for college, but meant to teach high school students the skills that will enhance their daily lives and open up their minds to the future. Let the colleges teach them college subjects when they get there.

REFERENCE NOTES

The sources are the Great Books series for the extended quotes and the Web for the shorter ones. Joshua test questions come from his tests at the Latin School of Chicago in 1992. The Committee of Ten material was taken from the Web as was the additional material I found for the participants. All the Harvard material can be found on their Web site.

7

Producing Educated Minds Is Not the University's Problem

While high schools busily prepare their students to go to Harvard in 1892, it is interesting to speculate why students go to Harvard at all and whether Harvard is actually interested in producing educated minds.

At the beginning of my classes each year (now I leave Harvard since I never taught there, but I did teach at Yale which is more or less the same thing) I usually ask students why they are in college and they tell me things like, "it is a four year vacation," "the parties are good," "it will get me a good job later," "it is what everyone does so I never thought about an alternative" and so on. The issue of learning never comes up. No student has ever mentioned it in class although I ask the question quite often. Why is that? School isn't really about learning at all. It is about certification. College students attend school to get a degree that they hope will get them something they want. They pick schools on this basis, and they attend school with the concomitant attitude. Students attend college (or any other school) to get a piece of paper, and they try to do well to get recommendations so they can get into the next school or get the job they covet. We never ask a student if he learned a lot, we ask how well he did. Self-evaluation is based on the judgment of others when it comes to "official" learning. Students feel they did well when others say they did well. It is the rare student who says that he learned a great deal and thus was very happy with his education. It is clear that education today means certification. The educated mind is one that has gone to Harvard. Who cares what he learned there?

Not so long ago, I attended the commencement exercises at Columbia University because my son was graduating. The valedictorian gave a speech in which she said that she had always disliked school and that while she felt that she couldn't help but work to be the best at it, she was sorry she worked that hard and would never do it again. It was an odd speech, and most people in the audience were upset by it. I was happy to hear someone tell it like it is. Education ought not be a competition. Learning should be more than memorizing answers for tests. An educated mind ought to be one that is prepared to do something with that education.

While I was pondering this young lady's speech I glanced at the program notes and was reminded of why school is the way it is. The notes mentioned that the commencement address had been given in Latin until quite recently. Of course we know why. The Latin department was pretty strong at every Ivy League university, not just Harvard. They held on tightly to every piece of legitimacy that they could for as long as they could. Change comes hard at universities.

The problem is not with the students. Students are malleable and will do what they are asked to do. The question is: What do we ask them to do and why do we ask them to do it? What is the conception of education that drives the curricula at Harvard or Yale? Maybe a better question is: Is there a conception of education that drives their curricula?

Many professors in today's universities are not motivated to provide high quality teaching. They do not see themselves as providing a service to a paying clientele. They know students will not act like consumers. They will not complain if a professor is ineffective, in part because they view effectiveness as the ability to entertain and in part because good grades counteract the potential uselessness of a course. Also, it is not irrelevant that it is the parents of the consumer who is paying the bills, thus making the real service provider's issue one of alcohol policies and dorm room quality, rather than of the quality of classes that parents rarely witness and would not deem themselves capable of judging anyway. Since students need the certification and recommendations that universities provide, professors are in a power position, not in a service provider's position. Anyone who can determine your ultimate fate does not consider himself a service provider who needs to please the consumer.

Professors understand that they can dominate students and create various hoops for students to jump through to get a good grade, but they don't really have to worry whether anyone has learned anything. In this model, it is all too easy to just lecture and test and forget about real education. My favorite example of this comes from the time when we were starting a cognitive science program at Northwestern and I asked that all professors in the program commit to never giving a multiple choice test. Now, every cognitive scientist knows that there is no value in such tests, nevertheless the faculty objected. "Who will grade all the papers that that students turn in?" they asked. "We don't have the money for more teaching assistants and I want to do my research." The idea was dead in the water.

This is all okay with students as it turns out. There is an implicit gentle-men's agreement about school. Teachers make demands, students satisfy those demands, and those who play the game by the rules win. "You give me the grade, I'll get the degree, I'm out of here." A student once told me that the reason he was a psychology major was not because he liked psychology but because psychology courses always have multiple choice tests and he had found that he was very good at multiple choice tests.

THE NATURE OF THE REAL UNIVERSITY

To understand why universities are the way they are it is instructive to at-tempt to understand the following 10 things:

1. Why professors teach
2. What professors teach
3. How university requirements get established
4. What students expect
5. How students decide what to study
6. How employers view the graduates
7. How graduate schools view the graduates
8. The role of grades and tests
9. The role of certification
10. Why university administrations do nothing about any of it

Why Professors Teach

There is a certain naiveté on the part of students in universities about why the professors who teach them are there. They assume teachers teach be-cause it's their job, and that the model they held in high school of the profes-sional teacher applies to the university as well. Nothing could be further from the truth.

Professors at the top universities teach because they feel they have to, or ought to, rarely because they see teaching as fundamental to their life's work. At Northwestern, where I worked in the 1990s, professors who don't get re-search grants or contribute to the university in other ways are "punished" by having to teach more. The worst professors, that is the ones who care the least or who have tenure but gave up research a long time ago, typically teach the most courses. A top-notch professor, one who is world famous and brings in lots of research dollars, may teach as little as one course every two years. Alternately, his colleague, who has none of these attributes, may teach as many as four courses a quarter.

It would be nice to imagine that this is a good system for students, hoping that the nonresearchers happen to be good teachers, but in fact the opposite is the case. Typically they are burnt out researchers, resentful of how they fared in the system and with little understanding of how their field has changed in the last 30 years.

The best professors in the U.S. may or may not be the best teachers. This is actually a complicated idea because the issue of what defines "best" is subject to question, and what defines good teaching is a very open issue. In the competitive world of American universities "best" has a clear meaning. Universities vie for the services of professors who have the biggest reputations. Top professors get great deals when they are sought after by the top schools. These deals include of course, higher salaries, but as universities can only go so high, other issues also matter. One of the biggest issues is teaching load. As a result, the best professors have teaching loads of nearly zero (and sometimes of literally zero). Clearly, in such an environment teaching is not valued despite what these same universities say to their prospective students.

Nevertheless, these same professors who happily avoid teaching are often the best teachers. The reason why this is so is not obvious to the prospective buyers of these services. Typically, for example when students attempt to decide between Harvard and Amherst, they say in Amherst's defense that the professors there are professional teachers, care more about the students, and pay more attention to teaching. Like any generalization this one can be dead wrong, but on the whole, it is true that a faculty member at Amherst is more likely to care about teaching than a faculty member at Harvard. The real question is: Of the professors at each institution, who knows more? On the face of it this seems like a silly question. A course in the classics is a course in the classics. The best teacher would teach the best course and the knowledge of any teacher is likely to be the same.

While this may be true for the classics it is not at all true for a field like Artificial Intelligence (AI). Artificial Intelligence as a field is being invented today. The people who are inventing it reside at big, well-funded research labs that allow them to build their toys and experiment with all kinds of hardware. They don't do this at Amherst. If you want to learn about AI you can take a course about it at Amherst, but the teacher of that course will be someone who read some books about it rather than someone who is doing it. (Actually Amherst students can sign up for AI courses at the University of Massachusetts nearby, which despite not being a university considered to be of the quality of Amherst, is far better equipped to teach them.) At the very best, the small college teacher is out of date on the subject; at the worst he really doesn't understand the issues all that well. I have been doing graduate admissions in AI for 30 years and can count on one hand all the applications we have gotten from students at the "best" small colleges. Students at these schools never even find out about this subject much less decide to make it their life's work.

Of course, you could go to MIT (where there is a very good AI lab) and take a course from the best professors in AI. But these are the very same people who don't teach all that much, who probably don't value teaching as much as they value research, and who, when they do teach, have classes with hundreds of students in them. The best professors in AI may or may not be good teachers, but they are not professors because they want to be teachers, they are professors because they want to be researchers. They want to build robots or explore how the mind makes generalizations or figure out how to get a computer to be world chess champion. Teaching is one of the last things on their minds.

So, the short answer to the question that heads this section is that in the best schools they teach because they have to not because they want to, and in the small colleges that are supposed to be very good teaching schools there is a very good chance that a faculty member is teaching something he or she may not understand all that well. Now, this is not true in say, English literature. In subjects where research doesn't play a big role and where labs are not costly and professors don't need graduate students to help with their work, good teachers can be found easily. In fact, those are precisely the fields where there is a glut of teachers on the market. So, it is possible to learn a lot about English literature at Bard because there are hardly any vacant jobs in that field so good people find themselves at odd places. Even so, most of them would jump to Yale in a minute. No matter how much professors say they like teaching, and many of them do like it a lot, they all recognize that teaching is not what they were hired for nor is it what they really do for a living. Professors are primarily interested in the academic issues in their field. They want to write papers and books and communicate with their colleagues. They want to be famous in their fields. They do not get famous for being a good teacher. Teaching is low on their priority lists.

What Professors Teach

When you tell a professor he is to teach a class, you might assume this means he will teach whatever any other professor might teach in that class. After all, one high school history course is like another, so one might assume that this is true of college as well. But curricula in college are professor-dependent. This wouldn't be such a problem if it only meant there was slight variance in how a given course was taught from year to year and professor to professor. Unfortunately, the issue is bigger than that.

Professors teach what they know. There is no standard set of things to be taught in anything but the most introductory of courses. So, introduction to psychology is pretty similar in every university, as is freshman calculus. But, any advanced course is subject to the professor's unique view on his field. This is fine because one goes to a university to meet interesting faculty and learn what their view of the field is. Or, one ought to. This is what universities have to offer, an opportunity to engage a world expert on his own turf to discuss ideas he created or is deeply involved with, and for just a few weeks to pretend that you are a world class economist or sociologist dealing with issues just as professionals in those fields do. This is the ideal. The reality is something else again.

One of the problems with this view is that students by and large don't share it. Most college students go to class expecting to learn the facts. They want to know how economics or sociology works. When I teach a class on how the mind works, students want to know how it works and I should please tell them. The difficulty with this view is that most professors don't actually know the answers to the questions students pose. Economics professors don't know how the economy works, sociologists don't know how society works, and I don't know how the mind works. What we all do have are deeply held beliefs about these subjects. We want students to understand the issues in the field, the controversies rather than the facts. And we all fervently want to get students to see things our way, to absorb our point of view and to understand why our academic enemies are idiots.

Students have no idea that this what they are getting into. They just want to know what is true. They don't want to hear one man's viewpoint. But that is what they get every time (unless the professor is a woman). For this reason one university is quite different than another and every course in AI, for example, is different at every school. This is the fun part of teaching. Professors like talking about their own work and their own ideas. They love trashing their enemies. They love talking about the research they are doing. The question is: *Is this what students came to learn?* It is if they want to become academics, but by and large, the career of researcher is not what undergraduates have in mind when they arrive at college.

How University Requirements Get Established

With this in mind we can begin to see how university requirements get established. When I was a graduate student at the University of Texas I was required to take a course in American Government. I was working on a PhD in Linguistics; I assure you there is no other school in the country that requires a government course to get a PhD in Linguistics. So why was this the case at Texas?

It turns out that, for whatever reason, the Government Department at Texas was very strong. (I don't know if this is still the case. I am pretty sure it

was the case then because the President was from Texas and planned to re-
tire at UT.) They had enough political muscle to get a university wide requirement passed that made it impossible to graduate from Texas without
taking this course. Why would they do that?

With all those students taking this class the requirement for extra faculty
increased, and more importantly, the requirement for teaching assistants increased and this meant more graduate students for each faculty member to
aid him in his research. This was a good deal for the Government Department, and who is to say that a little dose of American Government isn't good
for everyone?

At Northwestern all undergraduates must take a math requirement. Liberal arts students are notorious for wanting to avoid math, so the university
has set up a bunch of equivalents. One of these is linguistics, a field with
which I am familiar. When my daughter attended the university I was aghast
when she wound up taking linguistics to meet the math requirement and
couldn't imagine what she was going to get out of it. She told me the next
year that all she remembered from the course was the concept of an *infix*.
She remembered this because there is only one infix in English and that is
fucking as in *fanfuckingtastic*. Sounds like math to me.

Requirements get set in a university, from general graduation requirements for a BA to PhD requirements in any field, by a committee. This committee represents various interests. When I became a member of the computer science department at Yale, I noticed that to get a PhD in Computer
Science one had to take a course in Numerical Analysis (NA) and a course
in AI. I couldn't imagine a bigger waste of time for my graduate students
than to take a course in numerical processing by computers when they were
trying to build smart machines. One thing had nothing to do with the other.
The requirement was there because of political compromise. No one knew
what it meant to get a PhD in computer science, so they simply required a
little bit of everything of everybody. This could take an entire year out of a
graduate student's life for no reason, but no one questioned it. I got rid of the
requirement by making a deal with the top guy in NA. His students didn't
need to take our courses and ours didn't need to take his.

Now, it turns out that deals like this are very hard to make in a university.
The top NA guy was reasonable, and more important, he was someone
whose livelihood was not threatened by such a deal. When professors lose
students they may find themselves in deep trouble. Nontenured appointments can be eliminated and tenured faculty may wind up teaching subjects
they know little about. Unless your subject is very popular, the only way to
keep teaching your favorite subject is to make it a requirement. Believe me,
NA was not popular, but it was well funded so the NA guys weren't worried.
But there is no way to eliminate the Linguistics requirement at Northwestern

short of a revolution. Few students would ever take such courses otherwise. University requirements are about politics, not education.

What Students Expect

Of course, the students know none of this. Students tend to have the view that the university knows what is best for them and if they follow the recommended course of study their lives will work out fine. I once had a freshman advisee who asked me what courses to take. This was at Yale where course requirements were quite minimal. I said the world was open to him and he should take what he had always wanted to know about. He told me this was no good. He needed to know what would get him ahead in life and that he thought I was pretty successful so he wanted to know what courses I had taken my freshman year. I assured him that I went to school in the dark ages when one had no choice at all and that he should be happy he lived in such enlightened times. He insisted. So I mentioned that I had taken Western Civilization, English Literature, Physics, Chemistry, and Calculus, all required of all freshmen at Carnegie Tech. I said this had nothing to do with him but I was not convincing, because those are the courses he took.

I can only imagine the committee meeting that put that curriculum together in the 1950s. I had come to Carnegie Tech to study computers but they would have none of that. Everyone there had to take the same courses as those who were preparing to be an engineer, whether or not one was planning on being an engineer. There is some question about why one needs to know chemistry to be an electrical engineer, but compromise being compromise we can see how the basics got put in whether or not they might be relevant to a particular student.

Students expect that the curriculum set forth for them by the faculty is meant to help them get where they want to go after school. This simply isn't true. In computer science for example, the skills that will get students jobs include various programming skills that are used in industry. One might think that computer science departments around the country would make sure that all these employable skills are taught in their curriculum, indeed one would expect them to be the center of the curriculum. Sorry. Most computer science professors are not familiar with the commercial packages that are in use on a daily basis in industry, and even if they happen to know them, they consider them to be of little intellectual interest. So, a computer science student will learn the mathematics involved in making calculations about what is computable, they will learn the theory of designing programming languages, but they will not learn much of what they will ever use in the real world. Computer scientists want their field to be a science, and they want students to attempt to practice that science despite the fact that the students are there because they want jobs in industry. They are as concerned with preparing their students for the world of work as their colleagues in 1892 were about preparing high school students to go to work.

Why is *Introduction to Psychology* in every university a tedious survey of every aspect of psychology that no student likes and no student can avoid? This is a simple question. You can't get around this awful course because, as anyone who has taken it will recall, you are required to be the subject of psychological experiments to pass it. That requirement is made by the faculty because they need those subjects for their experiments. Without a course that anyone who wants to take psychology must take, there would be no subject pool. Psychology professors lobby long and hard to make this course required for graduation from the university so they will have even more subjects in the subject pool. They make sure every aspect of psychology is covered so that any faculty member can teach it, and thus, no one hogs all the subjects. A typical student signs up for a course in psychology because he wants to understand his parents, or his friends, or analyze his various personal problems. Universities make sure there is no way you can take courses on these subjects without having gone through other psychology courses that no one would want to take (e.g., on visual perception or on statistics). If departments responded to what students want, there would only be clinical courses offered and all those experts in experimental psychology would lose their jobs. When research interests of the faculty fail to coincide with students' course interests, ways are invented to make sure the faculty wins.

This conspiracy is not always supported by the faculty actually. I once asked some chemists at Columbia who were very interested in improving teaching in chemistry about the required first year chemistry curriculum. I asked what percentage of their students were premeds and got the unsurprising answer of 95%. I asked if the first year of college chemistry had anything in it at all that would be relevant to the life of a doctor. They said "no." I asked if there was chemistry that might be of importance in the career of a doctor. They said "of course." So why wasn't the chemistry curriculum revised to include the chemistry that might matter to doctors as opposed to the chemistry they will never need? Because medical schools and various certification boards and publishers had established what courses would be counted toward the requirements for medical school and there was no changing it. In this case even the chemistry faculty was frustrated by this, but there was nothing they could do about it.

How Students Decide What to Study

One of the serious problems with required courses, standard curricula, and other unchangeables in the current university system is the effect they have on the future of students. It is the rare student who comes to college knowing what he wants to be when he grows up. He usually knows what subjects interested him in high school, and remember those were from the 1892 Harvard catalog, not the current one so he is missing a few subjects. Maybe he knows something about the profession of his parents or other people he admires. But, those are usually the only guides he has. The fact that the high school curriculum is also unchangeable means that each student is familiar with having taken math, English, history, and some science and thus their first thought is to continue this course of study.

Students want guidance. However, the guidance they get is not necessarily what they need. My daughter loved biology in high school and had thoughts of becoming a biologist. When she went to sign up for college biology, it turned out that she had already taken the course in high school so she was told to take a required chemistry course that was a prerequisite for second year biology. She wound up hating the chemistry course, didn't finish the full year course, and had to find a new major. She never got to find out if she really liked biology.

Students are typically directed, either intentionally or through coercion by other students, into the majors that are "in" at their school. At Yale, vast numbers of students are English and history majors despite the fact that there is no call for such majors in the job market. They decide on these majors because it is well known that the faculty at Yale in these areas is first rate. Students at Yale have absorbed the ethic that a liberal education is what matters, not job potential. I was once booed at a meeting where department chairs advertised their departments to freshmen when I said "major in computer science and you'll get a job when you graduate." (This was in 1981. Most of our graduates in the next four years went to work at Microsoft. Most are very rich.)

This was not the zeitgeist at Yale. The theory behind college education at Yale has not changed much from the 19th century. A liberal education means a place to study the classics, not science or (egad!), engineering or business. Fortunately, the students of the 19th century often had daddy's business to go into. Today students get the same advice, but find themselves with only law school to attend when they graduate.

How Employers View the Graduates

There is tremendous dissatisfaction in corporate America with the products of many universities. Sometimes this dissatisfaction is right on and other times it is entirely confused. The dissatisfaction is real enough, but the blame is often oddly placed. What would employers like students to know that they don't know?

Corporations across America worry about students knowing basic business concepts like accounting, about how to work in teams, how to write well and make oral presentations, and generally how and why businesses work. But where would students learn all this? Even a major in business might not learn all these things, and many universities discourage undergraduate majors in business. So, a student interested in business is likely to major in economics, where he learns about macro and micro economic systems and learns next to nothing of what I have just listed.

Of course, I am not recommending that a college education ought to be proper training in business. (Although the idea that, in our world, understanding business is considerably less important than understanding Dickens is of some mystery to me.) The problem is really with the conception of a liberal education and the monopoly on education that is held by those who have that conception. Students think they should go to college to get a job and colleges think students are there for some other reason entirely. A compromise might be nice. Colleges do have some obligation to raise the consciousness of students beyond their initial aspirations. They also have the obligation to respect the practical exigencies that are extant in today's world.

Political science majors presumably want to work in politics and usually do not want to work on the theory of political systems. Psychology majors presumably are interested in the mind and might want to work in health related fields and are not likely to become experimental psychologists. Do these fields care about this when they design their curricula? Typically they don't. Professors often share the idea that they are really training their students to become academics like themselves and that their job is to cater to the one or two students who show promise in that regard. All other students, those who will become practitioners in these fields, are given short shrift and not taken seriously by the curriculum committee. Individual professors can and do work around the system they have set up, but by and large the system does not enable or even care about future student employment.

How Graduate Schools View the Graduates

Colleges prepare students for graduate study then, given this focus on making students into mini-academics, right? Well, no.

When a student enters nearly any PhD program the U.S. he is assumed to have learned little of value in college. The only time we ever give credit to PhD students for work they did in college is when they took the identical courses we offer to our first year graduate students. Given what I said about the idiosyncratic courses offered by professors around the world, this means in effect that only the undergraduates who went to our school, who actually took the identical courses they would be forced to take again, actually get credit for and can skip some courses.

All around the U.S., the best graduate programs believe that if a student learned anything in college it is a mystery to them how this could have happened and that they certainly couldn't have learned it the right way (i.e., "our way") so they better take it again. Given that this is the prevailing attitude in graduate school, and given that employers have roughly the same attitude, one is left to wonder why students go to college at all. The answer is simple: Both employers and graduate schools require an undergraduate degree. They don't much care what you studied in college because they know they have to teach you all over again. This is, of course, a vicious circle, one that allows colleges to continue their total disrespect for the needs of students since no one expects the product to be of value anyhow.

The Role of Grades and Tests

Deep down inside this drama of the disrespected student is the real villain in the piece: grades and tests. We assume there should be grades and tests because there always have been grades and tests, and school is almost unthinkable without them. After all, without them how will we know who is the best, who succeeded and who failed, who did the work and who sloughed off? How will graduate schools know who to accept and how will employers know who to hire?

To put this another way, everyone involved in the drama of indifferent education, faculty, students, and administrators knows that the real role of our universities is certification not education. The list of courses I gave you in chapter 6 from Harvard in 1892 was actually a list of examinations that each student had to pass to graduate. Certification is about testing, isn't it? What other choices are there?

Imagine a professor lecturing to a class of 500 for a semester course. How does the professor know if anyone is paying attention? In fact, it is a safe bet that most students are drifting off most of the time. Students know there will be a test and so they try hard to stay awake. No test? Then why fight the hangover? May as well stay in bed. Without tests, the system doesn't work.

Actually, tests are indicative of why the system needs fixing. The problem is that tests and grades are so ubiquitous it is difficult to imagine a school functioning without them. The problem stems from the certification mission of schools. As long as the next school or employer expects that the current school will tell them who is good, the system can't change. One wonders why the onus of certification is on our educational institutions at all. Why shouldn't employers figure out who is good on their own? One of things I have always been amazed by in this regard is the following: Accenture actually requires new employees (hired from college) to list their SAT scores. This might make sense if the SAT were something other than what it is—

namely, a test about geometry, algebra, synonyms, and antonyms—but there is little on the test that is germane to working at a consulting firm.

As long as tests are the yardstick in school students will go along with the measure. Students vie for grades and refuse to learn something if it won't be on the test. Students routinely inquire whether they are "responsible" for the material being discussed, and if they are not they turn off. They cheat, they compete, they wangle their way around, they argue for grades, they whine and complain to teachers about their grades, they stress out, they cram and then forget what they crammed. They do everything but love learning.

The Role of Certification

Universities will never grow out of their certification mission. Too much depends on it. It is hard to imagine that as many people would go to college as do now if no one really cared about whether you had been to college. No one would fight to go to Harvard if going to Harvard didn't matter. But what matters about it? Not the education. No one asks if you learned a lot, they just assume you are smart because you went there. It is time to rethink this.

We may not get rid of certification but perhaps we can contemplate new kinds of certification. Students should be certified as having accomplished something or as being able to do something. Like Boy Scout merit badges, Karate black belts, or pilot's licenses the proof should be in the pudding. A student should show his stuff, he should be able to do something and the attestation to the doing should be the certification.

Such changes are unlikely to occur in current universities. It is the rare faculty member who will willingly stop teaching the same old course he has taught for 30 years and design a new one that will be more work for him to teach, because it requires more individual effort. This will not happen unless the venue and the circumstances of education change radically.

Why University Administrations Do Nothing About Any of It

The most well meaning college president can change none of what I describe. The former Provost of my university used to say "with faculty, everything is a la carte." He couldn't ask a professor to do a single thing beyond his normal duties without being prepared to promise something in exchange. As they say, *tenure means never having to say you're sorry.*

The uproar amongst students and faculty alike would be enormous if grades and tests were eliminated, lectures were abandoned, tenure were abolished, and all requirements were dropped, although it is all these things that keep the universities forever promising real education and only partially delivering. There is simply no way to implement such things over faculty opposition and there would be plenty of opposition. Take tenure for example. No administrator thinks tenure is a good idea. Every first rate university is saddled with "dead wood"—professors who once were good but no longer are. There is no way to get rid of them. Northwestern employs an avowed Nazi who goes around the country denying that the Holocaust ever took place. Can they get rid of him? No. They can't even lower his salary (Although he hasn't gotten a raise in a long while, you can bet.)

If Harvard eliminated tenure other universities would surely follow, but even they can't take the first step. As soon as they did, Yale would get a great many more faculty applications. When requirements were eliminated at various schools in the seventies this was seen as the decline of standards and soon other schools were bragging about their "core curriculum" that centered on the humanities. When grades have been eliminated they have often been replaced by essays on student performance that were both onerous for the faculty to write and annoying for employers and graduate schools to read. When professors have been required to teach more than they do (in a good university they typically teach one course a semester), then the best of them went off to another school where they could get a better deal. Research universities hire great researchers, not great teachers, and they will not be motivated to stop this practice unless their very roots are attacked.

There really is no way to fix all this because universities are not motivated to change. There is no challenge to Harvard and Yale. They are not worried (except maybe by coming free market in education, which we discuss later).

College is a time of great joy and excitement for the young. It is often the best time of their lives. But it is not necessarily the highlight of their personal education. And a good college education is really not available to all. Furthermore, students are often frustrated by various professors, requirements, lack of availability, depth and breadth of offerings, and the great deal of tedium that goes with a college education.

Universities do not really have the answer to what constitutes an educated mind.

8

Structuring the Learning Experience

So, all the subjects we teach are wrong, and the way we teach is wrong, and colleges are run by and for academics and school has been in the hands of the wrong people. What to do?

Before we do anything we need to think about what learning is like, what students are like, and what school should be like. It is not unreasonable to consider ignoring school entirely when one wants to examine how learning works. A better subject to examine if one wants to learn about learning is what I like to call *natural learning*. How do humans learn naturally? What does natural learning look like?

No one takes walking and talking lessons. Prior to age six or so, very little attempt is made to explicitly teach things to children. Children are allowed to interact with the world and learn from those interactions. This phenomenon is by no means limited to children, of course. No one takes "how to be a CEO" lessons either. New CEOs learn their jobs by doing their jobs. We all have visible reminders of this every four years when we elect a new President. You watch the President learn each time how to be President. Of course, he's learning on our time. We would like to instruct him on how to be President. But, is he any more likely to sit still for such a course as a two-year-old who we misguidedly decided to sit down for a lesson on how to conjugate verbs properly? If we decided to give the new President a President's course, we would have to figure out what would be on it, who would teach it, and how we would measure the results. Could we really do such a thing? And, if we couldn't, what does this say about building any courses whose subject matter is not already set in stone?

In any institution, a new CEO has to be broken in from time to time. When they're clever about it, they pick someone who was high up in the organization for some years and the transition is often painless. Being the second in command is a real training course. It is this realization that can make us understand something of what should go into any course. Any course needs to be realistic, like the job it is preparing you for. The best we have been able to do in that regard is apprenticeship, an old method of teaching that always worked quite well. It was abandoned as a method of learning for social reasons, not pedagogical ones.

Apprenticeship is a form of what is called learning by doing, in this case, learning on the job. In fact, it's the best method of learning. One reason why companies don't employ this method of learning is that they don't always have the time to do so. Quite often, a good training course would take more time than companies have the patience for. Apprenticeship always took a very long time, not necessarily unreasonably. But, time constraints in education are a major problem. Getting the job of education done quickly often leads to not getting the job done particularly well.

So, how do we find out how learning works? Go watch a child learn. Observe a two-year-old for a day and take notes on what he has learned by the end of the day. As part of this day, attempt to teach him something. When you sit a two-year-old down and say, "Two-year-old, today we're going to review past tenses," his reaction is to be out the door as quickly as possible. When you say, "Kid, we're now going to have a discovery of the neighborhood lesson, so first I'm going to put up this map and you're going to study it," the kid will not be amused. When you want to teach him the principals of balance for him to build blocks he will say "Go away, I want to do it myself." When the blocks fall down, he doesn't care that much. He might be embarrassed and might cry if you're looking. But, if you're not there he goes back and tries again. If you want to teach him to ride a bicycle you don't give him a theory of physics—you give him a bike. We all know this, but we violate it as soon as we begin to invent the idea of a course of study in school.

This gets worse as we get on in life. If you've had the experience of teaching teenagers how to drive a car (which I have had twice and hopefully will not have to have again), you try to tell the kid stuff about driving the car and he doesn't want to hear a word you have to say. He just wants to drive the car. He's ready to hear what you have to say at the moment he has had, or almost had, an accident. Even then, he doesn't really want to hear you but he's been humiliated into listening.

Now I'm not proposing humiliating people into listening, but I am proposing that you don't tell them anything until they want to hear it. Of course, this puts a crimp into the style of lecturers, since a lecturer can only guess at what his audience wants to hear. But I do know what a company's employees want to hear. Employees want to understand what they're supposed to do in their jobs and what will constitute a job well done. Curiously, that's what employers want to tell them too. So business training starts off with employers and employees on the same page, and that's pretty good. But then everyone gets lost because many people think the answer is, "we'll tell them what they need to know." Unfortunately, this doesn't work. People don't like to be told anything. They have trouble listening. They aren't paying attention. They don't understand what you said.

I don't believe in lecturing. It simply doesn't work. Parents always wonder why kids do what they were told not to do, why they repeat the mistakes of their parents, why they can't learn from the experience of others. Why can't you just tell them? It is ironic that I believe that lecturing doesn't work since I spend a good deal of my time lecturing. I don't lecture in classes because I have found alternatives that work better, but quite often I am asked to give a public lecture to a large audience of people who have assembled for the purpose of listening to me, and I do it. One might ask why I do this? It certainly isn't because I think that it's the best method of communication. And furthermore, I know that no one in my audience thinks it's the right method either.

Let's imagine that a member of my audience was flying to the same meeting where I was about to lecture, and as chance would have it, they were seated next to me on the airplane on the way there. We exchange idle chit chat, and then when he asks me what I do, I proceed to give him my one hour speech. What would my seat mate be likely to do? Would he sit there quietly, happy he was so lucky to sit next to me? Or would he get up and leave, go to the bathroom, put a newspaper between himself and me, anything to avoid this barrage of verbiage? Or, assuming that he was interested in what I had to say, would he interrupt me? On the assumption that my seat mate really did want to hear what I had to say it is safe to assume that he would interrupt me. Why? The answer to this question holds the key to what we need to know about learning.

Learning is an interactive process. People interrupt other people because communication involves mutual story exchange. No one wants to be talked at for an hour, when the possibility exists for interruption that might cause greater comprehension. People do agree to be civil and socialized for an hour when they are in large groups but that is a matter of economics, not communication or learning. If a speaker will only agree to address large audiences, and will not agree to have an individual conversation with everyone who might want to have such a conversation (as is typical of professors), then you need to sit quietly and listen. But even so, sitting quietly and listening really doesn't work all that well.

A curious thing happens when you try to listen to someone else talk—you think about what they are saying. And, it turns out, you can't listen and think at the same time. So when a lecturer says something interesting, what they said will remind you of something you already knew. You will begin to think about what you have just heard and compare it to what you already thought about that subject. You will attempt to generalize. You will come up with some questions. Or, to put this another way, the more interested you are in what the lecturer has to say, the less you are likely to hear the rest of what he has to say. When you think, the lecturer doesn't stop and wait for you to finish thinking. He goes on speaking and you don't hear the next couple of words, which is why lecturing just doesn't work all that well. One reason we interrupt is to say what we have been thinking and begin to understand it better ourselves. We want to ask the questions we have come up with, or relate the stories we have been reminded of, to see if the connection we made in our minds was valid. We also want to stop the other person from talking so we don't forget our own thoughts.

One way to understand the communication process is as a method by which we map stories onto stories. Our minds are repositories of the stories we have lived. Our memories are compartmentalized into episodes that describe our personal experiences. When we hear the personal experiences of others we cannot help but connect them to our own. We understand others in terms of what we know about ourselves.

Let's imagine that someone comes to you with a personal problem. Suppose they say to you, "Look, I can't decide whether or not I should get married." They are not looking for you to say "you should" or "you shouldn't." This is annoying advice. What people are looking for you to do is to ask them for their story because they like to tell it, and when they are finished telling you their story they are ready and willing to hear some corresponding story.

Communication is basically story exchange which means matching stories onto stories. Why does this matter? Because it turns out that that is how the human learning apparatus works. Human beings have experiences which they tell to other people. Quite often, they have told them to other people many times and this causes them to collect in the mind as stories. We tell our favorites over and over again. When my father was 88, he'd lost all his stories but four, as far as I could tell. One day he started to tell me a story and I said "This is a new story." He said, "it is? You haven't heard it?" He was excited. It turned out he had just used a new introduction.

The lesson here is that any real educational experience must tell stories. The stories that are told must relate to stories the student is likely to already know. The stories must be told when the student is ready to hear them, not sooner and not later. Businesses have stories to tell—lots of them. This does not mean that a company's training program should involve telling the history of the company, the philosophy of the company, the principles of the company or any other official story concocted by the company to make it look good. Training for a real life situation should be full of actual people's experiences from which everyone else could benefit; those are the kind of stories that matter and that are difficult to find when you need them. If this is true in business, and it seems obvious that it is, then it is even more important in school. School must relate to real experiences and real stories need to be told about those experiences. That is what makes an experience memorable.

But when should these stories be told? Bear in mind that people don't remember what you tell them, they remember what they themselves experience. They don't remember what *you* say, they remember what *they* say. Watch people relate the events of their day to each other. They may say "I had a really interesting conversation the other day," but if you ask what it was about you are likely to hear "Well, I said . . . , and then I said . . ." If you ask "What did the other person say?" they are likely not to remember exactly.

Such poor recollection is not necessarily the sign of a person who is too self-centered. This is just the way human memory works. You have to do a lot of mental work to come up with what you want to say, and if you're excited about a conversation it's because you said something new. You said something you had never thought of before. We are excited by our own thought processes or good ideas. We remember our own ideas. So if you want someone to learn something you've got to get them to be excited about it, get them to think about it, get them to use what they have thought, and get them to tell about the experience. Asking them to memorize what they have heard will last a minute or a week, however long you make it last by constant repetition and examination. But, asking them to reflect on what they have experienced can last a lifetime.

School should tell stories. But before we go stuffing every course we build with stories we must think about whether the student can absorb the stories we choose to tell. Remember that people hear things as they relate to their own interests and experiences, so two different people are going to hear the same story in two different ways. To see what I mean by this, let me tell you one of my stories. To get a feel for how different people process the same story, I once pretended I was a character in the movie *Diner* (in which four guys about the age of 20 sit around in a diner complaining about their lives for most of the movie). I took one of the monologues from this movie and I read it to each of my graduate students one at a time. The monologue (paraphrased) went something like this:

> Gee, I don't know, I just got married and I have nothing what so ever to say to my wife anymore because prior to our getting married we only had two topics of conversation: we were either planning the wedding or we were discussing where and when we would we could have sex. Now we don't have to do either of those any more and there's nothing left to say.

I said this, as if it were me speaking, to each of my students in turn. (I told them it was a movie and to just pretend it was me.) I read the story to them asking them to make believe that we were in a conversation and that I was really saying this. I asked them to just say whatever came to their minds. Each and every one of my graduate students said, "Something like that happened to me, and it reminds me of a story." There's nothing random here; that's what people do all the time. It's called conversation. When you're on an airplane and decide to talk to your seat mate, you tell your story—they tell theirs—you tell yours. Each story reminds the other person of a new story to tell. In fact, if it reminds you too early, you can't listen to another word the other person has said. You sit there and hold it in. You can notice other people doing this. You can see them wanting to interrupt you. In such a case you may as well just stop talking because they're not hearing you. You may as well listen to the story they are reminded of because they are busy trying to remember it and they cannot hear another thing. People don't control their reminding processes.

Since getting reminded is an important thing in a conversation, it isn't all that surprising that my students got reminded of something in their own lives by what I said. What is interesting is what they were reminded of. One of them was reminded of a friend who had not graduated high school and gotten married very early. He said he was a very smart guy but now he works in a Pizza Hut, and my student thought this was really sad. Another one of my students said it reminded him of a love affair he had had, and how whenever he wanted this woman she seemed to be involved with someone else and whenever she wanted him he was involved with someone else. Another one told me it reminded him of his marriage because he had gotten married right out of high school. But the most interesting one was the student who said, "This reminds me of the qualifying exam for the PhD in artificial intelligence." He said, "I worked and I studied for a whole year and I didn't do anything else that year; everything was about planning for it and when I finally passed the exam I didn't know how to resume a normal life."

We need to understand that a good educational experience tells stories, or even better, is a story. Designing good experiences means controlling the situations that students are in, so that they get to live the right stories and are ready to hear stories that relate to what they are experiencing.

Natural learning, the kind we do every day (not the stuff of school) depends on our finding what we need to know when we need to know it. When we go to a new city we learn where the important landmarks are, our hotel, tourist attractions, the place where we will conduct business, in a natural way. We don't set out to learn this kind of stuff, we don't memorize it, we just learned it by doing it; after a few days in an new place we know the routes we need to know. After a while we can get around without thinking about it—that's natural learning. For natural learning to take place, we must fail. Failure is where it all starts. We are receptive to new stories, new information of any kind, at the failure points. If you create a course in which a student cannot fail (and by that I do not mean will not get a good grade), you will not enable people to learn. Failure is a difficult concept to understand, especially in a success-oriented society.

Natural learning depends upon failure. Not the kind of failure where we say "Oh my God I've failed." I am talking about failure of a different sort: *expectation failure*. People have expectations about nearly everything—what people will wear, what they will say, what they will do under various situations, and so on. When these expectations fail we need to reconsider them. We ask ourselves why we thought what we did and whether we now want to change the point of view we had. Changing our mental structures, what we think about how things work, is what learning is all about, really. Therefore, in any good school experience students must fail. By this I do not mean that they should be presented with an extremely difficult problem that cannot hope to solve and get very frustrated. I mean that there should be situations where a student's natural expectation about a correct course of action is seen to be incorrect, forcing the student to reconsider his basic beliefs.

When expectations fail, we have to explain to ourselves why that has happened. I'll give you an example. I was giving a lecture in Puerto Rico one day and I tacked on a week's vacation at the end. After the lecture I took a walk along the beach of the hotel I had reserved. As I walked along the beach there was a sign that said, "Danger, no swimming here." I kept walking and I saw a sign that said, "Danger, no walking here." I was really concerned. What kind of hotel had I selected? You couldn't swim at its beach, or even walk on the beach. The next morning I got up and I took the same walk and when I got to the sign that said "Danger, no swimming" there were lots of people swimming. I walked by where it said "No walking here" and there were lots of people walking. I had to explain this to myself; I was concerned; I didn't know what was going on. And suddenly I was reminded of the State of Connecticut, where I lived at the time. Why was I reminded of Connecticut? Along every single highway in Connecticut there is a sign which says "Road Legally Closed." When I first moved to Connecticut I noticed this right away and was worried. "Why is this road closed?" Of course, they can't all be closed and in fact none of them are closed, and they're all full of traffic jams and so on but nearly all the roads are legally closed. But if you read the fine print (which they've changed recently because it was really stupid and now it's only somewhat stupid), it says, "If we happen to be doing construction work, and if you happen to get into an accident because of that construction work, don't blame us; the road was legally closed." So it's kind of a liability limitation.

Now why was I reminded of this at this moment while I'm walking on the beach in Puerto Rico? The answer is very simple. My expectations have failed; I needed an explanation; I couldn't think one up consciously. There's a difference between conscious and nonconscious processing. My conscious mind was failing, it didn't know how to deal with it. But I had nonconscious knowledge that my mind began to seek out. And my mind found the story about Connecticut. Now my conscious comes back and it says, "What is the story of Connecticut doing in my mind? Why am I thinking about it?" And suddenly I realized why. Because I recognized that the hotel was trying to limit its legal liability by putting up this sign. My nonconscious mind served up a remembered experience, a *reminding*, that had the same kind of expectation failure in it that I was now experiencing. I had previously resolved this expectation failure with an explanation that was suitable here as well. The hotel was saying to me, if you drown don't tell us, we told you not to swim here. If you meet someone you didn't want to meet on the path, you're off hotel grounds and we told you not to walk there. They were limiting their legal liability. So my prior experience helped me think about a current experience. This is a key aspect of human understanding works.

The net result of this process is that an understander needs to constantly modify his expectations. The expectation that failed here was one that says, "when organizations put up signs saying that some behavior is prohibited, they should be obeyed." This belief needs to be modified to say that "if one can interpret those signs as an attempt to limit legal liability, then the sign can be safely ignored."

This process, the modification of existing belief due to expectation failure is called *learning*. We engage in this process all the time, through nearly every experience we have. We have expectations that are very detailed about how a given room will look or a certain friend will talk. When these fail we notice it and wonder about it. For example, whenever I see signs prohibiting various behaviors I wonder about them. I was recently in Paris and I saw a sign that said "Danger, don't walk down these steps." So I figured, "OK, I'll walk down the steps." It turns out I was in the Metro and the stairs went down to the tracks. So this was a sign that made sense. I am always working on this. Every time I see a sign that says don't do this I wonder if I should do it and whether someone is just trying to protect their liability and trying to figure out whether I should pay attention to the sign. This is my own particular quirk perhaps due to a childhood spent on the beach in Brooklyn which was dominated by a big "NO" sign that prohibits nearly anything one might want to do (it included NO newspaper reading, for example).

All expectation failure comes from trying to do something in the first place, even just trying to understand. So you're not going to have a failure unless you were trying to do something, mentally or physically. This is an important point to remember about school. If the student isn't trying to do something, he certainly won't fail at accomplishing it. All natural learning involves learning by doing.

Proponents of learning by doing (as opposed to learning by being told) have long lamented the school system's lack of understanding regarding the idea that people learn by doing as their primary way of learning. For example, John Dewey remarked in 1916:

> Why is it that, in spite of the fact that teaching by pouring in, learning by passive absorption, are universally condemned, that they are still so entrenched in practice? That education is not an affair of "telling" and being told, but an active constructive process, is a principle almost as generally violated in practice as conceded in theory. Is not this deplorable situation due to the fact that the doctrine is itself merely told? But its enactment in practice requires that the school environment be equipped with agencies for doing ... to an extent rarely attained.

The trick is to do something to begin with the set of beliefs that students have and get those beliefs to change through real experiences. Students need to change beliefs that don't work. When a student is feeling lost because his beliefs failed him, he is ready for instruction.

Actually, if you really want to understand education, it helps to think about the Department of Motor Vehicles. In the Department of Motor Vehicles, there are two tests conducted for you to get a driver's license. The first asks if you can drive a car. The second asks if you can memorize a set of irrelevant and boring facts about driving and keep them in your mind long enough to pass a multiple choice test. Every state, and as far as I can tell every country, has both of these tests in their Motor Vehicle Bureau. The school system thinks it is much cleverer than the Department of Motor Vehicles, of course. It has eliminated one of those tests. They never ask, "Can you do it?" They don't even understand the question. What does it mean to do psychology, biology, economics, and history?

It is easy to understand where the doing is if one examines the interests of students in signing up for a given course. For example, students who sign up for a psychology course in college want to learn to do psychology. They want to learn to deal with their family and friends and better understand themselves. What they get in the typical psychology course is nothing like that, of course. They all want to go find out what's wrong with them, what's wrong with their parents, and what's wrong with their boyfriend or girlfriend, but what do they learn? A lot of facts about experimental psychology and the history of psychology (good for testing on multiple choice exams). They want to come in and do something; they come back with a set of things they have to memorize on the way to becoming mini-psychologists, which isn't what they were trying to become in the first place.

What would it mean to do biology? The closest any of us ever came to do-ing biology was to cut up a frog. It turns out this never came up later in my life. Of course, there is a lot of biology that does come up in your life. For ex-ample, everyday you eat food because you have a sort of basic assumption that it will be good for you and you need food. You may have learned about this in biology. We need to learn about nutrition but instead we learn vari-ous facts about phyla and zygotes. I typically ask audiences that I lecture if any of them could pass a high school biology test if I gave it to them right now. Less than one percent of any (usually highly educated) audience that I speak to ever thinks they could pass such a test. They are right. I carry one with me and offer some of the questions to those few brave souls who said they could pass. They rarely know the answers.

What does this tell you about the state of American education? These people presumably did pass a high school biology test. They probably even got As. But they've all forgotten the stuff that they tried so hard to memorize to pass the test. Most school is about the temporary memorization of a lot of irrelevant and boring facts that never seem to come up again later in life. Why is that? I first discovered this when my son came home with an A on his biology test; he very rarely got an A on anything. So I looked at it and I realized that I didn't know the answer to a single question. I handed it to ev-ery professor who came into my office from that period on and none of them knew the answers. These are professors; they're supposed to be good at this stuff. The next year I gave him the test back and he didn't know the answer to any of the questions either.

There's an important lesson here. All real changes in education have been impeded by the dreaded "M" word. Measurement. All too often, when we are asked to design a new educational experience, the next question is to tell how success in the course we designed will be measured.

If you want to measure things you need to teach things that are measur-able. To teach things that are simply measurable there have to be simple an-swers. Why is my son's biology test so silly? Because it's trying to teach things for which there will be multiple choice answers or that can be answered by filling in the blanks. It may be that the course taught him some stuff besides that, I certainly hope so. But that's not what's on the test. And in the weak-est of courses teachers teach to the test. So what it means is that we are try-ing to measure because we are interested in specific results. Because we are trying to measure those results, we teach things that are objectively measur-able. Unfortunately, all the stuff that is objectively measurable is the least in-teresting stuff there is in the world. Real life knowledge is not so objective. Real life is full of "in certain circumstances this works but on other occasions you might try this." In real life, the right answer is rarely "b."

In fact, the real objective in teaching is to get students to figure stuff out on their own. You'd like them to be able handle complex problems by use of the thinking abilities they have acquired in the course you designed, by relying on stories that impressed them, not by trying to recall memorized facts.

We need performance measures, not competence measures. Who cares what people know? We're in a society that is hell-bent on what people know. Even our leisure games, like Trivial Pursuit or Jeopardy or many others you could name, are all based on spouting back irrelevant facts. You can impress your neighbors by knowing them, but does that matter a lot? Would the smartest people in the world do the best on Jeopardy?

So what should we be teaching? The primary goal is to teach skills. But we need to clearly define what a skill is because the word is used rather loosely in education. In business, skills are clearer. Dealing with an upset customer is a skill, it's not something you can teach memorizable answers about, you need to practice it, as is true of any skill. Selling is a skill. Managing people is a skill. In each case, the experts know how to do it because they have done it.

Listening is a skill. You can ask students to memorize the eight principles of listening, or you can have people try to listen and see what they miss. Being able to program your VCR is a skill. You could of course learn how to program you VCR by reading the manual, but who does that? People naturally use the learning by doing method; we try to do it until we screws up and then we try again. When we're left to our own devices we use the learning by doing method. Left to our own devices means there's no one looking over our shoulder in front of whom we feel embarrassed if we fail. The thing about failure that's so important is that it needs to be done in a quiet room all by yourself. You don't mind going on to a computer system and screwing up when you won't break it and no one is there to laugh at you. But if there's someone right there by your shoulder you suddenly get very cautious.

Skills can be acquired through practice, but when that practice is mediated by good stories told at the point of difficulties in the practice, the result is a really good learning situation. The first really good piece of educational software was the air flight simulator. Every time you get on an airplane you're real happy that the pilot isn't practicing with you. Now in fact he may be in his first real plane. But the air flight simulator he practiced on is so realistic it is hard to tell the difference between that and the real thing. (I once flew a DC 10 simulator and cracked it up in five minutes—I don't know anything about flying. I got to hear what it sounds like when you crash. But the thing is, it looked and felt very real. I wasn't trying to learn how to fly, I was trying to understand the value of the simulator.) Unfortunately when pilots practice on these things they don't crack them up, which is too bad. They don't do anything risky—they do it just by the book. In the end, they've practiced on the very plane they will be flying. They practice on a variety of conditions until they are very good at it, for which we all ought be thankful every time we fly. They don't get to hear the stories of others when they fail. In fact they don't fail at all, which means that while the simulator is wonderful, the learning situation in which it is used is less than perfect. The pilots ought to be hearing from other pilots who had difficulties under certain conditions so they could learn from their experience, but, unfortunately this doesn't take place.

The important lesson to understand here is that what everyone needs, in training and in school, is an experience simulator. For any job for which one is trying to train people one needs a simulation devise. Are simulation devices better than the real thing? Not really. The real thing is pretty good. But in certain jobs, practicing on the real thing could be very dangerous. People could die. The pilot might be marginally better off flying a real 747 for the first time rather than the simulator but if he crashes it's at great cost. The same thing is true of allowing employees to work on real customers or real circumstances without any training. It's actually the right way to do it, it's just that they might screw up, and the screw up might be costly. But if it isn't costly, then learning on the job can be the best way. Of course, when we learn on the job we don't have the stories of experts readily available to us. We also have a strong fear of failure that might disallow risk taking. So the real thing may not be better after all.

When we redesign school, there are certain things we need to think about. There cannot be any lectures or any passive listening without an active goal driving that listening. Don't tell students things that you are not sure they want and need to hear.

Natural teaching needs to be done within the context of something I call a *goal based scenario*. A goal based scenario has a goal clear and agreed on, which is to say I know I want to accomplish this job and you know I want to accomplish it, and it's clear what it is. No preaching, only teaching. Teaching only after failure; the only time. Discovery and exploration guide work. You're constantly in a position of trying to find out what you're doing, on your own. Success is clear to anyone in the course. When we rolled this course out, people signed up for it who weren't beginners. In fact all the experienced people signed up for it and we asked why. And they said you have a lot of cases in there that we've never experienced. So learning how to handle them successfully made them feel that there was something they had learned. So it's clear to them what's going on.

Learning is supposed to be fun. Have you ever watched a little kid, before the age of six, before he goes to school? Everything they learn—they're eager, they love it, they can't wait. Even school—they look forward to school, too, that first day. By the second day they're not so sure anymore. Because learning has always been fun, and you know what? It gets to be fun again when you finally leave school.

Really what we are trying to do is to teach people to think. To teach people to think you need to cause expectations to fail, tell stories, and induce goals. A student emerging from a goal based scenario may not be able to explicitly state what was learned, but articulation of added factual knowledge is not what education ought to be about. People don't always explicitly know what they've learned. A successful student in a well designed course should have learned how to perform. It's performance, in its broadest sense, not competence, that is what education is all about.

The School of the Future

Experience. Since we learn from experience, school should be an experience. Each day, every student should be part of a complex experience that may last several days, weeks, or the entire year. The experience should be structured such that it is very engaging, exciting to the student and full of roles to play, skills to learn and practice, and goals to achieve. Ideally, the student participates in this experience with others, as a team, working together to achieve the goal.

Failure. Since we learn from failure, the experience must provide many opportunities to fail. What to do should not be obvious to the student most of the time. The student should struggle, working in areas above his head, with advice from others students, from teachers and from real world experts.

Complex Problems. Inside every experience, there must be complex problems that are difficult to solve. These must be realistic problems that will come up again in his life or else will form the basis of experiences that he can draw on in his life. These problems must be couched in terms of something the students genuinely wants to accomplish.

Motivation. Students cannot be expected to perform well in situations they do not care about. Freedom must be given to a student to not work on a particular experience because it doesn't interest him. We cannot expect every student to have exactly the same skills upon graduation. people are individuals and school must be individually adapted. Beyond reading writing and arithmetic there aren't that many skills that need to be directly taught. All students need to know how to communicate, relate to others, and to reason, but these can be taught within any experience.

Accomplishable Goals. School should present accomplishable goals. Every student should understand what an experience is likely to teach him and what he will be able to do afterwards that he couldn't do before. He should be able to demonstrate what he has learned to do in public asking others to watch him perform and taking satisfaction in a job well done. Every skill students learn should be demonstrable.

Competition and Cooperation. Experiences must involve competition and cooperation. People are motivated by being able to keep up with and surpass others. School should be a social experience, full of the kinds of problems people have with others. Those problems need to be part of the curriculum, not something hushed up and dealt with away from school. School has a responsibility to teach students to deal with the world in which they live. This includes the people in it.

Satisfaction. Students should come away from school feeling that they are good at something. Everybody is good at something. Students should be allowed to move into what they are good at.

Feeling Smart. Students should begin to believe in their own thinking abilities. We feel ourselves to be smart when:

1. we realize something—have an aha experience
2. we can explain something clearly—we can teach others
3. we see connections between events that are not obviously the same
4. we know what to do in a crisis
5. we can do something we couldn't do before
6. we can figure something out for ourselves

Students should be called on to figure things out, to explain something to others, to handle crises, and so on, on a regular basis.

Feeling Capable. Students need to see themselves as capable. Again, everyone isn't capable of the same things. We feel ourselves to be capable when we have done more than was expected of us or we have been original in something we did or we got others to recognize our abilities. We feel capable when we wow people, or we make others happy, or we do what we set out to do, or we do something we couldn't do before. Every school experience should be focused on making students feel capable.

Feeling it Worked. We know the experiences we designed have worked when:

1. we want to do it again
2. we worked hard and saw the results
3. we made others happy
4. we laughed
5. we reached down for more than we thought we were capable of

The experiences must be designed to make students feel this way after having had them.

Last, we return to the issue of the educated mind. Students feel educated when:

1. they understand something they couldn't understand before
2. they are interested in something they found dull before
3. they can converse with someone they couldn't talk to before

To produce educated minds, we must create experiences in which students are motivated to accomplish goals while working in cooperative and competitive situations dealing with complex problems that are satisfying to solve, making them feel smart, capable, and wanting more.

REFERENCE NOTES

The material from *Diner* I got out of a famous movie dialogues book. The informal experiment I ran with my students is described in detail in my book *Tell Me a Story* (Northwestern University Press.) The John Dewey quote is from *Democracy and Education*.

9

Teaching and Testing
in the Modern World

How should a good teacher proceed? In the good old days, teachers simply talked and students wrote down what they said. (Unfortunately, to a large extent, those good old days are still with us.) Today, teachers fret about preparing their students for state administered exams that have serious consequences for those who fail. Neither lecturing nor test preparation should be confused with teaching. What should teaching be like?

I am always ready to learn, but I do not always like being taught.
Sir Winston Churchill

And therein lies the rub. It is great fun to learn something new. It is even fun to fail and try, try again while learning something new. What is definitely not fun is being embarrassed because you can't do something or don't know something. It makes you anxious to appear stupid in front of others. Teachers would be great to have around if they were there only when you needed them.

I'll be back when I need you again.

Hana Schank, age 5

I couldn't resist quoting my daughter here. I thought this statement of hers was so cute at the time that I wrote it down. Later I realized it was profound. It sums up any child's attitude toward being taught.

Socrates. Well, my art of midwifery is in most respects like theirs; but differs, in
that I attend men and not women; and look after their souls when they are in
labour, and not after their bodies: and the triumph of my art is in thoroughly
examining whether the thought which the mind of the young man brings forth
is a false idol or a noble and true birth. And like the mid-wives, I am barren,
and the reproach which is often made against me, that I ask questions of others and have not the wit to answer them myself, is very just—the reason is,
that the god compels-me to be a midwife, but does not allow me to bring forth.
And therefore I am not myself at all wise, nor have I anything to show which is
the invention or birth of my own soul, but those who converse with me profit.

Plato (theaetacus dialog)

Socrates was famous for his Socratic method of teaching and this is Plato's
recount of it. Socrates saw himself as a midwife, bringing birth to new idea in
the minds of his students, the seeds of which he claimed not to have planted:

Socrates: Some of them appear dull enough at first, but afterwards, as our acquaintance ripens, if the god is gracious to them, they all make astonishing progress; and this in the opinion of others as well as in their own. It is quite dear that
they never learned anything from me; the many fine discoveries to which they
cling are of their own making. But to me . . . they owe their delivery.

I have never bought this idea of Socrates, namely, that all the teacher
does it bring out what the student already knows by asking good questions.
But, what clearly is true is that asking good questions is more important than
supplying answers. A teacher's job is to help a student reason about things,
and they can do that job best by being there at the right time to make a student think hard about what they are trying to do.

It is the mission of the pedagogue, not to make his pupils think, but to make
them think right, and the more nearly his own mind pulsates with the great
ebbs and flows of popular delusion and emotion, the more admirably he performs his function. He may be an ass, but that is surely no demerit in a man
paid to make asses of his customers.

H. L. Mencken

The downfall of all teachers (I include myself here as well) is the assumption that there is right way of doing things, a right answer, a right point of
view, and that their real job is to get the students to see it. Naturally, it is
sometimes true that the teacher knows and the students does not. Two and
two really is four. So, teachers can hardly avoid getting into the habit of setting themselves up as authorities on this or that and expecting students to
learn what they are teaching. There is only one problem with this, it doesn't
work.

> It must be remembered that the purpose of education is not to fill the minds of
> students with facts . . . it is to teach them to think, if that is possible, and al-
> ways to think for themselves.
>
> *Robert Hutchins*

People who talk about education have forever been mouthing aphorisms
about teaching students to think for themselves. It is the Holy Grail of teaching. Everyone believes it, but very few do much about it. Robert Hutchins
was a radical in education. He transformed the University of Chicago. But he
didn't eliminate grades and therefore didn't eliminate the teacher as an authority figure whose views must be followed. As long as the teacher makes a
judgment about the student, the student will try to please him. It is simple
human nature. Then, original thinking goes out the window.

> The authority of those who teach is often an obstacle to those who want to
> learn.
>
> *Cicero*

This is not really an issue of grades, of course. The problem is deeper than
that. Children are constantly being asked "how are you doing in school?"
Supposedly, the askers of this question want to know if people who are supposed to be learning actually are learning. It seems a fair enough question. It
seems like a quite reasonable question. But, it is one of the most seriously
bothersome and difficult questions that our society asks. Inherent in the various forms of answers that we will accept to this question is the fundamental
nature and design of what we think of as our system of education.

The question is problematic in a number of ways. The primary problem is
with the basic assumption that educational achievement is measurable. As a
society, we believe this in such a strong fashion, that is very difficult for anyone to disagree with it. Following on the heels of that issue, is the question of
what the attempt to measure does to our system of education and to the way
we teach. Third, and perhaps most important, is the problem caused by the
idea that it is the role of our educational institutions to measure.

We want very badly to know that our investments in education are worthwhile. We want to spend our money wisely. We also want to know if students are learning anything. We need to know that they have been paying
attention. We don't want to award degrees or certificates or licenses to those
who were just faking it and are not really competent. All this makes a lot of
sense. When you invest in production you expect a return on investment
from the products you produce. And, this model would be just fine, if the
product we produced in education were something other than graduates of
the education system.

Factories produce finished products. The success of those products can be
measured in any number of ways from judgments of quality to profits on each

piece. But students are not finished products. In fact, finished students are merely entrants on the highway of life. Their success is yet to be determined. They simply haven't begun the journey. If we measured the quality of an educational program by results, then the fair measure would be the results after the lives of the students were over. "Yale produces more millionaires than Podunk" would be a valuable measure if we agreed that money earned was the right arena in which to judge and if we could control for the earning potential of the students prior to entering Yale or Podunk. Such a measure would, of course, take too long to be of value and would be highly controversial in terms of deciding what the measures of a successful life might be. Podunk graduates might be happier than Yale graduates, if we could assess that then we could decide on the relative value of these institutions based on our personal value systems.

But, alas, we are a society in need of speedy measures, so these issues will never be addressed. What we choose to substitute for the more lofty and impossible metrics is the issue. Basically we have two choices. Either we decide on a set of standards that measure the unfinished, untested, and soon to be released into the world student, or we don't. If we do, the question is *what measures?* If we don't choose to measure, then the question is: *what do we do?*

Of course, this choice has not been realistically considered. We all assume that there must be measures. Can we live without measures? If we cannot, how can decide on a reasonable set of measures?

To legitimately address these two questions we must first contemplate the idea of measurement.

Every teacher's nightmare, and in some sense every parent's and school system's, is that the student has gamed the system well enough to get a passing grade without doing the work. When a professor lectures, he knows that many students are sleeping, day dreaming, passing notes, and otherwise just occupying the physical space of the classroom without much caring about what is going on. Professors assign readings, grade homework, and administer tests to counter this state of affairs. "If they want to day dream, ok, but let's see how they do on the test!"

Tests exist in our system of education for a variety of reasons. They make the professors feel that something has been learned. They make the school system feel that degrees are awarded to those who deserve them. They make parents feel that their child is doing well or that they can help by motivating them to do better. They assure parents that something worthwhile is going on when their children are in someone else's care.

In some sense, tests seem like a perfectly fine idea. If we attempt to teach somebody something, it seems a reasonable idea to find out if they know what they were taught. This idea is only a fine idea until one understands that there is a big difference between *knowing how* and *knowing that*.

The difference between these two notions of knowing is best illustrated by the test given to obtain a driver's license. All around the world, in every state and country that certifies drivers, there are two driver's tests. One tests if you can drive a car by having someone sit with you while you drive. The other is a multiple choice test that attempts to determine if you have memorized a set of rules about driving that the state would like you to know.

No matter what differences there may be in countries around the world, they agree on this: There shall be a *knowing how* and a *knowing that* part of the driver's test. No matter how huge the cultural and systemic differences in this world, unanimity on testing in this one circumstance. Amazing! Why is there such agreement on might wonder? Or to put this another way, how did it come to pass that the knowing how part actually made it onto the test?

In most other state certification exams, there is no knowing how part, and in school there is almost never a knowing how part. So, why is this distinction preserved in driver's tests? How is it that there are two tests where nearly everywhere else there is only one?

The answer is easy enough to figure out. First, this stuff matters. We don't want our drivers to have only a theoretical knowledge of driving, we want to know if they can actually drive! Second, we know how to do it. We can administer this test. We know how to put somebody in the passenger seat and have them determine if someone can drive.

Now consider the same concept for a literature course. In the *New York Times* of November 30, 1998, there was an article about new English tests for fourth graders that has replaced some multiple choice questions with requests for students to write something of their own, analyze some literature, and so on. Not surprisingly, students and parents objected. They thought that this stuff was too hard for a fourth grader. Or to put this another way, testing knowing how is actually difficult, both for the student and for the administrator of the test. The motor vehicle department has to commit a great deal more manpower to the knowing how test than to the knowing that test. Multiple choice tests make everyone's life easier—except that you wouldn't want to fly on a plane piloted by someone who had never demonstrated to someone that they can actually fly the plane.

So, therein lies the rub. If want accurate tests, we need to decide what is important to test. If we want scores that make everyone happy then we can take the easy way out. Unfortunately this is not the only issue. The question is bigger than testing. What should we be teaching? Is it possible that because we know that tests will be about knowing that kind of stuff, then we only teach knowing that kind of stuff? How does this decision affect what we transmit to students as education? Is it possible that tests cause us to throw out the baby with the bath water?

The formal name for tests of knowing how is performance tests. Knowing that tests are usually referred to as competence tests. Thus, there are three alternatives: performance tests, competence tests, and no tests. One can make the case for each.

But beyond that, there is another more serious issue. When one designs a course or a curriculum that really seems to teach what one wants to teach, it may be difficult to test it in any way yet the no test answer may have no appeal.

To see what I mean here, let's imagine testing a two-year-old child. We have spent two years raising this kid and now we want to see how he is doing. An alternative to this issue, and something to think about at the same time, imagine we have sent a kid to a one week summer course and we want to see what he learned in that course so we can decide whether we might want to send him again.

Now one obvious way to measure a two-year-old is to compare him to other two-year-olds along a set of dimensions that we care about. For example, we might consider verbal ability, physical coordination, social skills, potty training, and so on. Some of these are easy to measure—potty training for example. Verbal abilities are easy to spot, but measurements can be unrevealing. For example, one could count the number of words that the kid says over a one week period. This number will vary widely from child to child. But how valuable is this measure?

For physical things, there are obvious tests. He could run a race and we could time him. We could ask him to carry a fragile object a certain distance and see if it arrives intact. Children will vary widely along these dimensions as well.

Social skills are harder to measure, but not impossible. Can the kid play with another kid for a certain amount of time without fighting? Can the kid negotiate with another kid for something he wants? Will the child do as instructed in a situation involving adults? Does the child need constant attention or can he play by himself? All of these are skills which can measured.

But, these measures break down in a school setting. Suddenly there are subjects and curricula and their committees and Boards of Regents who want to know how everyone is doing. In corporations, there are people whose job it is to determine how many people went through training and if the training time could be reduced without reduction in quality, but no one is quite sure how to assess the quality in the first place.

All this has a profound effect on teachers. Teachers are part of the system of courses and tests and naturally they fall into the traps set by that system. As tests increase in importance in our society, teaching, in the sense that Socrates or Hutchins meant, becomes more and more difficult.

When I taught undergraduate courses at Yale and Northwestern, I tried to take myself out of the role of authority figure by eliminating grades altogether. I asked students to write about a subject I chose each week that had the property that there was no known answer, so their answers could be interesting or not but they couldn't quite be right or wrong. Then I refused to grade their answers. I simply noted whether they had tried hard or not.

This was a very difficult concept for students who were used to being graded at every turn and were used to trying to satisfy the whims of the professor.

Here are some of the comments students made about this course the last year I taught it at Northwestern:

> The professor was incredible.
>
> Without doing too much work, you'll learn a lot about what you think and why you think it.
>
> Wow. I never know such a great class could exist. I'm afraid that now, I will be disappointed by all of my other classes at Northwestern.
>
> Take this class—Schank is great—it'll be the highlight of your semester.
>
> This is the most interesting and provocative course I have ever taken.
>
> Interesting class, but don't get fooled into believing you're learning.
>
> Easy A, but the most boring, pointless lectures.
>
> Don't take this class if you have any expectations to learn. My tuition was wasted by taking this class.

Students have a variety of expectations for what a course should contain and what it should accomplish. An entertaining professor may get high praise but he may be imparting very little. A professor who imparts a great deal of information in a dry way, may be formally fulfilling the criteria of the course but may leave the student knowing a lot less than the professor was trying to impart.

Being a good teacher means, in effect, fighting the system. And that system is enforced by everyone, including the students. Therefore, we need to give ammunition to teachers—metrics by which they can know how they are doing and students can know if the teacher has succeeded and metrics by which the student can be judges that have some real import.

THINGS TO MEASURE

> A teacher who is attempting to teach without inspiring the pupil with a desire to learn is hammering on a cold iron.
>
> *Horace Mann*

A Good Teacher Supplies Motivation

Every student, in every course, has the expectation that what the teacher is trying to teach will somehow be relevant to his present or future life. It is obvious, if one takes this idea seriously, why so many courses in school fail to really work.

A student who is learning about long division, or reading Dickens, or studying ancient Greece, has questions in his mind about the relevance of what he is learning to his own life. Some students simply grant the school system the wisdom to know what is relevant and dive in. Others suspend disbelief long enough to pass the tests that will get them to wherever it is they think school will get them in life. For them, the relevance to their own lives is in the grades and they do what they are asked. For others, the belief in the system, and the quest for grades does not supply the necessary motivation and they lose interest and fail to learn what they are being taught.

The problem here is more than one of paying attention or worrying about whether students have a good attitude. The problem is deeper than that. Motivation is an integral part of memory. To put this another way, even if you accept that you will not fight the system and will try to learn whatever it is you were asked to learn, you may have a great deal of trouble remembering for the long term what you were not inherently motivated to learn in the first place. You can't fool your memory into being motivated.

Memory is the name of the game here. The desire of any teacher is have the students come away having their memories permanently altered. Most courses cause a temporary memory alteration. In other words, students can pass the test and then have no ability to pass the same test, years, months, or even days later. College students report overwhelmingly that they could not pass the same tests that they passed a year earlier.

Now, compare this with exams that test whether someone can do a job that they already do. If that test is a good test, no studying should be required. Every employee who does his job well should know most of the answers to any reasonable question about his job. If he does not, then the test is bad. The reason for this is easy enough—practice makes perfect. Memory for new information requires motivation to pay attention in the first place and practice in the use of that information in the second place.

Even if a student plays along when he is not intrinsically motivated and does well, it will be very difficult for that student to remember what he has learned. To remember something we must know where to put that thing in memory. If I tell you a random number you can keep it in mind for a short while, but after some time you can't recall it, because it was meaningless, it didn't fit with any other information you had or any goals you were trying to achieve. If I tell you how to do something, how to do some operation on the computer for example, you will remember it as long as it takes you to do it and then, if you don't do that same operation for a while, you are likely to have to ask me for the same information again.

To really acquire new information one must recognize the need for that information. This is another way of saying that you must know where that new information will go in memory. Now, we don't know that sort of thing consciously, but we can know unconsciously what it is that we need to know. We know we don't need to know the date of the Battle of Waterloo, we know that we might need to be able to convince somebody of something in an argument. It is thus far easier to teach the latter than the former. If we should, for some reason, what to teach something that it is not inherently motivating to know then it is important to embed it within something that is motivating to know. (The date might be the key to winning the argument for example although this begs the question of why anyone would want to teach the date in the first place.)

A good teacher supplies motivation or builds upon motivation that is inherently there in the first place. If the material to be taught has no inherently motivating reason to learn it built in so that any student would want to be in that course, then the teacher must supply the motivation. No one has to explain to a student why they need to learn to drive or why they would want to know about sex, but one does have to explain why they need to know history. Since that explanation itself is still unlikely to supply the necessary motivation, it is incumbent on the structure of the course itself to supply the motivation. That is, we cannot simply tell students why they should be motivated as this will not motivate them. We must build on the motivation that a student naturally has and weave what we want to teach around it.

A successful teacher has the students in it clamoring for more. Students should be sorry the course is finished because they were so motivate to learn more. Measuring how motivated students are assesses both the teachers and a real student outcome.

> The test and the use of man's education is that he finds pleasure in the exercise of his mind.
>
> *Jacques Martin Barzun*

A Good Teacher Promotes and Enables Inquiry

When a child asks a question it is a wonderful thing. If they ask, it is usually because they want to know, and at least because they want to engage an adult in conversation. Conversation is, at its base, the root of learning. We learn in conversation because we have to play our role in the conversation. We have to keep up our end of the dialogue. This means that we must think of something to say in response to what we have heard. The process for doing that thinking requires that we analyze what we have heard sufficiently such that we can extract an index from it and match that index to something we already have stored in our memories. In other words, listening means matching what was said to what we know. If what was said is mundane and already well known by us, then we match to an identity and say something like "right" or "I already knew that" or "that's what I thought." When the match is partial, when we knew some of what we heard or found some accord with what we thought and some discord, or when we find something similar but not identical, then we have found something to say back. We can say what we were reminded of, or we can argue with a part with which we disagree.

This is the basis of dialogue, and dialogue eventually leads to the third possibility, that something someone says has no match at all in our memories. In such a case, we work hard at finding a place to put the new information. We need to store it someplace that relates to what we already know. So we become curious, we attempt to understand better, so that we can fill in the holes in our knowledge and effectively relate what we heard to what we had known. This means we must inquire. Our part of the dialogue turns into questions at this point. We ask if what we heard really happened, we ask for explanations of what happened, we ask for facts that would make clear what we didn't know that confused us. To put this another way, when we are confused we can learn because we suddenly want to know. Without inquiry there is no learning.

It must be the goal of every teacher to cause students to begin to wonder about complex ideas. This is not simply an issue of having students ask questions—since the desire to ask questions in a public forum is much more a matter of personality, perceptions of the teacher's receptivity to questions, and to some extent, showing off. No, the real question is whether students are curious about the subject matter. A successful teacher causes the students to become interested in knowing more and to begin to find ways to acquire the information they seek.

A Good Teacher Is Surprising

It may seem odd that we expect that a teacher be surprising. But if a teacher is not surprising, can there be any learning? We learn when what we expected to happen fails to happen. When things occur in life just the way we imagined they would, then we can say we already knew what would happen and there is little to learn from the experience. Knowledge is, to a large extent, about predicting events. The rise of the sun in the east in the morning is a predicable event if you know about that subject. To those who have no rules about such matters, each sunrise could be a surprise. Knowledge is the opposite of surprise. If the sun failed to rise we would want to know what was going on. Failure of predictions based on knowledge causes us to attempt to revise our knowledge base. We seek explanations from ourselves or from others, to help in our quest to make accurate predictions.

For this natural learning process, a teacher must surprise his students. But more than that, a teacher must put students in a situation where they are entertaining predictions in the first place. We are not surprised if we aren't trying to understand and predict some events that are unfolding in front of us.

Lectures are rarely surprising, although they can be. If a good speaker sets up a situation which the listeners are following closely, then they can be surprised if events don't turn out the way they expected. Careful listening requires prediction.

Comedians take advantage of this aspect of human understanding all the time:

> Last year we went on safari in Africa. We took pictures of the native girls but they weren't developed. We are going back next year.
>
> *Groucho Marx*

Jokes like this one count on the fact that a listener will have decided a particular sense of the word "developed" because of the context of "pictures." This is the kind of prediction we are talking about. Violating it, in this instance, simply makes one laugh. In more serious venues, when one is trying to understand something more complex than a one-liner, a failure in comprehension of this sort, makes one think about what happened.

To create an active listener, one who is paying attention to what is being taught, one needs to make sure that there are many surprises that force many explanations. This is another way of saying that a student can't simply be listening or reading. They must be predicting as well, and the teacher must make sure that the predictions the student makes are sometimes wrong so that thinking will begin.

But, the issue is more than simply making something think (or even laugh). The issue of surprise relates to the material to be taught as well. Some subjects don't seem to lend themselves well to the idea of surprise. Is mathematics surprising? Certainly, a good teacher can make it somewhat surprising by attending to those arenas in mathematics that are not obvious and predictable. But the problems is grander than that. Mathematics can be surprising in the sense that when one is trying to accomplish some task, what is needed to do that task may not be available to the student, The student may need to find something out because he may be surprised by his own lack of knowledge. This a more important kind of surprise in a course. To put this another way, a student needs to be made aware of what he doesn't know and the surprise is finding out that he needs to know it to do something he wanted to do. The issue again is prediction. We can fail to accurately predict what tools we need to do a job, and thus be motivated to learn what we need to know. This kind of surprise is very important in any course of instruction. Without it knowledge is flat, unrelated to real world needs.

A Good Teacher Causes Structural Changes to Take Place in the Memory of Students

All of the previous discussion has as its primary intention the formation of structural changes in memory. No person who enters a course of study unchanged by it has learned anything at all. Learning means structural change in memory. A student must change his beliefs, his point of view, his emotional stance toward a subject, as well as acquiring new knowledge. Knowledge is not acquired in a vacuum. Learning does not mean simply adding a set of facts to one's repertoire of knowledge. This inert view of knowledge is what underlies the current structure of courses in school. The idea is that people have a bank of knowledge and what a teacher does is simply add to it. Unfortunately it's not that easy.

What is actually the case is that people have attitudes, beliefs, procedures, and a range of other kinds of knowledge besides factual data. Learning means altering this less static type of knowledge as well. We need not only to inform in a course, but also to create structural change in memory.

People have complex memory structures that they use to help them understand the outside world and to function in that world. They know how airplane trips work and use that knowledge to help them understand stories about such trips or use that knowledge to help them take a trip themselves. They understand how human interaction works, and here again, they use their knowledge to guide their comprehension and their functioning. The knowledge that they have changes daily. Each time there is another trip or another human interaction there is the potential for change.

This kind of change happens through the use of memory structures that contain expectations about what will happen next. As these expectations prove to be wrong in some way, people change them, sometimes consciously and sometimes without realizing what they are doing. When a restaurant's food that was good is no longer good, we change our view of the restaurant. This how natural everyday learning takes place.

For some reason, learning in school has always had a different set of underlying assumptions. We act as if being told about the restaurant's food will change our point of view, when in fact, only eating will really cause a mental change to take effect. We learn very little by listening in the sense that what we learn can be repeated but does not become part of our processing apparatus. Memory changes when something causes it to change, when we experience something that makes us look at things a new way. A teacher must do this to be effective. No teacher that simply tells about the world will serve to change memory in any profound way. Memory change comes form actual experience. A good teacher must provide experiences.

Those experiences must be about something we care about (motivation), must cause us to become curious about them (inquiry), and must be unusual in some way (surprise) for memory change to take place.

A Good Teacher Uses Mental Imagery to Aid Memory

The idea of "visual aids" has been with teachers for a long time. Teachers often show students pictures of what they are talking about. Lecturers frequently show interesting slides. Parents, when reading to children, know to let the child look at the picture at frequent intervals. We all know intuitive how important mental images are. When we try to recall something we often find ourselves picturing a scene or a face. We think about past events in terms of mental images and our memory is, in general aided by them.

The pictures we recall best are, of course those that satisfy the above four criteria. They relate to things we care about, are curious about, things that we find surprising, and they things that cause us to view the world in a new way. There are of course, other properties of mental images in addition to these four. Images can be pleasing because they are pretty or interesting or even repulsive.

When we consider how teachers use imagery, we need to bear in mind that the primary criteria we care about is memorability. If we are likely to remember the image then it is of some educational value potentially. There are other criteria, like relevance to what we are trying to teach, for example. We can remember interesting sights, but what we remember about them must be germane. A good image should help us in doing, and that is the ultimate issue in memorability as well as in the potential usefulness of a course.

A Good Teacher Must Incite Emotional Responses in the Student

Emotions are the fundamental basis of memory. We remember what care about. We dwell on what we are really upset about. We recall happy days and sad days. We get excited and we get depressed and we remember why. We remember being angry or hopeful. In short, we remember that which has caused us to feel something. Conversely, if we feel nothing, we remember little. A good teacher must evoke emotional reactions in its students.

Now this is easier said than done. How can mathematics be emotional? Well, of course it is for many students, usually negatively so. The issue is to find a way to evoke emotional responses naturally. One such natural emotion can be found in the sense of accomplishment felt by someone who has worked hard to achieve a goal and achieved it. Students do sometimes feel this emotion, but usually that emotion is tied to a grade achieved or an exam that has been studied for and completed with success. The problem here is that what this means is that students are likely to recall the process of studying or the emotional reaction of getting the good grade and neither of these relate to recalling the content of the course.

The issue for teachers is to get the emotionality to be tied to the content in some way. What this can mean in practice actually boils down to one of two things: a powerful demonstration or a powerful reaction to doing—the frustrations associated with doing and the sense of accomplishment associated with achieving one's goal.

Put into practice, this means that in the telling model of education, memory alteration can be achieved and thus learning will take place, to the extent that the story being told or images being shown are emotionally powerful. One might expect that one could learn about the Holocaust for example, by seeing vivid pictures or hearing first-hand stories. Even without doing one could learn if the emotional impact was high.

But in a doing environment, what this means that one has to fell emotions associated with the doing. If it were possible, one could easily teach about the Holocaust by making students experience some of the same experiences. This would probably best be done in simulation given the rules of education under which we live, but from a memory point of view if you want students to remember, the more real it is the more easier it would be to remember.

A Good Teacher Encourages Practice in Doing

Doing is what learning is all about. We learn so that we can do. Everything in education tends to point the other way. The idea behind most schooling is that we learn so that we can know. But knowing without doing is a rather meaningless state of affairs. Not all doing is physical of course. Mental doing or social doing are also kinds of doing. Learning to do means learning procedures and practicing those procedures.

Most of school leaves doing out. Most courses are a kind of preparation for a doing that never take place. Sometimes, arguing about ideas, a kind of doing, does occur in a course. Sometimes laboratory work in a course allows some practice in doing. But in a standard lecture course, there usually is no doing at all.

A good teacher must not only encourage doing but he must make sure that all his teaching is centered around doing. The teacher should be about preparing students to do something, having them do it, and then having them reflect on how well they did it and prepare to try again.

A Good Teacher Encourages Practice in Reasoning

I have saved this for last because this is the most important. In the end, all education is about is teaching people to reason. If reasoning were a subject per se, then you could teach people to do it and they would be forever capable of reasoning. Unfortunately, reasoning in physics isn't exactly the same as reasoning in political science, although they do have some things in common. To learn how to reason in our daily lives we must practice reasoning in task specific situations. Reasoning on the job is the most important part of learning a job. It is easy to learn procedures, it is must harder to learn what to do when those procedures fail or when there are no rules that fit the situation. Being able to handle new issues that come up is the hallmark of intelligence.

Thus, it is the job of every teacher to help students figure things out for themselves. Yes, there are rules. Yes, there are ways of doing things. Yes, there are facts and cases and examples to be followed. But most of all there is figuring out what to do on one's own. Learning really means preparing oneself to go out into the world and practice what one has learned to do and this means doing it without help.

Mentoring

A good teacher is a good mentor. They don't teach anybody anything. They help as needed. Teaching is a bad idea. Mentoring is a noble idea. You really can't teach anybody anything they don't want help in doing.

The best way to mentor anybody is to let them loose and only say something when asked. The key issue in mentoring is when to tell. The question for a mentor in a learn by doing course is simple: At what point should the mentor tell the students how to do it?

In learn by listening courses, the answer is: *all the time*. We might be tempted to say therefore, that in learn by doing courses the answer is: *never*. This isn't quite the case however, so what we have written here are the exceptions to never. That is, there are times to tell students something. We are sure the list of when to tell is too long. When in doubt, don't tell anybody anything.

Rule #1: Be ignorant
When asked, a good mentor claims ignorance. Your favorite response to a student question should be: *I really don't know. What do you think?*

Rule #2: Live and let live

It is important to realize that not every student is suited for every role. In a well designed story centered curriculum, there will be many roles to play and every student will have different talents. It is not necessary, as it is in traditional courses, that every student have the same level of achievement. Some students will never get it about something. That is ok. It is important to let students move on when they are stuck. It is important to let students work harder at one thing than another because they are better at it or more interested in it. A good mentor recognizes when a student can be unstuck and lets him live if he can't be unstuck.

Rule #3: Know when to tell and when to run like hell

3a: You can tell a student the answer when the answer is a small missing fact that the student would have to spend inordinate amounts of time attempting to figure out on his own.

3b: You can tell a student the answer when his following the wrong course of action might lead to danger or a recovery period that is too long given the situation.

3c: Don't tell the student anything if you know he can figure it out on his own.

3d: Don't tell the students anything if the reason he does not know the answer is basic laziness of thought or deed.

3e: Don't tell the student anything if what he needs to know has been written down somewhere and that writing is accessible.

3f: Don't ever tell the student an answer when the performance objective of the exercise is the discovery of that answer.

Rule #4: What do you suggest?

Suggestions are good. In fact, the real role of a mentor is to make suggestions. Of course, there are suggestions and there are suggestions. When suggestions look like the gospel they are bad. When they are presented as something to think about they are good.

4a: When a student is misdirected and needs repointing, it is good time to make suggestion. If the student is headed south when he should be headed north, it might just take him a 1000 miles to realize his mistake. The 1000 mile journey is mostly a waste of time. After 10 miles it might be a good idea if the weather seems to be getting warmer.

4b: When the information a student needs has been discovered and somehow the student hasn't realized it. This is a good time to ask them if they would recognize their own nose if it were in front of them.

4c: When the student is spinning his wheels and accomplishing nothing. Putting him on a solid footing and letting him start driving is a good idea when he is so stuck he will never get out on his own. A mentor needs to recognize when this is the case. This is, in the essence of the art of mentoring.

Rule #5: Let it lie

This might seem like an odd idea: Lie to your students. We don't mean by this telling the exact opposite of the truth in a factual situation. But, there are times when a student has an idea and that the key issue is to get them to express that idea, understand its ramifications, play with the idea a bit. This will never happen if your response to an idea is to expand on it yourself or even simply to ask a student more questions about the idea. It is a better strategy to deny what the student has said by adopting what seems to him to be a patently absurd stance. Typically students get emotional in such a situation and get fired up in an attempt to show you what a dope you are. They work hard to come up with reasoned argument. You should work just as hard to show why they are wrong. It doesn't matter whether they are wrong. Say things you don't believe if it will advance the cause of the students thinking harder about how to defeat you. It is not your job to show the student how smart you are nor to earn the students respect for your good ideas. It is much better to make the student think hard.

Rule #6: I want to hold your hand

Holding a student's hand while they attempt to do something can be very tempting. While we like the Socratic method as a means of mentoring, Socrates, in the slave boy dialogue at least, was not actually being a Socratic mentor. It is possible to hold the hand of the student too much, to have them follow your lead and seem to understand, only to find out that when left to their own devices they cannot do it on their own. Don't put words in the students mouth and don't hold the hand that is doing the actual work.

6a: Generic strategies are worth telling to students (at the right time). Hand holding with generalities is more useful than hand holding with specifics. "Now turn the wrench another quarter inch" is exactly what not to say.

6b: Specifics that are about practice on the other hand can be suggested. Reminding a kid learning to hit a baseball to keep his elbow up is one of those things that you cannot say too often. It is easy to fail to do because you don't realize that you are not doing it and it has to become second nature. Helping a student get something to become second nature is what hand holding is all about when done correctly.

Rule #7: One more time, this time with feeling

Practice is the essence of doing correctly. Understanding when a student has gotten it right and when they have simply happened to have succeeded is critical in mentoring. Good mentors know when more practice is needed. Good mentors also know when the rest of what is be done can be skipped because the student got it faster than expected.

7a: Make the student do it one more time when the student believes they've finished but they can do better.

7b: Let them stop when feedback on the current attempt would make success trivial and tedious.

Rule #8: Stop in the name of love

A good mentor knows when a student needs to be diverted from frustration. Often this means simply telling the students to stop doing something and do it later or having the student do some other problem instead. Also, as stated in rule #2, sometimes this means simply letting the student realize that the problems he is working on are simply not his future career and letting him bag it altogether.

REFERENCE NOTES

The sources are the Great Books series for the extended quotes and the Web for the shorter ones. The Northwestern students' quotes can be found in an archive kept at Northwestern of student reviews of courses. They are available online but only to Northwestern people. The Groucho Marx quote is from *Animal Crackers*.

10

Horses for Courses:
The Story Centered Curriculum

A good teacher, no matter how good they are, is still guided by the curriculum that he is teaching within. We can make no substantive change in education without radical change in the curriculum. This is easy to say but difficult to do. Schools don't typically erase their curricula. There are too many vested interests in what is already there. The teachers are familiar with it, students expect it, states require it, testing services test it, publishers publish it, and, perhaps most important, we have all experienced it and have come to accept it. Schools are armored against change. But in the last few years, a chink has appeared in that armor. It may be possible to exploit it. That chink is the Internet.

In the last few years, universities have started to consider getting into the distance education business. They see the computer as vital to this enterprise but it is not obvious that they know why it is vital. They want to deliver courses via the Web. There are a few obvious reasons why a university might want to do this, ranging from additional student revenue to the exploration of new teaching methods, although in reality, the latter reason is not high on any university president's mind. For the most part, this has not been a successful venture. Newspapers are full of stories about how the idea of a virtual university didn't work, but it may be a just little early to write the obituary for the concept.

Most universities went into the online course building business without attempting to understand why students attend universities and what an online offering should look like. They naturally assumed that the courses they offer were very valuable and that students would flock to the online versions. But, as we have seen, students take courses in college because they are required to do so for degrees or other certification that they seek. Left to their own devices, students would rather not attend courses (and they often don't), because courses all too often feature lecturers who drone on endlessly about subjects that students know will never matter in their real lives.

Another reason that students attend college is for the experience of being with other students, including social events and intellectual discussions. Both are sought after by students and are not fully provided by a conception of online education that takes existing lecture courses, adds a pretty picture or two to their textual version, and allows students to take the exam at the end.

Universities shouldn't spend time or money copying what they now offer on campus and offering it online because doing so makes the assumption that it is the content of those courses that is valuable. Nothing could be further from the truth. Most of the content that they offer online is available in textbooks. Students don't simply buy textbooks and read them to get an education. The content is not the issue.

What universities offer is the possibility of exciting students to work on projects that faculty are involved in. They also offer one-on-one mentoring to help foster a student's ideas or projects. Or, they offer lively discussions on complex issues, informed by faculty. These are the things that must be put online. And these are the things that can be put online. To do so, requires building online experiences (not necessarily courses) that lead to degrees. This can be done by allowing students to work in teams with mentors on projects that are simulations of real life experiences and help prepare students for the real world.

One thing we know is that virtual universities will serve up online courses. But what exactly is a course?

As with most aspects of society that we simply take for granted, courses have been with us for so long that we simply accept that they have the structure, length, and characteristics that they should have, and leave it at that. Web courses can be different than what is there now. They can be different for three reasons: 1. Current college courses aren't very good and the new medium exposes their weak underbelly. Listening to a lecture online is a disaster. 2. The length, material covered, and general methodology in college courses was derived from practical considerations that are irrelevant in this new medium. Faculty only show up to teach some many hours per week. The room can only accommodate so many people. Buildings open and close at regular times. None of this matters online. 3. It's on a computer. This new medium has to change the very nature of how things are presented because it can. Just like movies ceased to be filmed plays quickly enough, online courses will cease to be online copies of what was there before.

What should a Web course be? For starters, the concept of a course is all wrong. A course is of arbitrary duration. Horses run on courses set up at preestablished standardized distances at various racetracks. Students are not horses. Students need to accomplish tasks, and having accomplished them, they should move on to the next task. Students needn't run through courses. They need to practice whatever skills they are being taught in a realistic environment. Such an environment is the kind of "course" that should be on the Internet.

A parable:

Every Curriculum Tells a Story

Once upon a time, there was a kingdom that was overrun with dragons. The people were terrorized by the dragons, so they decided to build a new curriculum in their finest university to train young warriors in the art of dragon slaying. The university they selected had a faculty that knew many different things that would be of potential use to a dragon slayer, so the faculty met and formed a curriculum committee to establish a master's degree in Dragon Slaying. The committee drew on all the wisest faculty in the university, so it had faculty from the arts and faculty from the sciences. There were business faculty and law faculty and medical faculty. The engineering faculty was represented and so was the humanities faculty. Surely from such an erudite group, the best and the brightest could instruct those who wished to learn how to slay the dragon.

At the curriculum-planning meeting, everyone agreed that each faculty member had something important to contribute. The business faculty was concerned that potential dragon slayers understand how to finance a dragon slaying expedition, and know how to create a business plan to market the story and lessons derived from a successful voyage. The engineering faculty wanted to make sure that the student warrior would know how to read maps, build bridges where needed, and launch missiles. The humanities faculty realized that dragons could be reasoned with and proposed a course in how to speak Dragonese and how to negotiate with dragons. The legal faculty was concerned with dragon rights and potential lawsuits, and suggested a course in law for the neophyte warriors. The arts faculty wanted to make sure that the public would be able to see what the dragon looked like, and suggested the use of photography and drawing courses. The scientists wanted to know about the habitats and evolutionary history of the dragon, and therefore proposed teaching a basic course in evolution and biology to the students in the program. The medical faculty was concerned that students might not know how to kill the dragon properly if they failed to understand how dragons were constructed.

As it happened, this university was the most prestigious one in the land. Consequently, its faculty were very busy working on government funded research projects and on traveling around the world giving invited speeches and consulting to businesses. They didn't really like to teach all that much, and they hated to have to develop new courses because these were a lot of work. They were willing to develop some new courses, but new courses for master's students were never a priority. They each decided to choose courses from existing curricula that would be appropriate for the novice dragon slayers. In this way, students would get a broad education that would serve them well. When they finished, this was the curriculum they chose:

First Semester
    Introduction to Dragonese
    Basic Legal Concepts
    Introduction to Photography
    Introduction to Anatomy
    Strength and Materials

Second Semester
    Introduction to Dragonese II
    Civil Liberties and Animal Rights
    Introduction to Drawing
    The Anatomy of Dragons
    Projectile Physics

All agreed that this was very good curriculum indeed, but that it was difficult to cover everything needed in a one-year master's program, so it was decided to make the dragon slaying master's a two-year program. This was the second year curriculum they agreed on:

Third Semester
    Basic Negotiation
    History of Warfare
    Introduction to Ethics
    Evolutionary Biology
    Introduction to Map Reading

Fourth Semester
    Introduction to Public Policy
    Basic Marketing
    Basic Finance
    Introduction to Computation
    Logistics

The faculty was very proud of this curriculum, and they agreed it was well balanced and covered everything a student would need to know. A student body of 20 was recruited, and they all graduated two years later, most of them with high honors. They then went out to slay dragons.

Three of them failed to win funding for their expedition, and they went into other fields. Five of the remaining formed a dragon slaying team, but they had great difficulty getting along with each other. One of the members killed another one, then the rest killed him. The other three ran away and were never heard from again.

The remaining 12 were more successful. They formed three teams of four, were well financed, and got along well with each other. Unfortunately, the first of those teams never could find a dragon to slay, although they did spend a lot of time looking. Eventually they formed a company that trained dragon slayers.

The second team did indeed meet the dragon. Unfortunately, this was because the dragon found them first. They tried to reason with the dragon, but only one of them could remember how to speak Dragonese, as it was a year since the students had taken Introduction to Dragonese. However, the graduate who had been good at speaking Dragonese had been the only student to fail the negotiation course. He succeeded in annoying the dragon by demanding that he not breathe fire while they negotiated. The dragon ate all four members of the team.

The third team did indeed find and do battle with the dragon. Unfortunately, they had never really tried to fight a dragon before, and the dragon was much faster and its flame much hotter than any of them had anticipated. The dragon chased one of the members of the team off of a cliff and then proceeded to melt first the weapons and then the body of a second team member. The last two team members had no idea how they to engage in a battle between the just the two of them and the dragon, so they negotiated a truce. They are now doing public relations for the dragon.

THE STORY CENTERED CURRICULUM

What went wrong in the dragon slaying curriculum that the faculty worked so hard to build? For one thing, there was no actual dragon slaying in it. Teaching actual dragon slaying can be very difficult because, among other things, it requires access to an actual dragon. But this was not the only problem. There are other issues that were not addressed by this curriculum. For example, where was the course in teamwork? Where was the course in planning a dragon attack? Where was the course in protecting oneself from a dragon, or enticing a dragon into entering into a vulnerable situation?

The idea behind the story centered curriculum (SCC) is that a good curriculum should tell a story. That story should be one in which the student plays one or more roles. Those roles should be roles that normally come up in such a story. The curriculum is intended to teach the student how to do something. The roles should be ones that the graduate of such a program might actually do in real life work environment or might actually need to know about (possibly because he is likely to manage or work with someone who performs that role).

The SCC is in many ways the antithesis of the idea of putting courses on the Web. To put a course on the Web, should one simply replicate the existing content for the courses and put that material online? Why would that be a good idea? Is there no more to education than handing out the materials? If that was the case, why were there ever classrooms in the first place?

But if the classrooms were so special, why not put the classes on the Web? One can replicate classrooms, creating virtual classrooms where people can hear lectures, get into online discussions, and ask questions. Many people think that that is the right thing to do. The problem is, of course, at its heart, existential. This mandate to create courses on the Web has made people question what was valuable about the classroom in the first place. Sometimes it's a good thing to ask questions like that.

To put education online, one needs to think about what stories you want your students to live and to build a story centered curriculum that fully uses your existing teachers and existing materials, but puts them in support of a story that students will live. To put this another way, we can build learn-by-doing curricula by making teachers into Socratic tutors and creating realistic tasks for students to do. Those tasks should come from the real life situations that they might be called on to do. Often real life situations include writing reports or building things, or make some sort of analysis. When that is the case, students are given tasks and pointed to materials that help them achieve those tasks and given tutors who can help them along the way. The beauty of this is that it can all be done online. Thus it can all be on the Web, be done anytime, anywhere, and significantly enhance the experience that the student has, making education seem very relevant.

Building the Story Centered Curriculum

To understand how to build an SCC we need to understand its components. To do this, we return to dragon slaying. What would building a good dragon slaying curriculum entail?

Step 1. Determine the career goals of the student for adult students or use goals that children have and design situations that exploit those goals.

Step 2. Determine the key activities that comprise the life of a person who has achieved the goal to which the student aspires.

Step 3. Determine what key events might occur in the life of a person who has achieved such a goal.

Step 4. Come up with a story that all the above fit neatly within.

Step 5. Determine what things a person entering the curriculum would need to know that are not particularly part of the story *per se*.

The story would be about a particular attempt to slay a particular dragon. The student would be part of a dragon slaying team that would prepare for the big event by learning to do small parts of the overall task, and by practicing on simulated versions of the task that have been simplified in critical ways. In this way, when a student attempts to slay an actual dragon for the first time, he will be part of a team of student dragon slayers advised by more experienced dragon slayers.

During the simulated voyage, obstacles would be thrown the student's way that he may not have anticipated. These obstacles *could* be overcome by good reasoning and planning with the help of a tutor, by working out a plan with the student's team that divides up the roles, by special purpose just-in-time courses that have been prepared to help students who have encountered obstacles, or by the faculty suspending time and going back to remedy any holes in a student's knowledge. When a student finally slays the simulated dragon, he is certified a Master Dragon Slayer and is ready to encounter real dragons on his own.

When an integrated story has been created, it is the job of the course designers to determine a set of tasks to be accomplished, and to decide how students are to be taught to do the assigned tasks. This is where the traditional notions of teaching get changed.

When books were moved to classrooms, they were not simply read to the assembled students. (Actually they were at the beginning, hence the word *lecture*.) New teaching methodologies evolved that were more appropriate to classrooms and books became supplemental materials for teachers. Different media require different methods.

Will the SCC work as one of those new Web-oriented methods? Only if we abandon the idea that education means providing courses to students. Once one thinks in terms of courses, it is often difficult to get into a different mindset. Many courses translate easily into an SCC, however. Consulting companies, for example, often train new hires with immersion courses.

These courses sometimes do simulate aspects of the job the trainee will eventually perform. In an SCC the entire story would be more fleshed out and typically trainees would train for a role higher than the one they about to begin, because in the long run it's easier to understand one's role that way. Simply put, the SCC encompasses more than one typical course, and thus would be appropriate where students are trained to perform roles in an organization that might entail learning many different skills.

The SCC will work in any complex learning environment as long as there are mentors available and realistic roles to learn. A great deal of work is required to build a realistic environment. This environment would be on the Web and can be used in a classroom or online. In either case, teamwork and mentoring as well as the successive evaluation of work products that are the result of activities are the *sine qua non* of the SCC. It is relatively cheap to build because there is no teaching in what is built. Teachers still teach, although they would do so socratically on an as-needed basis. Work is still evaluated by teachers. What teachers don't do is stand up and talk, nor do they tell people how to do things before they try to do them. Instead, they point students toward help (written or with tutors).

Courses

The problem with courses is simple enough to explain. Following are the college transcripts of a graduate student of mine. He went to Tufts for a year and a half and then transferred to Harvard. He graduated two and half years later.

What story do these transcripts tell? This student seems to have been very interested in art, especially photography, and in writing. He doesn't seem, from this transcript at least, to be the epitome of Fadiman's educated mind. He seems to have simply taken courses that interested him. There is no story, no coherency to what he did in college. He simply took what interested him. Not a bad idea really and it is nice that Harvard let him do it, but it corresponds in no way to Fadiman's view. Certainly, Harvard would have let him do nothing like this in 1892. The fact that he could do it in 1992 indicates a few things. One obvious thing is that Harvard has changed while the high schools have not. Another is that while Harvard has officially rid itself of old Fadiman-like notions, it has not necessarily replaced them with some other coherent point of view.

To what extent does the story centered curriculum make sense for college and high school?

We have used the SCC for master's degrees and for professional training. (The former is described in chap. 11.) Does the SCC work elsewhere? The premise of the SCC is that it is used to prepare students for a world in which they expect to live by having them live in a simulation of that world while in school. Master's students are training for a profession, so simulating the life of the professional they are training to be makes a great deal of sense. The fact that this hasn't been done before in master's degree programs speaks more to the lack of attention paid to them by universities than it does to a radical shift in perspective as to what master's degree programs are, or ought to be, about.

But what about undergraduates? Are they training to be professionals? Some might say they are, but many students do not feel that this is why they are in college. Nevertheless, the SCC is appropriate in college. To understand why let's take a look at the requirements for a Bachelor's degree at Harvard (taken from the Harvard Web site):

Course Requirements for the Degree

All candidates for the Bachelor of Arts or the Bachelor of Science degree must pass sixteen full courses and receive letter grades of C– or higher in at least 10.5 of them (at least 12.0 for a degree with honors).

```
----------------------------------------------------------------
                    T U F T S   C R E D I T S
----------------------------------------------------------------
  SUBJ NUM              TITLE          GR   CRS/CR    CR/PT
----------------------------------------------------------------


1987 FALL/FIRST TERM       ADVANCED PLACEMENT
   COMPUTER SCIENCE                    1.0
   MATH CALCULUS BC                    1.0

1987 FALL/FIRST TERM       TUFTS UNIVERSITY

  ENG  0001 EXPOSITORY WRITING          A-    1.0     3.667
  EXP  0009 FRESHMEN EXPLORATION        P     1.0     0.000
  FAH  0079 GERMAN EXPRESSION ART       A-    1.0     3.667
  FAH  0061 PHOTOGRAPHY II              A+    1.0     4.000
  FR   0004 INTERMEDIATE FRENCH         B+    1.0     3.333
              CR/AT  CR/ER  DG/CR  CUM    CR/TOT STATUS
  TERM         5.0    5.0    5.0   3.67    5.0    DL
  CUMULATIVE   5.0    7.0    7.0   3.67    7.0

1988 SPRING/SECOND TERM  TUFTS UNIVERSITY

  FAH  0132 ITAL RENAISSANCE 16TH C  B     1.0     3.000
  FAH  0168 FRENCH PAINTNG 1860-1986 B     1.0     3.000
  FAH  0062 PHOTOGRAPHY III           A+    1.0     4.000
  MATH 0012 CALCULUS II               C+    1.0     2.333
  TERM         4.0    4.0    4.0   3.08    4.0
  CUMULATIVE   9.0   11.0   11.0   3.38   11.0

1988 FALL/FIRST TERM       TUFTS UNIVERSITY

  COMP 0040 COMPUTER ARCHITECTURE     B-    1.0     2.667
  FAH  0120 SURVEY ARMENIAN ART       W    (1.0)    0.000
  FAH  0063 PHOTOGRAPHY IV            A     1.0     4.000
  FR   0031 MASTERPIECES FRENCH LIT   B+    1.0     3.333
  TERM         4.0    3.0    3.0   3.33    3.0
  CUMULATIVE  13.0   14.0   14.0   3.36   14.0
```

FIG. 10.1.

COURSE TITLE	GRADE full half
Granted 6.0 course credits for work done at Tufts University.	
1988-89	
FINART 97R Sophomore Tutorial	A-
LIT-ART A-14 Chaucer	B
FINART 154Y Albrecht Durer & His Age	B-
VES 145X Photographing People/Workshop	A
ANNUAL RANK GRP: II TOTAL COURSES PASSED:	8.0
1989-90	
Granted 0.5 course credits for work done at Boston Museum in N. Mex,summer.	
FINART 98AR Advanced Tutorial	A-
VES 143R Alternative Photographic Process	A-
EXPOS 18 Writer's Craft: Fiction/Drama	A-
SCIENCE A-15 Dynamics and Energy	B
VES 100B Analysis of the Art Image	A-
FINART 21 Am Photography, 1920 to Present	A-
FOR-CULT 48 The Cultural Revolution	B
FINART 267XR 17th-Century Dutch Art: Seminar	A-
ANNUAL RANK GRP: II TOTAL COURSES PASSED:	12.5

COURSE TITLE	GRADE full half
1990-91	
FINART 174Z Invention of Photog & Art World	A-
PSY 1195 Minds, Brains, and Computers	B
VES 10AR Fundamentals of Drawing	C
SCIENCE B-29 Human Behavioral Biology	C+
VES 172 Design and Human Use	B+
FINART 99 Tutorial: Senior Year	SAT
ANNUAL RANK GRP: III TOTAL COURSES PASSED:	16.0
CUMULATIVE RANK: II SATISFACTORY LETTER GRADES:	10.0

FIG. 10.2.

Quantitative Reasoning Requirement (QRR)

All students must satisfy the quantitative reasoning requirement. They may do so in one of the following ways: 1. A satisfactory score on a test on data interpretation; or 2. A passing letter grade in Quantitative Reasoning 10 or QREA S-10 in the Harvard Summer School; or 3. A passing letter grade in Statistics 100, Statistics 101, or Statistics 102. Because these courses are fast-paced and significantly more difficult than Quantitative Reasoning 10, they ordinarily are not appropriate for students who have been unable to pass the data interpretation test.

Writing Requirement

Degree candidates, whether admitted with Freshman Standing or transfer credit, ordinarily must enroll during their first year of residence in a prescribed half-course in Expository Writing offered by the Committee on Expository Writing.

Language Requirement

Degree candidates must meet a foreign language requirement in a language with a written component that is taught at Harvard or for which an appropriate examination can be given at Harvard or by the College Board.

The Core Curriculum Requirement

All students entering the College after 1981 must meet the requirements of the Core Curriculum in order to graduate.

There are ten areas in the Core Curriculum:

Foreign Cultures
Literature and Arts C
Historical Study A
Moral Reasoning
Historical Study B
Science A
Literature and Arts A
Science B
Literature and Arts B
Social Analysis

Each student must pass one letter-graded course in eight of the ten areas of the Core Curriculum, and all students are exempt from two area requirements on the basis of their chosen field of concentration.

I have abbreviated this list by quite a bit, but the message still comes across. Harvard thinks that you should know how to write, how to deal with statistics, that you should have some familiarity with a foreign language, and that you should take some history, some literature, some science, some moral reasoning, and some social analysis in addition to majoring in one particular area of academic study. Harvard's requirements are not particularly unusual because every college is influenced by them. Furthermore, as we have noted, high schools are held hostage by them.

Who could object to such requirements? This is what universities are about. This only looks odd to the observer who considers what has been left out. What's missing? I mentioned law and medicine earlier. How about human relations? Doesn't the average Harvard student need to know how to get along with other people—his fellow students, employers, a spouse? Why isn't this at least as important having him take a chemistry course? How about basic business? Won't many Harvard students be involved in handling money and perhaps occasionally wanting to make a buck or two? Introduction to Economics doesn't teach that any more than Introduction to Psychology teaches human relations. What about the principles of construction or electricity? Won't a Harvard student one day need to take care of a house? How about government? Might he not become President or at least a Senator? Might this not be more important than handling statistical data on average? How about communication? Yes, they have a writing requirement. How about a speaking requirement? Won't Harvard students need to talk to the public from time to time?

The issue, on the surface at least, is whether these subjects are academic subjects. That is not, of course, the real issue. The real issue is whether there is a political constituency at Harvard for teaching these courses. Every student at the University of Texas had to take a government course when I went there because the Government department supported itself through that requirement. I would assume that Harvard's Government department has better sources of funding or has no political clout. Either way, the students at Harvard have different requirements than those at Texas not because the students are different or their educational needs are not the same, but because the political climate is different.

What should every student know? I am not going to try to answer this, partially because there is no right answer. But, I do know that whatever the answer is it is not a subset of all the subjects that happen to be taught in the college of Arts and Sciences. Making sure every faculty constituency of the college is happy is not the job of the student.

Credit for What?

To get a degree at any institution, the relevant variable is time served, not knowledge gathered. It is possible to graduate simply by attending every class and doing every assignment and passing every test. Because the real issue is spending four years at the institution. In fact, any other measure, like achievement, causes chaos. For example, a PhD typically takes anywhere from three to seven years to complete. Often the only real requirement is writing a thesis and this can be done in two years if one works at it. But, most institutions won't grant the PhD if you have only spent two years there even if the thesis is acceptable. Why? Because they want the requisite amount of tuition. To get a degree faster than normal one actually has to pay extra (i.e., make up the tuition the school would have gotten). This happened to me when I finished my thesis in two years, and as a professor, I have seen it happen in each institution I worked for. Time served is the relevant variable in degree granting.

Now of course, this would be quite problematic in a learn by doing based institution. After all a course is, or should be, finished when you have learned to do what the course was teaching you to do. This is not a time spent issue but a goal achievement issue.

However, making school into a doing institution from what is essentially a listening and testing institution would certainly throw chaos into the system. It is obvious why it hasn't been done.

The remedy for all this lies in the SCC. The problem is simple enough— this random potpourri of courses does not an education make. It simply puts together a bunch of independent, unrelated events, each sponsored by a department and hosted by a faculty member, that do not work together in any coherent way. They are not intended to work together. The education of a Harvard student is simply a smorgasbord affair. More work goes into the planning of a first-class dinner than goes into the coordination of courses in a Harvard education. If Harvard is supposed to produce educated minds, and I am sure that Clifton Fadiman would have asserted that Harvard was doing exactly that, then the conception of an educated mind at Harvard is one which has done a little of this and a little of that, with no real plan.

The SCC is an alternative conception of how school ought to work. In the following chapters we consider some potential college and high school stories.

REFERENCE NOTES

My graduate student didn't want his name revealed. The requirements are from the Harvard Web site.

11

Rethinking College

WHY GO TO A GOOD COLLEGE?

College dominates high school. It dominated it literally after 1892 by establishing the precollege curriculum that is in place today. But it also dominates it psychologically by being the driving force in the motivation of every student and every parent. Whenever I suggest any change in the high school curriculum to any group of parents, the first question they have is about how the colleges will perceive this change. Parents are deathly afraid, long before their kids enter high school, that somehow whatever path their child has chosen will have been the one of which Harvard wouldn't approve.

Every year, thousands of loving parents agree to pay large sums of money to send their sons and daughters to college. They want the best, of course. They want Harvard or Stanford or Swarthmore. Actually they don't just agree to send their children to these schools, in most cases they cajole, encourage, and fret about this for years. Getting into a good college can be a theme in some families that takes up years of dinner table conversation. What extracurricular activities should their child engage in? What AP courses should he or she take? Will what they do in the summer look good on their record? All this in the name of getting into a good college. But do parents want to send their children to a good college? Whatever parents' responses to this might be we can be sure that they differ considerably from their children's reasons. And, it is certain that these both differ from what the college thinks either of their reasons should be.

In the end, most people think one should go to college to get a job. While colleges typically don't advertise themselves as job training programs, and certainly Harvard and Yale don't, nevertheless the expectation is that in our society one is basically unhireable without a college degree. Unfortunately, expecting college professors to help your son or daughter get a job, or teach them what they need to get a job, is like expecting good sex counseling from a priest. There may be some opinions to offer, but really it is not their particular field of expertise. Professors don't really live in the traditional world of work and are often quite unfamiliar with that world. As scholars, they are familiar with how to do research. If that is the job a student wants, they can certainly train him for it. Anything else is unlikely.

OK then. Maybe the right answer is that one goes to college to learn things one will need in life and some of what one learns may help one get job. Wrong again. Although the best colleges employ brilliant men and women in many different fields, you can be almost certain that the professors your child will meet will not teach them anything practical that your child needs to know. Professors can occasionally be cajoled into teaching something practical, but for the most part they resist this request. What professors know best, and what they want to teach the most, is esoteric knowledge that is of use only in their particular academic field that has little relevance to what your son or daughter might care to know.

If your child majors in economics, it stands to reason that he might want to go into business. Economists don't know much about business, and what they teach is only vaguely related to what you might need. Most top colleges won't let your child major in business. Too practical. Not academic enough. So they study economics from people who, for the most part, don't even like business very much.

How about psychology? Maybe your son or daughter wants to be a psychologist, or just wants to know what's wrong with him or what's wrong with you? Sorry, psychologists at the top universities are experimental psychologists. They teach your child how to design an experiment or use statistics. Most top psychology departments consider the kind of psychology your child might be interested in to be beneath them, and hardly worthy of serious academic consideration.

How about medicine? Suppose your son or daughter wants to be a doctor? Surely he has to go to college to do that? Indeed he does. Medical schools require it. And he will have to take courses in chemistry, physics, biology, and so on. Do these courses help prepare him to be a doctor? Well, no. In fact their intent is to make it hard for him to be a doctor by giving grueling courses that separate the wheat from the chaff. What percent of a first year college chemistry or physics course has information that will be relevant to the future life of a doctor? None. Is there information in such fields that might be of use to a doctor? Yes, but for the most part it is isn't taught. Too practical.

How about computer science? Now there is a practical field. Surely one can get a job after being a computer science major. Yes, indeed one can. Companies hire computer science majors willingly, because programmers are in very short supply and they feel very confident that their majors know something about programming, and that if they don't, they can be taught. Are they taught how to program in college? They are sometimes, but for the most part computer science departments hate teaching programming. Not science, after all. Computer scientists hate it if what they are doing isn't considered science.

All right, so maybe a good college isn't about getting a job. Maybe it is about opening students' minds and teaching them to think. Certainly this view of college is closer to the one held by the faculty of a good college. But is this what students can expect in a good college? No, not really. The dirty little secret of the good colleges is that they are really about job training after all. The job they are training your child for is the one they have. They are training their students to be professors. If a student isn't professor material, there is a good chance their needs will not be taken seriously by the faculty.

Well, what about the other colleges then—the state universities rather than the Ivies? Are they more realistic places? Do they provide better education for the students? Actually no. They aren't all that different. The professors at the big state schools are the same folks who teach at the Ivies. Sometimes they are not as good as their Ivy League colleagues, but in many cases they are much better than their counterparts in any given field. And because they play in the same academic playground, they have the same views about teaching. They differ in the sense that the classes they teach are so large that even if they cared about the needs of an individual student, they would have a great deal of difficulty satisfying those needs.

Do students know all this? Yes they do. But for the most part, they don't care. Mommy and Daddy are sending them to a four-year party, a vacation before the real world starts. Why should they argue? Anyway they know that a Harvard degree opens doors, which indeed it does.

One question is why it opens doors if the students who go there don't learn much of great value. Another question is how this situation of college being irrelevant to real life came to pass. The latter question is easy. Harvard and Yale were always like that. They were set up as Divinity Schools and they were intended to produce ministers. Ministers should know the classics and be generally educated. They need not function in the real world. Harvard and Yale were never about the real world. As they became playgrounds for the sons and daughters of the rich, they had no need to become more practical. Daddy would teach his son about business, Harvard should just keep him occupied until he grows up.

Harvard and Yale established the model, and others have copied the model. There is no need to change. There has been some competition, Antioch College and Goddard College come to mind, but their antics don't affect the main stream. There has been no need to change, so colleges haven't changed.

Real Colleges

New Haven, Connecticut is often thought of as a university town. Most people would imagine that the average college student in New Haven is a student at Yale. But New Haven is the home to quite a number of schools, some larger than Yale. These include Albertus Magnus College, Southern Connecticut State University, the University of New Haven, and Quinnipiac College. I know this because I was a professor at Yale for 15 years. I would not have known it otherwise. I would never have heard of these schools if I hadn't lived in the town.

Within an hour's driving distance of New Haven, there are the University of Hartford, the University of Bridgeport, Trinity University, Wesleyan University, Connecticut College, and a large number of branches of the University of Connecticut as well as a variety of state colleges and, I am sure, any number of schools that I haven't heard of. In fact, here is a list of colleges in Connecticut I found on the Internet:

Albertus Magnus College—New Haven
Central Connecticut State University—New Britain
Charter Oak State College—Newington
Connecticut College—New London
Eastern Connecticut State University—Willimantic
Fairfield University—Fairfield
Holy Apostles Seminary and College—Cromwell
Quinnipiac College—Hamden
Sacred Heart University—Fairfield
Saint Joseph College—West Hartford
Southern Connecticut State University—New Haven
Teikyo Post University—Waterbury
Trinity College—Hartford
United States Coast Guard Academy—New London
University of Bridgeport—Bridgeport
University of Connecticut—Storrs

University of Hartford—West Hartford
University of New Haven—West Haven
Wesleyan University—Middletown
Western Connecticut State University—Danbury
Yale University—New Haven

When we begin to think about the educated mind, we need to realize that while Harvard's conception of education has defined the characteristics of modern education, real education is carried out by institutions far removed from Harvard. Harvard and Yale are not where most people are going to college. There are many more Universities of New Haven in this country than there are Yales.

The problem is that we revere Harvard and Yale. And, those of those that were fortunate enough to attend highly rated colleges may well have had a number of courses and professors whom we genuinely enjoyed. There is a tendency for us to recoil in horror when we think that our alma mater was serving up the wrong fare, or that online education might eliminate forever the experience we had with old Mr. Chips.

One thing seems clear enough. When people who have great minds and great teachers take the time to share what they know with those who are interested and do so in a way that is motivating and exciting, learning will take place. An environment where there are many great minds who are also great teachers can be an enormously fulfilling place to spend time. This is the ideal. Now we must ask what is the reality.

The acknowledged best schools in the nation are quite often providing some very bad courses.

Yale doesn't have only quality professors and quality courses. I asked some former Yale students to tell me about the best course and the worst course that they ever took at Yale. Here are some responses:

alumnus #1. The best course I took was Perlis' CS221 class. We learned how programming languages work in that class by learning APL and T, and by building interpreters and compilers for baby algebraic languages. The way Perlis was able to tie what we were doing to the history of computing made it feel really valuable, and for the first time, I finally understood how computers do what they do. It was very hard, the hardest I'd ever worked, but for me it was very satisfying. On the other hand, I think it was a very different experience for most of the students. I was a junior in another dept., and they were all scared freshmen who were worried about whether they had what it took to be CS majors. They were so concerned about doing well enough on the assignments that I don't think they learned anything.

I took any number of worst courses at Yale. They all shared the quality of being intro level survey courses that were designed to lay the groundwork for subsequent work in that field—physics, chemistry, econ, math. They all presented an overview of the field according to a formal framework, and assigned decontextualized problems that taught me how to do problem-solving in the field, but never taught me why I'd want to. I didn't hate them because I could play the game well, but they didn't give me any appreciation for or enjoyment of the fields.

alumnus #2. English 29—Western lit. This had some of the obvious problems, they made us read a bunch of stuff and it was a mixed bag. Also there were once a week huge lectures that were very beautiful but I can't remember anything. BUT—the seminar sections were the first time I had ever really tried to read something closely and had the benefit of a discussion leader who actually knew how to do that (lit discussions in high school were ridiculous). And second, we did a LOT of writing in this course with heavy revisions and so this is where I learned how to write (to the extent that I know how to write).

Modes of Thought. I don't remember the professor. This was a course in the anthropology dept on cross-cultural cognition, I thought it would be interesting. I went to the first class, the room was packed. The prof had been expecting 15–20 kids, there were 50. Then he announced the work was 3 3-page papers, no exams. So the next time there were 150. He had been planning to run a seminar and had ended up with a lecture course filled with people who couldn't care less. A complete disaster.

alumnus #3. "Z-lab," run by a prof who ended up not getting tenure, maybe Chris Zornig was his name. This was for electrical engr. majors and was structured as a series of projects where you worked w/one other person to design and build something (a traffic light controller; a computer music generator).

Introduction to Mechanical Engineering. Standard dry lecture out of a textbook, then go read the textbook, then do the fairly simple problems in the back. Sort of the classic textbook-based class. This course changed my major: I came to Yale thinking I'd be interested in being a Mechanical Engineer. After this course I thought that electronics would be a lot more fun to create things with.

Is it a surprise that the good courses are often doing courses and the bad courses are usually lecture courses? (No, I didn't set this up.) There *are* good lecturers. Yale may have more of them than other schools, but I doubt it. The value of Yale and other schools of its ilk is shown in the good courses noted above. Having the attention of an individual who is very good at what he does can make for a very worthwhile educational experience.

Yale does, on the whole, provide a very worthwhile experience to its students. But, can the same be said of schools that do not have the same quality of faculty that Yale has? That kind of personal attention is very hard to find at a large state university. It might be possible to find at a small state college or liberal arts college but then the question is whether this is attention from people who are particularly expert at what they do.

Most students attend college for reasons that have very little to do with a search for knowledge. As I mentioned earlier, on the first day of class I usually ask students why they are there. They assume that this is a question about why they are in college and they proceed to tell me about how it is a kind of four-year vacation and how good the parties are and how it's good to get away from home, and how they will need to get a job and college will help and so on. I am all for this point of view. College is about all those things for a great many students. If a parent can afford this expense and send his child on a four-year vacation from real life, he should by all means do so. Much is to be learned from such an experience. But, and this is an important but, what is learned most of all is rarely stuff about physics or literature.

We need to differentiate in our minds the value of college as a personal growth experience and the value of college as an educational experience. Personal growth can be attained by joining the army or the Peace Corps as well. Education is the stated province of the university.

The Goals of the New Liberal Professional University

As we think about what makes an educated mind, we need to consider how we would like to see colleges change. There are two important reasons why they must change. One is that they are simply not providing what they are expected to provide, that is, job training. They need to be clear about what they do provide and reconsider actually attempting to provide what customers want. The second is that they are killing the high schools with their current attitude. If all of high school is about college preparation then it is impossible to be innovative in a high school curriculum. High schools must forever parrot the 1892 curriculum. This must change. Colleges need to change their requirements. They also need to stop insisting that high schools do their admissions work for them by telling them who the best students are. This simply makes high school a competitive experience instead of a learning experience. Colleges control education in this country and they need to relinquish that control for any improvement to occur.

Following are five goals I have set up for universities to adopt. These represent changes I'd like to see.

Goal 1: To challenge the best and brightest to become something other than academic researchers.

The problem is simply stated. The best universities are research universities. Their faculty are appointed because they have proven themselves as great researchers. When colleges create their curricula they are heavily influenced by the model presented by the best schools. In other words, even if they have no great researchers they still teach similar courses that great researchers tend to teach and often demand of their faculty that they publish research. Harvard's influence is felt at the lowest ranked schools, most of which really want to be just like Harvard and often claim to be the "Harvard of Western Missouri."

At research universities, students are considered successes if they model themselves after the faculty and do research projects. This is a fine model for some students. Faculty see no need to change the model because they benefit from it. But, many students are not having their real interests catered to. They don't want to do research and thus do not receive the full attention of the best faculty.

> Goal 2: To focus on teaching students abilities of value to the society of which the university is a part.

The research focus of the great universities causes them to lose sight of what students are there to learn. I can recall many conversation about the curriculum in Computer Science, for example, where I suggested that students were there to become computer professionals and therefore needed to learn skills that were needed in the workplace and was ridiculed and told that theoretical computer science was much more important than teaching them how to use a database. These conflicts come up in every department. Students want to know what they will need when they go to work and faculty want to teach what faculty know how to teach, which often has little to do with the world of work of which they have quite likely never been a part.

> Goal 3: To take seriously the notion that a college is a supplier of manpower to the most important and innovative corporations.

The majority of students will tell you that they go to college to get a job. How does one reconcile this with the concept of a "party school"?

Survey ranks Indiana University as No. 1 party campus in nation
SCHOOL SAYS IT HAS CURBED ALCOHOL USE
By Shannon Dininny
Associated Press

BLOOMINGTON, Ind.   Indiana University was crowned the nation's No. 1 "party school" Monday in an annual Princeton Review survey that school leaders and medical experts derided as irresponsible and unscientific.

Following Indiana in the rankings were Clemson University, the University of Alabama–Tuscaloosa, Pennsylvania State University and the University of Florida.

Indiana University officials questioned the No. 1 ranking. The school, which didn't appear on the list last year, has toughened its stance on student drinking since the 1998 alcohol-related death of a student.

In the past year, five Indiana University fraternities have been suspended or expelled for violations of alcohol policies, said Bill Stephan, the university's vice president for public affairs.

"There are some serious questions about the methodology of the study, and it really calls into question the credibility of the ranking," he said.

Indiana junior Erin Pritchard said, "I'd be surprised to hear we're No. 1. Even though most people party three or four times a week, this past year they've been a lot more strict."

The survey, conducted since 1992 and published in Princeton Review's "Best 345 Colleges" guide, ranks schools in 63 categories based on interviews with 100,000 students. The party school designation is based on student reports on alcohol and marijuana use, the amount of time spent studying outside of class, and the popularity of fraternities and sororities on campus.

Princeton Review, a test-preparation and college admissions company with no connection to Princeton University, defended its survey.

"We simply are reporting on the conditions that exist on those particular campuses, and if social life continues to be an aspect that students comment on, then I will continue to include that list in the book," said Robert Franek, the company's editorial director.

Franek noted that the survey also lists the top 20 "stone-cold sober schools," where students say there is little drinking. Brigham Young University topped that list for the third straight year.

While it may be important for students to let off steam and grow up while away from home for the first time, this process tends to take away from the educational experience. Learning is not necessarily a key goal for college students. When they do sober up and realize that real life awaits them, learning is still not a key goal. Job preparation begins to matter to them. Corporations have had to create large training departments to teach students what they could have learned in college had anyone been willing to teach it. But, while students know full well that they can slough off their "rocks for jocks" course or their English Lit course because they know this stuff won't matter in their lives, they feel quite differently when it comes to job skills. Colleges need to take seriously the idea that at a real part of the curriculum must be preparing students to enter the workplace.

Goal 4: To change the listening-based university curriculum into a doing-centered curriculum.

At the core of the problem is the lecture system. As long as professors feel they can simply talk and then test to see who was listening, no real education is taking place. Students remember their experiences. The more they are active, the more they remember. It is not simply a question of changing passive courses into active ones. The subject matter determines how a course can be structured. The intent of the course has to be teaching students to do something in the first place. Determining the things that students will one day do and having them try to do them first at school necessarily changes what is taught at school. A modern real world skills curriculum with modern, that is, less academic, goals would be radically different than what exists now at most colleges.

> Goal 5: To emphasize building useful skills, creative minds, and preparing students for real life challenges.

Living in the real world has a number of aspects to it. Typically, colleges have felt responsible primarily for the intellectual aspect of life. However, people still get married, raise children, hold jobs, and are part of their community. Why is this not the subject matter of college as well? When we tried to get developmental psychologists to focus on child rearing issues in an online course, they refused, insisting that the course had to be about recent research. Never mind that the students were more likely to become parents than to become researchers. But when do students learn about parenting? When do they learn about showing up on time for a job or working in a team and delivering a work product? These nonacademic skills matter a great deal in real life. Why aren't these part of a university education?

Going Forward

The time has come to build a new kind of university education—one that focuses less on building scholars and more on building intellectually alive citizens who are prepared for the world of work and day-to-day living in the modern world. We must build schools that challenge the best and brightest to be something other than academic researchers—that allows the average student to learn something of value to society within the university setting. To accomplish this vision, we must create a new university curriculum and explore new methods of delivery for that curriculum.

There are three ways in which we can make the changes we need: we can build a new university; we can build an entirely online virtual university; or we can change an existing university. There is also the tantalizing possibility of mixing the virtual with the campus and allowing universities to share resources with each other and stop replicating economics 101 3,000 times across the country, allowing schools to focus their energies on what they do best.

With any of these options, since certification is one of the main things that a university provides, it will be necessary to have brand name universities take leadership roles in demonstrating feasibility and desirability of this radically different approach to Learning resulting in degrees from this new experimental university.

A key element of this new kind of college would have to be its relationship with corporations. The planning for the curriculum of this college would have to be done in cooperation with sponsoring corporations who agree to provide funding for the school, internships for the students, and hire its graduates. One tenet of any professionally oriented university is that the courses it offers would be industry friendly and doing-centered. This means that not only would learning by doing have to be the underlying philosophy, but also that all graduates from this school would come out with a set of skills that the sponsoring corporations deem as being valuable to society.

Skill Types

The courses offered by a liberal professional university would fall into four broad categories:

Life skills entail the basics for being a functioning adult in modern society. Some subjects that are typically not covered in college that belong to this set are child raising; basic medicine, basic law, dealing with government, the basics of business, interaction with people, and other such skills that are part of everyday life in the modern world.

Mental skills include reasoning, argumentation, research, experimentation, invention, exploring new uses for technology and mental exercise in general. These courses would be taught opposite of the way modern universities teach. Most universities present complex, new problems only to seniors or graduate students, once they have already taken years of basic subjects. Younger students are forced to take general survey courses as introductions and may never get to the hard problems in a field, the problems that are unsolved. Instead, students are only taught the facts that are well known. It is our intention to reverse this.

Hard problems of a field should be presented first. Students would be encouraged to learn the basics of a field on their own, when they determine their need for them. Instead of learning calculus as some kind of rite of passage prior to learning economics, for example, students will learn calculus at their moment of need—when they decide that it will help them in pursuit of a goal in economics. This means that courses will have to be taught "just in time," which is quite feasible when such instruction is online.

Real world skills involve general issues, like communication, and specific ones, like programming. Students will need to learn to write, speak, and use and build technology. Corporations would help determine which of these skills are most needed.

Job skills are both general and specific. Students would learn to function in and to manage organizations by practicing within organizations set up in the school. They would learn general skills by practicing them. Individual sponsoring corporations will help teach specific skills, both by providing their criteria for what students need to know how to do, and by providing the instruction to do it. Industries, in consultation with the faculty of the university, will provide tracks within the job skills part of the curriculum. These tracks would lead to employment within the specific industries who helped design the tracks.

Students will engage in a variety of activities intended to teach them certain concepts and skills. A variety of support would be available to help students attain those skills: tutors (both present and virtual), professors who set up challenging situations and help students look at problems in new ways, software that teaches certain skills, and internships that teach real world skills and job skills in an apprentice mode. Students would be judged on the skill level they have mastered. They would choose which skills to master by coupling those they find interesting with the skills sponsoring potential employers want them to have. The role of the university is to help students obtain the skills that the parents, students, and employers (i.e., the customers) have determined that they need rather than the professors. This last idea alone is so radical that there is hardly a university that is capable of restructuring its educational programs to be responsive to this need.

Student Life

Why would a student want to come to a new college of the type we have been discussing? Many people enter college because they see it as being in the natural order of things, part of the process of growing up. As a result, much of what they do in college in the first few years is to enjoy all the liberties that were not available to them while living under their parents' roof. College is indeed a great deal of fun for most students. Unfortunately, the fun quite often interferes with the education. Students skip classes because they partied too hard the night before, they focus on extracurricular activities like sports or fraternities, and their studies suffer as a result. Often it is not until the last year or two of college that most students realize they were supposed to be preparing for entry into the real world and begin to take their schoolwork seriously.

For this reason, it is best to focus the first year of this kind of college more on the life part of the curriculum than on the intellectual part. Students will be learning by doing, so one of the main things they will be doing is being involved in the general administration of the activities of their university. From a technical point of view, this means they will be learning how to maintain the hardware, software, and networking used by the campus. They will also administer and take part in the intramural sports and social events of their school. Far from being extracurricular issues, these activities will be part of the curriculum.

Coursework in the first year would stress the social, legal, medical, and personal issues involved in such activities. Students would learn to work in an organization by working in one, and they would study how to behave in social settings like the ones they are in. They would be encouraged to do, and also to think about what they do. Psychological counseling, for example, will not be simply available to students to discuss how to cope with the new situations they encounter, it will be part of the curriculum, teaching about handling stress, dealing with other people, understanding oneself, and so on.

Student life would be both fun and part of the curriculum. The goal of the first year is to make students into adults by having them cope with the transition into adult life in a context where traditional intellectual coursework plays a back seat to emotional, social, practical, and psychological issues. This balance would shift each year so that intellectual issues become more strongly emphasized in the middle years. In the last year, as students prepare themselves to enter the real world, practical, job-related issues would become the focus.

We are talking then about having the students live three basic stories (in the SCC). These stories described next fall into the following categories:

The Career Story
The Academic Story
The Life Story

The idea behind this division is that college is about three kinds of preparation. The *Career* part of the SCC is focused on preparing students for the world of work by having them live in a set of scenarios designed by the faculty to look and feel like a real job while teaching the skills necessary for such a job. The story is meant to look as much as possible like the life one would live after graduation thus providing practice in the world of work as well as skills useful for real employment in some IT field.

The *Academic Story* is related to courses students typically take in college but differs in some very important ways. The first difference is that the student does not take courses but instead is involved in a small number of stories. These stories are not meant to give students a smattering of facts in a given discipline. Rather, they are intended to have students live in given discipline for a short while—attempting to participate in that discipline without having to take tedious introductory courses in order to do so. The intent of the participation differs from typical college courses as well. It is quiet common for academic courses to be offered as if the students were about to become researchers in a given field. The first and second courses students take in a given field in college are often the beginnings of a long journey into that field, one that very few students actually complete.

So, while we believe that students should be learning about various academic disciplines we have a different view as to why they should be learning these subjects and therefore it follows that we have different view of what they should be learning about these subjects. For example, in science courses in most universities the introductory course is either for non-majors, in which case they are watered down versions of the majors course meant to entertain and give basic facts or else they are courses intended for majors, in which case they are full of first principles and surveys of the field meant to introduce basic concepts of a field. We believe that neither of these are the right course of action.

The future professional would be a citizen of the community and would also likely work in some area of software that may require some knowledge of science. But what knowledge would be required? There is no way to know. So rather than teaching the basic facts of various sciences, our science story attempts to teach scientific reasoning. Students are asked to play roles that require a knowledge of science and to make decisions based on that knowledge. They do projects and submit reports based on their findings in an attempt to actually do science and reason about scientific issues rather than learn scientific facts. They live a science story for some months in an experience meant to be memorable and exciting.

Similarly, the graduate would want to be literate, and familiar with social issues. Here again, this does not mean that the student would take general courses in literature, art, or social science. Rather, we want students to be able to function in the world in which they live and not be one dimensional. So, while we might want them to learn about how to deal with ethical issues for example, would want those to be set in a context that may have some bearing on their future lives. Similarly, we would want them to think about issues in law and business that might matter to them both professionally and personally later on.

Some of these issues are dealt with in the Life part of the story. The *Life Story* is not handled in classes, courses or even in assignments in projects. Rather, it is handled by living. Students are expected to be part of various organizations on campus that provide life experiences. These include social organizations, athletic organizations, living situations, and various aspects of running the daily life of the community in which they live. These things would be required as part of their education. Furthermore, there would be regular mentoring through these situations. Students would regularly discuss and plan how to deal with various issues that arise in the operation of these organizations, and would receive counseling on how to deal with complex situations.

The Story Centered Curriculum for Electronic Commerce

Carnegie Mellon University is already using the story centered curriculum idea in its West Coast campus. One degree that is offered this way is the MSIT, with specialization in E-Commerce. Here is what the story looks like in that curriculum.

Enabling Electronic Commerce at Berkshire Foods

Introduction

Berkshire Foods is a multinational food company with revenues around $4 billion. The Berkshire name is most widely associated with salad dressings and innovative mayonnaise products, but their business owns many more widely recognized subsidiary brands of food products. Berkshire is known for quality. Their products tend to be at the somewhat higher end of other similar product lines in terms of both ingredients and price. Over the last 50 years, Berkshire has grown steadily and maintains a favorable image to its customers, but it also has strong competition from larger food companies. Berkshire aims to continue to grow and become more widely recognized world wide, while still maintaining it's upscale image and high quality standards. Berkshire Foods today is an enterprise involving more than 19,000 people in over 95 major locations worldwide, with leading brands on 4 continents.

Currently Berkshire Foods is lagging with regard to developing ecommerce business practices. The company's only online offerings at present is a brochure-type website that presents general information on Berkshire, including:

- Key subsidiary brand names, without specific product listings
- Main office locations and key contacts
- Investor information
- Press releases
- Career opportunities

They do not provide any mechanism for buying or selling transactions at this time.

Scenario Beginning

The CEO of Berkshire Foods, Dara Griffith, recently attended a conference conducted by a leading strategy-consulting firm. The firm discussed ecommerce as a potential driver of organizational growth and increases in shareholder value. Excited about the possibilities ecommerce might bring to her company, Griffith hired on a new ecommerce task force to research and possibly develop ecommerce at Berkshire.

To lead the task force, Griffith hired a new ecommerce manager, Len Walsh. Walsh was chosen for his proven ecommerce success record at several other companies. Once at Berkshire, he brought on board the members of the task force, a small team of expert ecommerce practitioners, to help fulfill the mission.

The students in the ecommerce curriculum play the role of the expert practitioners on this ecommerce task force. They often work in teams to accomplish each task.

Project 1: Preparing a Business Case

Griffith asks the task force to conduct an analysis and make recommendations to help determine whether it makes strategic sense for Berkshire Foods to undertake an ecommerce initiative. If they determine that it does, they must specify which aspects of its supply chain ecommerce should address. Griffith also asks the task force to assess the specific benefits ecommerce would provide to Berkshire Foods.

Griffith requests that the team provide her with a formal recommendation report on an ecommerce initiative for Berkshire Foods, including a business case for any development in this area.

In order to accomplish this task, the task force, or student teams, must study what accounted for successful and unsuccessful ecommerce companies thus far, and compare the key attributes of both to Berkshire's business. They have to figure out whether Berkshire can sell products in such a way that they can become profitable; they have to find other areas in which ecommerce practices have enhanced standard business processes at similar companies; and they have to determine whether Berkshire could adopt similar new ecommerce practices to increase efficiency within their business. Finally students have to make concrete recommendations to Berkshire Foods, and defend their recommendations in a detailed business case. Students write up their findings and business cases in a formal presentation, which they give to the board of directors and CEO of Berkshire Foods.

Increasing Visibility

The results of the task force's study showed that over the next five years a significant amount of Berkshire's commerce should take the form of electronic commerce with the major entities in its supply chain. Walsh begins to plan the overall initiative of developing ecommerce at the company, when Griffith announces that out of curiosity she did a search on the Internet for salad dressing. She found that the Berkshire name did not appear in any of the top results on popular search engines. She requests that as an immediate step she would like the task force to make the brochure-ware site more visible on Internet searches. That will at least enable customers to find the company and associate the Berkshire name to its major products types, while the more functional ecommerce site is under development.

Project 2: Making an Existing Site Visible

Walsh sends an e-mail to his team asking them to modify the existing website so that it ranks higher in search engine results. He asks them to submit to him:

- A modified HTML version of the existing brochure-ware site that ensures better search results

- A report describing the before and after site modification search rankings, including an analysis of the results for a specified search engine(s), and a list of terms most likely used by customers to find Berkshire's products.

In order to complete this request successfully, the student teams must first learn how the various search engines rank pages in order to optimize the rankings for the Berkshire site. To test the effectiveness of their modifications, student teams submit their versions of the site to real search engine services (e.g., Inktomi) and can then test the results on the search engine sites.

Building the Site

Now, with the basic site more visible, Walsh sends the team a memo setting a vision for the first major step in developing ecommerce at Berkshire: to build a website that advertises all of Berkshire's products, and that allows customers to select and purchase products online. He proposes the following phased development plan:

Conduct a requirements analysis for the new system
Build the system and database design models
- Create the user interface for product purchasing
- Develop the catalog application
- Select an electronic payment solution provider
- Conduct user testing of site
- Select an ISP to host the site

Each of these development phases constitutes a separate student project.

Project 3: Specify System Requirements

To begin the site design process, Walsh asks the team to capture the user-perspective design requirements and client perspective system requirements. These will serve as critical inputs to determining the look and functionality of the new Berkshire website. Specifically, Walsh requests from the team the following deliverables:

To capture the user perspective requirements:
- Cultural model of users
- Flow model
- Sequence model
- Breakdown analysis
- User requirements summary
To capture the client perspective requirements:
- System requirements specifications document (SRS)
- Use-case analysis
- Use-case diagram

To construct the deliverables associated with the user perspective requirements, students will first have to use some information that the manager will provide to them about Berkshire's intentions for the website. For instance, they will learn that Berkshire's consumers need to learn through the site about their product offerings, but only retailers may purchase their products online. This information will help students to construct the cultural models of the expected users of the new website.

Next students will need to sit with people that they find in the world who would be likely to use such a site. Students will guide the users in conducting searches and choosing products to purchase on a competitor's website. Students will study what the users do to accomplish the tasks on the competitor's site, and the students will create diagrams that show how information flows around those sites (flow model); what steps users take to accomplish their goals on the site (sequence model); and finally the students will capture the places in which information flow had areas of breakdown, and where users had difficulty accomplishing their goals within the competitor's site (breakdown analysis). Students will use this information to inform their new site, enabling them to improve upon what competitors currently do in their sites. They will capture what they learn in the "user requirements summary" document.

Once students have a clearer understanding of what users look for in these types of websites, and how they conduct searches, the students will take information from fictional client members who will tell them the system requirements. Students will decide which of the client recommendations to follow and which to make recommendations against, based on what they learned from users. They will take the whole of their information gathering to prepare an SRS document, detailing all critical functionality and capacity the new system should allow. They will also create a use-case analysis and diagram showing specifically how users can maneuver through the system, and how the system will respond to user actions.

Project 4: Create the User Interface for Product Purchasing

Walsh reviews the user and system requirements documentation. Once the task force reworks the documents to meet Walsh's high standards, he asks them to use their preparatory work to help them develop a navigational flowchart and then a prototype of the catalog as an HTML mock-up. He explains that the prototype needs to be approved by the CEO before the database design and development begins.

Because the look and feel of the site is so critical to how it will be received by consumers, and because the site is intended to influence the company's growth over the next several years, Walsh decides to have an interface design contest, in which teams of designers from the task force will compete to arrive at the strongest possible design. He is clear, however, that it is in everyone's best interest to help each other make all of the designs as strong as possible. He explains that first, whichever design wins will influence the growth of the company, which will in turn affect its stock value, and thus the potential earnings of all employees as stock holders. Second, the team members who will be selected to work on future projects of high importance, such as version 2.0 of this site, will be chosen both for their design abilities, and for their critiquing abilities.

Walsh structures this competition such that each team must first submit to Walsh:

- A site-map of the navigational flow of the website catalog
- An HTML mock-up user-interface prototype of the catalog

Walsh will then send these documents on to another team who also created similar documents of their own. Each team will have to do a thorough heuristic analysis of another team's design, and submit:

- A heuristic analysis report

Walsh will review the reports to assess each team's critiquing skills, and then he will send the reports along with his own feedback to the teams who created the interfaces the reports address. Finally each team will revise their interfaces based on the heuristic analysis reports and his feedback. They will have to also justify their final design decisions if they choose to disregard a recommendation from the reports and feedback.

Project 5: Conduct User Testing on the Interface

Once teams improve upon their interfaces based on the heuristic analyses, Walsh will ask them to conduct user testing to add final refinements to their designs. Students will find users to search for products using the interfaces they constructed. They will first design the process by which they intend to test, they will sit with test subjects and document issues that users had when working through the interface. Students will then make final adjustments to their interfaces based on their test findings, with a brief report defending their final design decisions. Students will submit to the manager:

- User testing plans
- Test results documentation
- Revised prototype interface
- Design justification report

Project 6: Build the System and Database Design Models

Given the system requirements, use-case analyses and diagrams, and a strong interface design, Walsh assigns the task force to build the system and database design models for the catalog. He asks the task force to submit to him the following deliverables:

- Database model
- Sequence diagrams for use-cases in UML (Unified Modeling Language)
- Class diagrams in UML

To create the database models, students will have to first analyze the requirements of the application, based on their own SRS documents, as well as the data dictionary that their manager will provide. They will use these documents to inform their drawing of entity-relationship (ER) diagrams using UML. They will also have to remove any redundancy in their models. Finally, students will map each model to a set of database tables. Then students will submit their models to the manager for review.

To create the sequence and class diagrams, students will again refer to their SRS documents and use-case analyses to create a UML activity diagram for every major user action (case). Then they will build a dynamic model, showing the objects in the system and the messages those objects send to one another when an action is being taken. For the dynamic model, they will build a UML sequence diagram. At the same time, they will capture useful information from the static model to generate class diagrams. When finished with these diagrams, students will submit them for review.

Project 7: Develop the Catalog Application

The completed database and system design models give the task force teams all they need to build the catalog. Walsh requests that the teams begin development immediately. He requests that they submit to him:

- An application architecture diagram
- Source code for catalog application
- Retrospective risk analysis

In order to develop the application, students will begin by using the database designs they prepared in the previous project, and they will create database tables. Then they will set up the web server environment and develop the first web server program of the prototype that connects to the database following coding standards. Next they will develop and run the whole web application. Students will submit the application for review. When they have approval on their applications, they will conduct a retrospective risk analysis for the project.

Project 8: Analyze Potential Security Threats

Dara Griffith, CEO, requests that the ecommerce task force conduct a security analysis on the Berkshire ecommerce process, as it starts to take shape. She is quite concerned that electronic commerce will make Berkshire Foods susceptible to numerous forms of fraud, burglary, and generally threaten Berkshire's credibility as a stable and reputable company. She cannot let anything harmful affect her company due to careless disregard for the risks associated with putting a business online.

Griffith has the IT department develop a block diagram of Berkshire's online processes. She then asks the task force to conduct a security analysis of each aspect of the process. She assigns the ecommerce manager to oversee the analysis.

The manager, Walsh, explains the assignment to the task force, and asks them to study the process diagram, assessing any potential threats to the following:

- Integrity
- Privacy
- Availability
- Authentication
- Accessibility

He asks that the task force deliver to him a report identifying all potential threats, associated risks to Berkshire, and viable technical solutions or other methods of eliminating the risks.

To accomplish this mission, first students will learn to conduct IPAAA security analyses, enabling them to evaluate security risks of anything, not only Internet connections. Then they will research the specific types of security threats that affect an Internet presence and electronic commerce functionality. Students will identify solutions to each attack type, and then determine which of the threats to protect against, depending on the plausibility of attack and the cost of the solution. They will present all of their findings in a formal report for their manager and the CEO.

Project 9: Managing Payments

The website is nearly fully functional, but it still does not have the functionality of managing financial transactions online. Walsh developed a plan in conjunction with the accounting department to make a billing section of the website that allows suppliers to submit electronic invoices. This would make it so that Berkshire would receive all invoices in the same format, saving a tremendous amount of time for the billing department. As an incentive to the suppliers to use this system, Berkshire promises to pay all invoices received electronically within five business days. In addition, the ecommerce task force needs to determine the most ideal payment options to offer to its business customers who make online purchases.

Walsh requests that the team determine which forms of payment Berkshire should allow online to businesses making purchases on their site. He asks them to select three forms of payment, and to write a report justifying their selection, and comparing their choices with other options they considered. He also asks them to begin to design the interface for online invoice presentment. (Not sure they get enough out of designing this interface. May drop this. Also may combine this with the current shipping task. Could use same XML stuff.)

As they begin their work, they receive a memo from the CFO of Berkshire Foods who is concerned about the new online invoicing and payment functionality being implemented in the new website. He requests that the task force prepare a presentation about how these new electronic processes will affect his ability to manage his cash flow, and in what ways it will make his job easier. He also requests that their presentations address both domestic and foreign currencies.

To accomplish the tasks within this project, students will begin by studying various forms of payment that are available for online transactions, determine which are most likely to be used by businesses, and why. As they do their research on potential forms of payment to offer to customers, students will also look into cash flow as a general concept to begin considering how electronic cash will affect cash management at Berkshire. Students will learn how money moves, and what payments really mean. They will also learn about how businesses deal with foreign currencies, and how decisions about managing foreign currencies affect the business as a whole. Students' work will result in two deliverables:

- A presentation to give to the CFO regarding how electronic financial transactions will/will not make cash management more efficient at Berkshire Foods.
- A report recommending the payment options Berkshire should offer to customers on their website, with a justification for their decisions, and comparisons to options they did not choose.

Students will give their presentations before the CFO and accounting department.

Project 10: Select an ISP to Host the Site

At this point the website is nearly complete, and Berkshire is getting ready to go live with version one of their new ecommerce business. In order to do so, the system must be hosted so that it can reach customers in all parts of the world in which Berkshire does business. The ecommerce manager made the decision to have an external ISP host the site, but he has not decided which one. He sent an RFP (request for proposals) to several ISP vendors; now he needs the two returned proposals evaluated and needs one to be recommended. Walsh asks his team to review the proposals, and to write a report that compares them and recommends one based on an articulate rationale.

To conduct an analysis of the two proposals, students will need to learn the fundamentals of networking, taking into consideration issues such as bandwidth, reliability, and security. They will need to weigh the difference between two reasonable proposals, based on the needs of their business.

- Integrate suppliers with negotiation system
- Where orders are in the shipping process
- Mcommerce
- Site evaluation for ongoing maintenance/improvements
- Security breach

In fall, 2002, CMU West opened, using two story centered curricula for master's students (the other is in software engineering).

Their experiences were quite different in this new kind of school, as we shall discuss in the following chapters.

REFERENCE NOTES

The Connecticut schools were found on the Web. The Yale alumni quoted were former students of mine whom I stayed in contact (typically because they continued to work for me). The quoted news story appeared in 2001. Details of the CMU courses can be found at www.west.cmu.edu.

12

The SCC at Grandview
(2002–2003)

A FUNNY THING HAPPENED . . .

A funny thing happened on my way to Carnegie Mellon West. Carnegie Mellon University (CMU) asked me to oversee the educational mission of their new campus in California. I designed the Story Centered Curriculum (SCC), which I described in chapter 10.

As it happened, I had been talking to a K–12 school in Florida (Grandview Prep) for some time about adding new technology based projects to their curriculum. I realized that we could redesign the CMU master's degree in E-commerce and make it into a full-time senior year in computer science for high school students. They liked the idea at Grandview and said they would send all their seniors to this program. Much as that appealed to me, I thought that not all students would want to do computer science (although there is heavy business component to the curriculum as well, it's still not right for every kid). So I contacted the University of Chicago, and they said they would love to help design a senior year in writing. We began to design both for delivery in September.

This is when the funny thing happened. Grandview asked me to be academic dean of their school. They have bought into my ideas about education and want to do more. I suggested we immediately prepare curricula for eighth and fifth grades for September, and then proceed to do more. And, that is what we have done.

These curricula ignore what was there before. They make no attempt to cover the material normally covered in those grades (although material that is critical is still used in the normal course of the scenario). We are trying to change things, not modify them. The new curricula are all built in the form of story centered curricula which are elaborate goal-based scenarios (GBS's), grand scenarios in which students play active roles that emulate some aspect of the real world and learn by doing. These GBS's are built on the Web so they can be exported to other schools. The teaching is done in the form of mentoring by experts who may or may not be teachers at the school. The idea is to have students live in a story for a while, helped through that story by materials we have prepared or can point to and by mentors who can advise and suggest strategies, as well as review work and suggest improvements.

So, we began to create the story centered senior year in high school. The first thing we did was attempt to adapt the CMU E-Commerce MS.

THE COMPUTER SCIENCE SCC
FOR HIGH SCHOOL SENIORS

Senior year of high school is currently structured just like freshman, sophomore, and junior years. Students take a variety of courses that do not intersect in any coherent way, and none of the classes mirror what people do in the working world. Senior year is a critical year of transition between either college or working life, in which students have to make decisions about what they will do once they graduate. But high school does not prepare students to make the choice wisely because it doesn't give them experience testing potential careers. As a result, students do not have adequate skills to move from high school into specialized jobs, and if they choose to attend college, they waste the first few years trying out different courses of study as they move from what they thought they wanted to do to what they actually enjoy.

By senior year of high school, many students have developed interests in specific areas of practice that they believe they want to do for their careers. Rather than wasting time taking more courses in areas they don't care about, high school seniors should have the chance to do concentrated work that mirrors what they would do as professionals in a chosen career. That way they will learn whether they really like that type of work, and they will get a head start learning usable skills to either get jobs right out of high school, or excel in a college program that specializes in their career area.

For this purpose, we created a one-year, story centered curriculum (SCC) in computer science to serve as the senior year of high school for students interested in careers in computer science. Working in groups, students are given detailed information about a simulated company for which they are working, together with authentic projects they are expected to complete.

This intensive year-long curriculum lets students experience first-hand how Internet technologies are transforming the way businesses are run. Students working in teams play the role of a newly formed e-business technology task force at Moffett Foods, a fictional company with real-world problems. Their mission is to help Moffett Foods leverage technology across their entire business. But they have a long road ahead of them: Moffett is in the dark ages technologically, with only a simple Web site.

Later, as the students build their skills, they may be promoted to the role of technical director of the eCommerce division of that company. Alternatively, students may be a part of a special eCommerce Task Force brought into this company specifically to improve the company's Internet presence and online offerings. Student roles are selected to be ones that the graduates of such a program might actually do in real life, or might need to know about because he or she might manage or collaborate with a person who performs that role.

Students in the Computer Science SCC work for a fictional company that requires them to do various projects over the course of a school year. Each project requires that students submit deliverables (work products) that are assessed fictionally by their boss, and in reality by their teacher, who serves as a coach and expert reviewer in this curriculum. As students work to accomplish each task within the projects, they receive help when they need it. The help (which is really the instruction) comes from a variety of sources, including suggested readings selected by the faculty, Web-based resources, and close mentoring by their own teachers, who will be specially trained to teach in this curriculum.

In the Computer Science SCC, students do not take separate courses to teach individual subjects. Instead, they have a job in which they work with a fictional company that is designed to maximize learning. In this job, students gain experience in all critical aspects of computer science that freshmen in college might learn in a first-year computer science curriculum. However, the SCC students are further ahead of the game, as they also learn how to apply the concepts they learn in the context of accomplishing real world tasks. Students graduate from the Computer Science SCC with concrete experience, and they will learn in the context of doing meaningful tasks.

A Detailed Example

In a traditional college computer science curriculum, students may take some set of the following courses:

- Introductory Programming
- The Internet
- Data Structures

- Object Oriented Modeling
- Software Engineering
- Human Computer Interaction
- Introduction to Computer Systems
- Computer Networks
- Rapid Prototyping of Computer Systems
- Algorithm Design and Analysis

In the Computer Science SCC, instead of taking these courses separately, students will use the related skills and concepts in the context of a realistic project that closely mirrors the types of tasks they would be asked to do in a real job.

Example Story

Continuing in the example of students working for a computer games manufacturer, this fictional company, perhaps called, "Zapster," may be just beginning a new initiative to further grow the company by developing its Web-presence, and by using Internet technology to expand the services it offers to consumers. Zapster may want to begin offering:

- An extensive online catalog of products
- Online purchasing of games
- Free versions of online, Web-based games
- Pay-for-service games for enhanced features
- Chat groups for serious game players

To start in their curriculum, students, playing the role of the new Zapster eCommerce task force, might begin with an assignment from the fictional eCommerce manager, Sharon Kladis. The story might reveal that Kladis recently conducted an Internet search on computer games, and found that Zapster did not appear in any of the highly ranked search results. The company has a glitzy Web site that provides general information about its offerings, but consumers would not find Zapster's products if they did a simple Web search by product type. Instead, competitors would get the business.

Example Student Task

Kladis assigns the task force (the students) to improve Zapster's Web visibility. This assignment is written for students in a detailed memo. To do this project, students will have to learn about search engine technology to help them modify the existing Web site so that search engines will retrieve Zapster and place it high on the list of search results. The students study lessons traditionally taught in "*The Internet*" course to learn the critical concepts and skills to achieve this initial task successfully. They work in teams, each team having its own Web site to modify. Teamwork is critical as it both makes learning more effective and fun, and because in real life, this type of work is frequently carried out in teams.

The task might begin with students doing research on search engine technology by going through some recommended readings. Teams will then prepare an initial plan for modifying the site, including an analysis of the problem and steps the team expects to take to fix the site. The teams might also prepare a list of critical open questions to bring to class for discussion. Students will submit their plans and questions to their teacher for review.

Student Support

Students are supported in each task they do with interim deliverables, such as the aforementioned plans and questions, check-points, whole class discussions, and one-on-one and team meetings with their teacher. For example, in addition to reviewing teams' plans and questions, at this point in the assignment process, the teacher might lead a discussion about the first task, asking students to suggest some techniques they expect to be effective, and giving the class an opportunity to answer the questions each team listed. The teacher uses the Socratic method in the discussions, working to have students teach each other, and as a group find ways to learn what they need to know to complete their task successfully. The teacher also provides answers to questions and guidance to other resources when students require such assistance.

Assessment

As their final deliverable for this task, students submit to the task force manager a report describing the before and after search rankings of the company Web site, an analysis of the results for several search engines, and a list of terms likely to be used by consumers searching for products the company sells. They will also provide a modified version of the old Web site.

The teacher actually reviews each deliverable, but the feedback is in the voice of the fictional manager, to help students feel they are submitting their work to their boss. This is meant to facilitate the continuation of the story narrative to help students build an emotional bond to their work in relation to their fictional job. The more engrossed students are in the story, the greater their motivation will be to do their work well. In this way, playing up the fiction serves an important function and should be emphasized. For instance, schools with more than one teacher running this curriculum may have one teacher play the role of the coach, while another plays the character of the eCommerce manager. This would provide students with one person from whom they should aim to learn as much as possible, while the other they should aim to impress with their knowledge and skills—as one might do in a real job between an experienced colleague versus one's boss.

Students should expect that the first time they submit deliverables for any assignment, they will have to do some revisions to get each one right. The revision process may involve several rounds when related to particularly critical skills. When students have successfully completed the deliverables for the first task, they have demonstrated their understanding of search engine technology, and they have programmed in HTML to modify a Web site effectively. Similarly, at the conclusion of every task in the curriculum, students have demonstrated their ability to practice a useful set of skills. When they complete the full curriculum, they have proven they are skilled practitioners in various areas of computer science.

Students do not receive grades on their work, and similarly, neither do professionals. Instead, they receive feedback, and they are expected to revise each deliverable until it shows an acceptable level of competency. This form of assessment is far more useful to students than letter grades, and also more closely resembles the type of assessment working professionals receive on the job.

Courses Represented in Tasks

Each time students complete a set of deliverables for a task, the story progresses to the next set of deliverables the company requires. In the Zapster story, once the task force makes the existing Web site more visible on the Internet, it will be time to begin executing the high level mission of expanding Zapster's online offerings. The CEO of Zapster may want to begin by enabling consumers to find detailed information about each of its products through the Web site, and then, as the next step, allow customers to purchase Zapster products online. To do this, students have the following progression of assignments given to them by their manager:

1. Conduct a contextual inquiry to determine the best way to shape the interface for optimal usability.

This task captures one of the critical lessons from an HCI (*Human Computer Interaction*) course. It teaches students to consider how users think about the tasks they want to do on the Zapster Web site, so the students can construct the interface to be most compatible with users' needs.

2. Conduct a requirements analysis to determine such factors as, e.g.,

    a. Which products and services to offer through the online catalog,

b. How many users Zapster aims to support at a time,

c. Which locations the Web site is expected to cover.

The deliverables that students have to prepare in association with this task, such as a system requirements specification document (SRS), a use-case analysis, and a use-case diagram, draw from the lessons taught in a *software engineering* course and, at a high level, students would begin to think about lessons in *object oriented modeling*.

3. Create the user interface for the Zapster online catalog.

This task continues the lessons from the HCI course. Students learn to categorize Zapster's products and organize all of the content they plan to present within the catalog. They also submit a prototype of the catalog in HTML, providing more practice with programming.

4. Build the new system's catalog and database design models.

This task is a continuation of *software engineering* lessons. Students will have to create the following deliverables in this task: database design document, database design model, class diagrams, and sequence diagrams. In preparing these deliverables, students will have to learn object oriented design techniques, content design, and unified modeling language (UML), to enable them to model their object-oriented program visually.

5. Develop the catalog application and conduct user testing for the catalog application.

In this task, students begin to learn about *Web-application development*, while they continue their work in HCI and *The Internet*. In the process of developing the application, they will install a Web server, use Web development tools, server side technologies, and scripting, for example. As they conduct user testing, they will have the opportunity to study the effectiveness of the site from the HCI perspective, and they will continue to develop their understanding of how the *Internet* works, as they bring their new Web site to life. Students will also learn about *rapid prototyping*, as they develop parts of their system to be tested early in the overall development process.

6. Select an e-payment solution provider.

In this task, students will have to evaluate proposals of various providers of e-payment systems. In the process, students will learn about the complexities involved in the payment systems that enable electronic commerce, and as a part of that effort, they will be introduced to issues in *Web security*.

7. Select an appropriate ISP to host the eCommerce system.

For this task students have to evaluate the differences between ISP providers and figure out which one most suits the needs of the company for whom they are working. This is a challenging task that involves knowledge of *computer networks*, as well as *security*. Students will learn such concepts as: interconnectivity, transmission technologies, intranets, internets, networking technologies, and messaging technologies.

As always, in addition to working through CMU's recommended readings on each of these topics, students will work closely with their teacher as coach. The teacher will help students to break the task down into small chunks of information, and they will work together to construct an understanding of each area to make the task manageable. When they complete this task, students will be useful to many companies who need help making similar difficult decisions.

Once the Web site is hosted, the fictional eCommerce manager will request that students add additional functionality to the Web site to provide the other services mentioned earlier: free versions of games, pay versions of games, chat rooms, and so on. Zapster may want to do various types of customer tracking through a customer database, for instance, in which case students would need to learn about *data structures* and *algorithm design and analysis*, to implement such functionality. Each task is formulated to provide students with experience practicing key skills in the major subject areas related to computer science. Tasks are placed in order of both how they fit chronologically into a real-life project, as well as in consideration of skill building overall.

At the high school level, tasks may take from two to four weeks for teams to complete. In addition, throughout their time working on the story based projects, students will also have one parallel course in computer programming, to gradually develop their programming skills throughout the year. At times the fictional manager will require students to apply the programming skills they learned in their parallel course to accomplish tasks within the ongoing story.

At the conclusion of the year, students will have developed critical skills, and they will have a clear picture of when and how each one fits into the framework of real life projects. Students will also know whether they enjoy computer science as a field of study and practice, and they will be able to make informed decisions to allow them to find jobs that require the skill set they learned, or to make the most of a college major in computer science.

Students learn HTML and Java programming, enabling them to tackle a number of projects, including: studying the flow of goods, money, and information on a global level within the global food service industry, and within Moffett Foods, and recommending improvements; designing and building a new e-business Web site including the system and database design models, and user interface for product purchasing; developing a database-driven catalog application; and conducting user testing of the completed site.

The year concludes with a significant externship project where students identify a local nonprofit or community organization and work with them to redesign and improve their Web presence and related business processes.

UNIVERSITY OF CHICAGO SENIOR
YEAR IN WRITING

In this dynamic curriculum developed with experts from University of Chicago's top-ranked writing program, students divide into groups and play the role of an editorial committee responsible for producing a monthly online magazine focusing on pressing social issues. Topics for the periodical include the social, environmental, and economic consequences of transportation policy; the effects of the Cuban revolution on American policy and identity; the ethics and logistics of natural resource protection; and the escalating tensions between civil liberties and security concerns in a technology enabled world. Students approach these topics with a multidisciplinary and multimedia sensibility, building their stories from research drawn from newspapers and journals, as well as from interviews with experts in the field, field trips, and sources in literature and the arts. As they explore their questions and consider the needs and expectations of their readers, the students will expand and integrate their learning in science, government, law, history, philosophy, ethics, and aesthetics.

Each student contributes two topic-relevant pieces to each issue, as well as publishing a monthly column of their own design. The students are responsible for both the content and the production of the magazine—they consider questions of design and accessibility of written materials on the Internet as they hone their writing for a critical public audience. After brainstorming ideas for articles in an editorial committee, the students engage in critical discussions of key sources recommended by experts. These discussions, and subsequent writers' workshops, inspire ongoing research and revision to strengthen the articles as they are written. This dialogic input serves to focus the students on the role of writing as a communicative medium, with the capacity to inform, expose, persuade, and enlighten. A public forum in which representatives from each student magazine argues their editorial position in front of schoolmates, teachers, and parents follows the publication of each issue.

Projects Outline

Project 1, Critiquing Zines: Students will spend the first week evaluating the content, functionality, and visuals of existing Web sites. In the mornings, they will be learning HTML, and in the afternoons, they will be surfing sites and putting together a critique of one site, pointing out its strengths and weaknesses. Then, they will present their critiques to each other.

Project 2, Webzine Proposal: Having drawn up a list of what works and what doesn't on existing Web sites, students will write proposals for their online magazine and create mock-ups of the proposed site, which they later present to the class. The design for the magazine will come out of this section of the curriculum. This project will take one week.

Project 3, Summer Literature Review: The first issue of the online magazine focuses on the students' summer reading assignments. The core texts for this project are taken from the summer reading list, but the project resources tab will also include information about book clubs, citywide reading initiatives like those in Seattle and Chicago, and Oprah's Book Club. Students will write two articles for this issue and put the magazine online for teachers, parents, and other students to read, and hopefully, respond to. The project takes three weeks.

Project 4, Reflection and Evaluation: Following the publication of their first issue, students will spend the next two weeks evaluating the site, drawing up a "lessons learned" document, and coming up with ways to improve content and layout for the next issue.

Project 5, Society in Transit: Students will begin their first substantive research for the "transportation" issue. They will be interacting with experts in the field and learning more about the topic as it relates to their community and the world at large. They will write two in-depth articles and one column for this issue. The project takes four weeks.

Project 6, E Pluribus Unum?: Acculturation vs. Assimilation: For the third issue, students will focus on culture and community with an emphasis on Cuba. They will research various topics for their articles. Each student will write two articles and one column. As in the previous projects, students will spend some time putting up the online magazine. The project takes four weeks.

Project 7, Reflection and Evaluation II: This mid-term review happens before the winter break. Students will take two weeks to evaluate the site and work on ways to improve on content and layout.

Project 8, Nature Clash!: In the month following the winter break, students will work on the fourth issue, which focuses on Everglades restoration. In addition to writing and putting up content, students will be preparing their report to the Governor's Commission and a report to Congress.

Project 9, Report to Congress: Students will finalize their reports and learn more about presentation skills that will enable them to present their information before the Governor's Commission and the U.S. Congress. They will be making two field trips, first to Tallahassee, and then to Washington, DC.

Project 10, Privacy and Piracy: The fifth issue of the online magazine looks at file sharing, online surveillance, hacking, and intellectual property rights in the computer age. Students will spend the month of March researching and writing on this topic. Each student will be writing two in-depth articles and one column for the magazine.

Project 11, Experience as Education: Students will take a month at the end of the school year to assess their experience with our curriculum as well as research various educational approaches for this issue. In their sixth issue of the magazine, students will have the chance to weigh in publicly about what they liked and what they didn't like about their precollege education.

Project 12, Designers for Hire: Preliminary work for this project will begin midyear and will culminate in the "externship," in which students will build a Web site for a local business or not-for-profit. Here, students will have the opportunity to take their Web-building skills to the larger community.

Field Trips

Students do not spend all their time in the classroom. In fact, they will need to go outside the school to conduct research, including interviewing experts, visiting sites for stories, and filming on locale.

In addition to weekly forays into the field, students make two field trips: The first trip to the state's capital will take place in January. Students will present their findings on Everglades restoration to the Governor's Commission. The second field trip, tentatively scheduled for late February, will be to Washington, DC, where students will present their findings to Congress as well as make side stops to their state representatives' and senators' offices.

Finally, for the externship, students will need to go into greater Boca Raton to offer their services as experienced Web designers to businesses and/ or not-for-profit organizations. Although most of the work for the externship will happen at the end of the year, students will need to start on this assignment at least three months before the production schedule.

Eighth Grade Year in Writing and Web Application Development

The eighth grade curriculum transforms students from passive classroom learners into active participants in designing, programming, and publishing a monthly Web magazine. Each issue of the magazine focuses on a different issue, including self-image, U.S. foreign policy in Cuba, environmental protection of the Everglades, and MP3s and intellectual property rights. Students are divided into teams; each team is responsible for all facets of publishing their own online Web magazine, including writing literary reviews of related literature, doing fieldwork and interviews, conducting research for investigative articles, and writing editorials. Students not only must grapple with the underlying scientific, mathematical, cultural, and historical issues, but they learn to organize their work and thinking and communicate it in both written and oral formats. Following the publication of each issue, students present their editorial positions in a town hall meeting format in front of schoolmates, parents, and teachers.

To enable students to publish their magazine on the Web, they spend half of each day learning HTML and Java programming. Using Java to connect to a database, students create Web interfaces for increasingly complex features such as displaying scores and schedules of school sports teams, a calendar displaying important dates and birthdays, and ultimately a mechanism for storing, indexing, and searching back issues of their magazine.

The year concludes with a final issue of the Web magazine that each student publishes individually on a topic of his or her choice.

Eighth Grade Year in Writing and Web Application Development

Course Overview

For the 2002–2003 school year, you and your class will be learning how to design and develop content for an online Web magazine. Students will spend half of their time learning HTML, Java, and graphical Web design. Throughout the year, they will apply these skills to building their own magazine.

In addition to learning more about Web design, students will learn how to do in-depth research on topics of concern to them and to the larger community. Using a dynamic writing curriculum developed with experts from the University of Chicago's top-ranked writing program, students will learn how to write with skill and confidence.

The research and writing components of the curriculum are model-centered. By reading and analyzing good journalism, students will learn how to write their own articles, including feature stories, editorials, commentary, essays, and reviews.

The major topics covered this year are:

- self-image and peer pressure
- the Cuban-American experience
- water pollution and distribution
- intellectual property rights

In addition to publishing the Web magazines about these topics, the students will also conduct debates after each issue is launched, covering a real social issue related to the topic (e.g., school uniforms in the self-image unit, a new local policy in the water pollution unit).

Research materials are available through the course interface, but students are encouraged to pursue outside resources. On the site, students will find bibliographies, tips on how to brainstorm ideas and workshop their writing, and procedures for getting the magazine out on deadline.

Fifth Grade Year in Science, Technology, and the Law

Fifth grade students in this curriculum are not just elementary students— they are scientists, lobbyists, lawyers, writers, researchers, documentary producers, and Web designers.

During the first half of the year, students undertake an intensive course of study of environmental issues facing the Everglades and South Florida using an integrated set of research-based curricular units developed at major universities. Over the course of the semester, students are assigned to one of three groups: Developers, Farmers, and Environmental Activists. Through research, scientific experimentation, and interviews, students develop rich, deep understandings of their own group's point of view as well as the others. They express these views in a variety of media: writing, video, and the Web. At the end of the semester, the students present their group's point of view on how to protect the Everglades to a visiting official from the U.S. Environmental Protection Agency.

In parallel with their work on the Everglades, students are commissioned to create a video documentary of the curriculum they are participating in. Students are responsible for all aspects of production, including storyboarding, writing, shooting footage, and digital post-production. At the end of the semester, they present their curriculum evaluation documentaries to a school curriculum design committee.

During the second half of the year, in a curriculum designed with experts from Harvard Law School, students take on new roles as lawyers. They research and argue both sides of a landmark case in which an indigenous tribe from Papua New Guinea sued the U.S. government for patenting genetic material allegedly stolen from members of the tribe by visiting U.S. scientists. Through the process of investigating the underlying biological issues and writing and presenting a legal brief, students will have the opportunity to learn about the legal process and how it works, basic biology of cells and genes, ethics, cultural imperialism and politics, the pharmaceutical industry, and the nature of federal government. At the end of the semester, students participate in a mock trial adjudicated by practicing attorneys, legal experts, and scientists.

The School of the Future

Experience: Since we learn from experience, school should be an experience. Each day, every student should be part of a complex experience that may last several days, weeks, or the entire year. The experience should be structured such that it is very engaging, exciting to the student and full of roles to play, skills to learn and practice, and goals to achieve. Ideally, the student participates in this experience with others, as a team, working together to achieve the goal.

Failure: Since we learn from failure, the experience must provide many opportunities to fail. What to do should not be obvious to the student most of the time. The student should struggle, working in areas above his head, with advice from others students, from teachers and from real world experts.

Complex Problems: Inside every experience, there must be complex problems that are difficult to solve. These must be realistic problems that will come up again in his life, or else they will form the basis of experiences that he can draw on in his life. These problems must be couched in terms of something the students genuinely wants to accomplish.

Motivation: Students cannot be expected to perform well in situations they do not care about. Freedom must be given to a student to not work on a particular experience because it doesn't interest him. We cannot expect every student to have exactly the same skills on graduation. People are individuals and school must be individually adapted. Beyond reading, writing, and arithmetic there aren't that many skills that need to be directly taught. All students need to know how to communicate, relate to others, and to reason, but these can be taught within any experience.

Accomplishable Goals: School should present accomplishable goals. Every student should understand what an experience is likely to teach him and what he will be able to do afterward that he couldn't do before. He should be able to demonstrate what he has learned to do in public asking others to watch him perform and taking satisfaction in a job well done. Every skill students learn should be demonstrable.

Competition and Cooperation: Experiences must involve competition and cooperation. People are motivated by being able to keep up with, and surpass, others. School should be a social experience, full of the kinds of problems people have with others. Those problems need to be part of the curriculum, not something hushed up and dealt with away from school. School has a responsibility to teach students to deal with the world in which they live. This includes the people in it.

Satisfaction: Students should come away from school feeling that they are good at something. Everybody is good at something. Students should be allowed to move into what they are good at.

Feeling Smart: Students should begin to believe in their own thinking abilities. We feel ourselves to be smart when:

1. we realize something—have "an aha" experience
2. we can explain something clearly—we can teach others
3. we see connections between events that are not obviously the same
4. we know what to do in a crisis
5. we can do something we couldn't do before
6. we can figure something out for ourselves

Students should be called on to figure things out, to explain something to others, to handle crises, and so on, on a regular basis.

Feeling Capable: Students need to see themselves as capable. Again, everyone isn't capable of the same things. We feel ourselves to be capable when we have done more than was expected of us or we have been original in something we did or we got others to recognize our abilities. We feel capable when we wow people, or we make others happy, or we do what we set out to do, or we do something we couldn't do before. Every school experience should be focused on making students feel capable.

Feeling It Worked: We know the experience we designed have worked when:

1. we want to do it again
2. we worked hard and saw the results
3. we made others happy
4. we laughed
5. we reached down for more than we thought we were capable of

The experiences must be designed to make students feel this way after having had them.

Last, we return to the issue of the educated mind. Students feel educated when:

1. they understand something they couldn't understand before
2. they are interested in something they found dull before
3. they can converse with someone they couldn't talk to before

To produce educated minds, we must create experiences in which students are motivated to accomplish goals while working in cooperative and competitive situations dealing with complex problems that are satisfying to solve making them feel smart, capable, and wanting more.

In any case, that was the plan. The reality was something else again, as we lacked money to complete our plan and we ran headlong into those enemies of educational innovation—parents.

13

Teaching Realities

It is all well and good to be in favor of learning by doing. It is easy to say to teachers that they are now to use learning by doing, that they no longer can lecture or give multiple choice tests, and that learning should be fun and relevant for the students. It is easy to say. But teachers, like the rest of us, know how to do what they always have done and find freedom intimidating. That having been said, there are two things that seem to be true all the time. When asked, teachers know full well what the real value of the subject they teach is in the lives of their students. And when pushed, they will try to retreat to teaching something other than that real value.

When I met with the Grandview teachers the week before school started, those not doing 5th-, 8th-, and 12th-grades, I told them that I expected them to stop lecturing and to start emphasizing writing skills, critical thinking skills, argumentation, and real life doing as much as possible. I said that I would be available to help them and that they could ask me via e-mail when I wasn't around, about any ideas that they had or ways they were considering approaching in the coming year. This meeting was one week before the start of school.

I received only one e-mail the next day. This was it:

Hi Dr. Schank,

I am the new Upper School Social Studies teacher at Grandview. I was wondering if you might be able to assist me—This is my second year teaching and I have been assigned to teach Political Science for the first time. Presently, there are no curriculum guidelines for me to follow to get some ideas. I was wondering if you might have any suggestions/resources/ideas to help get me started.

Heather Anderson
Upper School Social Sciences

Here was my response:

There are three things I would like to see form the basis of the political science curriculum. First, there is the Model UN. Second there are the elections being run this year. Third there is student government. These three should form the essence of what is done this year. The Model UN is usually ancillary to the curriculum. At Grandview I would like it to be central to the curriculum, taken seriously, and worked on in class. There are many elections going on this November. Every student should be involved in a campaign of his choice. There are two aspects to this. There is something (not much) to be gained from volunteering at the campaign. Let them stuff envelopes etc. for a bit. But, I would also like them to write position papers and engage in debates about any local candidate who they are backing. They should research the issues and choose sides in each campaign. The third is harder. I want them to run their own campaigns for positions and issues at Grandview. You will need to discuss these with the students to see what interests them. Then try and teach them the political process by having them engage in it.

In fact, I was surprised to find that they even had a course in Political Science. I had no preconceived notions about the subject, other than the usual "let them actually do something" perspective.

I awaited other e-mails. After all, I had just rocked the world of these teachers by saying, in essence, that I expected them to create a learn by doing curriculum on their own in the next week. But no e-mails came.

I returned to the school three days later and again met with the teachers. They were all quite nervous about the grading policy. I had told them there would be no grades, and they were collectively quite nervous about just giving written subjective reports about how the students were doing. They were afraid the parents would demand more and they thought there should be detailed guidelines about how they made judgments about the students, probably so they wouldn't be accused of failing to be objective by an angry student.

I calmed them down a bit by saying that high school would still have grades (this year at least—as I was unprepared to fight the colleges just yet.) Furthermore, I said that all work to be turned in could be judged acceptable, unacceptable, or outstanding, and as long as that wasn't seen as A, B, or C, I had no problem with work done by students being looked at and judged. I did have a problem with students working for grades, so I encouraged the teachers not to be too numerically detailed about how they came to these judgments and to avoid arguing with students about a grade. Grades in K–8 don't matter to anyone fortunately, so I suggested that they learn to be write very detailed evaluations and get on with it. They quieted down some.

I then proceeded to have meetings with various groups who wanted to see me.

The first meeting was with two Spanish teachers. They told me what they had been doing, emphasizing all the talking, songs, visits to restaurants and such that they had done last year. Of course, this was what I like and they knew it. I figured they were leaving out the grammar instruction and vocabulary tests etcetera that haunt all language education. One of the teachers had spent quite a bit of time at the local school whose main function is to prepare students for Harvard, so of course, she had been spending her time there on getting students to pass the Spanish AP exam and achievement tests. I mentioned to her that my daughter who was fluent in French after living in Paris for a year, barely passed her French achievement test and then they both agreed that they had learned English by immersion, that they thought even Americans would have a hard time with the TOEFL test of English language competency for graduate school, that explicit instruction in grammar was a real waste of time and they were happy to be rid of it. We will see how it goes, but they seemed to be totally on board with the idea that our goal was to teach speaking. Then they told me that they also taught Spanish culture by showing movies that were in English. I said there was to be no English in the classroom whatsoever and that culture, to the extent that it would be taught at all, would come for free by watching movies in Spanish or otherwise learning about Spanish speaking countries through books they read in Spanish. Again they were happy and we left the meeting seemingly on the same page.

I moved on to the English department.

I started by asking the English teachers to each tell me why one should study literature. Each teacher said more or less the same thing: that there were complex issues in life that had been dealt with by many people before and that reading about what various people had to say about these things would help students make more informed choices in their lives. Having to deal with these issues in class would be good for them and help them to reason. I agreed.

They then asked me, because they had read what I said about teaching literature earlier in this book, if students could really choose any book they wanted and wasn't it a good idea for every student to read the same book so that they wouldn't be alone in what they read and experienced. It is fun to have a common experience, they said.

I replied that that was a fine sentiment but that if it meant that every student had to read *Silas Marner* or *The Red Badge of Courage*, then I had a problem with it. I suggested that they pick a set of issues germane to the lives of the students they were teaching and then find a range of books that covered those issues. If a student really only cared about sports, I said, I was sure that there were sports books that covered a number of complex life issues and the student could focus on reading those and still be able to contribute to a discussion on that issue as well as be able to write something arguing a point of view.

They then decided that they had left something out—that the literature course was also about instilling a love of reading and wasn't it ok to simply have them read a book that addressed no real issue, just for fun? I said that I thought fun of that sort could be had outside of school and they replied that kids don't read outside of school. I said that I thought that reading novels on the best seller list was of no practical value that I could see, and that a literature course was probably not about getting students to do so. They said that some of those books did in fact address real issues in life and I suggested that to the extent that was the case, they should suggest that students read them when a relevant issue was being discussed. Then the hidden bomb exploded.

What about teaching plot and theme an irony and other literary concepts? When were they going to teach those? Never, I replied. But it is important to know that stuff. Why? I asked. Because that was how you analyzed a book and talked about a book and understood how to write a novel. How many students were going to go and write novels, I asked. Well, someone might and where else would they learn to do it, they replied. I suggested that there was plenty of time for that and that junior high wasn't likely to be the place where they would start their novel. But here, of course, is the heart of the issue.

What is the issue? Namely, that teachers have always taught what is testable. Further and more important, it is relatively easy to teach terminology to students, have them memorize it, and then have them use those terms for a while. The problem is that there is no value in it (unless they are going to become literary critics or English professors.) The latter remark is of course, not really a joke. What is going on, and this is going on in every conversation with teachers although sometimes it is buried and does not come up, is that teachers want to teach the intellectual aspects of their subject. They want to do this in part because that is what they studied when they went to school and they want to do this because it certifies them as intellectuals of a sort and they want to do it because the professors who dominate their fields do that and claim that it is what these fields are all about. Literature courses without plot structure analysis? Unthinkable.

But why should a student study such things? If the real issue is getting students to think hard about issues in the world that they confront on a daily basis or get them to understand that people before them have had important things to say about these issues, why not concentrate on that? Why isn't that more important than the terminology of literary professionals?

I suggested that if the teachers wanted to use that terminology them-selves, they should do so. In fact, people learn vocabulary by using it and they that they should feel free to use it and explain it, but that is was simply not the point. If school is to both fun and relevant then school has to revolve around issues that are on the minds of students at the time or that are any-way not far from where students are headed. The idea that students are somehow preparing for careers that they will either never have, or will have to prepare for yet again when they go to college, is simply wrong. High school should be about opening the mind in ways that it can be opened, not in ways that professors at Harvard have deemed important.

I then went to the fourth grade.

The fourth grade teachers were ready and willing to do what I wanted, but that didn't mean that they knew what to do. They told me that they didn't like school except when they had a nice teacher and that all they remem-bered from fourth grade was their teachers. They obviously wanted to be nice teachers and I believe that they are probably successful in that.

Their problem, they said, was they had been handed this curriculum which they didn't much believe in. They said they were required to teach government and local history and the various regions of the country and as far as they knew this was standard across the country in fourth grade. I don't know if that is the case, but it is silly enough to be the case.

They suggested having the kids simulate the legislature and try to get a bill passed and they wanted them to dress up like conquistadors and simulate the capture of Florida. They knew where I was coming from and bought into it. In passing, one teacher mentioned that she had had the students be travel agents last year and it was the best part of the year, that the kids had really gotten into it. I suggested that they make that a good chunk of the beginning of the year and use that as a way of teaching the various places in Florida and the rest of the world. Allowing students to book trips and plan travel would cause them to have to learn about the places they were going to of course. Moreover, I suggested that they organize the kids into different travel com-panies and have them pursue business by making pitches about the advan-tages of trips they had planned, as well as marketing places by writing bro-chures, making posters and Power Point presentations extolling the virtues of the places they were looking into. They asked about math and how much they had to pay attention to the book they were using. I said that I had agreed to use the standard book this year but that that shouldn't prevent them from having the kids use math in running their business and working within the budgets of customers. They asked about science, apparently some-one had bought them science kits that they were being asked to use (I can only imagine what is in them), and I suggested that some of their customers would demand science tours, history tours, or whatever, and they had to research this stuff and plan out good itineraries and be able to explain what visitors would learn there. Then I went off to history.

The history folks included the woman who had written to me and she said she liked my idea but now she was worrying about history and felt lost. She mentioned that she always thought history should be taught backward, starting with the present day (because there isn't usually time for it), but that she wasn't sure how to do that.

I replied that her idea was right-headed but not radical enough, that I think all history is relevant only insofar as it informs present decisions and that she should start with real present day issues that require history to understand. As an example, I mentioned the electoral college, this being Florida only two years after the controversial 2000 election. Have the students decide the issue of whether there should be an electoral college, I suggested. Certainly that is a question that depends very much on history and would get you into the Revolutionary War period quickly enough.

The real issue I suggested was breadth versus depth. You can't cover everything in depth, so the usual answer is to quickly cover everything lightly. This is again backward. Light coverage leads to memorizing dates and places. Deep coverage means real issues but a lot less information. Schools always err on the side of breadth. We need to err on the side of depth. They may never get to the Mexican War, but they may understand something about why our country is the way it is. Memorizing the name of the Kings of England does not teach European history. Understanding why there are so many Irish in America might teach more about Europe and England than all the Henry VIII stories ever will.

And then there was physics.

Physics presented a peculiar problem. We had produced an on line physics course with Columbia the previous year and I wanted to use it at Grandview. In the mean time they had hired a physics teacher. He had come out of retirement to teach physics and he wanted to teach the course he had always taught up north. I wanted him to help mentor our on line students. The Solomonic decision the school had chosen was to create two physics courses, Columbia for bright kids, teacher standard physics for dumb kids. I asked why dumb kids would be better at a standard physics course that would bore them to death, and he said that he had understood where I was coming from so instead of simply teaching Ohm's law he would have them play with circuits first and then derive Ohm's law. While this is clearly preferable I wondered why they needed to know Ohm's Law in the first place. He responded that the parents liked it this way, which made me wonder if any of them knew Ohm's Law. He assured me they did.

I was having none of this. Somehow this teacher and his chairman had convinced the parents that dumb kids were better off with the regular course because the Columbia course was too hard for them. In fact, they had never seen the Columbia course and had no idea what was in it. What they did know was that this new teacher wanted to do what he had always done and they didn't want to lose him since physics teachers are hard to find.

But why do dumb kids need to take physics at all, I asked? What is the point? Well, the point was easy to guess. They only had so many courses to offer. This is a small school. Physics is what there was and they needed this guy for other science stuff so they needed to make him happy. This was clear enough from the vociferous support he received form his chairman.

Time to go to work, I thought.

I asked him why students should study physics. He said something about understanding the world they lived in. I asked why that mattered. He said they might have to make a decision that involved knowing that. I asked what kind of decision. He said that maybe they should know about global warming because it might matter to them. I asked why. He said that they might need to help make policy decisions. I asked if that was all he could think of. He said that they might need to understand how their bodies worked as well. I asked why. He said that something might go wrong. I said, so what? He said that were medical decisions to make and that they should be informed about them. I asked if there was anything else. He said they might want to know about whether it as ok to kill off species from the face of the earth. I asked why. He mentioned something about the balance of nature.

I then said that I thought he had roughly outlined a very nice science reasoning curriculum but that it didn't sound much like physics to me.

Again I asked why students should know physics. He said that they should know about how the physical world worked and I asked why and he sat silent.

The chairman then piped up about lightning strikes and moving heavy objects he saw in the room, one of which was a refrigerator, and I asked if he thought they should understand how a refrigerator worked and he said yes.

I suggested they design a relevant physics curriculum, and they agreed. I left after apologizing for being so Socratic (but hell, its what I do).

I met with the third grade teachers the next day. It seems that the third grade has always focused on disasters (The Titanic, Pompeii, and the like). I am not sure why they have done this, the teachers claim that they kids love it and it isn't too hard a stretch to imagine that they do, but still I am not sure what the point is.

But, as I believe that nearly anything can be made relevant of done correctly, it was low on my agenda to change what they were doing. These teachers had learned something about goal based scenarios when the idea was introduced to them last year and they were trying to do the best they could with the idea. They told me they were going to have the kids lay out the measurements to the Titanic on the field adjacent to the school so the kids would get an idea how big the Titanic actually was and could learn to use various tools to accurately measure distances.

Of course, the kids had probably seen big ships since they live in Florida and measurement, while important, is probably more important to do on small things that are more manageable, but I decided to leave well enough alone.

Next, I was informed that learning the State capitals was a big part of the third grade curriculum and that the kids really looked forward to this activity. Well, so much for my good humor. I wondered what kind of life the kids had in school that would make memorizing State capitals its highlight. I asked, of course, why this mattered for anyone to know and received blank stares from the teachers. I suggested that if they wanted the kids to learn about the various states they might have the kids plan trips to those states using maps and travel brochures, and decide what to see and what might be worthwhile to find out about a few of the state capitals by writing to the Chambers of Commerce and viewing what was sent, and so on. I also suggested that, as this was Florida where a lot of folks have retired from somewhere else, they could probably find people who would like to visit the school and talk about where they had come from and what its like there and at least they would get to look at and talk to someone who sounded like he was from Maine and might know offhand the name of its capital.

I suggested that if measurement was to be taught, and I can't see why this is a bad idea, perhaps the kids might try building a scale model of something and measure it precisely. I suggested Pompeii, since they were already into that, and pushing on with teaching about Roman life, and so forth. I added the caveat that this should only be done while considering some modern analogies, allowing discussion on the kinds of building the Romans had and the kinds we had, and why Rome died and whether we are making similar mistakes and so on. I am not sure why Pompeii is important to study except to find out more about Roman life, which is exactly not why they were studying it. I think it was the whole volcano thing, which is ok too of course, but then I suggested the kids might try learning about Montserrat about which there is a heck of a lot more information and real survivors to talk with.

Of course to really make no difference whether they study volcanoes or empires, what matters is that they do something more than pass over this stuff in the night in a mad rush to cram in lots of breadth and no depth. The teachers understood this point and were happy to get into Rome in more detail, but asked what they could throw out. They suggested grammar, which was certainly fine with me. They had been teaching grammar for years and had no idea why. One teacher told me she just learned what an adverb was last year, because up until then she had been teaching first grade and it hadn't come up. I told them they should concentrate on having the kids write, and they should correct what they write for grammar, but that explicitly learning about gerunds and predicates was waste of time and they needn't be bothered, they seamed quiet relieved and asked if that went for spelling as well. I assured them it did.

I emphasized the idea that the kids should spend a great deal of time reading but that they should read for a reason related to something they were trying to find out, in an effort to persuade someone about something. They agreed that it would be good if kids could make good arguments and we discussed having debates and such. The teachers are certainly right-headed and want to do the right thing. The question is how easy that will be.

I went back to visit the fourth grade teachers again. They were deeply into the travel agent idea and were considering various issues connected with it. They were trying to set the kids up to build competing businesses but didn't really know how to do that. They wanted them to compete on their plans and logos etcetera. I suggested that they simply would try to win business that the teachers presented to them, and compete by who made more money. They liked that idea and began to think about having the kids earn (fictional) salaries and so on. These teachers really want to do the right thing, but yet again, we are flying by the seat of our pants here.

On Monday, school began.

14

Fifth Grade Follies

We decided to change fifth, eighth, and twelfth grades in September, 2002. This decision was taken in the summer of 2002, so we had little time to prepare or to smooth the way with parents. This latter issue came back to bite us. Those grades were chosen because, in the words of the headmaster, those years were basically review years owing to their place at the end of the lower, middle, and upper schools. We had time (and money) to redesign eighth and twelfth, but we had no resources for fifth, so we decided that rather than using the SCC approach in fifth we would simply employ good methods that had been invented by other educational innovators, combining them in as coherent a way as possible.

Working with several of education researchers (John Bransford of Vanderbilt University, Elliot Soloway of the University of Michigan, and Allan Collins, of Northwestern University) we decided on one coherent theme (the survival of the Florida Everglades) to bring a sense of a story to the overall semester plan. We also decided to use one curriculum that would not fit into the theme perfectly, but would add value nonetheless. The curricula we chose to use were:

1. The Adventures of Jasper Woodbury (math); (John Bransford: Vanderbilt University)
2. Water Quality and Model It (earth science); (Elliot Soloway: University of Michigan)
3. Betty's Brain (earth science); Nancy Vye: Vanderbilt University)

4. Video Crew (writing, video production, and visual analysis); (Diana Joseph: University of Chicago, Center for School Improvement)
5. HTML Programming (Chris Riesbeck, Northwestern University)

The Everglades Story

The Florida Everglades is a serious issue for South Florida. Since students live near the Everglades and it is an essential part of their lives, this seemed to be a captivating topic for them to study.

Currently people have widely inhabited the areas around the Everglades and have impacted the water and the ecosystem as a whole. Who is really polluting the Everglades? Should they be allowed to pollute or to use the water in the interest of the work they are doing there, and the populations of people who have migrated to the area? Who is most affected by the changes, and who cares to solve the problems? The dialogue involves numerous parties and is highly political. Two critical components of the Florida economy are land development and sugar production, each of which affect the quality of the Florida Everglades water.

The goal is for students to grasp the issues and defend the interests of different parties involved in the debate. The story has enough depth to allow students to practice a myriad of useful skills. They can practice research skills, conduct science experiments related to water quality, develop arguments—making claims that they would have to defend with evidence, address counter arguments of other parties. They can practice written and oral communication, and they can learn how to dissect and analyze an issue.

We wanted the students to work in teams with the idea that teamwork is in and of itself a critical performance objective for the semester. Working in teams is something that does not often happen in traditional school instruction, but is something that often happens in the workplace. This meant that the teams had to be large enough to provide complexity, but small enough that no one could hide in the background without participating.

The Adventures of Jasper Woodbury

All of the curricula we chose to use were able to contribute fairly well to the Everglades story except the first one: "The Adventures of Jasper Woodbury," designed by John Bransford and his colleagues at the Learning Technology Center at Vanderbilt University. This was a curriculum designed to teach math skills, but we couldn't modify it to teach the skills so that they'd be related to the study of the Everglades. The curriculum was already designed around adventure stories that had nothing to do with the theme we chose. However, we liked the curriculum because it was goal driven, centered on a story, motivating, and also thoroughly tested for several years prior to our adoption of it.

There are twelve adventures in the Jasper series, each targeting different skill sets in mathematics. Each adventure is presented as a movie that sets up a complex problem. Once the problem is fully staged, the movie is shut off, and students are asked to work in teams to solve the problem.

We chose to use four of the Jasper adventures:

Journey to Cedar Creek
Rescue at Boone's Meadow
The Big Splash
Bridging the Gap

The skills of the first two related to complex trip planning, and the second two involved statistics and business planning. In traditional instruction students have problems broken down for them, so they know which parts they have to solve, and the chapter of the math book gives strong clues as to which operations to employ. One of the key features of Jasper is that students are presented with a complex situation and to solve the problem, they have to determine how to break it down on their own.

Water Quality and Model It

The Water Quality Curriculum was developed by researchers at The University of Michigan's Center for Highly Interactive Computing in Education, or "HI-CE." The philosophy behind the curriculum is project-based science focused by a "driving question." The driving question poses a problem that motivates instructional tasks and activities. Students in project-based science investigate real world problems that are intended to be interesting and important to them. Once the problem is set up, students engage in investigations to answer their questions. In the process, students develop various work products that demonstrate their research work and provide answers to the questions the students pursued.

In the course of their work in this curriculum, students first develop an understanding of what water quality is. Next, they perform scientific experiments, including building a watershed model and performing water quality tests, to analyze the various factors that affect water quality. At the end of the course, they do a presentation of their findings on water quality in the Everglades and apply their conclusions to the Everglades Project. The driving question in this course is "What is the quality of water like in our river?"

Once students have a sense of what factors contribute to the quality of water they study, they work to create computer models of the water, and the elements in and around it. The University of Michigan recommends using a tool called Model It with the Water Quality curriculum, but we chose to use an alternative tool from Vanderbilt University called "Betty's Brain."

Betty's Brain

Fortunately, at the same time as our development team began to learn about Water Quality, we were also learning about another modeling tool that Vanderbilt University was developing and researching, called Betty's Brain. This tool is geared toward a younger audience, and is less quantitative and more qualitative in nature.

Betty's Brain is a software program that involves a character named Betty. Typically, teachers provide students with a story about Betty that explains her motivation to learn about what affects water quality, so that she can help to save the river she loved to swim in since she was very young. We wrote a new story that provided motivation for Betty to learn about the Everglades instead.

As students construct their models, they can ask Betty questions about the parts of the ecosystem they've modeled, and check to see if she draws appropriate conclusions. If she does, then they know they constructed their models appropriately. Students can also test Betty for her overall understanding. Students love to teach others, and Betty provides feedback as often as students desire, so they can check how well they understand the concepts themselves, and to check how well they are teaching them to Betty.

Video Crew

The Video Crew curriculum was developed by Diana Joseph, a PhD student of mine now at the University of Chicago, as an example of a "passion curriculum." By producing videos, and playing various roles on the production team, students learn reading, writing, planning, budgeting, and film/video specific skills such as storyboarding, scriptwriting, camera operation, lighting, editing, directing, and acting.

A cornerstone of the Video Crew curriculum is the certification process. Students aim to become certified in areas of their interest, allowing them to play particular roles on the production team. Joseph created worksheets that provide students with activities that are required to achieve certification. The activities give the students practice with the skills related to each of the roles on the production team. Students can work at their own pace to master the various roles. Once certified, they are to be empowered and trusted with video equipment or leadership roles, such as director, scriptwriter, or storyboarder for student productions.

HTML

All students at Grandview who were in story centered curricula were meant to learn the HTML programming language. Empowering children with the ability to program their own Web pages is a skill that they can build on over time, and that is relevant for today's world.

Chris Riesbeck, a professor at Northwestern University, originally developed the HTML curriculum for his undergraduate and graduate students. He supervised the modification of this curriculum for Grandview, but even the modified curriculum required additional, special modification to work within the Everglades story.

> The basic tasks in the HTML course include: building a basic home page with formatted text, adding images to the Web page, creating new pages and linking pages together, creating links to other Web sites, applying style sheets to create a consistent look and feel across the Web site, and adding lists and tables. The course instructions were all to reside on a Web site, and the instruction was to primarily come from a book that the students would use as a reference guide.

Designing the Curriculum

In July, 2002, we had a meeting with all of the teachers and development staff that were to be a part of transforming the fifth, eighth, and twelfth grades at Grandview.

The fifth grade teachers had a very positive attitude in the meeting, though they somewhat lacked confidence in their ability to think of ideas that would appropriately meet the requirements of a strong learn by doing, story centered curriculum. They were excited to help however they could, by informing the development team of the character and abilities of the incoming fifth grade class, or telling us about strategies or field trips they'd experienced in the past that seemed relevant.

After some initial brainstorming about issues related to the Everglades, and how each curriculum might contribute to the students' work in the theme, we plotted specific curricula and events on a calendar, providing us the backbone for the design. Of course, when the curriculum was actually delivered, the schedule required ongoing updating and refinement, as each part took the classes significantly longer than we had initially planned.

Once all of the design decisions were made, we had approximately five weeks to put it all in place, at least well enough to launch. We would be able to spend some time while the curriculum was running developing any unfinished parts that would come later in the semester.

The Curriculum in Practice

Once the school year began, the teachers found that we packed the semester with so many new curricula that they had a significant amount of work to do each day of the semester just to prepare to teach in the coming day or days. It seems that mastering what we had designed was difficult enough; showing additional ownership through inventiveness or modification was perhaps more than was reasonable to expect, and it's not clear that it was necessary. Some of the researchers who provided us with curricula warned us that introducing too many new elements at once was a recipe for failure, but the fifth grade teachers rolled with the punches extremely well. They maintained a high level of organization, preparing their own binders of information that we'd provided for each unit, and working together to figure out what they'd teach together and what they would instead divide and conquer.

Their positive attitude ultimately enabled them to teach to our design, and use our materials quite well. They also certainly did adapt pieces of curriculum when they needed to, without guidance. In some cases they added small amounts of their own curricula that they'd used in the past to layer on some additional learning objectives, but they managed to use the Everglades theme as a launching pad for most activities.

On the first day of school, the teachers took the students on a surprise field trip to the Everglades where they took a guided airboat ride, in which they learned various points of interest about the Everglades and the nature (plant and animal) that make the Everglades home. Students took along special notebooks that they would continue to use throughout the semester to capture their research. They were called "Field Notes." The teachers explained that the students were to be researchers who had to be good observers and good at asking questions about what they see. The students took, in some cases, copious notes about their experiences on the boat ride. That same afternoon they also began to read the novel *The Yearling*, a story about backwoods Florida, aloud, as a class.

In preparation for the second day of class, the teachers made a short video that raised questions about the quality of water in the Everglades. The teachers showed the students the video to kick-off a discussion about the Everglades and the importance of its water. The students were divided into their "special interest groups" related to the Everglades, and they did some activities designing their field notebooks and doing some warm-up observation exercises. They continued to read *The Yearling* daily until they finished the book.

Later in the week, they began their HTML course and programmed their first Web pages representing their teams' identities. We realized at this point that HTML would take the fifth grade longer than the other grades because they needed to write original texts about their groups. In original HTML course, the written parts are already complete for the students. Even if they were not, higher grades would find writing less challenging than fifth graders do. The writing process for younger students was much more time consuming, but added an excellent additional learning opportunity for the students.

The students also did some activities related to observing and collecting data, and they continued using their field notebooks while they worked. Through discussion, the students reflected on what good observation skills entailed. They began to read brief articles about the Everglades, took notes, and started to ask questions about information they lacked with regard to their own teams' concerns.

The second week of school was only a four-day week (there was a day off for Labor Day). The first three days were spent on a field trip to an outdoor education company named Pathfinder. For many of the students this was to be their first time sleeping away from their parents at all, let alone for three days. Pathfinder was planned to teach the students some basic facts and issues related to nature in Florida and issues that closely related to the Everglades theme. One activity, "The Developer's Dilemma," put the students in teams, in which some were developers who wanted to put new construction in fragile areas in Florida, including the Everglades. Students learned about their positions on the problem and debated each other to find a solution. Students were highly engaged in the activity, and it was a great kick-off to our theme.

Another important aspect of the Pathfinder trip was its focus on teaching the students teamwork. We discussed with the teachers in July the problem of fifth grade children becoming more and more cliquey and unkind to their peers. Scheduling Pathfinder early was meant to begin preparing the students for some of the intense teamwork to come in the new curriculum design. Pathfinder gave students an introduction to issues that would arise during the upcoming teamwork, but in a game context, it did not fully prepare them for the real situations that they were soon to face. Teamwork would prove to be one of the most difficult aspects of the curriculum for the students.

In the next weeks, one by one, each new part of the curriculum was introduced. We decided to separate the mornings and the afternoons, such that mornings were the time for Jasper and math skills, which we were unable to link well to the Everglades curriculum, and the afternoon focusing on curriculum aspects related to the Everglades theme. Jasper started in the mornings the week after the Pathfinder trip, and in the afternoons students progressed on their research about the Everglades, they worked on their HTML course and filled in their Web sites with information they learned about the Everglades, and they also began their video crew curriculum. After a couple of weeks, they started the Water Quality curriculum to get into scientific research about their Everglades issues, and eventually Betty's Brain would be used in conjunction with Water Quality.

Since the environmentalist group had plenty of ammunition to defend their perspective on the Everglades as backed by the Pathfinder trip, the airboat ride, much of the literature on the Web and in the papers, the students who really had to work hard to defend their positions were the farmers and the sugar growers, both of whom were being targeted as threats to the future of the Everglades. The students on these teams felt personally attacked when they had no way to defend their teams. They needed some help. An exciting opportunity came to the rescue.

On hearing about the curriculum through one of our course developers, Judy Sanchez, the Public Relations Director for U.S. Sugar was excited to speak to the class to defend the sugar grower's work. She helped to arrange a field trip to the U.S. Sugar plant, where she explained how the whole process of farming and processing sugar works, and the great lengths the sugar industry in Florida goes through to protect the environment around them. The students and the teachers were mutually impressed with the overall message. They left feeling that many opponents to the sugar growers are missing critical information. The students were given such hope by Sanchez's message that it inspired them to go deeper into their research to find additional defense for the sugar industry that they could add to their own arguments. An example of data they found is that U.S. Sugar reduced the amount of phosphorus they use in their fertilizer three times more than they were asked to do. The group became excited by their findings, and excited that there was a fight to be had.

Next, Dr. Joel Howard, an environmental scientist, came to speak to the class. He works with development companies to help ensure that their development is carried out in an environmentally sound way. For instance, before any land goes through development, he helps the team to do ample background research on plants and animals that are part of the habitat before any shovel is turned. If there will be 300 acres considered for development, they will ensure that some percentage be allotted as a preserve. They will also have some percentage of man-made lakes in the development to handle run off, so it doesn't eventually run into the Everglades. However, Dr. Howard also explained that there are developers who proceed without taking these precautionary steps, and without at all working with such scientists to help them protect the environment. The students learned the good and the bad realities of developers.

Teacher and Parent Reactions to the Curriculum

Overall, the teachers have had a positive experience with the new curriculum. It was a challenge for them to keep up with parts that require more preparation than others, which in some cases has prompted them to find easier solutions to implement the flavor of the original plan, without fully using the plan as intended. They believe that the kids have done some great work and had some truly valuable learning experiences, and they seem to enjoy the curriculum overall.

The teachers agreed that one of the most difficult day-to-day challenges has been facilitating effective teamwork amongst the students. The teamwork issue first reared its head during the first Cross Talk of the semester. Students came together excited to discuss and share their findings, but when it came to deciding what would be said to the full group of students, and who would say it, the disputes began. The teachers did not panic or put a stop to the discussions. Instead, they saw the event as a teaching opportunity, and they allowed the students to come to the group unprepared and without selected leaders, and as a group, the students reflected on the problems of arguing rather than making progress.

As a result, some teams have found their way over time to smooth working relationships resulting in strong work products, such as beautiful, clear Web sites with good arguments for their side of the debate, while others continued to argue and have made little progress in their overall research and Web site development. The teachers have tried to continue using the intrateam disputes as a learning experience for the students, exploring how give and take and showing respect for one another leads to strong work products and bickering leads to nothing getting done. They also did some activities early in the year of having teams lay out their own ground rules for working together, so that they could troubleshoot their own shortcomings. Unfortunately, as children, acting out on visceral responses is sometimes difficult to overcome.

Parents and students alike were frustrated when teams could not perform well together. It made the day-to-day experience for those students somewhat stressful, and they felt frustrated about their lack of progress. Reflecting on this difficulty, the head mistress of Grandview School noted that she knew that this group of students did not have a history of getting along well, and that many of their parents were easily perturbed at anything in school that did not feel smooth for their children, or that felt different for them. She decided that perhaps it was a mistake to start this curriculum, which required significant amounts of teamwork, on this particular class. However, teamwork, as mentioned earlier, is a critical performance objective that should not be avoided just to keep students and parents happy.

The teacher's willingness to allow the students to have difficulty at times, showed their understanding of the idea of notion of learning through failures. They built on the idea further by taking a suggestion to make a special bulletin board in one of the classrooms dedicated to "Useful Failures." When students ran into trouble in their work, they might decide that there was something important to learn from their mistakes. When this occurred, they would write out the failure and the lesson learned, and the teacher would cut it out of the paper in a fun shape and post it to the board. The board was filled with mistakes and lessons of the children, celebrating their mistakes and what they'd learned rather than instilling shame in them, as is done in typical school situations.

The Parent's Reaction

At the start of the year, the parents were nervous about the whole idea of having the old curriculum changed. They wanted school to be the way that it was when they signed their kids up for it. They heard that there would be no homework, grades, or tests and they decided that meant that it was neither serious nor good. They worried their kids would not be as prepared for college as children in other schools. They feared their kids would not learn about responsibility and diligence. They worried that with all the teamwork and project work, the students wouldn't learn to sit still, be quiet, and listen. The parents wanted school to look like what they were used to it looking like, and the change made them uncomfortable and upset. According to the headmistress, some parents might have gone with the flow much better, had other parents not been so outspoken about how upset they were. They felt their children were being used as experiments, and they did not approve. Over time, small changes were made to the curriculum and many parents relaxed.

There were rare cases of parents who were fully onboard from the start though. The headmistress recalled one set of parents who came to the school to express their gratitude and belief in the new approach. They pleaded with her not to cave into the other parents' fears. They knew their child was learning, and they knew that working on meaningful projects rather than focusing on memorizing facts was a better approach to schooling. Parents like these were few and far between. This set up a pattern in which, unlike in years past in which parents would regularly be invited to the classroom or on fieldtrips, in this case the teachers kept the parents away from the class as much as possible. When they were there, they caused trouble. The teachers had faith in the curriculum and knew the students would learn a lot—but they did not want to fight the parents the whole way through.

The Everglades Theme

At the start of the second semester, the students were scrambling to complete their second video projects and make the next round of improvements to their Web sites. At this point, they said, the students for the most part had connected well to their teams and to their issues.

Those who before were upset to be on the teams that had no defense for being destructive to the Everglades had new found ammunition from their visitors and subsequent research. They were energized to make progress, and to work quickly to meet the deadline for their videos, but overall they were collectively getting ready to be finished working on this project. The teachers noted that a few of the students who especially enjoyed the technology parts of the project, such as making their Web sites, would have been happy to do this for a lifetime, but it's not clear that they were as connected to the environmental issue as the production work they were doing.

The teachers also felt that it took a long while for the students to get up to speed on what they needed to do in this part of the curriculum. They believe that some more level-appropriate materials are required to bring the students up to speed much faster at the start of the school year. Only recently have the students really developed a command over the issues and the vocabulary that describe them, and only recently did they develop a thorough understanding of their roles and their mission. While this was laid out for them early, it took time for them to fully grasp what the story of the curriculum was about, and more specifically, what it was asking of them.

The teachers also felt that the class lacked sufficient structure. Once it was running, they felt the need for more frequent deliverables, more specific research activities, and more of a sense of accountability. Accountability ended up being an issue for a couple of our grade levels. When we did away with grades and homework, we were not clear about what these would be replaced by. We knew that we wanted written evaluations about the students that were more descriptive than grades, but the formal structure was no in place by the start of the school year. This was upsetting to the parents and left the students feeling that it was a "free year;" they didn't have to do much work and they wouldn't be punished for laziness. Many students worked despite the lack of structure, but for those who did not, the teachers did not have recourse that would effectively motivate the students to try harder.

Although the teachers were instructed to not give students any homework, parents were overtly concerned about their kids not practicing math skills at home. They also felt that some students needed to learn to solve problems with less help than they received from her during the school day. To solve both problems, she did create worksheets for the students to bring home, and she made special requests of the parents that they not help their kids to finish them. They also needed a way to assess which students were adequately grasping which skills, so the worksheets helped her to assess their abilities and to provide additional support and practice opportunities for the students who needed them.

The high degree to which the students grasped the material is evident through an example from an assessment test they gave to the students to see who knew what material, and how well. One problem she gave mirrored a scene from a Jasper episode in which several of the characters have dinner together, and they have to divide the bill and pay their parts, including tax. She created a word problem in which a guy she named Jeff goes to a CD store and purchases three posters and two CDs. She gave the dollar amount of the purchase and explained what bills Jeff used to pay. She asked the students how much change he was due. Many of the students knew how to solve the problem, but one went above the call of duty, adding Florida state tax onto the purchase amount to figure out a new total, and thus a lesser amount Jeff would receive in change. The problem did not mention tax at all. The student simply knew this would be a part of the payment.

Parents were very concerned about Jasper because they had never heard of it before and they did not understand the work products their children came home to show them. On parent's night, they began to complain emphatically that this new program was different and they did not want it tested on their children. As designers, we found their concerns to be ironic, since Jasper had been formally tested over many years and was already available through a publisher to any school who wanted it.

Several of the parents went so far as to purchase a standardized test preparation book from a teacher supply store. The book was intended to cover skills that fifth graders should learn in their classes. A parent opened the book to an early page and asked her child to solve a problem in the book. The child did not know how to do it, and the parent was enraged. The teacher explained that the skills may not all be covered in order, but she assured the parent that after teaching math for more than 10 years, she had complete and total confidence that Jasper was teaching all of the critical skills, and teaching them better than is normally done. Furthermore, by the end of first semester, she felt that many of the students were ready to move on to Jasper episodes that entailed sixth grade level work.

The Water Quality curriculum required tweaking as the curriculum was not geared toward a body of water that was like the Everglades. With our tight development schedule, we did not give the teachers revised materials for the curriculum often until they day before they were supposed to teach particular units. The teachers found that they did not have enough time in their day to prepare to teach the new curriculum the next day. Also, neither teacher had taught science before, so all of the material and experiments were entirely new to them. They needed significantly more training and time than they had, so they did not implement this curriculum quite as fully as originally intended.

This is not to say that they did not use Water Quality at all, though. They did do some of the experiments exactly as planned, and they worked well for the class. They found them to be both fun and interesting. They also would often use the topics from the Water Quality curriculum and then find outside resources that had prescribed experiments for the class to do with regard to the Everglades. The students not only enjoyed the experiments, but they saw direct relevance between the experiments and their larger Everglades project work. Also, the students serendipitously found a relationship between their experiments and their daily lives at one point in the year.

In the Water Quality curriculum, the students did a test in which they checked the Everglades water for coliform. Coliform is a bacteria that is dangerous when in drinking water. The students did not find coliform in their Everglades water test, but in the middle of the semester a news story broke about how coliform was found in the Boca Raton drinking water, and the students were not allowed to drink tap water for several days. They were very excited that they knew what coliform was, they knew about its dangers, and they knew how to test for it.

Their parents were curious how they knew so much, but they were not ready to embrace the curriculum quite yet. Still too much activity and not enough discipline, it seems—not enough standard memorization of set facts to make the parents comfortable. The parents were not comfortable with anything that might be different from what kids at other schools were doing. Often the concern they expressed related to what would happen if their kids were to transfer to another school. They just wanted their school to be like any other school.

Overall the teachers like the Water Quality curriculum, but they need more time to work with it and learn it properly. They continue to use the units from it as launching points from which they find other, clearer, perhaps more locally relevant curricula to take its place.

Betty's Brain had an unfortunate turn of events that rendered it out of sight for the teachers, and therefore mostly out of mind. The problem was that the computers in the fifth grade classrooms did not have sufficient memory to run the Betty's Brain program. They worked with technical support staff at the school trying to get the software to run on the classroom computers, but to no avail.

In the end, they had to install the software on the library computers. We trained the teachers on how to use Betty, but because they would have to set up special library time to use it and they were already straying from some of the Water Quality structure, they only took their classes to work with Betty's Brain once by the start of second semester.

The video crew curriculum ran smoothly from the start. The students made their first videos a little too long, but they had a lot of fun making them, and they were all certified on some part of the production process by the time of the taping. In the end, most students did not try to get certified on more than one thing, perhaps because the teachers did not make this a daily commitment. But students seemed pleased to have a role and to be the leader on some aspect of their teamwork.

After viewing the Web sites, all of the students sat together as a group and the teachers played for them each team's video. An example was a video produced by one team (the environmentalists) called "The Man in the Field." This video made an argument through a comedic piece, in which the claim was that South Florida is sinking.

One issue that arose for the teachers during the running of video crew was that the design team did not adequately figure out the timing of how video sessions would be run. While some students were scripting the videos, other students had nothing to do and they would mess around instead. This should not have been the case, as they always could have been either achieving certifications on other video-related skills, they could have continued to do research on their team issues, and they could have worked on their Web sites. They also could have kept working on Jasper or any other part of the curriculum. Also, the teachers ultimately felt that the whole curriculum did not provide enough opportunities for formal writing. The designers always believed that all parts of the curriculum provided opportunities for writing, but we were not always explicit about when and how to work writing assignments into the schedule. The teachers did not seek opportunities to work writing in more on their own.

While the students thoroughly enjoyed creating their videos and becoming certified on parts of the production process, the parents did not ever comment on whether they did or did not like this aspect of the curriculum. It seems that they saw it merely as fun activity, and not as useful skill building of the sort they would normally expect from state standards. While visual literacy is something some states and some countries value highly, because western culture regularly experiences television, movies, and other visual media regularly, the Grandview parents chose only to focus on how well, or how traditionally, the fifth grade was working with the standard subjects of math, science, language arts, and social studies—the strongest focus being math.

The HTML curriculum was one of the hardest parts for the fifth grade teachers to implement, primarily due to lack of sufficient training prior to the course delivery. Since they did not have the time or enough training (though they did have a little), they were mostly learning together with the students. When students were stuck and frustrated, the teachers could not help much more than to say, "let's look in the book together." This was time consuming and sometimes left the teachers with further questions that no one was there to answer. Eventually the 8th and 12th graders, who were moving through the course faster than the 5th graders, came in periodically to help the class. The teachers appreciated this assistance. Despite the frustrations, though, some students took to HTML quickly and soared with their skills. They loved to design their team Web sites, adding fun graphics and effects. These students would be happy doing HTML all year long if they could.

Parents saw the HTML pages as a part of parent's night. All in all, the parents felt the same about HTML as they did about video crew. Even though learning to program is clearly a useful skill in this day and age, the parents saw it as a fun activity and not much else. Those parents whose children loved working with HTML were pleased they had the opportunity to do it in class, those whose children were frustrated by HTML were frustrated that their kids had to spend time working with it during school, and those parents whose children were of average skill in programming did not seem to care much one way or the other.

So was the curriculum a success overall? The teachers believe that it was. The students got to know their issues well over time. They have learned a lot about teamwork, research, and defending an argument. The various aspects of the curriculum were linked together nicely and motivated by the overall theme. There were bumps along the way that can be worked out in the future, but rather than wanting to scrap it and start over again next year, the message from the teachers seems to be more about tweaking and refining than starting over from scratch.

The Head Mistress of Grandview's perspective is centered primarily on parent reactions to the changes in the curriculum and to the school as a whole. She admitted that she had not seen the curriculum in action almost at all because she is thinly spread across the K–12 grades. She did know a lot about the plan for the curriculum, and had faith in it and the teachers who were teaching it completely. However, she heard an earful from parents throughout the semester about it, and the feedback was by far mostly negative. Her perspective is less about the curriculum and more about how the message of change was delivered to the parents—a question of marketing.

There were two main parts that she wishes were done differently. The first is the original message delivered to the parents, and the second is the overly speedy development schedule. The original message about changes to come started out with a letter home to parents. It explained, at a very high level, the researchers and university professors who were joining the school's advisory board, and would be coming to the school to help it achieve its original mission. It explained the grades that would be involved in the most major changes the first year and invited all parents to an informational meeting in August. In other words, the first parents would hear in detail about the plans for the school would be in August, and school was to begin at the end of August. The intention was that after one general meeting, everyone would be good to go. It was a plan that may have ultimately been, simply, unrealistic. However, many parents wondered if their children were to be guinea pigs, or they questioned the premise; after all, traditional education worked for them. Many of the parents left feeling threatened and upset, and they wondered what happened to the sweet little school in which they had the power.

The other part of the headmistress' concern, related to the speed with which we developed and delivered the curriculum, had to do with the infrastructure of managing the changes. As mentioned earlier, while we had a strong sense of what we wanted to avoid—extrinsic motivations like grades, separate classes for math and other classic subjects, and tests, we did not have in place at the start of the school year all of the policies and forms that would take these standard processes' places. Parents confronted her from the start about how these things would work, and although she did her best to dance around the issue to buy time for further development, parents saw through the smoke and mirrors and grew more and more skeptical overall. She believes that had we had answers to their questions and communications pre-prepared, they would have been fine and much more ready to go with the flow.

By the second semester of school, she continued to believe that the curricula we brought to the school were ultimately the right thing to be doing, but with the lack of parent buy-in and infrastructure details yet to be worked out, she started making some minor changes to some of the courses, although not to the fifth grade in particular, as parents have become happier since math homework has been assigned. Her plan for next year is to allow students to volunteer for the new programs, and these programs are likely to run less than the full school day. Some periods will be traditional classes. She sincerely hopes to someday reach the vision we set out to achieve in the first year, as it was originally conceived, but the parents pay the bills in this small private school and she feels, they leave her little choice.

Test scores were much higher for these fifth graders than for any other fifth grade in the school's history. As we certainly were not preparing these students for tests, the results surprised everyone.

15

The Eighth and Twelfth Grade Writing Curricula: A Study in Contrasts

We had received some donations to fund our work in developing new learning-by-doing curriculum at Grandview, but not enough to field full development teams for fifth, eighth, and twelfth grades. We had to find a way to make a little go a long way. The strategy we used for fifth grade was to use existing high-quality curricula and integrate them into a coherent storyline. However, there really wasn't anything available that we liked for the eighth and twelfth grades. Besides, the whole point was to do something new and different.

We decided to adapt the CMU eBusiness Technology master's curriculum for use in twelfth grade, but we knew not all of the students would be interested in a computer science curriculum. So, we needed another option for twelfth graders. And, we figured that whatever we tried in twelfth grade could be further adapted for eighth grade, so we decided to give that a try as well.

We had been in discussions with the University of Chicago about doing something with them in the humanities so we asked about high school and they were willing to lend their name and expertise to develop a new kind of writing curriculum. We decided to develop a "University of Chicago Senior Year in Writing" curriculum to provide the seniors an alternative to the eBusiness curriculum. We then decided that we would adapt portions of both the eBusiness and writing curricula and combine them to create a curriculum that would work well for eighth grade.

THE UNIVERSITY OF CHICAGO SENIOR
YEAR IN WRITING CURRICULUM

We had had a great deal of experience developing Business Writing courses for Columbia University in a Web mentored format, where students produce deliverables and receive mentoring from experts about what they have produced via the Web. Writing is after all, simply a context in which a range of other issues can be explored. So, the question was: what other issues were appropriate? The challenge we faced was to find a way to allow students to write on topics that interested them in order to keep their motivation high, but at the same time to cause the students to have to delve into key topic areas that the school felt obligated to address. We also wanted a curriculum that would result in deliverables that students themselves could see and be proud of, and that could be shared with other students, parents, and friends.

At the same time we were thinking about the writing curriculum, we had also decided that we wanted all students doing the new curricula at the school (in 5th, 8th, and 12th grades) to learn how to build Web pages using HTML. This would allow all the new curricula to kick off the year on a similar note, would give students practice working in teams on a very immediate, concrete task, would build a sense of accomplishment early, and give students the skills to use in presenting their project work later in the curriculum.

We decided that students would publish a Web magazine that would have monthly issues focusing on different topics (e.g., environmental science, politics and government, etc). This would allow for a natural integration of the HTML skills with the concept of a writing curriculum. Each student would be required to write 2–3 articles for each issue, along with one or more columns on a topic of their own choosing (e.g., sports, cars, fashion, music, movies, etc.). Even for the required articles, students could still select story assignments that resonated with them the most, preserving a sense of choice even within a structured curriculum.

For the first few weeks of the school year, the students worked on the HTML tasks in the mornings and the Web magazine curriculum in the afternoons. Once the HTML tasks were completed, students devoted all of the available classroom time to the Web magazine curriculum.

HTML Tasks

The development team worked to craft a introductory HTML curriculum that could be integrated into the Web magazine storyline. The students would work in teams to craft some basic pages in HTML that would form the basis for a more full-fledged Web magazine design that would be developed later.

The student teams would access the curriculum Web site where they would receive (fictitious) email messages from a senior programmer at the magazine publisher who gave them their assignments.

The HTML curriculum consisted of eight tasks:

1. "Who We Are" page
2. "Upcoming Issues" page
3. First Site Prototype
4. Standardized Look
5. "Contact Us" page
6. Site Navigator
7. Form-Based "Contact Us" page
8. Quality Assurance and Code Review

Each task was designed to teach students basic HTML constructs for text formatting, links, images, tables, forms, and frames. These concepts are learned in the context of an extended realistic Web site development project.

For example, in the first tasks, students were asked to create a simple "who we are" page for the webzine that included:

- A brief description of Grandview Press—where it's located, how many employees it has
- A mission statement for the webzine—who it's for, what its purpose is
- Brief profiles of the management team

Attached to the email giving them their assignment, students also had access to a number of documents that described the fictitious Grandview Press, the company's mission, and bios of the management team. They used this information in building the Web pages.

After each task was completed, the students had to submit the completed Web pages to the teacher for review; not only of how the page looked, but how well the HTML code was written behind the scenes. Students had to write the HTML code by hand, they were not allowed to use commercial HTML editors that automatically generate HTML code.

Web Magazine Projects

The Web magazine curriculum consists of a set of projects where students learn how to research, write, program, and produce an online magazine. The content for each webzine is theme-based and interdisciplinary.

The curriculum materials were created in conjunction with the University of Chicago to ensure a rigorous writing component that challenges students to become good researchers and writers as well as independent learners. The learning objectives in writing are similar to those demanded of students enrolled in the university's writing enrichment program.

During the development of each webzine issue, students participate in workshops designed to improve their writing and research skills. They identify strategies for developing news stories by reading and analyzing the work of professional journalists, and model their writing on real-world examples. They also read selected literature related to the theme of that webzine issue.

Professional writers (some from the nation's leading publications) were available in person or online at different points during the year to answer students' questions about the craft. In addition, students had the opportunity to interview experts in the fields of transportation, the environment, and education, which they may use in their articles and reports.

The high-level learning goals for the curriculum included the following:

- Work cooperatively in teams
- Manage complex projects
- Demonstrate leadership
- Read and analyze current events
- Interpret statistical data
- Read and analyze core texts related to project themes
- Write analytically and critically about current events
- Master key genres in journalism
- Edit writing in a way that demonstrates an understanding of standard conventions for spelling, punctuation, grammar, and style

The curriculum consisted of the following sequence of projects:

1. Webzine Critique
2. Webzine Proposal
3. Summer Literature Review
4. Reflection I
5. Society in Transit
6. E Pluribus Unum?
7. Reflection II
8. Nature Clash!
9. Privacy and Piracy
10. Experience as Education
11. Designers for Hire (Externship)

Projects 1 and 2 build up to the production of the first issue of the webzine in project 3. Additional issues are published in projects 5 through 10, for a total of 6 webzine issues published during the course of the year. The year concludes with an externship (project 11) where students offer their expertise in writing, design, and programming to local businesses or not-for-profit organizations.

Here is what each project consisted of:

1. Webzine Critique

In preparation for publishing the first issue, students spend time analyzing existing web sites and online magazines. The students are asked to critique the sites in terms of content, navigation, and design. As a deliverable for this project, the students make a presentation on the one site they feel comes closest to their vision for their online magazine. They are also asked to include their thoughts on how to improve on the site.

2. Webzine Proposal

As the second step in preparing to publish the first issue of their own webzine, students are asked to use the analysis they did in the first project along with their newly acquired HTML skills to develop a proposal for what their webzine will look like. In addition, the students are asked to come up with a name for their new webzine. The proposals are presented to the teacher (and other teams), critiqued, and revised accordingly.

3. Summer Literature Review

For the initial dry run issue, they wrote articles related to their summer reading assignments and editorials on their feelings about summer reading requirements in general.

In this project, students:

- Learn how to write a clear thesis statement
- Practice summarizing information
- Become proficient in online databases
- Organize information to support a story's main idea
- Relate literary themes to personal experience and/or current events
- Learn how to quote sources

The students publish this issue of the webzine to a server in their classroom. Before actually posting this issue of the webzine on a publicly accessible server, however, students proceed to the next project to conduct a review and reflection.

4. Reflection I

In this week-long project, students step back from the publication of the first webzine and reflect on their work. They review the first issue using the guidelines developed for content, navigation, and design in project 1. Students also consider ways to streamline the project plan for the upcoming issue.

Specifically, students:

- Conduct a webzine evaluation where identify strengths and weaknesses in their webzine's content, navigation, and design. Then they list possible solutions for each problem.
- Hold a "lessons learned" meeting where they review the project calendar for project 3. Students are asked to assess how effectively they managed producing the first issue and adjust the next issue's project calendar to help streamline the production process. Students explicitly list lessons learned from putting up the first issue.
- Meet to exchange staff roles in preparation for working on the second issue. Predecessors revise the original role descriptions and add a list of "tips and traps" to them. Successors learn about their new responsibilities and discuss with their predecessors how best to handle problems that may come up in the next issue.
- Develop a webzine style guide for the webzine. Students review the first issue's articles and the site design to identify recurrent problems with punctuation and mechanics. The style guide also serves to standardize formatting features like font style, size, and colors used in section headings and article titles.
- Apply the lessons learned, and style guide to the Summer Reading issue of the webzine and post the webzine on a public server.

5. Society in Transit Issue

This issue of the webzine focuses on topics related to transportation. Students will write two articles and one column for this issue, which will build on the original design. This month-long project involves extensive research and analysis of the subject.

In this project, students:

- Study the pros and cons of energy sources, from fossil fuels to hydrogen fuel cells
- Analyze the impact of physical geography, demographics, and development on transportation
- Examine the automobile's influence on American culture
- Trace the history of transportation initiatives from the invention of the wheel to the liftoff of the space shuttle
- Analyze current events in terms of the nation's dependence on foreign oil
- Assess the efficacy of public transportation initiatives

- Critique the latest automobile designs and learn more about new modes of transportation like Dean Kamen's "Ginger"
- Investigate Boeing's funding of antigravity research and its application to transportation

6. E Pluribus Unum

The third webzine issue, "E Pluribus Unum," looks at our multicultural society and the way that individuals and communities preserve cultural identity, while adapting to mainstream American culture. Students read a variety of fiction and nonfiction books in preparation for researching this topic. They also follow the debates on "hot-topic" news items like racial profiling, affirmative action, and recent actions by the Office of the Attorney General to track terrorists.

In this project, students:

- Investigate state and federal laws on immigration
- Study the history of immigration in our country
- Examine language as an expression of cultural identity
- Compare the United States' concept of the "melting pot" to Canada's idea of a "cultural mosaic"
- Research demographics and analyze census data
- Acquire a knowledge of basic statistics and use algorithms to calculate data sets
- Practice interviewing techniques in preparation for writing oral histories
- Conduct surveys and tabulate the results

7. Reflection II

In this project, as in the previous reflection project, students step back to review the webzine issues published so far, and work through a process to identify lessons learned and suggest improvements for subsequent issues.

8. Nature Clash!

Following is a multifaceted project on the environment, "Nature Clash!," which directs students to examine the dynamic between conservationists and developers in regions like the Florida Everglades. Students not only devote an issue of the webzine to this topic, but they may also prepare a report to present to the state or federal agencies.

In this project, students:

- Conduct experiments to test for water and soil quality
- Analyze how urban sprawl is encroaching on our national parks
- Track the impact of invasive species like the snakehead fish

- Synthesize secondary sources to write a balanced piece on a key environmental issue (e.g., water safety, biodiversity, global warming, etc.)
- Collect original data on restoration of the Florida Everglades and present findings to the Florida State Assembly and the United States Congress
- Profile spokespersons for both sides of the preservationist vs. development debate
- Explore local environmental issues through a series of field trips to hot spots in their area

9. Privacy and Piracy

In this issue, students do in-depth research on the topic of intellectual property rights as it relates to the practices of online music downloading and sharing. Students share their research and opinions through writing thought-provoking articles and commentary.

In this project, students:

- Research laws regarding copyright and intellectual property rights
- Do a comparative analysis of our laws vs. those in other countries (e.g., United States' position on freedom of speech vs. French and German restrictions on access to hate speech and extremist propaganda)
- Learn how spy software is built and understand the technology of online surveillance
- Trace the history of the Internet from academia to corporate America
- Study the history of Napster and debate file sharing and other challenges to intellectual property right law
- Study the history of Napster and debate file sharing and other challenges to intellectual property right law

10. Experience as Education

The last webzines issue is an opportunity for students to reflect on their experiences with the writing curriculum, how the year's experience differed from that of other school years, and what they thought they learned that would be useful to them in the future. In this project, students compare and contrast various educational initiatives like Roger Schank's "learn by doing" approach or the "back-to-basics" movement with traditional approaches to schooling.

11. Externship

In the final project "Designers for Hire," students take their newly acquired programming and writing skills into the larger community by offering to design Web sites and write copy for local businesses or not-for-profit organizations. In this externship, students also are responsible for managing the relationship with the "client," analyzing client needs, developing and presenting a proposal, organizing a project plan, and completing the project on time.

Eighth Grade Year in Writing and Web Application Development

The curriculum for the eighth grade followed that of the twelfth grade very closely. This was intentional since we did not have additional funds to deploy a separate development team. The year began with the same HTML curriculum used in twelfth grade. The eighth grade spent the mornings working on the HTML tasks and the afternoons working on the webzine projects. Once the HTML curriculum was completed, students were to move on to the Java curriculum borrowed from the senior computer science curriculum. However, due to lack of funding this segment of the curriculum could never be implemented. Therefore, students ended up working on the webzine projects for the full day.

Like the senior writing curriculum, eighth grade students produce six issues of the online magazine during the school year. In addition to writing content and programming the site, students participate in public debates on the issues raised in each issue of the webzine.

Students begin the school year by analyzing existing sites and developing guidelines for producing their webzine. For the dry-run issue, they will write articles related to their summer reading assignments.

In this project, students:

- learn to how to write clear thesis statements
- practice summarizing information
- become proficient in online research databases
- organize information to support a story's main idea
- analyze the structure of two key genres: reviews and columns
- relate literary themes to personal experience and/or current events
- learn how to quote sources

The second project, "The Clothing of the American Teen," focuses on topics related to self-image. This topic was chosen specifically for the eighth grade and was not part of the twelfth grade webzine curriculum. Students write two articles for this issue, which will build on the original design. This six-week project involves extensive research and analysis of the subject, concluding in a debate about school uniforms.

In this project, students:

- evaluate the pros and cons of school uniforms

- review current legislation about dress codes in schools
- analyze portrayals of teenagers in the media
- explore the effects of media portrayals on teenagers' self-image
- investigate the mechanisms by which something becomes "cool"
- explore the nature of social groups and gender norms in middle school
- profile unconventional individuals

The third project, "Big Cuba & Little Havana," examines the Cuban Revolution and its effects on life in the United States. Students also consider our multicultural society and the way that individuals and communities preserve cultural identity while adapting to mainstream American culture. Students read a variety of fiction and nonfiction books in preparation for researching this topic. They also choose a topic for the debate that coincides with the launch of this issue.

In this project, students:

- study the history of Cuba and its relations with the U.S.
- critically evaluate the Cuban Revolution
- compare the political philosophies in Cuba and in the U.S.
- examine the ways that the Cuban diaspora has preserved its cultural identity and ways that it has developed a new Cuban–American identity
- research demographics and analyze census data
- acquire knowledge of basic statistics and use algorithms to calculate data sets
- practice interviewing techniques in preparation for writing on oral histories
- conduct surveys and tabulate the results

Following is a multifaceted project on the environment, "Nurturing Nature," which directs students to examine the dynamic between conservationists and developers in regions like the Florida Everglades. Students explore the problem of invasive species in natural environments and they debate a current issue in environmental policy.

In this project, students:

- analyze how suburban sprawl is encroaching on our national parks
- track the impact of invasive species like the snakehead fish
- synthesize secondary sources to write a balanced piece on a key environmental issue (e.g., water safety, biodiversity, global warming, etc.)
- collect original data on restoration of the Florida Everglades

- profile spokespersons for both sides of the preservationist vs. development debate
- explore local environmental issues through a series of field trips to hot spots in their area

The last two webzines deal with intellectual property rights ("Intellectual Property Wrongs") and education issues ("Experience in Education"). Again, students will do in-depth research on each topic, write thought-provoking articles and commentary, and debate a key issue in these areas.

In these projects, students:

- research laws regarding copyright and intellectual property rights
- compare U.S. laws vs. those in other countries (e.g., United States' position on freedom of speech vs. French and German restrictions on access to hate speech and extremist propaganda)
- learn about spy software and explore the technology of online surveillance
- trace the history of the Internet from academia to corporate America
- study the history of Napster and debate file sharing and other challenges to intellectual property right law
- compare and contrast various educational initiatives like Roger Schank's "learn by doing" approach or the "back-to-basics" movement
- research cognitive science and learn more about the human brain's functioning

At the end of the year, students produce their own individual webzines. In the final project, "My Own Private Webzine," they take their newly acquired programming and writing skills and design their own homepage and content.

Students:

- manage the building of their own websites
- schedule development to meet a timeline
- build the site and development content

Building the Curriculum

In late May and early June, 2002, we began the process of brainstorming what the writing curriculum would look like, and assembling a team of developers. We were fortunate to be able to re-assemble the core part of the team that had developed the writing courses for Columbia University. These three individuals not only had worked together before, but also deeply understood our approach and what materials needed to be produced to make it work. As an added bonus, all three had previous experience teaching at the K–12 level so were able to much more easily make the shift from developing college-level courses to eighth and twelfth grade courses.

Through our partnership with University of Chicago, we were able to add an experienced writing educator, Judith Stein, to our team. With Stein's input, we were able to capitalize on the collective experience that the University of Chicago writing program had on the process of teaching writing. Stein participated in numerous conference calls and meetings with the team as the curriculum was developed.

In July 2002, we had a meeting with the teachers and development teams at Grandview Prepatory School in Boca Raton, FL. This meeting was critical because it allowed us to fold the eighth and twelfth grade teachers who would be delivering the curriculum into the development team. These teachers contributed greatly to the team by, among other things, researching and recommending the books that students would read for each magazine issue, and reviewing the curriculum based on their knowledge of the skills and interests of the students that would be in the fall classes. For example, the idea of a doing an issue on cars and transportation arose out of discussions with the teachers about what kinds of topics the students were interested in.

One early issue the development team faced was what to do about the summer reading assignments the students had been given at the end of the previous school year. Our initial plans for the curriculum did not include any reference to summer readings, and the teachers on our team raised a concern about how the students would react if nothing were done to follow up on the reading assignments. One option discussed was simply holding a traditional discussion of summer reading separate from the rest of the Web magazine curriculum. This was ultimately dismissed, because it was thought that having a separate assignment would just add to the confusion at the beginning of the webzine projects and prevent the students from getting off to a good start. The compromise solution that was finally arrived at was to add a summer reading issue as the first project in the webzine curriculum. This would allow students to feel that their readings were not neglected, and give them a chance to warm up to a more full-blown issue of the magazine in the second project. Had it not been for this issue of what to do about the students' summer reading, we would not have included that as the first project in the curriculum.

The first thing the team did was to adapt the existing HTML course to fit into the webzine story. The team kept the core learning objectives of each task, but replaced the story surrounding those tasks to be one consistent with designing some simple pages that would eventually be part of the webzine students were to create. Having these tasks in place early would also help by giving the development team extra time to complete the webzine projects while the students worked through the HTML tasks.

To build the eighth grade curriculum from the work we did on the twelfth grade curriculum, we started the full development team working on just the twelfth grade curriculum. After a month, we selected one member of the team to be in charge of the eighth grade curriculum. His job was to "follow behind" the twelfth grade team and work with the eighth grade teacher to adapt the twelfth grade curriculum to make it appropriate for eighth graders. This involved changing some of the topics that students would write webzines about, simplifying some of the required workshops, eliminating some intermediate deliverables students were required to produce along the way, and replacing the book selections with titles appropriate for eighth grade readers.

The team worked from June through October (when the funding ran out), and was able to produce eight tasks in the HTML curriculum and half of the ten webzine projects for the twelfth grade. For the eighth grade, the same HTML tasks were used, and five of the ten webzine projects were completed.

The Curriculum in Practice

To help insure that things got off to a good start, we arranged to have a member of the development team be onsite at various times during the beginning of the school year. This would allow them to help the teacher get up to speed on this just-produced curriculum, to help the teacher get the classroom and kids organized, and to troubleshoot any omissions or problems in the curriculum materials.

The start of the year was both very rewarding and very frustrating due to a number of issues that had to be ironed out. The eighth grade class got off to such a great start, that by the fourth day of class the students refused to go to lunch because they were so caught up in what they were doing. When they were made to go to lunch, they snuck back in the classroom and went back to work and skipped recess!

This was a terrific validation of everything we had been working for in building the curriculum. A big part of the success of the eighth grade was the enthusiasm and commitment of the two teachers, Judy and Rob. They jumped into the new curriculum with both feet, and not only embraced it but picked it up and ran with it on their own, extending and adapting it to fit the needs of their students.

Unfortunately, along with the good came a number of challenges. Unlike the enthusiasm of the eighth graders who skipped recess to keep working on their webzine, the twelfth grade students got off to a very different start. We discovered dramatic differences in the skills and attitudes of the teachers between eighth and twelfth grades. In addition, based on early observations of and feedback from students, we made some changes to the curriculum and to the organization of the Web site. There were also numerous issues related to the computer and network technology at the school, as well as the physical classroom layout. I discuss each of these issues in turn.

Perhaps the biggest obstacle we faced in the twelfth grade was an entrenched culture in the school of seniors not having to work hard, if at all. This was a carryover from the curriculum and practices of previous years where seniors spent at most a half a day in classes. One of our team members, on observing the class during the first weeks of school, commented that the students "will do everything they can not to work" and "have the sense that they'll graduate no matter what." In addition to having to combat this deeply ingrained belief that they were not required to do any work, we also had to deal with students adjusting to a curriculum that asked students to work productively in teams and asked them to shoulder a much greater share of the responsibility for organizing their own work. While some of the students rose to challenge and truly flourished in this new environment, others saw the decreased structure as an invitation to goof off, listen to MP3s on their laptops, or gossip with their friends.

Compounding the problems we faced with the attitudes of the seniors were the poor skills and attitude of their teacher. Originally a Spanish and Psychology teacher, she lacked skills in writing to really teach the core content of the curriculum. Her reviews of the students' writing were not sufficient to help them improve their skills. In addition, she lacked the organizational and process skills needed to manage a project-oriented curriculum and support students in organizing their own work effectively. For example, during one visit to the classroom, a team member suggested that one way to help students get more organized would be to post a project timeline on the wall. This idea came as a big revelation to her. Beyond just lack of skills, the teacher also lacked the enthusiasm and commitment shown by the eighth grade teachers. She preferred to sit at her desk and work on her laptop rather than circulate among the student teams and coach them on their project work.

The team members who visited the classrooms during the early weeks of the school year came back with some important insights that prompted some changes to the curriculum and to the design of the Web site. One early change to the curriculum was adding a final task in the HTML curriculum. We discovered that because the teachers were not very experienced in HTML, they were not able to give the students adequate feedback and comments on the HTML code they were writing. As a result, mistakes were going uncorrected and a number of the learning objectives from the earlier tasks were not being met. We decided that we would add an eighth task to the HTML portion of the curriculum that would require the students to conduct a thorough code review—something that professional programmers often due to insure the quality of their code. To do this, students were required to check that their HTML would work in a number of different browsers

(Internet Explorer, Netscape, and others) and on different platforms (Windows, MacOS). They were also asked to use automated HTML checking tools available on the Web. This new task helped students uncover and correct problems in their HTML code that had gone unnoticed before.

We also observed that the students did not find the cover story of working for the fictitious Grandview Press to be that motivating, and that the organization of the Web site was not doing enough to help them organize their work. It turned out that once the curriculum got underway, doing the real project work to publish their webzine was more compelling to the students than the back story about Grandview Press. In a sense, the students very quickly adopted the webzine publishing story as their own—they considered it to be "their" webzine—and didn't need the fiction of working for an imaginary publisher.

In addition, we saw that the students needed more structure to help them organize their work, and this was reinforced by comments from the teachers. The Web site as originally designed introduced students to their project via an email from their "publisher." Project plans were included, but were buried further inside the Web site and were not "front and center" as it appeared they needed to be. This, combined with the feedback about the lower importance of the Grandview Press back story, inspired us to reorganize the way each project was presented on the Web site and to add detailed week by week project plans. Instead of leading with an email, each project got a new "home page" with a more functional layout that provided a high level overview and direct pointers to the new weekly project plans.

We also faced numerous technology related issues that slowed down the initial momentum of getting the students and teachers going with the new curriculum. The most serious of these was how long it took to get every student a laptop. Even though all students were notified prior to the beginning of school that they were to bring in a laptop, many had not yet purchased one. The school administration also had to scramble to deal with the issue of how students who could not afford to purchase a laptop would get one. The school finally decided to purchase laptops for these students. But the delay in resolving this issue, and in getting the "stragglers" to get laptops, cost us valuable momentum in the early days of the school year.

As if procuring laptops was not enough of a problem, getting the laptops connected to the Internet so that the students could access our curriculum Web site proved to be an even thornier endeavor. The school had just decided to move toward a wireless network solution from their existing wired one. That meant that in addition to buying a laptop, all students needed to acquire a wireless network card that could work with the school's network. Students would come in day after day asserting that their parents had in fact ordered the cards and that they were "in the mail." When the cards did arrive, many were not compatible with the school's network (despite specific instructions about which card to buy). As a stopgap, we suggested that these

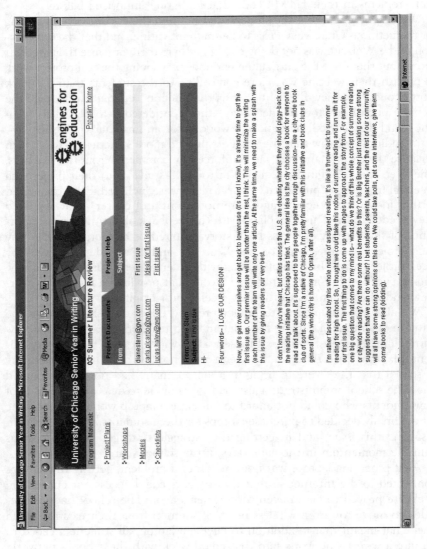

FIG. 15.1   Original Layout Showing Email Introducing Project.

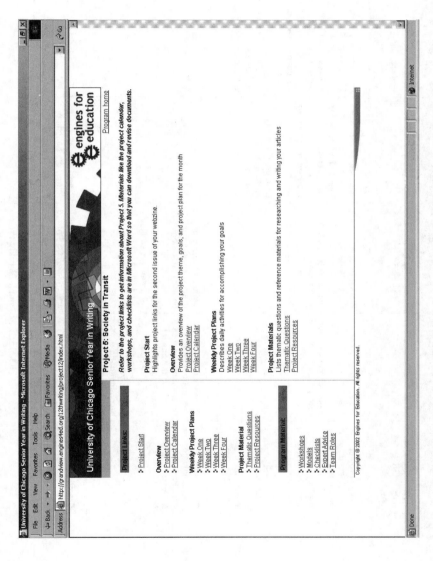

FIG. 15.2 New Layout Showing Functional Organization Highlighting Project Plans.

	September 9	September 10	September 11	September 12	September 13
AM	HTML Task 4 Cascading Style Sheets	HTML Task 5 Lists and Tables	HTML Task 5 Lists and Tables	HTML Task 5 Lists and Tables	HTML Task 6 Frames
PM Content	Create Project 3 file folders on your hard drive (include folders for core reading, workshops, and your article) Core reading discussion: Text 1 Workshop 1: Brainstorming	Workshop 2: Genre Analysis Research the topic for your article	Workshop 3: Content/Audience Research the topic for your article Core reading discussion: Text 2	Workshop 4: Sources Research the topic for your article Work on pitch for your article Hold project status meeting about the webzine	Core Reading Discussion: Text 3 Workshop 5: Pitch Session Set up interviews with sources Email questions and/or comments to gv-12thwriting@engines4ed.org
PM Design	Create an additional folder in your Project 3 file folder for design issues	Review webzine design from Project 2; recommend changes based on the project theme (e.g., color palette, font size, etc.) Discuss your recommendations with the managing editors	Write up a report of yesterday's site design and style decisions Send your report to the programmers so they can build a basic site framework and create a CSS		
PM Programming	Create an additional folder in for design issues		Create site framework and the new CSS based on the report	Create basic framework based on website proposal	

FIG. 15.3. Example Weekly Project Plan.

256

students simply plug into the old wired network. Incredibly, we found that although all the network jacks were still there, they had been disconnected because of the school's shift to a wireless network!

Finally, the school purchased a large supply of network cards, and students took their computers down to the support desk at the school to have a card installed and configured on their computer. The school charged each parent's account for the wireless card instead of waiting for parents to purchase one on their own. This (seemingly obvious) solution finally ended the network connectivity issue. Or so it seemed.

To further aggravate the situation, the school's connection to the Internet went down for several days. So while the student laptops could connect to the local area network, no one in the school could access the Internet (and hence, our curriculum Web site). The school's Internet service provider had just gone out of business and the school had to scramble to line up a new provider. In the meantime, we were reduced to having to print out copies of the Web pages and fax them to the teachers, who then made copies and distributed them to the students. Welcome to the twenty-first century!

Parent Reactions to the Curriculum

The parents reaction to the curriculum was most concretely demonstrated during a series of "parent's nights" at the school and was similar in many ways to that of the fifth grade parents. Some parents of eighth graders were concerned about how their children would be ready for high school without doing algebra. Others worried what would happen to their children should they ever transfer to a different school with a more traditional curriculum— they were afraid their children would "be behind." It seemed at times that these parents were more worried about comparing their child to peers than they were about the learning and motivation of their own child.

However, many eighth grade parents had seen how excited their children were about the webzine curriculum and couldn't wait for an opportunity to come in and learn about it first hand. When they walked into the eighth grade classroom, they saw it organized into three work tables—one for each team. Each of the teams had decorated their work area with pictures of their favorite movie, music, and TV stars cut out from magazines. Some had put up colorful Christmas lights or flowers. It was immediately visible that the students felt a tremendous amount of ownership in and enthusiasm for the curriculum they were engaged in.

One parent found this quite frightening, however. His child had been the seventh grade star because she studied hard to pass tests, but she had no social skills. As a result, the eighth grade seeming disorder in the classroom isolated her and made her acutely aware that her school skills didn't work in

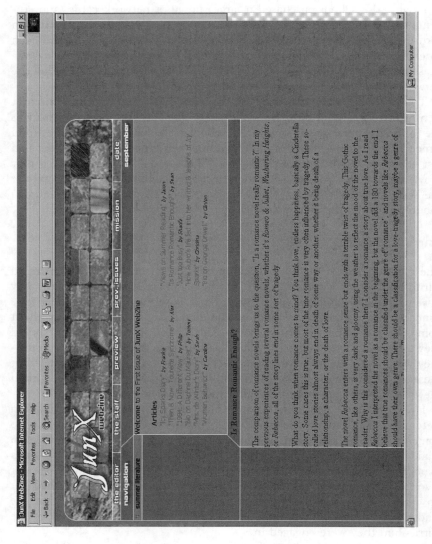

FIG. 15.4 Sample Screen From the Twelfth Grade Webzine.

this new world. Her parents withdrew her from the school and sued the school (and me.)

The twelfth grade parents were extremely apathetic—very few showed up for parent's night. It was an indication of where the seniors' attitudes may have come from. One set of parents was anything but apathetic, however. They came in to parent's night to thank us for the dramatic turnaround they saw in their son. Prior to this year, he was not very engaged in school, and was not doing that well. This year, his parents reported that he was, for the first time in a long time, excited about coming to school to work on the webzine curriculum. This student was an extremely talented graphic artist, and in fact had run his own business designing websites for local companies. He had taken on the role of designer for the senior webzine and had emerged into a leadership role in the class. He became the focal point because everyone had to send their materials to him to get posted into the webzine, or to implement suggestions or ideas they had to improve the webzine's design. His graphic design skills allowed him really shine in the eyes of his peers and due to his abilities, the seniors were able to produce an extremely professional looking webzine.

A Study in Contrasts

Despite the fact that the eighth and twelfth grade curricula were almost identical, the story of their delivery in the classroom could not be more different. The differences were due to the triangle of teachers, students, and parents. In the twelfth grade, the teacher was not right for the job, and didn't exercise the leadership necessary to make the curriculum work. The seniors were not at all motivated to do any schoolwork, a sentiment that was not necessarily contradicted by some of their parents. The result was a relatively uninspired implementation of an otherwise exciting and innovative curriculum.

Yet, working from essentially the same curriculum, the 8th grade was a roaring success. The teachers were engaged and motivated, understood what it would take to make the curriculum work, and really owned the curriculum from day one. The students were a much more motivated group, as evidenced by their attempt to skip both lunch and recess the first week of school. Finally, their parents, while perhaps less enthusiastic than the teachers or students, picked up on the excitement and learning that was taking place in the classroom, and for the most part were supportive of the new curriculum.

As with the fifth graders, the eighth grade test scores were way up at the end of the year. Isn't irony grand?

REFERENCE NOTES

These curricula were built by Engines for Education, a nonprofit that I set up. They can be viewed at www.engines4ed.org.

16

Redesigning the Curriculum

We have read what the great minds have said about education. Collectively, they all believe in the key role that experience plays in learning and tend to agree that schools have it wrong. Most of the people I have cited were philosophers not educational theorists. They were simply observing that education seems to bear little relation to what they have observed the learning needs of children to be.

Why does school, in its current form, fail to be effective, exciting, or even interesting most of the time? The answer, simply, is that most schooling fails to relate to the actual goals of children or the needs of the society in which they will eventually function as adults. There is an old adage about leading a horse to water—but not being able to make him drink. A better way of putting this might have been to say that you can't make him thirsty. In fact, in school we do make him drink. That is what all the testing is about. We can make him learn the Pythagorean Theorem, we just can't make him care about it. If what you learn in no way relates to a goal you have you cannot possibly remember what you have learned nor would it matter if you did. New information has to be useful in some real way to the person who has acquired it or it will be forgotten. That information will not be used unless a goal to which it relates drives that use. To put this another way, if you don't want to know something because there is an activity you are going to pursue that requires that knowledge you will not remember what you learned. School typically ignores this principle of inherent use.

Every aspect of human behavior involves the pursuit of goals. Sometimes these goals are rather simple, like brushing your teeth to prevent decay. Sometimes they are quite unconscious, like having your mind search for similar experiences when you encounter some new experience. And, sometimes they are quite complex, like trying to build high quality educational software as a means to effect change in the school system.

When goals are simple, we really don't think about them much. When they are unconscious we don't think about them at all. And, when they are complex, we may think about them, but find the going so rough that we hone in on the simplest ones and lose the forest for the trees.

Why would anyone learn anything if not to help in the pursuit of a goal? Why would anyone try to understand anything if not because they had the goal of learning new information from what they were trying to understand? The desire to change one's knowledge base, to comprehend what is going on about you, and to learn from experience, are all pretty much different ways of saying the same thing. And, all of these are goal-directed activities.

NATURAL LEARNING

If goals are at the base of the human thought process, then it follows that learning must be a goal-dominated arena as well. This is certainly true of the learning processes of small children, who are quite goal-oriented. One-year-olds want to learn to walk because there are places they want to go or because others around them also walk. Their learning to walk follows the goal of walking (which may well be in service of some other goal). Similarly, a two-year-old learns to speak a language because he wants to communicate. Four-year-olds can find any room in their home and they know the neighborhood in which they live; in general, they understand and can plan in their own environment because these plans are in the service of goals the child has.

Children have natural learning mechanisms, ways in which they progress from babies with innate abilities and no actual knowledge to children with a great deal of knowledge about the physical, social, and mental worlds in which they live. And, these mechanisms, like the understanding mechanisms of adults, are goal-dominated.

Small children do not have motivation problems. They are excited by learning, eager to try new things, and are in no way self-conscious about failure (though perhaps no less surprised by it). In short, they are perfect examples of goal-based learners. Consequently, we never see a two-year-old who is depressed about how his talking progress is going and so has decided to quit trying to improve, or a two-year-old who has decided that learning to walk was too difficult and thus has decided only to crawl.

The natural learning mechanism that children employ is not very much more sophisticated than trial and error. Children learn by experimentation, by failing, and by being told or copying some new behavior that has better results. Inherent in this model is the idea that children are trying to learn to do something, rather than to know something. Failure is not frustrating in this context; in a deep sense, learning, until age six, depends mostly on failure.

But somewhere around age six, all this changes. Children try to avoid having to learn. They fear failure. Their educational goals are no longer in pursuit of some personally motivating goal. Instead, they work to please authority, or they do less work. Furthermore, the instruction they receive is more like 30-on-one than one-on-one, which includes tremendous social difficulties inherent to peer group dynamics. What has happened to cause all this? The six-year-old has started school.

The goals that are the basis of understanding and of learning ought to be the basis of schooling as well, but they are not. In school, natural learning goals are replaced by artificial ones. Instead of trying to learn something because one wants to be able to do something (like get places, communicate, or use objects) children learn in order to please the teacher (in order to avoid ridicule, get good grades, or get into a good college). In other words, natural learning goals that have to do with increasing understanding or increasing one's power to operate successfully in various endeavors get replaced by artificial learning goals that have to do with acceptance, approval, and socialization. It is simply a matter of intrinsic versus extrinsic motivation.

Learning in school rarely looks like learning in the real world. While learners in the real world struggle to learn to achieve their goals, learners in school struggle to learn material their teachers and school administrators insist they must know to achieve the goals of getting good grades and credit for courses and degrees.

Do schools have the right to set learning goals for children? Of course they do. But these goals must be set in a way that fits with the natural goals of the child. These goals should be ones set by the needs of the society in which the child lives, rather than by the needs of ancient concepts of the educated mind.

Redesigning School

School offerings need to be created within a context that enables students to pursue their own interests for as long as they want to, without disallowing the possibility of switching interests at any time. Of course, it is the job of the school to try to expand the child's interests at any point. This does not mean telling him what he has to be interested in. Rather, the idea is to offer enough situations that a child can find his own level and his own place.

Any curriculum must be based on an understanding of how any given academic materials pertain to a child's specific interests and how such materials might convey general issues independent of a specific context. Once a student selects an interest, then accomplishable goals, in terms of visible projects, should be pursued. Much of the kind of knowledge now taught explicitly in school will be taught implicitly, within the context of helping the student achieve the goals of the course he has selected for himself. In other words, if arithmetic matters then it ought to matter within a context where it is needed. When that context has been selected by the student (e.g., running the student store), the reason to learn arithmetic becomes much clearer. Teaching will occur as the student discovers his own need to know to accomplish whatever his current task is, and in order to serve his higher-level goals.

A key factor in education is motivation. To the extent that a student feels he has selected for himself what he is going to learn, he can be expected to feel empowered by that selection and be more self-directed about learning. It is important that a student select courses and curricula based on his own interests. The particular student's subject matter choices are really irrelevant from an educational design point of view; if we want to teach reading for instance it hardly matters what material is being read. But the more interesting the material is to the student, the more likely he is to want to read it. Similarly, in business, it really doesn't matter what industry a student chooses to study when he learns to deal with accounting issues within that industry. What does matter is that whatever a student studies must be grounded in some context. As much as possible, students should be using real cases and real situations, and should avoid abstractions. It is important to appreciate the lesson of case-based teaching: real stories, real contexts, told by real people, at the right time. The more the situations being studied relate to the student's area of interest, the more likely it is that the student will want to know more.

For many years, we have build computer simulations for education in the form of Goal-based scenarios (GBSs). GBSs allow students to pursue well-defined goals and encourage the learning of both skills and cases in service of achieving those goals. Goal-based scenarios may be quite artificial in the sense that they may ask students to do something they would never do in real life as a way of getting them to understand something. It helps if the scenario is something that someone actually does however. For example, we built a program to teach history by asking a student to play the role of the President of the United States at a particular period and presenting him with decisions that need to be made. Accomplishing this goal caused the student to need to know certain cases, learn certain skills, and understand certain processes. The idea is that while the student is unlikely to end up in the Oval Office, he will find use for the reasoning, decision making, and other skills he learns and practices in this GBS, and it is fun. We extended this idea in a course we built for Columbia University in Economics where the student plays the role of an economics advisor to the president. The student helps to decide national economic policy, goes on (simulated) television to defend that policy, meets with advisors to make compromises, and so on. We have built more than a hundred programs of this sort. Students find them engaging and we have used them as pieces of courses and to replace entire courses. But, as I have said, I am not sure courses ought to be the building blocks of education.

For a course to be effective, students should know what the goal of the course is, and the designer should construct a GBS that causes the student to accomplish that goal. As long as the goal is of inherent interest to a student, and the skills needed in any attempt to accomplish the goal are those the course designer wants students to have, we have a workable goal-based scenario. That may lead to an interesting course, but what does an interesting course lead to? Students who find themselves taking five courses in parallel have a disjointed school experience that in no way corresponds to what real life is like. In real life we have sequential experiences, not parallel courses. School needs to provide experiences that are germane to student's future life. This entails elimination of the parallel courses idea.

Learning to communicate, function with others, and reason are the most important parts of learning experience. It is really not possible to teach these subjects directly. A course in reasoning that emphasized some arbitrary "principles of reasoning" would not accomplish much. But, nearly every real life situation involves reasoning. Having students reason in a situation is very important. The subject matter or domain of the situation is less important. Thus any goal-based scenario constructed to teach various skills must, first and foremost, teach communication, human relations, and reasoning.

But in many ways, it doesn't matter what subjects are taught. What matters is that certain skills are practiced within a context that is motivating to the students. It is very difficult to learn about things that you don't feel you need to know and that have no real excitement for you. A school's job is to make exciting contexts to learn in. By this I do not mean a classroom, but, as an example, a hospital (chap. 19) or a construction site or a day care center. Learning must take place in a context, within a set of goals to be accomplished. Much of school probably shouldn't take place in a school at all. For children to learn about the real world they need to be in the real world. This means finding roles for them in the work place and then letting them discuss and learn from those roles in the school. The students must have selected those roles and not have had them thrust on them. Choice is therefore a key idea here. Students must have many contexts from which to select.

There are two kinds of GBSs, natural and artificial. A natural GBS is something like learning to drive a truck. While there are many ways to teach this skill, they don't vary all that much. Alternately, in an artificial GBS, one constructs a fictional goal and uses it to package a skill set. In an artificial GBS, the skill set drives the design of the GBS, as opposed to having the

GBS drive the design of the skill set. (But, we need to be aware of knowing what it is a student ought to know. Business trainers and school administrators alike often feel they know what their students need to know. Further analysis indicates that they are often quite mistaken.) Simply put, if a student wants to accomplish a goal, there are skills he will need to learn. And if there are specific skills we want to teach, the designer of the GBS must create a goal that packages those particular skills.

A curriculum can consist of either natural or artificial GBSs. It follows however, that since we often want to teach a set of skills related to a non-naturally occurring goal (because the goal is sometimes just a design for motivating the learning), creating an artificial GBS is necessary most of the time. This would be true both in school (where designing a rocket ship that could get to Mars and then simulating actually flying it there might be a great way to teach physics), and in industry (where designing a course that taught proposal writing might be a valuable way of packaging skills but might not be the job for which any one person was being trained).

The key idea here is to embed instruction in such a way that it occurs at the point where the student has developed the need to know what will be taught. When students want to know something to help them in a task, they will be determined to learn what they need to know if their motivation to accomplish the task is strong enough in the first place.

In short, we would want to teach skill sets that are normally packaged under titles such as design, politics, physics, economics, math, reading, history, geography, or biology. Remember that we want to teach the skills needed within these subjects, not the subjects themselves. In traditional school settings, biologists teach biology and historians teach history. These teachers are concerned with their subject and protective of the field of inquiry to which they belong. They cannot help, therefore, to attempt to create little biologists or little historians, when their real goal should be the creation of people who can think clearly in a given context. All of these are worthy contexts within which on can learn, but the skills that are taught within these contexts need to be re-examined.

In school, curricula ought to correspond to the interests of children of different ages. As a start, and merely as point of departure for discussion, I propose the following potential curricula based on my own perception of some of the interests of six-year-old children. It is my contention that any of these curricula could be made to encompass a variety of goal-based scenarios, covering skills encompassed by the subjects and the three processes named described previously. Here are some of my favorites contexts for six-year-olds: dolls, pets, travel, vehicles, food, dinosaurs, sports, music, houses, and clothing. Any of these can teach all of the above (and more academic) subject areas. Many other curricula could be devised that would do the same. The issue is finding out what children really want to know about, and using those natural interests as a springboard to teach reasoning skills, engage in processes, and kindle new interests.

Goal based scenarios can be constructed by examining all the skills deemed important and putting them into some natural situation around which a scenario can be constructed. There is no one right format for a GBS. The scenarios can take as long as the instructors want them to, from a day to a year. They can be built into software, or partially instructor-led, or completely paper-based. Case libraries, used to tell stories about previous encounters in a given context, can come in the form of real live experts or video recordings, in electronic media or in paper format. Human experts ought to be available for the teaching of processes on an as-needed basis. The point is that skills ought to be taught by the most appropriate method, and that determination depends on the particular skills. Learning occurs when students want to know. It is the job of the instructional designer (and the teacher) to do what they can to cause students to care about knowing something.

The intent of a goal based scenario is to provide motivation, a sense of accomplishment, a support system, and a focus on skills rather than facts. Facts can be deceptive, they give the sense of knowing without the significance of knowing. Understanding why you are doing something, having a clear goal that is more than the recitation of facts, truly knowing why and wanting to know more so that one can become curious about more "whys" is what education is all about. Goal based scenarios, interrupted by good telling of important cases, offer a reasonable framework for courses that are meant to be the means of education. To put this another way: expectation failure plus storytelling allows for reminding, explanation, and the subsequent reorganization of a dynamic memory. School needs to provide sets of skills that students can learn that would be ones they would use regularly in real life. Some of those skills students know that they need. They may need to be convinced that they need others. This means that the current curriculum is almost entirely without real value.

We must ask ourselves what skills are important and then construct contexts in which those skills might be exercised. The subjects don't matter. Providing students an opportunity to practice various skills in simulations of real world situations where those skills are employed is the cornerstone of a good educational system.

The Skills

So what is it that intelligent humans know, that constitutes the basis of the educated mind? The educated mind should be characterized not by what it knows but what it can do, this much is clear. But, what is it that the educated mind can do? Here are some key mental skills:

- An educated mind can use its memory and experience to come to reasonable generalizations.

Children need memory structures. It isn't that they need to know where China is and what it produces. They need to know how to travel, how to deal with people different than themselves, how to order food in a Chinese restaurant, and how to understand and help create foreign policy. People acquire memory structures about such issues simply by living and functioning in the world. They can't help but learn from their experiences. This leaves two questions for educators. First, what kinds of experiences do children not naturally have that it would valuable for them to have from the point of view of what we hope they will learn? How do we create such experiences? Second, what experiences do they naturally have that they do not fully comprehend or effectively reflect on, that they would learn better from if there was teaching available? How do we enhance experiences that they already have by allowing them to reflect, communicate, and generalize about their experiences? Schooling must be designed around precisely these questions.

The ability to form generalizations that serve as hypotheses for future experiences is the basis of all human learning. So, our first key skill is generalization. The purpose of that skill is to build memory structures that are rich in both experience and hypotheses.

- An educated mind can determine connections between events.

When children experience an event they may not understand how it is related to some other experience they might have had or others might have had before them. Good teaching helps students make connections between their own lives and the lives of others, and between events currently being processed and those they have previously processed.

The key issue is making sure that are events to connect. School must provide a set of experiences and must allow for the connections to be made. This means that in addition to creating contexts in which significant experiences can be had, time must be allowed for reflection on those experiences and attempts must be made to communicate those experiences to others. Thus, any good curriculum would entail having goals that students pursue followed by writing and speaking about the experiences. Learning what causes what, and how to reason about possible causes and effects of actions is a key issue in education. Experiences need to be mediated by a teacher whose job it is to cajole the student into re-examining his assumptions and seeing his experiences with a new perspective.

- An educated mind can use principles that enable seeing one event as being the "same as" another.

To understand the world we must be able to predict what will happen next with some accuracy. To form effective predictions, we must learn how events taking place in different places at different times can be seen as the same. This is simple enough for recognizing that when we enter a restaurant, it is indeed a restaurant and thus we can expect a set of events to take place that happen in restaurants. But it is much harder to recognize "imperialism" when we see it. Good teaching helps students appreciate similarity across contexts. Thus, a problem in the hospital curriculum can be seen as same as a problem that occurred in the Web magazine curriculum. Power struggles and interpersonal issues for example, transcend any given context. These must also be seen as the province of the curriculum.

- An educated mind can predict the outcome of various courses of action by use of evidence gleaned from similar situations.

One very important problem for education and for the creation of educated minds is prediction. Explicitly teaching predictive skills enables students to learn to become good decision makers. We cannot learn to predict without some real experience, the job of the curriculum is to provide that experience. The job of the teacher is to ask for predications and help students reconcile what happened with what was expected.

Children need to do things, and to learn to think about what they did and why it worked out the way it did. To do this well, they must have experience planning in a complex environment, and reflecting on the complexities of achieving their goals. This requires careful attention on the part of the teacher to making sure the goals children are trying to achieve are ones they are truly interested in achieving.

- An educated mind can deal with abstractions.

Underlying all of the above is the process of abstraction. One cannot generalize without abstracting common elements from different events. One cannot recognize the applicability of a plan without generalizing between situations. Abstraction is the highest form of thinking, but we cannot teach it directly. Rather, students needs to reflect on commonalities, to discuss abstractions they see or hypothesize. Here again, this depends on real world experiences and real world goals that drive those experiences.

- An educated mind is self-aware.

One of the key real world experiences we can examine is our own thinking process This is very hard to learn to do, and indeed most people are quite bad at it. We often don't know why we do what we do, and we fail to understand what we want and what we should do to get what we want. Self-reflection must be the stuff of schooling because it is so important to all the other processes mentioned above and is part of becoming a healthy person.

- An educated mind will learn from expectation failure.

When our experiences fail to predict future behavior correctly we need to know what has gone wrong. Quite often we resort to the idea that someone else has made a mistake and we can simply ignore what has gone awry. Children need to understand that their preconceptions can be wrong and that they must be constantly vigilant to avoid assuming that the memory structures they have are the same ones everyone else has. We can only change our own conceptions when we are prepared to admit they were in error. Since expectations fail all the time and it is this failure that gives rise to learning, a good curriculum will cause expectations to fail. A good teacher will encourage students to reflect on those failures.

- An educated mind can handle exceptions.

Seeing exceptions as things worthy of interest is what separates the curious from the self-satisfied. We need to account for exceptions. Indeed we need to revel in them. Appreciating differences and explaining them is part of what intellectual growth is all about. Indeed good science education depends on this. Too often we try to teach students the facts in science when what they should be dwelling on is the open problems in science. It is what is confusing to scientists that is potentially the most interesting to children. Understanding how to form a new hypothesis and seek evidence that would prove or disprove that hypothesis is the key lesson from science that is valuable in any other are of life.

- An educated mind can recover from failure.

We cannot let failure get us down. Lack of understanding can be a beautiful thing because it allows for creative thought. Students need to learn to revel in their failures. Having things not work out the way you expected is what starts the creative juices flowing. School should be about causing expectation failures and helping students to recover well. School is quite often about avoiding failure. Any really educated person is likely to have failed many times. Failure was a vital part of their education. Successful people always have interesting stories to tell about their failures. Creating situations in which it is permissible to fail is an important part of good curriculum design.

- An educated mind absorbs new cases.

Knowledge resides in cases (and in interconnected memory structures), not in facts. Students need to learn cases. The educated mind is one that has many cases in a variety of domains to draw on. It is not the cases themselves that comprise the basis of an educated mind but the ability to draw on those cases in new situations to make predications and generalizations. But one cannot do this without the cases. This is known by the old educational system which has endeavored for many years to teach cases absent of their use. The cases are important but secondary. The first issue is understanding how to learn from a case. In that context, cases can be taught but it is much better if they are experienced.

Students need to have a library of experiences to draw upon and to examine when they are looking to generalize, to predict, to abstract and to explain. We need to learn cases from our own experiences but also from the experience of others. Teaching cases is an art and one teachers need to learn to do effectively. Teachers need to be good storytellers and they need to help students become good story analyzers. A student with a large set of cases is prepared to understand the world in all its complexity.

- An educated mind seeks explanations.

All of the previously discussed processes depend on explanation. We explain the world around us all the time as we create the memory structures that contain those explanations. Teaching children to accept the explanations of others and then later to venture out and make explanations of their own is what real teaching is all about. When we stop creating new explanations, when we are self-satisfied and rely on all the old explanations we were taught or those we created for ourselves when we were young, that is when we have stopped learning. Good teaching and effective schooling depend on putting students in situations that require explanation and then letting students come up with explanations on their own. Being wrong doesn't matter as much as learning to rely on one's own thought processes. Schools stress being right. They should stress having an opinion of one's own that is founded on solid thinking.

Educated minds are made up of the skills I have just listed. It is impossible to acquire new knowledge in a useful way without having these skills. The fact that, in general, we do not teach the basic stuff of human intelligence, the stuff that allows us to acquire, absorb, and integrate knowledge, comes from the fact that the school curriculum was designed by people with little feel for how people's minds work.

There is also, of course, another set of behaviors and skills that is important in determining intelligence and knowledge acquisition that is less easy to enumerate. This set includes playfulness, interest, attention, perception, rule breaking, and individuality.

These behaviors and skills are idiosyncratic. They are critical in the acquisition of new knowledge, and it is differences in these arenas that accounts for many of the differences in human intelligence and the ability to learn. These reflect a given student's personal characteristics and their particular learning style. It is, of course, possible to enhance these capabilities to a certain extent, but one must recognize their significance first.

In short, we must teach students to absorb and analyze their experiences. We must value their observations, generalizations, and creative points of view. We need to de-emphasize the idea that there are right answers and take careful heed of the idea that any individual has his own way of seeing the world. We must come to understand that human memory has a wonderful mutable quality and a teacher's job is to help it evolve and grow.

17

K-12 Stories

WHAT SHOULD K-12 LOOK LIKE?

If schooling means participation in various GBS's, which are part of a story centered curriculum, we need to ask what the makeup of the entire school experience should look like. Before we begin, we need understand that is no one set of things that need to be taught to all students. In fact, the scenarios that I propose are not to be taught at all. They are to be lived. The goal is to give children experiences, or more accurately, to encourage them to have a variety of experiences. Ideally then, there would be hundreds of experiences to choose from and each child would participate in a many different ones, finally selecting those to concentrate on that were of the greatest interest to him or her.

We want students to have experiences so it is the school's job to enable those experiences. But, we also want students to learn to do certain things. What they learn may not be the intent of the experiences per se. Rather, they are the sorts of things that will be learned in the course of any well designed experience. Thus, we create experiences for students that take place within a story but we do this keeping in mind that there are certain abilities we want to make sure students have at the end of their schooling.

The first issue concerns what we want students to be able to do. As before, the question is not about knowing but about doing.

What are the key things that an educated mind should know how to do? Perhaps that is the question that Fadiman should have asked. In any case it is the question that we ask. The answer to this question will not only be different than we are used to, it also will be at a different level of abstraction than we are used to.

Below is a candidate set of things we want K–12 students to be able to do (they should be able to do these at any age, better as they grow older of course):

- make a scientific judgment
- use mathematics to make a decision
- use modern technical tools
- write a descriptive piece
- make a judgment based on ethical precepts
- make a sound argument
- reason about the prose and cons of a decision
- make a decision based on historical precedent
- analyze a situation and come to a conclusion
- use knowledge of the physical world to create a plan
- research something to come to a conclusion about it
- discover facts about something
- create a compromise in a situation
- plan a course of action
- set goals
- adapt to new environments
- make oral presentations
- make value judgments
- handle people
- analyze the goals of people in a situation
- deal with and take into account cultural differences
- make a moral judgment

Some of these are very similar. Differentiating between them is unimportant. They are simply loose guidelines to remind us that whatever stories we create they would be charged with covering a great deal of this territory. These are the kinds of things that educated people can do well.

As a way of making some broad generalizations, here are the key elements of any curriculum. Because we need a name for these elements, we will call them "threads." The main threads of any education must be as follows:

- communication
- human relations

- reasoning
- development of curiosity
- development of a healthy attitude
- use of available tools
- comprehension and employment of principles
- learning to plan, prioritize, and execute
- decision making
- being able to operate in the physical world

There is little disagreement among scholars who have thought about education over the centuries that each of these threads are critical to forming an educated mind. I believe that there is nothing here with which Plato, Descartes, Montaigne, Locke, Mill, or Dewey would disagree.

There are, of course, many other ways to compile such a list and other ways to look at this issue. We can consider this is a first pass at undoing the damage done by the Committee of Ten. These should be the key items in any curriculum. These are what the conferences should have been about. The 1892 Committee never thought about what educated people did on a daily basis, they simply thought about what subjects Harvard faculty explicitly taught. That was an issue of scholarship rather than education. There needs to be a reason to study algebra. One cannot simply start with the premise that it is a subject worth studying. To put this in another way, an educated mind will be able to:

- communicate clearly with others
- relate well to other people
- reason about complex issues and come to reasonable judgments
- revel in one's native curiosity and pursue courses of action based on one's own interest
- have an attitude about the world and one's relationship to the world that enables one to develop and pursue well thought out courses of action
- have a familiarity with the tools that are available in one's world and be able to know when and how to use them
- understand the principles that govern various aspects of the world and be able to operate well in the world because of that knowledge
- plan a course of action in pursuit of a goal and execute steps to implement that plan
- make personal, professional, and political decisions that use rational arguments and can make use of evidence to support an action
- understand and be able to operate in the physical nature of the world in which one lives and one's own physical make up and needs

It is within this context that we must place the curricula we have already designed for Grandview. The computer science, writing, and legal and scientific curricula are not actually about those subjects at all. Those are simply the stories that are intended to hold the students interest, forming the context that enables the students to get better over time at the threads that weave through the context. The context is also important in its own right however. Working on a magazine may well teach the skills listed previously but it also does, in fact, teach one what it is like to work on a magazine, to meet deadlines, to work as a part of a team, and to play roles, like those of editor or art director. So, the context is an experience to be had which is valuable as well.

To put this another way, there are things one must learn to do to operate effectively in this world. In addition there are experiences worth having from which one can learn. An educated mind is one that knows how to do the skills listed earlier and which has had a variety of experiences in which to practice those skills. To educate a student one must open that student to new experience and help him enhance his skills within that experience. In our first year working with Grandview, we created three stories that drove the idea of learning within a contextual experience:

the technology of an e-business
the creation of a Web magazine
the arguing of a legal case

It is within these contexts that the traditional subjects can be found as well. Bear in mind, that while these subjects can be found within these contexts, it is really not all that important that they be found there. We have developed a way of speaking about education that forces me to address that issue but I do not consider it to be an important issue at all.

So, to the question, "Where is history taught?" for example, history would appear in any number of places, in many contexts. You can't argue a legal case without finding and being able to argue from, certain relevant history. You cannot write certain magazine articles without knowing history that might pertain to the subject you are writing about. You cannot use technology in a business context without understanding some history as well.

Where is science taught? One can teach science by making sure that the magazine covers certain scientific issues. One can embed science into a legal case to make sure that science is the basis of the case. In a fictional e-business, products can depend on certain scientific issues having to do with shelf life, decay or their very creation in the first place.

In other words, it is possible to embed any traditional subject within a context that make that subject both useful and relevant to the student who is learning about it. If we must follow the standards set down by some state school board then we can do so. But, we need not teach exactly the facts and materials that will be on the tests typically in place in those subjects. Our curriculum is not intended to help students memorize facts for tests. We can cover the terrain of the traditional subject matter while keeping our eye on the threads that constitute the abilities to be found in an educated mind.

With this having been said, we can now begin to talk about what contexts might work for students of various ages and the stories that will make those contexts enjoyable and memorable.

Before we talk about possible curricula for each grade, we need to realize that we want to students to have choices. Ideally, there would be many curricula available to choose from. Also, ideally there would be no grades, simply roles to play that are age appropriate. We want students to have a variety of experiences and be able to build on those experiences as the students get older. But we also want them to be able to change paths and try different things out when they have had enough of what they are currently doing. We will not achieve this state of affairs until we have built a great deal of material.

What we are proposing here are story centered curricula for students designed on the assumption that we will be able to build them as resources allow. So, initially this can be seen as a plan for grades 6–12, because there are six of them. Ideally, there would be hundreds of them and going to school would entail participation in as many as were of interest for as long as they were of interest, allowing specialization if a student really loved a given story. Teaching in these curricula would entail mentoring the tasks in each story but it would also involve helping students move from story to story so that they could experience many different activities. Thus, the stories listed below are really just a beginning, a set of suggestions for the kind of things that can and ought to be built.

The Travel Agency Story

There is a point where children are ready to comprehend the larger world around them. At about age ten or eleven, students are ready to consider the idea of travel, politics, and the world. This readiness to consider these issues does not mean that these issues are less relevant for older students.

The eleven-year-old is old enough to become interested in the world around him. He is less childlike and more open to finding out about people and places different than what he has known. This provides a good opportunity to use this natural curiosity to provide a story that covers that terrain.

The travel agent story can be used in sixth grade but older students can work on the more complex aspects of the story, as well as a real version of the story at any time. The students would work in teams, each of which is a small fictional travel agency. Their goal is to try to make their business flourish. To do so they would need to advertise and write brochures. They would need to learn to plan trips and to sell their ideas to their customers. The customers would be teachers early on, might be real travel agencies (as they make realistic plans for real customers), and might morph into a real travel agency run by the school's older students. Students would need to learn the economics of the travel business and of business in general. They would need to understand the various means of travel and to understand why people travel. They would need to see the world themselves (in simulation or in reality if possible.) They would need to interact with people in other countries, perhaps by e-mail or phone if they can't actually go there. They would need to learn at least some of the various languages and customs of their destinations. They would need to deal with government policies, visas, and travel restrictions. They would need to comprehend the history of the places they visit and what is unique about each place. They would have to plan various specialty tours, a science tour, a castle tour or a battlefield tour for example.

The major academic subjects covered in the Travel Agency Story are: world politics, cultures, languages, writing, business, history, geography, and basic business mathematics. Other areas covered include the internet, planning, teamwork, and communications.

This story might not be equally interesting to all students of course. But aspects of it transcend the story, business, writing, and planning for example. In addition, the geopolitical issues are relevant to all. For this reason, some student participation in some aspect of this story makes good sense for everyone, at least for a small amount of time.

The Techno-Future Story

As children reach age twelve or so they begin to define themselves more by gender, and are at a stage of life where they have a tendency to withdraw because they are confronting various changes in themselves that are complicated for them to understand. There are many advantages to separating the genders at this age in school. We are proposing two stories that would be of interest to twelve-year-olds, each gender-specific. We are not suggesting that one is for girls and one is for boys by any means. However, one would expect that they might choose them for that reason.

The first story is about space travel, robots, computers, video and phone technologies, and whatever other new technologies may be available to us. The intention is to use what already exists, the Space Camp run by NASA, the Robot Camp run by CMU, a simplified version of the Columbia online physics for poets course, as well as new things we will create about phones, computers, and video. They will all be put into a coherent story about deciding future government policy on technology, making decisions about investment in research, and making laws about controversial issues (like cloning and stem cell research). The emphasis of this curriculum is on science, technology, the mathematics necessary for those things, as well as policy issues, politics, government, legal issues and the writing of arguments.

From Home to the Mall

This story is meant to help students analyze the world in which they actually live. How does their town work? How does the home they live in fit in the community? What are the economics of the community they live in? Special attention is paid to the small businesses within their community. A new mall is planned by a developer. Should the town try to stop it? How will it affect local business? How will it affect their neighborhood? After such questions have been researched and analyzed, the students will be asked to suggest a business they could start, in an existing shopping mall. They will find out what it takes to start such a business and will begin to plan it. They will compete in a simulation to make their business work better than the businesses of other students in the class. They will deal with the creation of business plans, the spending of a personal budget, and playing the role of local government to help regulate the proposed business. They will write their own daily journals about their experiences and about their feelings in dealing in this competitive situation.

The emphasis of this curriculum is on decision making and learning about their community. The history of the community and other communities would be relevant. Basic financial and economic issues as well as sociological issues are emphasized as well.

The Webzine Story

This has been discussed earlier. Students create a Web magazine. They learn to write, and do simple programming and graphics. They write about complex issues that they must learn to reason about. These issues span a range of subjects. This curriculum can be done at a variety of ages. Eight-year-olds can create a magazine as can adults. Learning to write, research, edit, and create an on time production are issues that come up in this story on a regular basis.

The World Trade Story

The role of the students in this story is to create an e-business that can function on a world wide scale. To do this they will learn about how e-businesses function and learn to build the technology needed for their business. They will need to learn about world trade, computer technology, foreign languages, basic engineering, and transportation. Students will create their own businesses. They will write business plans and modify them. They will put their businesses on the Web. They start by analyzing existing Web businesses. They first offer a service. Later they create a product. They must get the product built. They must ship the product. During this story they travel on cargo ships to learn how to transport their product and how to sell their product in foreign countries. While the Web is emphasized, it is not the only methodology employed. The main idea is to teach about technology and about world trade. Creativity is emphasized and attention is paid to coming up with a new idea and bringing that idea to fruition. Engineering and the mathematics associated with the engineering issues play a key role.

The General Contractor Story

This curriculum is meant to teach traditional academic subjects within a very clear reality. Students design and build a real building. To do so they must learn architecture, drafting, as well as the politics and local laws that govern the world in which they live. They also must learn practical science and mathematics. In the first part of the year, they work part time doing the low level chores on a real building that is already underway. This is meant to teach them practical skills like carpentry, masonry, and such. In the mean time they are learning in school about electricity, foundations, air conditioning, design, and architecture. These are learned in simulation within a story about house building. They learn the science behind these things and implement other people's designs. Eventually they learn to create their own designs. They criticize the work of others and focus on the aesthetics, practicality, economic basis, and significance of their designs.

The goal here is to teach students how to take care of themselves and their own environments, while embedding real world scientific knowledge within its practical implementation. History is taught through studying designs throughout history. Readings emphasize arts and design issues as well as basic engineering issues.

The Hospital Story

Continuing on with the idea that academic subjects are best learned within a real world context, more grown up students can spend their school year in a local hospital. The students are concerned with issues of biology, medicine, health, social problems, foreign languages, economics, and law. The students learn to work in and consult on problems in a hospital. They start out learning to help out in a real hospital. They meet real people and do menial tasks. At the same time they are learning the basics to make themselves more useful in the labs and with patients. They consult with the directors of the hospital departments on various issues in the hospital starting with simple issues like where to put the benches in places where they are needed, and later dealing with a hospital's economics and life and death issues both physical and ethical. They also learn to deal with law suits, how to deal with health insurance companies, and must decide policy issues with respect to the drug companies, the AMA, and HMOs.

The idea here is to again to marry the practical and the theoretical. They learn science in context, politics in context, economics in context. Mathematics is used to help make financial decisions as well as scientific decisions. Social issues are confronted daily in dealing with real patients and past cases. This curriculum is presented in detail in chapter 19.

The Pre-College Story

Before students go to college they are traditionally taking "college level courses" in high school. I have never understood why they do this because the college invariably does a better job of teaching college courses than does the high school. We suggest that this last high school year be focused on getting students ready for college in a variety of ways. They will take some actual college courses online. They will also start to deal with living on their own. They will deal with issues of personal freedom, time management, psychological issues, and doing research. They will participate in a variety of special stories built in concert with various universities. The overarching goal is to deal with becoming a grown up, and in that way, being prepared for the onslaught of personal issues that beset every college student.

THE THREADS AND CONTEXTS

In the end, it really doesn't matter what the contexts are. In the diagram here there are five contexts that might be of interest for children to participate in. As educators we are less concerned with these contexts than we are with the threads that pervade those contexts (written as arrows across them in Fig. 17.1).

In all of these contexts, state requirements can be met. However, those should not be confused with the real issues which are the threads that weave through each story. These are listed next together with a list of particular instances of the kinds of skills included within each thread. These constitute the real curriculum that underlies each story above. The contexts described here (hospital, general contracting, space) are important, but one can go through life without knowing much about any of them. This list includes what one must be able to do to function successfully in this world.

Communication: oral, written, psychology, argumentation, conversation, description, debate, negotiation, persuasion, and artistic expression

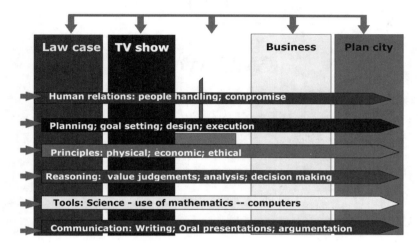

FIG. 17.1.

Human Relations: psychology, practice, groups, people handling, compromise, motivation, conflict resolution, and family issues

Reasoning: inventiveness, figuring it out on your own, analysis, judgment, values, decision making, scientific, and logic

Curiosity: inquisitiveness, creativity, seeing both sides of an issue, discovery, adaptation to new environments, and designing experiments

Attitude: gumption, ambition, pride, cooperation, time management, doing what you promised, empathy, and teamwork

Tools: scientific method, computers, construction, evidence gathering, research, reading, observation, arithmetic, languages, and case-based reasoning (history)

Principles: physical, ethical, moral, mathematics, and economics

Planning: setting goals, finding help, creating a plan, execution strategies, design, and project management

Physical: health, exercise, sports, competition, and the arts

The stories we propose are only a few of the stories that ought to be offered to children. Ideally, there should be military stories, biotechnology stories, home making stories, parenting stories, administration stories, invention stories, political office stories, literary critic stories, archeology stories, and dozens more. In time, schools will offer a range of stories and allow students to pursue those they want to pursue, at whatever age they want to pursue them.

18

CMU West

Carnegie Mellon University (CMU) opened its West Coast campus in September, 2002. When CMU decided to open this campus (CMW) it did so for a variety of reasons. The educational motivation was to try something experimental without spending much money. So, while it was, and is, a possibility that faculty will be appointed solely to the West Coast campus, this had not yet happened in 2002.

Nevertheless, students were expected in the fall of 2002. Approximately 60 part- and full-time students signed up for two masters degree programs in Computer Science. There was some idea that faculty would fly in and out from Pittsburgh to handle the students or that the students might watch videotaped lectures from previous semesters, but when I suddenly found myself in charge of the educational operation at CMW nothing had yet been decided.

As is obvious to the reader, I do not believe that lecturing makes sense as an educational delivery method. It may have made sense to lecture in medieval times when a monk could read and his audience could not, either because they were illiterate or because they had no books, but such are not the conditions today. Professors continue to lecture because it is easy to do, and they often enjoy it. Universities support lecturing because the economics of having 500 students and one professor work out very well. While there are some fascinating lecturers to be sure, at best, lecturing is just good entertainment that could possibly inspire students to look into something more deeply later on. At its worst, lecturing is dull and students find themselves cramming for exams that test if they remember anything they heard. Typically they don't remember and, more importantly, they can't make use of what they heard years later when it might matter in their lives.

We had two reasons not to have lectures at CMW. We didn't believe they were educationally effective, and we didn't have anyone to lecture. Of course we could have hired some local industry experts to lecture—we were in Silicon Valley after all—but this seemed less than ideal if we were trying to create a new educational experience that was to be at least as good as its big brother in Pittsburgh.

So, we came up with the *Story Centered Curriculum* (SCC). The SCC offers some real value in the delivery of on campus programs because it provides a way to implement learning by doing, it provides one-on-one instruction and mentoring for students, it is realistic and practical in what it tries to teach, and the material is both relevant and accessible to students. Feedback is usually quick, and students get the chance to rework what they produce before receiving a grade.

Of equal importance is the idea that the SCC can also be delivered online. Students can work in online teams and receive online mentoring and evaluation. It is so unimportant that the SCC be delivered on campus that we only found out, some months into the running of our first programs, that some of our students had moved and were doing the program entirely online. (We hear from them later.)

The significance of the possibility of high quality online education should not be underestimated. Education that is available online suddenly changes the notion of what it means to "go to a university." People who were limited by geography are no longer limited. People who were limited by available hours are able to work when they want. Opening up programs to a wider range of students also means opening up programs to more students. Typically a university would not consider a masters program that had one thousand students because they have neither the faculty nor the space to deal with such a program. Now, things have changed. There is now the possibility of delivering a quality education to many students across the globe who might not otherwise be able to get it and the possibility of real revenue to the university that offers such online programs.

INITIAL PROGRAMS

We decided to provide only masters degree programs at CMW to start. The reasons for this were simple enough. PhD programs are too faculty intensive and undergraduate programs are too long. Master's degree programs offer a nice opportunity to try out new ideas for a variety of reasons. First, as they are professional degrees, the professional orientation of the SCC makes sense. Second, they are good income producers for the university. Third, companies are likely to pay for students to attend programs that enhance professional skills. Fourth, they are short, so we could build them more quickly.

We started with two: Software Engineering and E-Business Technology. Software Engineering was selected because CMU has a terrific reputation in this field and because it is a sought after skill. E-Business was selected because we had a willing faculty at CMU in Pittsburgh to help us design it.

The first problem one encounters in building an SCC is, of course, the faculty. Faculty tend to abhor change. Moreover, they love the lectures they give and are reluctant to abandon them. But, there are two problems even more significant.

The first problem is both ubiquitous and easy to explain. In every field of academic inquiry there are one or more courses in the fundamental principles of the field. In computer science these courses are usually math courses or else they look a lot like math courses. In other fields they are called theory courses (they are called that in CS too). These courses are the results of theoretical work that lay the foundation for the ideas in the field according to the faculty. They are usually taught first, before any practical courses may be encountered. It is both this ordering and the idea that such courses must naturally matter to master's students that is problematic for the SCC.

The second problem is, of course, related to the principles problem. Faculty routinely teach various subject matter in a course simply because they always have or because the course they took as students contained that material. In designing the SCC one must develop a series of projects and situations that might come up in a (graduated) student's life. One does this by asking faculty what a graduate of their course is supposed to be able to do that they couldn't do before they took their course. Now, this is an unusual question for faculty, and they often take quite some time to ponder it. They want to answer that students will know certain things, but we object. What will they be able to do with that knowledge? Sometimes this causes a faculty member to stamp their feet and insist that that knowledge is important even if you can't do anything with it. Other times it causes a faculty member to find ways in which that knowledge might be used. Failing that, they concede defeat and attempt to address the question we have asked.

This interaction is most problematic when we are engaged in dealing with the principles problem. Typically the principles compiled by a field are of little use to its practitioners. Rather, they constitute a set of knowledge that theoreticians in a field value for a variety of reasons. Such principles are taught first for arcane reasons but rarely because they will matter in the life of the practitioner. We, of course, suggest eliminating them completely. This often causes problems. Our next suggestion is to teach them "just in time," that is, we will stop and teach them when they are needed.

Getting faculty to go along with the SCC can be an issue. It is not, however, an issue for faculty who are real practitioners. We have learned to select faculty who have a practical orientation and who really like training future practitioners.

In Software Engineering we chose to work with people who wanted to work with us, thus allowing us to work with practically oriented people who believe in the value of learning by doing. We were able to create a coherent year-long story in the life of a software engineer in a fictional company. Within that story, the faculty we had access to were professional software engineers and had done all the things that were in our story. Thus, we did not have to work with a large number of faculty to design and build the curriculum.

This was not true in e-business, however, as there were a range of different skills that were taught in the original MS program and no one professor knew them all. While this did not make it more difficult to design the story, since one could create a story that had students having to do many different kinds of things within one year, it did make the development quite difficult. Getting ten faculty members to agree on anything is like herding cats. Getting them to all deliver their projects and supporting material on time was a small nightmare.

The lessons from these two very different experiences clearly point to having a masters program that has one (or maybe two) very committed faculty members in charge. This may not work so easily for masters programs that are conglomerations of skill sets that no one faculty member has. Such programs are not great candidates for building an SCC. The best candidate masters program would be one that creates practitioners in a field where any faculty member is likely to have all the requisite skills that any graduate is supposed to have. If no faculty member can do what any graduate of the program can do, then the situation is probably too complex and therefore, too costly to try when funds are limited.

It is important when choosing a masters program for the SCC treatment to choose one that is really about building skilled practitioners. Since the evaluation of a student's success focuses on the quality of the deliverables that he or she has prepared, it is best if the masters program is one that really does have deliverables and is not one that is intended to familiarize a student with the basics of a field. While it is certainly possible to build an SCC for such programs, still focusing on deliverables, the faculty acceptance of such a program is likely to be lower since it will diverge so greatly from what has previously been in place.

First Semester

After months of preparation the program opened its doors. The students had a variety of different backgrounds, but most had at least a couple of years of professional experience. On the first day, the students went around the room, explaining their backgrounds briefly and what had brought them to Carnegie Mellon West. Everyone spoke of their respect for Carnegie Mellon University, and some students talked about how exciting it was to be able to attend such a prestigious university and still fulfill their obligations that required them to stay on the West Coast. All the students, to some extent, were motivated by the practical nature of the curriculum, but few, if any, really understood what it would require of them in the months ahead.

After several days of orientation, students jumped right into their teams and began working on their first task. It was clear immediately that old habits die hard. Initially, students were clamoring for lectures. When pressed, these students would acknowledge that they had never really learned much of anything from a lecture course.

One student acknowledged:

> I think back to my undergraduate schooling, and I was constantly cramming for exams and forgetting it ten minutes after I walked out of the exam.

But when faced with the difficult problems this new program presented, they could only think in terms of how they had traditionally been taught. They missed what had become familiar. The tasks in the CMU West masters programs were designed to stretch the students and to force mistakes from which they could learn. Not surprisingly, this turned out to be an incredibly uncomfortable experience for students coming from a traditional school system.

In the next several weeks, as the tasks continued to build, and it became increasingly clear that, although the teams were working hard and were fairly successful at completing their tasks, many students were floundering. More importantly, they did not feel like they were learning anything. We began to interview the students, and it became obvious that some of them were very confused and unhappy. It also became clear that many of the resources we had put into place were not being used very well.

"Where's My Professor?"

In a story centered curriculum, the idea is to put students into complex circumstances that they do not readily understand. Then, they are supposed to think about what to do. But, when students who are not used to being self reliant in their education encounter difficulties, their tendency is to ask for help. When the CMW students encountered problems and did not understand how to approach their tasks, they immediately looked for faculty assistance. Because faculty members are not based locally, their first thought was that they were getting cheated in some way. "If we were in Pittsburgh," they said, "we could go ask the faculty for help." Of course, in reality faculty members at most universities are not available on an as-needed basis to master's students. In the case of the CMU West students, we had deliberately set things up so as to make faculty available at the right time, but that may not have been the time the students felt that they needed them.

The students felt like their access to faculty was heavily restricted and were understandably upset by it. We kept hearing, "I want a real professor on site to be able to talk to when I have problems." In their role play as bosses, the faculty members are open to making appointments whenever the teams need help, but the students have to set the agenda. To utilize the faculty in this framework, a student has to know what he does not know. So, when students are bogged down in the middle of a problem, they might not even know enough about what they need to be able to ask specific questions.

We had thought that we could explain the roles of the supporting faculty and staff at orientation and that would be sufficient, but we underestimated the extent to which the forms of traditional schooling had become automatic in student's minds. In the story centered curriculum, students must direct and account for their own learning processes. It is one of the main goals of the curriculum to produce self-directed learners, but none of this was the norm for our entering students, and they were confused and frustrated.

One of our students mused:

> In classical education, where you have class and listen to lectures, it's kind of like being babysat because it's up to the professor to contribute to the session. Here, it's up to the students to contribute. We're not taking cues from the teacher.

Structuring one's time and seeking out the information that you need to accomplish your goals is a key skill within the program. Knowing how to get the help you need is a key part of the experience. Given some time, our students were able to acclimate to the self-directed learning style.

Another student reflected on the transformation:

> Where as some of us may have felt earlier that some of the more traditional academic aspects, like lectures and whatnot, were lacking, now, we've learned to teach ourselves material and to look up what we need when we need it.

As the tasks continued to move forward, the faculty members were not necessarily responding in a timely fashion with their feedback to students. The students increasingly felt abandoned as tasks kept building on another without receiving any comments on their initial stages. In truth, the deliverables were more difficult and time-consuming to grade than we had anticipated, and the level of detailed feedback we were providing was extremely labor intensive.

A faculty member commented on the SCC grading process:

When you teach the old way, you come up with dramatic simplifications because you think if I teach that point, and that point, and this point, it's relatively easy to come up with "either they know it or they don't know it." When you do it in a realistic setting, they have to produce real documents. These things tend to be big. And they tend to consume lots of time on their part, and I feel obligated to not just look for the few things that they're trying to do for this particular deliverable but address all of the issues that seem to be present in the document. And that's a lot of grading. That's a lot of time. I think it's good. I think they're getting a lot more out of it than the old way, but it requires me to change my mental image about what it is to produce a grade and produce feedback to the students. And that's taken some time and energy.

To resolve this problem, we worked rapidly to train more people to grade the products, and we established a task checklist that makes grading a smoother, more time efficient operation. Keeping the students constantly updated about their progress became crucial to their adjustment within the program.

"What Does a Mentor Do?"

To further facilitate the students' opportunity to get answers to their questions, we also created a meeting with subject matter mentors on a regular basis. Mentors are the staff members with industry experience particular to the specific task the students are working on, so they have just the right kind of expertise to be able to advise students and give the students examples from the real world. But students would rarely show up for these meetings, and when they did, they were not prepared to ask questions. They just wanted the subject matter expert to lecture on the information contained in the readings.

School is rarely taught using examples from everyday life, but we had asked our mentors to provide a context for the students by telling stories from their own professional lives germane to the task at hand. To deal with the problems between the subject matter experts and the student teams, we created a mentor meeting that made the subject matter experts more aware of the requirements of the specific task, so that they could giving more specific advice.

One student told us:

Subject matter mentors would be more helpful if they knew more about what is coming, the top learning objectives, and what they will be graded on, so he can help them prepare. He needs the goals to help them prioritize.

Another said:

He needs more familiarity with the task. When he draws on examples to help us, they are from the outside which is great, but it's hard to relate to the task, and he needs to know the task to help with this.

The subject matter mentors became more useful to students after we realized that we had to teach the mentors also. One can't simply teach in this curriculum simply because one is an expert. Experts cannot give good guidance without having been filled in on the particular details of a task. We also established a forum for the teams to make contact with the subject matter experts before they ran into problems during their tasks. This gave the teams greater respect for the subject matter expert's skill, and made the subject matter expert seem more accessible to the teams.

Students also had difficulty with the idea of a team coach. The team coach is a special kind of mentor involved in the team's planning process, but the students became frustrated with their team coaches because they did not see their usefulness. The team coaches do not have a high level of experience with every phase of every task, so often their role was Socratic in nature. When the students would ask questions, the coaches were trained to ask them more questions to see if they could figure out where to go for help together.

But one student complained:

He [the team coach] tends to be more passive unless he sees we're clearly going down the wrong track. Or we can ask him what he did when this came up in his experience at work. That is really valuable. If anything I'd love for him to draw more stories from his experience. The stories are pretty priceless.

The model of interaction was moving away from teacher as expert toward teacher as facilitator.

One of the mentors explained:

I try to figure out where the team is at. I'm trying to figure out where they've progressed, why they've made certain decisions, how they are doing with their end goal. Do they have a plan? Are they meeting that plan?

But, at first, this approach was frustrating for some students. The difficulty is rooted in the student's lack of familiarity with the open-ended nature of these tasks. Because the curriculum consists of real world problems, the tasks do not have a "right" answer. The most important piece of the task is learning to think it through, justifying your processes and your decisions. Many of the CMU professors impressed on our task designers that the "CMU Way" included being able to select from a toolbox of different strengths and strategies to use tools intelligently, not simply by rote. The most important part of an implementation is being able to give a well-reasoned explanation for the strategy used. The team coach is there throughout the program to talk through the process of planning and strategizing with the teams.

In retrospect, it seems pretty obvious that our teams would have difficulty with the new role they played in the student–teacher relationship. And while we tried to address these new roles during the orientation period, it was not an easy adjustment for the students (or the mentors, for that matter) to make. For each of these relationships, we had to explicitly highlight the differences between the roles in a traditional school environment and the story centered curriculum. And we had to do it over and over again.

Over time, many teams effectively coordinated their relationship with their team coach:

> We used to meet [our team coach] for an hour after we were done with our team, to chat about what's going on and what help we need. Now he comes in earlier and sits in on our team meeting, and we discuss issues after the meeting, so we don't have to brief him. It helps to be able to quickly ask him, in a meeting, "How does this play out in industry?" And, "What do you think about this?" He gives us really helpful insights.

In addition to trying to retrain the students' expectations for the student–teacher relationship, we also had to retrain the faculty's perception as well.

A faculty member comments on the experience:

> It's taken me awhile to figure out how to undo about 25 years of teaching experience, of standing up in the front of a room and talking. I really enjoy interacting with students. It's much more satisfying to be dealing with smaller groups, more of a one-on-one type of interaction.

It was difficult for some faculty as well, to understand their new role in the story centered curriculum. Professors often have the idea that the information they know is what makes school valuable for students—after all, students are paying to hear faculty talk about what they know. The mentors, who were all the products of traditional school environments, have difficulty knowing how much help to give students when they are struggling with a problem. There was a great deal of discussion among faculty and mentors about how to offer feedback this last semester, and it is sure to continue. Training mentors will be an ongoing project of ours for some time, and we are learning many new lessons through our experiences at Carnegie Mellon West. Overwhelmingly, we are learning that mentors and faculty at all levels need to be convinced of the power of learning-by-doing. Because the program requires a radical change in one's perception of learning and education, leaders at all levels have to buy into the process to avoid inconsistency.

"There's Too Much to Read"

In addition to the trouble that students had identifying their relationship to the coaches, mentors, and faculty, they also had difficulty navigating the on-line resources. As the tasks got harder and harder, some of the students were feeling really overwhelmed.

From one student:

> Things are really well laid out but it's overwhelming. We need to figure out what we can ignore. It's been hard to do this. It's hard to know what to pay attention to.

There were certainly lots of opportunities on the program Web site to get more information about topics or areas where a student lacks expertise, but students did not seem to be using these resources. Certain teams would attempt to do all the reading before ever beginning the task or they would skip the readings entirely and attempt to do the task without doing any research. Neither of these methods is the optimum way to use the story centered curriculum. But we just kept hearing from the students: "There's too much to read."

Another student suggested:

> The help is very rich, but it throws a lot at you, like an infinite reading list. If it was organized around mandatory stuff and optional recommended stuff, it would make it less infinite.

In this kind of educational experience, the resources were not meant to be covered from A to Z. We had to explicitly tell students over and over that they did not have to do any readings at all. When they need help, they should go to the library of resources and get the answers to their questions. Our program offers students choices, instead of learning a little bit about a lot of subjects, we wanted them to choose where they would focus within the context of their project work, and get narrower and deeper coverage than they would in other programs. They needed to monitor their own level of understanding. Students, of course, are not used to doing this. They understand the concept of required reading. In the case of the SCC however, reading is there if you think it will help you do what you are trying to do. This was a new idea to students.

"There's Not Enough Time to Read"

Some of the students felt that there was not enough time built in to the curriculum for them to investigate the answers to their questions. They felt that they were so busy "doing" that they didn't have time for "learning."

One student complained:

> I still think the reading and lectures seem like drinking out of a fire hose. You give us so much all at once. We need to look at everything so quickly and there's only so much you can do. You quickly have to mobilize and come up with a plan or schedule to get the task done, and so a lot of the readings and lectures fall off by the wayside.

One of the difficulties here is that most students are not used to depending on teammates. It was extremely helpful to offer the example of students in medical school, where students have to divide up the readings and summarize them for each other because there is too much information to be responsible for on your own.

We ended up offering a 50/50 rule, where students could give themselves the guideline of spending half of their time producing their deliverable and the other half of their time researching and reading about their process. To accomplish this, however, each team would have to renegotiate the scope of their own projects based on what they expected to accomplish. One of the explicit performance objectives was to practice tracking one's own progress to understand how long it took to do certain things, and to represent your work accurately to your boss and your other teammates so you could plan accordingly.

But the students were embarrassed to ask for less. The students thought they would be perceived as remedial if they had to scale back the scope of their project to accommodate their own research and reflection on their task. They were ashamed to take control of their own learning; it had been in the hands of professors and teachers for so long. They worried about being compared with the other teams and the other students and did not want to admit that they could not accomplish everything set out for them. They even worried that if they renegotiated the scope they would not be meeting the requirements of the master's degree, and they would not deserve the diploma.

This was a particular issue in the software engineering program because as the program began the faculty and mentors said repeatedly that they were going to be given too much to do. The software industry often takes on too much and simply cannot deliver on its promises. It seemed extremely important to the faculty members that these students be trained to monitor their own progress and negotiate the scope of their own projects in accordance with a realistic schedule. It took some time for the software engineering students to accept that they could renegotiate the scope of their tasks. It was against their belief in the standards of school that they could create their own goals in parallel to the strengths and weaknesses of their own teams.

One student explained the process:

The emphasis is very much on negotiating on a promise and delivering on that, once you've come to an agreement. So in that sense, it's of a fundamentally different nature [than traditional schooling]. We're pretty much in charge of what we say we want to deliver. The scope is pretty much what we can convince our stakeholders, the faculty, to accept. And that's the give and take that has gone on throughout most of the semester.

"I Don't Know What to Read"

The students said they did not know how to find what they needed "just-in-time." For some tasks, there was a tremendous amount of information available on the program Web site.

Students reported:

There's too much information and no guide on where to look. It's like a needle in a haystack.

How do we know that what we are looking for is there? It's kind of a blind info spree.

The readings and lectures were not always stored in the format most appropriate to the way the students were dealing with the problems. So, sometimes the most pertinent information was buried within eight hours of video lectures. While the task designers felt that managing information and being able to discern between two sources were important skills to teach in any course, the students' ability to find the answers to their questions was seriously impeded by the presentation of the resources. If the students were going to be able to use these resources as intended, we had to make them easier to navigate and manage. We are currently working on ways to annotate and index the resources to make using them more immediately satisfying.

But, the difficulty of this task is relevant to the general issue of the uselessness of lectures. We already had videotaped lectures available to us and made them available to the students. Of course, what we wanted to do was make the relevant ideas available to students on an as-needed basis. We had done this in the computer simulations we had previously built, but doing this is quite expensive. It involves asking a professor for his favorite stories about every subject he knows about, and then indexing these stories so they would pop up as needed. While we know how to do this, we could simply not afford to do it.

The basic premise of the SCC is that if you can do the tasks adequately and you can justify your decisions, then you have the appropriate skill level. The readings and lectures are there when you need help. We learned throughout the semester that the students wanted to place the responsibility for managing the readings and video lectures onto the faculty.

A student comments on the experience of looking through the resources:

> As we read, what do the readings have to do with the task? We didn't learn anything that helped us with the task. Towards the end, we found helpful stuff but after wasting a lot of time. We're getting better at skimming to see if it's worth reading or not, but it would be a lot better if the professor told us up front.

They wanted to be told what to read and when to read it, but we were consistent about forcing the students to manage their own process. Over time, some of the more successful teams developed strategies that helped them manage the research that needed to be done. Some teams would assign all the readings at the beginning of the task, and then each team member would be responsible for reporting on those readings at the appropriate part of the task. Other teams would wait until they were in the middle of the task to create a reading schedule when they had more of an idea as to where their team might require additional information. There are many ways to navigate the information in the readings. The important thing is that students take responsibility for the process themselves. We believe that this is a key issue in education.

"How Am I Being Graded?"

In addition to using the mentoring and online resources appropriately, it is important that the teams learn to use each other's expertise.
One student perceived:

> People fresh out of their undergraduate degree think that when you're working on a team you are cheating.

Throughout the semester, the challenge of team dynamics threatened to get in the way of collective progress. One particular sticking point for many of the teams is something deeply ingrained in the traditional educational system: competition.
Another student's perception of the grading process:

> It seems no matter how well or poorly we work, we get an "A" anyway. There's no way to distinguish if you are doing a good job. If one person is working harder, both will get an "A" anyway.

In the story centered curriculum, it is not very productive to compare your evaluation with the evaluation of others because everyone contributes in slightly different ways. If the team has been successful, then everyone has been successful. But many of the team members became excessively worried about how they could be accurately assessed in comparison with their teammates if they were turning in assignments as a group.

At the start of the semester, we initiated something called a 360-degree evaluation, where students evaluated the performances of their teammates. This was a kind of peer review. Because students were still in the mode of a traditional schooling environment, they had difficulty using these evaluations as they were intended. They are typically used by role-playing professionals in a corporate setting, but it was difficult for students to provide concrete examples of performance as a true professional would. Instead, they aired personal grievances and made sweeping generalizations about each other.

This was all about student obsession with grades, of course. There is, somewhat understandably, a lot of difficulty with the idea that people can put in differing amounts of work and get the same grade. The thing that is incredibly difficult to convince students is that grades are not really that important. We counseled them repeatedly to focus on themselves, on the skills they were acquiring. Despite all of our insistence that students participate in this program as if it was a year spent working in a corporate setting, grades are still required (because the university says so), and it is difficult for students to switch back and forth between professionals seeking a good review and students seeking a good grade. (This was particularly true of students seeking tuition reimbursement from their employers, who needed to maintain a certain GPA in order to get the money.)

To deal with the frenzy around how grading works in a story centered curriculum, it was most important that we de-emphasize grades as the ultimate arbiter of who is performing adequately. Accomplishing the tasks and accepting the feedback one is given are the most important markers of success. In addition to trying to de-emphasize grades, we are improving the way that the 360-degree evaluations are constructed based on a more complete accounting for each phase of the work product. We are asking the teams to build a more complete plan of the subdeliverables involved in any one task and determining who is responsible for that deliverable. Being able to reference a specific portion of the work plan should give students more concrete ways of giving feedback about one another.

Students have come to see the benefit of the 360-degree evaluation:

> Because we don't have daily interaction with faculty, the 360 evaluations are a way for each of us to get that feedback on ourselves. I think that's really valuable. Because people tend to be averse to competition, it helps to say objective things like you need to be more open-minded about this point. The 360's are a good neutral way of getting this out.

"My Teammates Aren't Working Together"

Another challenge for team dynamics is the variety of skills and backgrounds that each team member brings to the group. Many frustrations arose, in part, due to the disparate strengths of individual members of the teams. Certain people are often prone to taking the lead in group projects, and certain people often fade into the background. In the story centered curriculum, you really need all the team members to take their share of the responsibility or you simply will not accomplish your goals.

A number of teams had some amount of difficulty establishing a good working relationship with each other. The problems were certainly more acute when the team had a limited amount of work experience. Students are not usually given much experience in working with teams in school environments, and many of the students did not have the skills to communicate effectively amongst themselves. In fact, there was a student for whom working as a member of a team was so uncomfortable that he simply refused to put the effort into learning how to do it successfully. Because working as a team is such an important piece of job training, we brought in an organizational psychologist to help the students work through their struggles constructively.

With the help of the organizational psychologist, the teams discovered ways to speak constructively to one another and voice their concerns in terms that can be remedied:

> We could look at how we can change how we act rather than trying to make others change. That's sound advice and the hardest thing to do.

The teams eventually realized that one rarely gets to choose the members of one's team in a work environment, and you simply have to deal with it constructively. Communication and negotiation skills are some of the most frequently discussed in these story centered curricula. And, they are the most frequently dealt with in the workplace as well.

As one student concluded:

> People who are individualistic and don't like the team approach, that's maybe something they have to work on for this program or choose another program, but that's really stressed. I think time management is a big issue, if you're the type who likes to procrastinate it will be hard, not impossible, but you have to understand the parts of the project you have to dissect and get them done.

The End Result: Learning Looks Like Life

Throughout the program, the students have acknowledged that what they are working on is tremendously applicable to the workplace. Working on a complete project life cycle is extremely meaningful because it is not just about a school assignment. The work is directly relevant to problems the students know they will face at work. Many students cite this as the number one reason that the story centered curriculum appealed to them:

> Since our project work is so realistic, the story centered curriculum can even be a selling point on our resume as additional "work experience." We have a portfolio showing what we did. If it's positioned correctly, it's really quite an advantage over a more traditional graduate program.

Students have also become aware of the communication skills they have learned along the way. One student said:

> The skills don't jump out at you, but because you are doing a lot of reports, for instance, that you would have to do on the job, you realize in the end that there are skills you acquired about report writing.

In the story centered curriculum, this type of incidental learning applies to the acquisition of numerous skills including verbal and written communication, problem analysis, and project planning.

Another student compared the experience to learning a new language:

> I like the realism. It's immersive. That's how you learn a language, so that also makes sense here.

The part-time students, in particular, have found that their studies at Carnegie Mellon West impact their experiences at work to a significant degree. Because they are continuing at their daytime jobs, they can apply what they are learning right away. Furthermore, because their work gives them a larger sense of purpose, they feel more motivated to push themselves to really understand the content and processes. It is these students who can really articulate the strength of the story centered curriculum.

One part-time student reported:

> [The story-centered curriculum] is actually giving me more exposure to these skills than on my job where I do mostly just software testing and would need to get trained in these other areas, and yet at school I'm getting to go thru all the phases (of the software development life cycle), like software design and requirements and analysis, and using the same tools as at work . . . Before I would take the schedules (my manager established) and would just accept them and get things done by the date but now I actually understand the purpose and why a project takes so long; to manage a project it takes time to make sure everything is on track and what goes into doing this.

As mentioned earlier, we also have several part-time students on a remote team. These students are particularly appreciative of the flexibility that the story centered curriculum provides. They have really responded to the efficiency in time-management that this program allows them. They can focus on work and family, yet return to their school work at even odd times from the comfort of their homes. This team communicates via e-mail and telephone five days a week; they are convinced that the frequency of communication is critical because it adds to the morale of the team. They have really made online education work for them.

The practical nature of the story-centered curriculum keeps them motivated. As one student explained:

> I am already taking a lot away from my schoolwork and applying it to my job, because I can leverage it right away.... What I learn on Monday I can apply on Wednesday.... Here I feel we will use everything we learn.

Learning, Redefined

Overall, the changes we made in the curriculum in Carnegie Mellon West over the first semester amounted to educating the expectations of the students and supporting those expectations with concrete improvements in processes.

We found ourselves often having to highlight the differences between this program and a traditional educational experience. These differences need to be discussed early and often. Furthermore, we are working on explicitly articulating the relationship between students and mentors, the role of the reading and lectures, and the optimum composition of the teams in a format that will always be available when problems arise.

When we hear students say "Where's the learning in the learning-by-doing?" there is a fundamental misunderstanding. It is difficult to explain to students who have always understood that what they were learning could be explicitly stated, that much of the most important things we learn are implicit and nonconscious. In the story centered curriculum, the "doing" and the repeated practice and reflection constitutes the "learning."

Students need to understand that the process is the goal. Our objectives here are not primarily knowledge-focused. Our objectives here are related to performance of a specific set of skills. We want our students to learn to do something, something that they want to learn and that will bring them success in the job role they desire to have.

We also want students to know that mistakes are a part of this process. It's expected. It is even desired. Students are set up to fall short, with the understanding that they will be able to make sense of their mistakes and recognize how they can be avoided in the future. False starts do not have anything to do with grades. Really, grades do not matter at all. Learning how to fail and progress through failure is one of the most important outcomes of a story centered curriculum.

In the End

In the end, the students had only positive things to say about the program. On job interviews, employers were impressed by how much relevant experience they already had.

As one student reports:

> I've been able to give them [potential employers] brief demonstrations of what we've done with Moffett Foods. They've been very impressed, and they've understood that I'm able to come in and bring in an instant value add to their company. They really think that what we're doing here is revolutionary.

The students understood that they had gone through a grueling year of work that looked good to outsiders. The mentors began to say that they wished they had had this kind of education when they went to school, but they thought it was a lot more work.

A mentor explained:

> I'm almost jealous, in a way, because I see that they are gaining skills more readily than I could have gained them in my program . . . They get exposure to things that we just talked about in a lecture hall, where as they are actually implementing, building software, putting designs into practice where as we mostly did homework and talked about it in a lecture hall.

The faculty who taught in the program loved the involvement they had with students as opposed to the distance one feels from students in a lecture hall.

A faculty member described his experience:

> I get the feeling that I know my students in this format much better than I ever did in my previous teaching experience.

The faculty who did not teach in the program were another issue altogether. CMU has a large faculty back in Pittsburgh who were concerned that something was going on in California that was strange, and therefore, worrisome. Nevertheless, in the Fall of 2003, CMU's President opened the new building with praise for the success of the "learn by doing" approach at CMU West.

REFERENCE NOTES

The student and mentor report gathering was undertaken by Franci McFarland and exists now as a set of unpublished notes. Their public availability may change at some point.

19

The Eleventh Grade
Hospital Curriculum

The Hospital Curriculum is designed for eleventh grade students in high school. It was designed by a team from Carnegie Mellon University, the Veterans Administration, Engines for Education (a non-profit that builds new curricula for schools) and is intended for use at Grandview Preparatory School in Boca Raton, FL, as well as any other high school within the vicinity of a VA Hospital that wishes to be part of this experiment. It was designed in the form of a Story Centered Curriculum.

It is an experiential curriculum, intended to alter our conception of what schooling should entail, the relationship of young people to their community and the relationship of the community to students. In this curriculum the students' time is divided between a hospital and the school classroom. The curriculum provides students with hands-on experiences in a variety of roles within a real Veterans Administration hospital, as well as other health care centers the VA provides. Through their work, students will gain experience practicing skills relevant to a number of professions, including writing, math, science, reasoning, human relations, decision making, and communication. Students will also have a myriad of profession-specific experiences, working closely with adult professionals to learn about the vast world of health care work.

Students will work with mentors who are staff members at the hospital staff, both medical and administrative, as well as becoming familiar with patients and visitors, accomplishing meaningful responsibilities, gaining familiarity with the life and culture of the hospital, and working to solve ongoing, critical issues with which the hospital administration genuinely grapples every day.

The students will be part of a fictional consulting group whose mission it is to examine every aspect of how the hospital conducts its business, from economic decisions to political issues to medical, social, technological, and ethical choices. Students will become specialists in an area of the hospital that most interests them. At the end of the year, the consulting team will issue a report and make a presentation to the hospital administration about how to improve services at the hospital. The year is intended to provide enough knowledge to the student about a range of issues so that they will be competent to issue a report that will be taken seriously by those in charge.

THE PROGRAM

Weeks 1–3: Greeting

At the start of the program students will receive a formal orientation to the hospital in which they will work, and to the roles they will play within it. As a part of the orientation, they will learn about the Veterans Administration and meet and listen to the stories of veterans of war and former prisoners of war. The idea is that as students work in the hospital and see the patients coming and going, they should develop a sense that there is a story behind every person there. They should become curious about the patients, and develop sincere compassion for them before they begin their work. Throughout the year, students will have a chance to get to know veterans, collect their stories, and contribute to their care.

During the orientation, students will also learn about illnesses common to veterans, such as post-traumatic stress disorder, and they will begin discussing the issue that all veterans' hospitals confront such as the struggle to achieve balance, as there are limited resources available for the vast population requiring service. At the conclusion of the orientation, students will receive official hospital badges, and they will be given a job to do.

Students will work as "greeters" for the hospital, welcoming visitors, and helping them find their way to patient rooms or hospital resources. This will enable the students to begin working in a helpful capacity for the hospital, meeting real people who come to the hospital on a daily basis. Also, it will require that the students become familiar with the geography and structure of the hospital, and it will provide exposure to the wide range of health-related issues for which the hospital provides care, and administrative services required to support the system. In addition, it will give students real responsibility, and practice representing the VA in the work they do.

While they work as greeters, the students will also have a specific problem to solve: The hospital will ask the students to propose places both inside and outside the hospital to place benches for people to sit on. As they walk through the hospital, students will study where people tend to want to congregate or linger, or they'll notice places that patients or visitors frequently must wait. They will collect data on their findings and propose the most needed placements for benches, taking into consideration the hospital's limited resources.

To further contribute to students' sense of context about the VA hospitals, their purpose and their patients, students will watch relevant films (e.g., HBO's *Band of Brothers*, *Storming the Beaches at Normandy*, *One Flew Over the Cuckoo's Nest*, and *Saving Private Ryan*). They will also read books published by the VA (e.g., *The Greatest Generation* and *Ring the Night Bell*), which chronicles the early Veterans Administration, as well as other books that tell the stories of American prisoners of war.

At the conclusion of the first three weeks, students will write several reports about their experiences, including for example:

- Report on bench placements
- Report from the greeter's perspective: visible issues in the hospital that require attention
- Report on patients' life histories
- Report on a problem that a patient is having within the VA system. The student may take on an advocacy role on the patient's behalf.

By the end of the three-week orientation, and their work as greeters who frequently move around the entire facility, students will have had exposure to many departments within the VA hospital, both health and administratively oriented. Students will be asked to select and rank their interest in working with one of several departments for the upcoming week. Students will be grouped in pairs, each pair working in different departments throughout the hospital. Each pair of students will be grouped with a professional mentor who will structure their experiences for the week.

Week 4: Select a Department of Interest

In the fourth week of the program, students will do concentrated work in one department of the hospital, working with a partner–student and hospital mentor. They will start the week learning about the department and meeting the staff and/or patients in that department. The mentor will meet with the students to discuss the issues and responsibilities that the department faces, and will provide the students with meaningful work experiences each day. The goal is to provide students greater and greater insight into the work of the department, the professionals who work there, and when relevant, the patients who receive care. At the end of each day, all students will regroup for a debriefing about their experiences. As the conclusion to the week, students will write and present an oral report about their experiences working in each of their departments.

Week 5–6: Problem Analysis

In weeks five and six, students will be given several real world, complex problems that VA hospitals have confronted in the past or that they currently face. Often the problems have to do with patient safety, physician or nursing errors, and injuries caused by misuse of common hospital equipment. The stories tend to be interesting and emotionally charged, since real people were often harmed. This will increase students' motivation to find good solutions to the problems they study.

Some of the problems will come from a database that the VA maintains containing real problems and lessons learned from past experiences. Others will come from the National Patient Safety Foundation, The Institute of Medicine Reports, and veteran experiences that have been captured on video. Fictional but realistic problems may be posed as well, such as some seen on television shows like *E.R.* or films like *One Flew Over the Cuckoo's Nest*.

Students will work in teams to analyze the problems and propose solutions to them. They will write reports for each problem containing the team's analysis of the problem, the proposed solution, and a justification for the solutions chosen. In conjunction with their work, students will read and discuss a book about the realities of mistakes that people make, called *Human Error*, by James Reason.

Week 7: Root Cause Analysis

After students complete their work doing analyses of problems using their best intuitions about finding good solutions, in week seven, students will receive their first introduction to a formal method of problem analysis currently in use by VA hospital staff, called *Root Cause Analysis* (RCA). RCA is a method supported by a software tool. An RCA team works together to research and troubleshoot problems that arise. In this case, students will become the RCA team for a simulated problem, and they will learn the RCA software to solve the problem they face.

The simulated case may be shown with a video, for example, that presents multiple perspectives on the same event. Students are able to see various sides of the problem, and they can start to dig into the analysis. Students will receive training on the RCA tool and training on hospital safety, so they know the benchmarks from which hospitals should start. Working as an RCA team, the students will conduct formal, in depth analyses of the problem using the RCA tool, and they will write a summary report of the problem, articulating the key issues involved in the process and proposing well-reasoned solutions.

Students will present their findings in a presentation to the full student body and participating hospital staff. In addition, an attorney may be present to discuss issues of risk management, particularly highlighting solutions that the students developed as conclusions to their reports.

Week 8: A Patient Falls

A frequent problem in hospitals is that patients fall and hurt themselves. In addition to the trauma to the patient, the hospitals are liable and falls can be quite costly. Week 8 will begin with a real problem taken from a past event in which a particular patient falls under specific circumstances. Students will work on the problem from both a medical and a prevention perspective.

Students will first work through the medical diagnosis, working with physicians to read x-rays, MRI, and CAT Scan results. Students will then consider such injuries in a broader context, outside the realm of falls per se, but rather focusing on repair of bones and joints. Students may observe a live hip surgery or other bone repair surgical procedure. Students will then work with physicians considering issues of post-operative healing, such as the dangers of infections or pneumonia.

Next, students will work with the administrative team who must manage patient claims filed due to falls. Students will begin to understand the massive problems that simple issues like accidental falls can create for a hospital, building their motivation to take preventative measures.

Finally, students will work on an RCA team to troubleshoot the issue of patients falling. They will consider issues related to hospital equipment and procedures, and they will consider solutions to some of the more frequent causes of patient falls. Students will write a report proposing their solutions.

Weeks 9–10: Medical Imaging

In the last week, students had the opportunity to see medical imaging technologies at work. In these two weeks, students will take a step back from their hands on hospital experience to learn more of the science behind imaging technologies. Working with imaging experts, students will learn the physics and technology involved in x-rays, MRIs, and CAT Scans. They will also learn about radiation and related biology, machine reliability and the potential for improvement, nuclear medicine, and other upcoming technologies.

Students will receive and analyze test results from various types of imaging technologies and write diagnostic reports. They will compare their reports with those of the experts who analyzed the same images for patients.

Weeks 11–12: Microbiology

In these weeks, the students return to the patient who fell in the hospital. This patient develops an infection and is moved into an acute-ward room. An x-ray of the patient reveals a lung with pneumonia. Students have to answer how the patient got pneumonia, what an appropriate treatment would be, and whether the illness is at all related to the fall. In the process, students will confront the difference between viral and bacterial infections, and will have to choose a treatment that is appropriate for the patient's type of infection.

Weeks 13–15: Small Pox Policy

At the start of week 13, students are confronted with a brand new problem—a fictional but realistic scenario. The president of the United States issues an order for medical personnel to be vaccinated for smallpox in case of a terrorist attack. The VA hospital begins to prepare for the vaccination of all of their staff, when the workers begin to protest outside the hospital. The media begin to flood the hospital with questions about how the staff will work with patients if they have the smallpox vaccine in them, which can spread the smallpox virus to those with whom they come in direct contact. They want to know how long staff will be kept away from patients.

Students will be asked to prepare a cost benefit analysis of providing this vaccine to the hospital staff. In the process, they will learn some economics and statistics to use in their analysis. They will also develop a plan for administering the vaccine and controlling spread of the disease. Finally, students will create a media plan, so the hospital's reputation is not damaged by reporter's questions.

While students work through their reports, they will learn relevant history (e.g., the French and Indian War in which Jeffrey Amherst, a commanding general of British forces in North America, sent smallpox blankets and handkerchiefs to Native Americans surrounding his fort as a form of early biological warfare). Students will also read relevant books (e.g., Richard Preston's *The Hot Zone* and Laurie Garrett's *The Coming Plague*), as well as special reports such as the Center for Disease Control's paper documenting what Israel is doing to prepare for biological warfare. Students may also watch relevant films, such as *Outbreak*.

Week 16: Intensive Care Unit Experience

During this week of the program, students will have an intense, hands-on experience in the ICU of the VA hospital to learn about acute care. Students will work with an assigned nurse as assistants in the ICU, tracking a patient and all the services they receive, and meeting the patient's simple needs for one week. Students will consider the patient from a personal and medical perspective. When possible, students will talk to family members about the patient's situation, and about what it is like to have a close family member in the ICU. Students will write a creative narrative from the patient's perspective about what it feels like to be in this situation. If the patient can and wants to talk to the students, they may reveal answers to specific questions.

Students will also talk to the nurses with whom they are working, to learn about what is happening technically and medically to the patient. They will learn some nursing skills and some basic physiology, taking simple measurements such as oxygen levels and heart rates. They will also consult with the nurses about the plans for healing the patient, considering why various solutions are or are not effective. Finally, students will write a report proposing decisions that should be made for the patient, and next steps that should be taken.

Week 17: Paramedic Course

In week 17, students will work with a paramedic team, and learn some of the life saving procedures that paramedics use in their work. In addition to numerous other techniques, students will learn CPR using an advanced type of simulator, and will learn to use a defibrillator.

Week 18: Effective Communication

The focus of this week is learning to communicate with team members, sometimes under high-pressure conditions that may require speed and accuracy, and that also may entail varying levels of experience and rank. Students will begin by viewing one or more examples of situations that required good communication, and the results of failure, including, for example, *Charlie, Victor, Romeo*, an off-Broadway show in which a flight recorder tape is played to the audience after a plane crash. In this case, the pilot chose to pull rank and follow his own opinion despite his co-pilots pleading with him to maneuver the plane differently until the moment of the crash. Students may also view the film *The Abilene Paradox* and read an adjoining article discussing the issues at play.

Next the students will participate in ICU Simulation Training, in which participants of various levels of authority work together under simulated ICU conditions. Students will work with a team of physicians and nurses, both participating and observing behaviors. Students will consider how to be an effective leader under such conditions, as well as the dynamics of working with a doctor or other leader's orders when you question those orders. The week will end with a debriefing about students' experiences in the simulation, and students will give an oral report about their experience and communication lessons learned.

Weeks 19–20: Internships

Students will have two weeks to do internships in which they can study and work in particular areas of interest, guided by professionals who work in those areas within the VA hospital. These internships may also take place outside the hospital in nursing care facilities, mental care facilities, or working with VA homeless services.

For example, students may choose to work in extended care facilities (nursing homes) with geriatric patients and others who need extended care. Students will work as the nurse's assistant for a particular patient, also serving as the patient's playmate and friend. The students will work with the patient to deeply understand his/her physical and mental limitations, and to determine the full range of day-to-day care the patient requires. Students will write a life history of their patient, and prepare a discharge plan that accounts for the physical and mental limitations the student recognized. A professional home care nurse will critique the students' discharge plans.

One possible twist is that, after students worked in detail on people who accidentally fall in hospitals, they might be assigned to a patient who has recently fallen. The student can track the long-term care needs that such patients sometimes require.

Weeks 21–32: Case Studies

The remainder of the school year will entail students problem solving through a number of case studies. Following are several examples of such cases:

Case 1: Placing patients in need of non-emergency care.

It is late at night and the emergency room is filled. A patient enters who is in need of care, but the care required is not urgent enough for an emergency room. The hospital staff has to decide what to do with him. Under the circumstances, they send him home. Three days later, he comes back, now requiring acute care. (Alternatively, perhaps this patient is given a bed in the ICU, but someone else comes in who really needs the bed, and the rest of the beds are taken. What should be done?)

Students must study the problem and propose a solution. They must grapple with the delicate balance of patient needs versus available resources. As a part of their research, students may access a database of information that provides details about how often such incidents occur. They must determine what services patients in similar situations require and what is appropriate for a VA hospital to provide. Students may consider extenuating circumstances, such as where the patient's family members reside—whether they're near the patient, or near a nursing home facility into which the hospital might place the patient. Alternatively, if the family is far, students might decide that the hospital should transfer such patients, providing transportation to a facility closer to the patient's family.

For students to settle on a solution plan, they must do a cost analysis of their ideas. Their plans might detail which hospital staff members should be involved in making plans for new patients (e.g., social workers, nurses, doctors, administrators, organizations from outside of the hospital, etc.). Students might also determine whether a team approach to solving care issues is appropriate under various circumstances, and what structures could be in place to support team decision-making.

Case 2: Prioritizing patients—health care in limited resource situations.

This case will pertain to an issue such as organ donation, when certain patients become more eligible for care than others and determining which those should be. Currently, there are inequalities along gender and race lines with regard to who receives available organs from donors. Students will study such issues and propose processes for prioritizing patients when limited resources are available.

Case 3: Mental health.

This case will approach issues related to mental health, possibly among homeless populations and/or patients with addictions. Such "dual disorder" patients are common in the VA mental health care system. Students will study places that particularly work with these populations, possibly visiting homeless shelters, serving food, and getting to know the population. They may sit in on a group discussion session with patients in a rehabilitation group. Students may also work with outreach groups within the VA, working with a variety of potential patients or clients.

In their work with each care center, students should consider what service gaps exist in helping the patients and design a plan to build a bridge where such gaps exist. Students should also consider what the nation's responsibility should be to these populations. Students may express their findings in a written piece, or perhaps they will create documentaries telling the story of what they saw, and relay how the students' own perceptions of homelessness and/or mental illness have changed due to their experiences. During this work, students will also read books that are relevant to the overarching themes of the case.

Final Report

In the last weeks of the curriculum, the students will work as a team to create and deliver the final consultants report to the VA on the changes it deems necessary at the VA Hospital that has been the host for the year.

REFERENCE NOTES

The basics of this curriculum were deigned in a meeting between people who work for me and experts from the VA at a meeting in West Palm Beach, FL, in 2003.

20

Toward a New
Conception of Education

Technology has the capability to fundamentally reshape the world's education system. When we begin to conceive of education as inherently experiential, in the way that Plato, Kant, Spinoza, Galileo, Wittgenstein, Einstein, and many others have noted, we need to realize that today, the technology of experience and the simulation of experience is the computer. Computers are where experiences can and will be had in the future, and thus computers are a natural venue for education.

In a world where computers provide the context, the role of teachers radically changes. No longer are teachers information providers. Information will be provided far more effectively, through the computer. No longer are teachers the ones who open up new worlds to students. That too, will be done far more effectively through the computer. What computers cannot do, at least until Artificial Intelligence is far more advanced than it is today, is to help students figure out what is confusing them, or share and comment on a new idea, or encourage a point of inquiry. This is the new role for teachers, not as authority figures, but as mentors.

The technology to deliver high quality educational experiences is rapidly becoming a reality, and the impact will be pervasive. The availability of courses delivered over the Web will lead to a shift in teachers' responsibilities from teaching academic subjects to teaching social and interpersonal skills. All academic subjects will be taught online, and as a result, teachers will no longer be expected to be experts in these subjects. Instead, the role of teachers will evolve into one that combines the skills of a social worker, guidance counselor, and camp counselor. Teachers will move away from a role of authority figure to one of a learning facilitator or guide, as well as providing one-on-one mentoring.

The widespread availability of online curricula inside and outside of school will lead to a fundamental change in the role of schools as well. The school's most important role will be counterbalancing the social isolation and alienation that will come from the increasing amount of time students will spend in front of computer screens. The purpose of time spent in school but not on the computer will change to emphasize social learning and group activities.

The delivery of education via online curricula will change the entire landscape of curriculum development. We will be able to realize tremendous efficiencies by developing top-quality learning experiences once for every student in the country, rather than having every teacher in the country repeatedly doing lesson planning for the same courses. The fiction of local control of education will become evident and a panel of experts in various fields of inquiry instead of local groups of well-meaning, but uninformed, parents will develop the curriculum.

WHY ONLINE DELIVERY MATTERS

The primary driver of change in the 21st-century education system has already been created. It is the creation and delivery of courses over the Web. Plato could expound on how education should work, but Plato was never in charge of any school system. He could say that children should practice building houses, but how realistic was that? Suppose Plato had had funds and the Web. Might he have created a course in how to do various jobs that children could practice at? His words indicate that he would have done just that. While plenty of money is needed to build all the range of human activity in simulation, it would not be a recurring expense. Some of these courses, those that emphasized reasoning through Socratic dialogue for example, might have lasted forever. Simulated dialogues with great minds might teach generations of children.

The real value in on line delivery of education is in its portability. There have been good schools created throughout history. Today, for example, we see Montessori schools throughout the country that do a good job of keeping children excited about learning. But allowing every school to offer myriad opportunities to focus on any interest a child may have, to debate his ideas with him, to expand his horizons in ways he might want to go, to critique his work, this would be too much in a traditional school environment. Create such an environment once on a computer however and every child in the world can take advantage of the opportunities it provides.

Such online environments will first be developed for the university and continuing education marketplace. The reason is simple and unfortunate.

These environments cost a great deal of money to create. While the government could certainly afford to create them (the state of Florida, where I live, spends $100 million simply to grade its standardized tests) it will not do so for reasons that many of the great minds I quoted earlier have pointed out. The government typically does not really want to create citizens who can think for themselves in any deep way. No government ever has wanted that in any case. Governments want docile citizens and school is quite good at producing those. In fact, sitting still and not making too much trouble is the hallmark of success in school. As we have seen with Grandview parents, the status quo is enforced by the citizenry, not by the government. Parents are sure their children need algebra, they just don't know why. The same is true of faculty of course. Professors at universities and teachers in high school are usually quite certain that what they teach is important and that they way they teach it is right. What the government does is make it even harder to produce change by setting standards that parents are sure to reinforce.

New learning environments will gradually be developed by universities who feel that they can make money on them in some cases. But universities have other goals as well in creating on line courses. Universities are location bounded, or were before the advent of the Web. Soon there will be real competition between universities. One can imagine that Harvard and Yale are big competitors but apart from the gridiron and some key faculty appointments, they really don't compete all that much. This will soon change, perhaps not between Harvard and Yale but possibly between CMU and Florida Atlantic. If CMU offers online degrees in computer science (a field in which it is ranked number one in the world) in Florida, can Florida Atlantic compete? What if the universities that are best in the world in each area of study opened up on line branches available in Florida? Would Florida Atlantic need to exist at all? The answer is simple: if the online degree programs are better than what Florida Atlantic can offer than Florida Atlantic will have to close down. Such an event would harm no student and might save the taxpayers of Florida quite a bit of money.

While it may not be CMU's goal to close down Florida Atlantic, there are some important things that can be done when on line degree programs are of sufficient quality. Students who live where there is no university at all, or none that could possibly teach the subjects being offered on line will suddenly have educational opportunity in front of them. If the best dental schools in the country banded together to build an online dental school, then only the clinical practice facilities would have to be local. This might matter because there is a world wide shortage of dentists. If the engineering schools decided to build a great four year engineering curriculum online, suddenly high quality engineers would be educated around the world. These are both projects that I am working on as I write these words. I don't know if they will come to fruition or if they will be waylaid by lack of funds of lack of acceptance. But, things like these will come to pass and the world will be better off for it.

We mustn't allow ourselves to get confused by what online courses look like today. Now we are seeing the equivalent of the filmed plays of the early movie making era. This will not be the case for long. When sufficient funding is available, and it will be available when the success of these things has been proven, these new learning environments will be high quality major productions.

One has to accept the fact that traditional academic courses will no longer be taught by local teachers. Mentoring will become a profession, practiced online, one-on-one, that will allow experts around the world to help students around the world. Mentors may very well be the same people who are now teachers, but their jobs will be different. They will not be providers of information, they will be providers of support.

The computer enables the creation of learn by doing courses rather than perpetuating the delivery of traditional learn by telling courses. The computer allows the designers of these courses to be the best and the brightest in any given field. Moreover, these courses will be very engaging, nonthreatening, diverse, and fun. Once the very best physicists in the world sit down and create a physics course, there will be little use for local physics teachers.

The same will be true for every academic subject and for many subjects that are not now seen as academically relevant. Companies will create courses and guarantee employment to those who pass them. Quality universities will put their names on these courses. This will create tremendous change for everyone involved in the education system, from students, to teachers, to administrators, to government education agencies.

The teaching of traditional academic subjects, first at universities, later on in high school and still later in elementary school, will be increasingly done via online curricula. Once the initial set of these curricula become successful, there will be more of a push to make the technology available and people will be increasingly accepting of them. Eventually what you'll have in school is a library of hundreds of curricula. The teachers are going to have to do things that the teachers themselves are better at doing than the computer. What can they do better? What they can do better is personal one-on-one tutoring, teaching kids how to work in a group trying to accomplish something, and teaching crucial interpersonal relationship skills. Schools should be stressing the kinds of things children and adolescents really need to learn: how to get along with each other, how to communicate better, how to deal effectively with stress, and how to function in society.

The role of teachers is going to evolve away from being the expert in math, science, and other subjects. We've been evolving that way for a long time. Today, most high school teachers could hardly claim to be the expert in physics or history or literature in their communities. In the future, the best minds in the country, in the whole world, will be sitting there at your desktop. The initial knee-jerk reaction is likely to be that schoolteachers are going to feel disenfranchised. But there is an opportunity to start teaching those social skills that students desperately need. I think what's going to happen is that teachers are going to understand they can do a better job in these areas. A lot of teachers are doing it already, even though it is rarely part of the formal curriculum. They do it because they have to do it. In the future, these social skills will become the central focus of what teachers will teach. Today there is a push to measure teachers by the test scores achieved by their students. Tomorrow, teachers will be judged by more meaningful measures as we begin to value teachers for their human qualities.

The trends we currently see in this country only reinforce the need for this change in teachers' roles. Children are growing up in households where one or both parents are working all kinds of hours, leaving little time to provide the kind of guidance children need. Teachers will increasingly be needed to step into this role, and the sooner we as a society acknowledge it, and address this need openly and honestly, the sooner we will be able to effect positive change. I'd like to see teachers seriously trained in social work and guidance counseling. They need to understand how to effectively deal with a wide range of psychological problems. This is really a failure of our current approach to education. We need teachers who are specifically trained to remove their own personal feelings about a student and understand how to deal with that student in a complex situation.

Not only will teachers act much more as social workers or guidance counselors, but also they will lead courses that explicitly focus on developing social and interpersonal skills. In many ways these course will resemble the kinds of programs provided by Outward Bound. Let students participate in teams and deal with the team decisions that have to be taken care of. The students go off on a trip and they try to accomplish something. The teacher becomes an advisor to the team, or a guide on an expedition.

I have always believed that summer camp is a more valuable experience than school. Certainly many children look back on their summer camp experiences with much greater fondness than on their school experiences. Personal growth takes place more easily at camp, and personal growth is what high school ought to be about. With so many students going to college, high school as a kind of watered down college is really an archaic idea. So, I say let school become more like camp. At summer camp, the counselors have to get the kids to function together. They work on things that they love doing. A good counselor helps them learn from their experiences. The model of camp counselor is very valid for the role that teachers will assume. Right now teachers are authority figures. They have the power to assign grades and pass or fail students. This is why teachers, for the most part, are bad guidance counselors or team leaders. A camp counselor who doesn't have that power over students is actually more useful, specifically because the authority relationship is completely different. Once teachers move out of this authority role, they will eliminate a roadblock that prevents them from connecting with the students who need the most guidance.

The changes in elementary schools will be similar to those I envision for high school, with variations in the relative proportion of time devoted to academic subjects versus social interaction. While I believe that physics, algebra, European history, and such subjects are for the most part irrelevant to the needs of the average high school student of 2003 (as opposed to his 1892 counterpart), and thus the high school curriculum must change, elementary school isn't all that broken. Of course, it is getting more broken daily as each state mandates multiple choice exams that test trivial knowledge. But, reading, writing, and arithmetic should still be the staples of elementary school education. Nevertheless, as we have seen there is an important attitude adjustment that must go on in elementary school education. When Plato talked of refutation as being the hallmark of educational practice he wasn't exempting small children from the exercise. When Kant talked of experience being the best teacher he didn't mean small children. The debate of ideas needs to be the basis of elementary school, not the blind acceptance of ideas.

Small children should probably should spend less time sitting in front of a computer than would teenagers. I don't think little kids should be sitting much. They have too much energy for that. I think they should be going out and doing stuff and exploring the world and talking about it. There's plenty of time for them to sit later.

In fact, one of the biggest problems we have in elementary school is the amount of time kids are forced to sit still. It's so hard. It's the last thing they want to do. I'd rather see the kids play a lot and have a little bit of instruction. I'd like them to be spending more time playing than doing academics. I think the idea that you're going to sit down and instruct a seven-year-old with something complex is a mistake. A seven-year-old can sit there and do endless math examples, but what we are really teaching is how to follow instructions and how to sit for long periods of time. (This was originally part of the scheme of training factory workers.) While I think there is a valuable lesson in teaching a seven-year-old to sit down and focus on a task, it shouldn't be about doing hundreds of multiplication tables.

In the old days, they'd send eight-year-olds out to work in real jobs and they weren't worse off for it educationally. They were worse off for having their childhood taken away and they were worse off for being in sweatshop conditions that were oppressive. Yet many of them succeeded very well in life by learning good work habits early. To a large extent, I think that's what elementary school should be about. It should be about reading, writing, arithmetic and good work habits. Also it should be about instilling a love of

learning. So, the software should be available for the curious to follow wherever their interests take them.

Think about what parents do when they have a six-year-old at home.
They build stuff, they draw stuff, and they look at stuff. Parents don't sit
down and try to tell them something. They interact. You want kids to be
physically engaged in activities. It's the sitting them down that's torture.
When we sit them down we think we're going to instruct them. Well, get
over it. We don't have to instruct them. We should focus on the basics that
kids have to come out of elementary school with so that they are prepared to
begin taking the online courses they will get in high school. Aside from the
basics of reading, writing, and arithmetic, learning in elementary school
should focus on core skills such as communication, human relations, and
reasoning. All those can be done without sitting down. You can go to the zoo
and learn how to communicate, to relate to others, and to reason. Students
should learn how to stand up in front of people and talk about their ideas.
You can only learn how to develop these kinds of public speaking skills by
practicing them a lot.

In addition to field trips, I believe that team sports should be a big part of
the school day, much as it is in summer camp. A lot of what in today's school
system is considered extracurricular, like putting out a school paper, ought to
be the curriculum. You learn more that way than any other way. The
extracurriculars should become the curriculum.

Another advantage that comes from the creation of online learning environments is that students will be able to learn about topics that interest them
at their own pace. The idea that there is a second grade curriculum consist-
ing of lots of stuff kids will be taught that they could care less about is archaic. The lists of subjects that I discussed earlier that I took from
Grandview have got to go. The only students who should be learning about
Vasco da Gama are those students who really are curious about Vasco da
Gama. But, how do we make them curious about da Gama? By having a really good explorers online course that is fun and exciting that a student can
take when he wants to for as long as he wants to. Those who take this course
will learn about Vasco da Gama (and hopefully more important issues).
Those who don't will learn something else. Everybody wins.

Every year there is a story in the paper about an eight- or twelve-year-old
who is going to college. A typical reaction to this story is Oh, my God. Why?
Not because people are worried that he or she can't handle the intellectual
issues. People are worried he or she can't handle the social issues. With the
advent of online courses we will be divorcing the intellectual issues from the
social issues. Any child at any age who is intellectually ready can engage in
high school or college curricula. Actually, these should be designed so that
little kids have a role in the curricula that bigger kids are engaged in as a way

of apprenticing within a curriculum. They can take calculus when they're six if that's what they're ready for and if what they want to do entails learning calculus. Whether it's da Gama or calculus, children really do learn about these things only when they feel the need to do so and an interest develops. The job of the school is to try and create those feelings of curiosity and interest and then nurture them.

The role of schools will change in ways similar to the changes in teachers' roles. As I've said, one of the really big problems we have coming in the future of this country is a tremendous social alienation problem. We are moving in a direction where everybody is staring at a computer or a television all day and all night and not interacting with other people in a meaningful way. I think the schools will have to be the counterbalance to this trend, to actively provide opportunities for social interaction and to teach the skills required for successful interaction with other individuals and within a group or team. If not, we will see more school violence and alienation. Part of the job of the school is to help students learn how to work together and be a functional part of society.

The school itself should evolve into a sort of student or community center, where kids are engaged in a variety of activities and projects. Perhaps they will be on a team building houses for disadvantaged members of the community, or maybe going out on a trip or having a discussion. There will be a tremendous range of activities, but these will not be purely academic activities as they currently are. When students are not participating in these activities they will be having experiences online in school or at home. Schools will provide the space and resources for students to access the online courses but classrooms are a really archaic idea. It will take a while to get rid them but they have to go. They will be replaced by team meeting rooms, discussion rooms, activity specific rooms, and individual work spaces.

With schools serving as more of an activity or community center, I think that we will see them becoming much more connected to the community around them. Student activities will involve working on community service projects that bring students into contact with the community they live in. Schools will also become more connected to local businesses, as students have the opportunity to engage in real-world jobs with local employers. The school will become the center of the community in a much deeper way than it currently is.

The advent of ubiquitous networking technology will lead to the centralization of key functions in the education system, just as it has in the business world. I see this happening in three key areas.

First, the delivery of education via online courses will change the entire landscape of course development and control of the curriculum. Consortiums of academic experts, educational technologists, and businesses will work to develop, update, refine, and improve these courses. As a society, we will be able to realize tremendous efficiencies by developing these top-quality curricula once.

In addition to eliminating the redundant effort of reinventing the same courses across the country, we will also realize a tremendous improvement in quality control of the curriculum. The era where we have countless numbers of students who have been turned off to physics, math, chemistry, or literature because of poor teachers teaching bad courses in these subjects will be over. Every student in the country will be able to select from a wide range of top-quality curricula in any subject that interests them.

Second, the fiction of local control of education will become evident. Mark Twain knew what he was talking about. School boards were idiotic 150 years ago and they are still idiotic. Parents need to be kept out of the educational process. It is only human to resist change and to assume that what you learned was worth learning. But we cannot go on this way. The reverence we have as a society for certain subjects, especially mathematics, history, and some bizarre notions about what constitutes science education have kept education irrelevant and boring to the majority of students for years.

What will be the point of local school boards arguing over which courses should or should not be offered, when every imaginable course is available? A central body, comprised of the country's best experts on education and learning, with representatives from the various academic fields, will assume control over the curriculum represented by the online courses. By that I mean control in creating online materials. The idea that governing bodies should determine which material is more important than another is simply wrong. Yes, everyone should learn to read and write. But beyond certain simple skills, the driver must be natural interest. Graduation from school should mean that a student has attained a certain set of abilities and demonstrated that he has those abilities. Choosing from a wide range of possible subject areas and experiences, the student's task should simply be to accumulate experience in what interests him.

If Yale decides it only wants to admit students who have had certain experiences then that is up to them. But, the top colleges cannot be permitted to dictate a set of irrelevant requirements that simply make their admissions decisions easier to do but still are reminiscent of the 1892 curriculum. We rush to teach math so kids can do well on SATs and get into Yale where most of them will never encounter any math at all. Does this make sense?

Third, the advance of technology, in particular live video conferencing, will lead to the creation of a centralized pool of tutors for various subject matters. Just as today's companies have centralized phone centers where customers can call for service, we will see the creation of one-on-one tutoring services provided through live video conferencing. Having trouble with learning calculus for a simulated bridge construction project? Just connect to the calculus tutoring center for a face-to-face session with an expert tutor.

These learning service centers will provide students across the country, no matter what community they live in, with access to the best coaches available to help them with their work in an online curriculum.

These changes will happen gradually. How will they happen? Initially, progress will be slow. For example, right now a physics professor who wants to put an introductory physics course online usually just puts his or her lecture notes and some quizzes or tests online. This really doesn't do much to improve the course, but schools feel good that are making use of new technologies.

But, what eventually will happen is that the courses are going to improve. Physicists and educational technologists will sit down to redesign the physics course and ask important questions. Why do we learn physics? What does a student know how to do after having taken physics that he didn't know how to do before? What is the value to him in his future life with these new abilities?

Questions like these will force teachers and experts to confront the key issue underlying all education and educational reform: *Why are we learning this stuff?* Every kid asks this question and they are always right to ask it. But, they rarely are answered in satisfactory ways. The answers are not satisfactory because typically the course designers have not asked themselves these questions. These courses were last designed in 1892, after all. Redesign is the issue and online is the causal change agent.

What the Government's Role Should Be

The tremendous changes that technology will bring to our education system will necessitate an equally radical change in the role the government should play. Initially, I see four key things the government can do to facilitate needed changes in our education system. They are as follows:

1. Changing from a focus on goal and standard setting to a more active role in recruiting the country's best experts and designing the best online courses.
2. Supporting development of new curricula, particularly those that may have expertise already within the government, like using the VA for the Hospital curriculum.
3. Investing in new software technologies that can facilitate the creation of story centered curricula by people without training in instructional design.
4. Thinking about and planning for a vision of school that does not revolve around, or even include, classrooms. The government should begin to

pilot test the new role of school as activity center even before all the technology is available.

5. One of the most important things the government must do is to rethink the limitations imposed on the Department of Education, from exercising direct control over curriculum decisions at the local level.

At some point, the federal government has to understand what its job really is. The idea that local education is being run by a group of well-meaning, but uninformed parents on a school board is insane. They don't know what we should be teaching. As we saw at Grandview, parents are the problem not the solution. The idea that a local school board is in control of education is really a farce. Control is really in the hands of book publishers, colleges, and the Educational Testing Service. The government needs to actually lead, not follow the uniformed views of the electorate. This is one place where democracy has no place. Parents may well approve of the continued emphasis on testing. How would they know better? Parents surely believe that it is important for their children to know science, and history and mathematics. They have never thought about an alternative model, after all. Governments cannot continue to respond to what parents want if they want to make significant change in education.

The government must take an active role in recruiting the country's best experts and work with them to design the best online curricula. If the federal government decided to get all the physicists in front of cameras to get their physics knowledge, and design science reasoning, learn by doing curricula for all ages, it would be quite likely to succeed. There will be a tremendous amount of prestige associated with being asked to help shape the physics course that all the students in the country will take.

But this requires the government and the Education Department in particular, to move away from a focus on goals and curriculum standards toward helping to shape the curriculum and courses themselves. Let's face it, the government's standard setting is just a thinly disguised way of influencing the curriculum anyway. To help guide this country's education system into a new, and much more productive paradigm, the government must take an activist role. In other words, it must lead, not follow.

What Is an Educated Mind?

We started by wondering about what it means to have an educated mind. We saw that Fadiman's conception, familiarity with great books written by great men, was largely seen as wrong by the very great men most admired by Fadiman. Plato didn't think being educated was about reading. In fact, Socrates thought that books were a generally bad idea:

Socrates: Now you, who are the father of letters, have been led by your affection to ascribe to them a power the opposite of that which they really possess. For this invention will produce forgetfulness in the minds of those who learn to use it, because they will not practice their memory. Their trust in writing, produced by external characters which are no part of themselves, will discourage the use of their own memory within them. You have invented an elixir not of memory, but of reminding; and you offer your pupils the appearance of wisdom, not true wisdom, for they will read many things without instruction and will therefore seem to know many things, when they are for the most part ignorant and hard to get along with, since they are not wise, but only appear wise.

To ponder what it means to make a mind less well educated than Fadiman's, one must first understand that Fadiman claimed to have read over 25,000 books in his life. Obviously he saw reading what others said as the hallmark of the educated mind. Of course, he is not alone in this conception. He bragged about his reading attainment after all because others admired that level of erudition. The "more you have read the more educated you are" is not an unheard of idea. But, the curious thing is that considering what Montaigne said about memory and Plato said about refutation and Kant said about experience, it seems to follow that having read all those books guarantees nothing whatever. Who knows what he remembered of what he read? Who refuted what he thought about what he read? What experiences did he have in life besides reading? If experience is critical, as Kant said, and memory is faulty, as Montaigne said, and refutation is the key to erudition, as Plato said, it seems that Fadiman might not have been very well educated at all.

Still, I met the man. I admired the man. He was well educated by any standard definition of the term. And that is the problem.

Being well educated simply doesn't matter if one follows Fadiman's conception of education. It follows from Fadiman's beliefs that education would entail a great deal of reading. Mortimer Adler made this clear when he invented the Great Books Curriculum, still in use in a some colleges today, that essentially analyzes and criticizes a set of literature. There is no reason to criticize this idea. The Great Books Curriculum really does help teach one to think and analyze ideas. Taking what has been written before, and considering the ideas presented there, is a fine way to be educated.

So, what do I mean then? Is the Great Books idea good or bad? Which am I advocating?

I am suggesting that while analyzing what others have written certainly has its place, such analysis is no substitute for experience. While learning by reasoning is fine, because reasoning is after all a kind of doing, in fact an important kind, it is not all the doing that there is. A student needs to do many more things than analyze what others have said. Students need to experience what life has to offer. And while life does indeed offer great books written by great thinkers, it offers quite a bit more than that. When schooling is conceived of as a way to help people read, it leaves out all that has not been written and takes less seriously that which has not been written well.

I asked Adler how it could be that most of the Great Books in the series he edited were written centuries ago. As I stare at the volumes in front of me in my office, I see only six out of sixty that include 20th-century authors and those are, for the most part, small bits from a lot of people. Adler told me that all the great ideas had for the most part already been thought up long ago and not much of interest had happened in the 20th century. I admit that as a computer scientist I am a bit put off by this view. My own view is that all the really interesting ideas probably haven't been thought up yet, but that's just my opinion.

The real issue is the meaning of education. I have tried to show in this book that education has long been understood as being about doing. Fadiman had it wrong, and the society in which he was a literary icon had it wrong. Perhaps the 19th- and 20th-century educated mind was one that could quote Aristotle and had read 25,000 books. But that is not what the educated mind of the 21st century will be (nor should it be). The educated mind in the 21st century will be one that can do many things: relate well to others, think hard about new and complex issues, communicate well in a variety of media, interact with and use tools that are available to the society, make decisions based on scientific and technical knowledge, and so on. In short, as we are now educating everyone, not just those who will go to become intellectuals, we must create a new conception of education that fits everyone.

That conception must value abilities more than knowledge. That conception must enhance capabilities rather than pure intellect. That conception must help students become contributing members of society rather than deciding who does the boring jobs by first seeing who is good at math and relegating the losers to construction jobs. We must have realistic criteria for success, ones that depend on the ability to perform rather the ability to recite. Passing tests can only matter if those tests are performance tests. Education can only matter if it is education about how to live or how to make a living, as John Adams said 200 years ago.

It isn't that things have changed so much that causes us to need to reinvent education. Really things have changed hardly at all, as the quotes I have cited throughout this book make clear. What has changed is that education was defined by the elite in 1892 and was created as a province for the elite. This cannot continue to stand. Fadiman did well in that world, as did Adler, and I might add as did all the people in charge of education today (I include myself here).

But if we plan on educating everyone we must change the definition of what it means to be educated. We must educate minds less well than our own, to use Fadiman's phrase. We must think about the millions of people in this world who have had little or no education at all, and ask ourselves whether what they need is to learn to read Plato or do algebra? Perhaps they simply need to learn to lead lives lead by reason, as Spinoza said. Perhaps they simply need to learn how to make a living. What it means to be educated needs redefinition. The modern definition, in use in the 20th century, cannot continue to stand.

EPILOGUE

What's a Mother to Do?

Technology may very well have the capability to fundamentally reshape the world's education system but one can't help but wonder if there is any way that change will actually happen. Our experiences at CMU West and at Grandview were not entirely wonderful.

Teachers are not always happy about having to teach differently. To be fair, some have been quite excited about the changes we made. Lynn Carter, our primary Software Engineering Professor at CMU West, struggled with the learn by doing concepts in the beginning, but wound up loving this new way of teaching and feeling that he was a much more effective teacher. The mentors at CMU West, graduates of the more standard programs at CMU in Pittsburgh, worked hard to learn to teach Socratically and felt that their students were learning more than they had. Mike Shamos, the head of the eBusiness program at CMU, thought that the CMU West program worked well enough to consider taking it back to Pittsburgh and stop teaching the old way.

That's the good news.

The bad news is that many of the CMU faculty, mainly those not involved, were not so sure of our success. It makes faculty work harder and prevents them from lecturing, something they really like to do, and it often fails to teach sacred theoretical constructs that have no practical application. It remains to be seen if the faculty at CMU will allow CMU West to continue to offer a learn by doing, classroom-free curriculum.

At Grandview things were much worse. The parents, worrying continually about whether their kids would get into college, a curious worry since most colleges take any high school graduate, insisted that the normal curriculum should be taught and eventually the school caved in, frightened of losing tuition revenue.

So, what's a mother to do? What do you do if you know school is not really going to work for your child? One answer has been homeschooling. I have not been a great fan of this answer because I felt that it was just too difficult a solution to implement. It only works for children who have a stay at home parent who is sufficiently educated and motivated to pull it off. I also worried about whether it was too socially isolating for the child.

But I have changed my mind.

Homeschoolers seem to have worked hard to take care of the socially isolating features of homeschooling by banding together in a variety of ways. That is the good news.

The bad news is that parents are in search of curricula. Those who can make it up as they go along might be doing fine. Who would know? But those who want to get a curriculum they can use are left with the usual choices: so much American history, so much biology, so much math. They may as well be in school. (Well, not really. At least the kids aren't in fear while they learn.)

Homeschoolers who attempt to replicate the school curriculum are making a serious error. Why do they think that school has everything wrong but the curriculum? Those who want to sell curricula to the homeschoolers are worried about standardized tests and state regulations that enforce the existing sad state of affairs in our schools.

The solution is obvious. The right and proper place to try out these new curricula would be with homeschoolers, perhaps with parents acting as mentors and with experts available online as mentors. Either way, the growth and success of the homeschool movement offers the only real hope for educational change.

So, that is our challenge: prepare online curricula that are exciting, learn by doing approaches to a variety of experiences interesting and relevant to children's needs and get them into the hands of homeschoolers. When we succeed there, the schooling world will take notice.